D1123356

Design for Manufacturability & Concurrent Engineering

*How to
Design for Low Cost,
Design in High Quality,
Design for Lean Manufacture, and
Design Quickly for Fast Production*

Dr. David M. Anderson, P.E., fASME, CMC

*www.design4manufacturability.com
www.HalfCostProducts.com*

CIM Press

Design for Manufacturability & Concurrent Engineering
How to Design for Low Cost, Design in High Quality, Design for Lean Manufacture, and Design Quickly for Fast Production

By Dr. David M. Anderson, P.E.,fASME, CMC

Published by   **CIM Press**
P.O. Box 100
Cambria, California 93428-0100
(805) 924-0200 phone & fax
e-mail: andersondm@aol.com

Library of Congress Cataloging in Publication Data:

Anderson, David M.
       Design for Manufacturability & Concurrent Engineering; *How to Design for Low Cost, Design in High Quality, Design for Lean Manufacture, and Design Quickly for Fast Production*
       Includes index.
       1. Design, Product design, etc.
       2. Engineering, Concurrent Engineering, etc.
       3. Manufacturing, manufacturability, etc.
       4. Cost reduction, etc.
       5. Quality improvement, Quality assurance, etc.
       6. Time to Market, etc.
       7. Lean Production, etc.
       8. Competition, Competitive advantage, etc.

Printed in the United States of America

10 9 8 7 6 5 4

ISBN 1-878072-23-4

Cover Design and Graphic Art by Lin Marie Graphics

COMPANIES THAT USE THESE PRINCIPLES

DFM BOOKS

Allergan-Humphreys *
Applied Materials
Asyst Technology
Bayer Corporation
Beckman-Coulter *
Bio-Rad
Boeing
Boston Scientific *
Bristol-Meyers Squibb
Brooks/PRI Automation
ComDev
EG&G Instruments
Fisher Controls
Freightliner
Hewlett-Packard **
Hoeffer Scientific
Hollister
KLA/Tencor
Loral **
Measurex
Parker Hannifin
Physics International
PRI Automation*
Rainbird
Smiths Aerospace
Stanford Telecom
Storage Tek
United Technologies Corp.**
W.L. Gore

** These companies bought over 100
 * These companies bought over 50

IN-HOUSE SEMINARS

Ansitsu
BAE Systems
Ball Aerospace
Bausch & Lomb
Beckman Coulter (3)
Becton-Dickinson
BOC (formerly Airco)
Boeing (4)
Crane
Emergency One
Emerson Electric
FMC
Freightliner
GE
Guidant
Hewlett-Packard (7)
Intel Systems Group (10)
Invivo (3)
KI
L-3 Communications (2)
LG Group (Korea)
Loral
Medrad
NCR (2)
Northern Telecom
Plantronics (5)
PRI Automation-Robot Div.
Sloan Valve
Smiths Aerospace (4)
Storage Tek
United Technologies
Winegard (2)

*** See seminar description, page 407

Dedicated to my loving and supportive wife, Lin.

TABLE OF CONTENTS

PART I – DESIGN METHODOLOGY

PART II - FLEXIBILITY

PART III - COST REDUCTION

7. TOTAL COST   219

PART IV - DESIGN GUIDELINES

8. DFM GUIDELINES FOR PRODUCT DESIGN   239

PART VII - APPENDIX

TABLE OF FIGURES

PREFACE

This book shows companies how to design products that are manufacturable *the first time* and enables companies to quickly develop low-cost, high-quality products that satisfy customer needs *by design*.

It might seem obvious enough to ask: why would anyone do otherwise? Many companies think that since elements of the opening sentence are in the corporate goals and mission statements, this will automatically happen by decree. Therefore, why would any company need a book on design for manufacturability? Unfortunately, there are many reasons why products are not automatically designed for manufacturability.

Engineers are generally not taught DFM or concurrent engineering in college – the focus is usually how to design for functionality. Further, they are typically trained to design *parts,* not *products* or *systems*. Most design courses don't even talk about how the parts are to be manufactured. And engineering students rarely follow through designs to completion to get the feedback on the manufacturability of their designs.

Similarly, powerful computer-aided design tools help engineers design *parts,* not *products*. Sure, CAD tools can assemble parts into products for *analysis,* but that does not generate the most creative product design, the simplest concepts, or the most optimized product architecture. Since engineering training and tools are more adept at part design, engineers and managers tend to skip through the critical concept/architecture phase and "get right to work" designing parts.

This behavior is reinforced by far too many managers, who want to see "visible progress" which may mean a quickly constructed breadboard which, after it "works," is drawn up and sent into production.

Product development "management" usually stresses *schedule* and *cost,* but, if not measured right, may further reinforce all the above sub-optimal behavior. Pressuring engineers to complete tasks "on schedule" is really telling them to "through it over the wall on-time." In reality, the most important measure of schedule is the time at which the product has ramped up to stable production and is satisfying all the customers who want to buy the product.

Similarly, the only "cost" metrics usually emphasized are part cost, assembly cost, and development budget, which are usually a small percentage of the only cost metric that matters – *the selling price.* Overemphasizing only these costs, just because they are the only ones measured, encourages engineers to specify cheap parts, cut corners, omit features, move assembly to low-labor rate countries, and other short sighted actions that make the product less desirable.

In addition, too often engineering education and computer tools emphasize *individual* efforts, instead of emphasizing teamwork. Further, college deadlines may be loose and, if not, the traditional college all-nighter might just compensate for procrastination. Traditional homework assignments issue all the data needed – not too much, not too little – and there is single answer – and often students don't even have to get the answer right as long as they have the right approach.   However, real life adds many constraints beyond functionality, such as cost and quality. And the designers have to do all of this quickly and efficiently. Further, the designs have to be manufacturable. Very few individuals, especially right out of college, have enough experience to pull this off.

Fortunately, companies can compensate for this with multifunctional teams that have enough specialties to successfully address *all* the goals and constraints. Teamwork may have never been taught or practiced by many engineers or managers, but their companies need multifunctional teams that can work together to design products for manufacturability.

One goal of this book is to overcome shortcomings in current engineering practices, education, tools, and management. It shows the importance of thoroughly optimizing the concept/architecture phase, designing products as *systems* – not just collections of parts – and how multifunctional teams can accomplish this quickly.   The book has hundreds of design guidelines to help development teams design manufacturable products. It shows how to design for lean production and build-to-order and *design in* quality and reliability. The book has a "big picture" perspective that emphasizes designing for the lowest *total cost* and time to production when volume, quality, and productivity targets have been reached.

If engineers practice the principles of this book, they will be able to spend a higher proportion of their time doing fun, productive design work and less on change orders and firefighting.

BOOK OUTLINE

Part I: Design Methodology

Chapter 1 introduces the concept of design for manufacturability and shows the problems that can be avoided when products are designed for manufacturability. It also discusses roles, focus, and how to overcome resistance, understand the myths and realities of product development, and motivate engineers to design for manufacturability, avoid arbitrary decisions, and *do it right the first time.* The chapter concludes with benefits of DFM.

Chapter 2 shows how to use *concurrent engineering* to develop products in multifunctional design teams. Such teams are most effective when they have early and active participation of all specialties. The chapter shows the problems when this does not happen and how to ensure availability of resources. Just as Chapter 1 showed that the majority of the cost is committed by the concept, the key to getting products quickly to market is a thoroughly optimized concept/architecture phase. Product development phases are presented with the tasks that enable good DFM including: defining products to satisfy the *voice of the customer* with QFD; optimizing the product architecture and strategies for operations and supply chains; raising and resolving the issues early; concurrently designing the product and processes; and launching into production.

Chapter 3, *Designing the Product,* focuses on thorough up-front work, optimizing the concept/architecture phase, and a wide scope of design considerations. The chapter also shows how to use creativity and brainstorming to develop better products and how to develop half-cost products.

Part II: Flexibility

Chapter 4 shows how to design products for lean production, build-to-order and mass customization

Chapter 5 shows very effective procedures to standardize parts and materials, save time and money with off-the-shelf parts, and implement a standardization program.

Part III: Cost Reduction

Chapter 6 emphasizes the importance of minimizing the *total cost* and then shows many ways to minimize total cost *by design.* It also shows why cost is hard to remove after products are designed.

Chapter 7 emphasizes the importance of quantifying total cost and then shows easy ways to measure total cost.

Part IV: Design Guidelines

Chapter 8 presents 55 design guidelines for product design, including assembly, fastening, test, repair, and maintenance.

Chapter 9 presents 64 design guidelines for designing parts for manufacturability. The chapter also has a section on tolerance step functions and how to specify optimal tolerances.

Part V: Customer Satisfaction

Chapter 10 shows how to *design in* quality and reliability with 47 quality guidelines and sections on mistake-proofing (*poka-yoke*) and designing to minimize errors. The chapter also shows product quality is a function of the cumulative exponential effect of part *quality* and part *quantity.*

Part VI: Implementation

Chapter 11 shows how to implement DFM including: determining the current state of how well products are designed for manufacturability; estimating much could be improved by implementing DFM; getting management support and buy-in; arranging DFM training; forming a task force to implementing DFM; stopping counterproductive policies; implementing DFM at the team and individual levels; and implementing standardization and total cost measurements.

Chapter 12 summarizes key DFM principles in a graphical or bulletized format including: definitions; myths and realities of product development; when cost is committed; how to cut in half the real time-to-market; best and worst resource allocations scenarios; summaries of several other DFM principles; summary of DFM methodologies; and a summary of DFM benefits.

Part VII: Appendix

Appendix A presents effective methodologies for Product Line Rationalization to maximize resource availability for product development and increase profits immediately. Appendix B summarizes design guidelines without explanation to help DFM task forces create customized design guidelines and checklists. Appendix C contains several useful forms for obtaining feedback from customers, factories, vendors, and field service. Appendix D provides resources about the reference books that were cited the most in this book and information about the author's web-sites, customized in-house training, workshops, consulting, commercialization, and design studies.

PREFACE FOR INSTRUCTORS

This book can be especially effective for use as a textbook for a senior/graduate level course on Design for Manufacturability and for company in-house training. The book contains the latest material from the author's 25 year in-house DFM seminars at manufacturing companies.

The book evolved from his experience initiating and implementing the DFM program at Intel's Systems Group and teaching internal courses. That evolved into college courses on DFM at the University of Portland and later in the Management of Technology Program at the U.C., Berkeley.

Various editions of this book have been used for courses at Cleveland State University, UC Berkeley Extension, University of Colorado, University of Dayton, Eastern Michigan State University, Morehead University, New Mexico State University, North Carolina State University, North Central Michigan State, Northern Illinois University, Oregon Institute of Technology (2 campuses), University of Portland, San Jose State University, Sinclair College, South Alabama University, Southern Methodist University, St. Thomas University, West Carolina University, Washington State University (4 campuses), and Worchester Polytechnic Institute.

The industrial orientation of this book should give practical direction to college students to help them adapt quickly to the "real world" and design manufacturable products. Additional reading assignments can be selected from the references listed at the end of each chapter.

This book can also be used to supplement courses on Machine Design, Project Design, Engineering Management, Engineering Economy, Value Analysis, or other courses in Business Administration or Mechanical, Industrial, or Manufacturing Engineering.

A complimentary instructor package is available from the publisher that includes a college course outline, term project suggestions, homework, and exam questions with answers.

ABOUT THE PUBLISHER

CIM Press is the publishing arm of Dr. Anderson's consulting practice. Cooperation between author and publisher enhances the flow of reading with abundant headings, optimal page breaks, sensible figure placements, and the arrangement of related material on facing pages whenever possible. The book is thoroughly researched with 324 references, conveniently placed at the end of each chapter. The book will be easy to read, browse, search, or use as a reference with 400 headings and over 2000 cross-referenced index entries, with topics broken down so that each entry rarely has more than two page references. For example, there are 75 entries under "Cost Reduction."

This book is continuously updated every year or two based on Dr. Anderson's ongoing experiences teaching DFM & Concurrent Engineering to manufacturing companies and doing concept/architecture studies (for more on his design studies and DFM training, see Appendix D).

ABOUT THE AUTHOR

Dr. David M. Anderson is the world's leading expert on using Concurrent Engineering to Design products for Manufacturability, which he has honed to an effective methodology for accelerating the real time to stable production and significantly reducing total cost. A partial client list, with the number of multiple seminars cited, appears on the page opposite the copyright page.

His book-length web-site, *www.HalfCostProducts.com*, presents a comprehensive cost reduction strategy (summarized in Chapter 6) consisting of eight strategies, all of which can offer significant returns as stand-alone programs and even greater results when combined into a synergistic business model. DFM is a key strategies because it supports most of the others. Dr. Anderson shows clients how to apply these strategies for cost reductions ranging from half cost to an order-of-magnitude when commercializing research.

In the Management of Technology Program at the University of California at Berkeley, he wrote and taught the course as an adjunct, *"New Product Development, the Management and Design of Manufacturable Products."*

He also wrote the opening chapter in the DFM Handbook published by the Society of Manufacturing Engineers (Tool & Manufacturing Engineers Handbook, Vol 6) and the chapter on "DFM and Mass Customization" in Wiley's *Quality Function Deployment Handbook*.

His second book on Mass Customization is *Build-to-Order & Mass Customization; The Ultimate Supply Chain Management and Lean Manufacturing Strategy for Low-Cost On-Demand Production without Forecasts or Inventory*, 2004, 520 pages (see description before the Index).

Dr. Anderson has more than 35 years of industrial experience in design and manufacturing. For the past 25 years, he has been providing corporate seminars, workshops, and consulting on DFM (the third page of this book presents a partial client list and a list of companies who bought multiple DFM books).

For seven years, his own company, Anderson Automation, Inc., built special production equipment for IBM and OCLI and did design studies for FMC, Clorox, and SRI International. As the ultimate concurrent engineering experience, he personally built the equipment he designed in his own machine shop. He has been issued four patents and is working on more.

Dr. Anderson is a *Fellow* of ASME (American Society of Mechanical Engineers) and has been certified a Certified Management Consultant (CMC) by the Institute of Management Consultants. His credentials include professional registrations in Mechanical, Industrial, and Manufacturing Engineering and a Doctorate in Mechanical Engineering from the University of California, Berkeley with a major of Design for Production and minors in Industrial Engineering, Metalworking, and Business Administration.

Web-sites: *www.design4manufacturability.com*
www.HalfCostProducts.com   *www.build-to-order-consulting.com*

Phone: 805- 924-0100   e-mail *anderson@build-to-order-consulting.com*

DESIGN FOR MANUFACTURABILITY

Design for manufacturability is the process of *proactively* designing products to: (a) optimize all the manufacturing functions: fabrication, assembly, test, procurement, shipping, service, and repair; (b) assure the best cost, quality, reliability, regulatory compliance, safety, time-to-market, and customer satisfaction; and (c) ensure that *lack of* manufacturability doesn't compromise functionality, styling, new product introductions, product delivery, improvement programs, strategic initiatives, and unexpected surges in product demand.

Concurrent Engineering is the proactive practice of designing products to be built on standard processes, or concurrently developing new processes while concurrently developing new products. Concurrent Engineering with multifunctional teams is discussed in Chapter 2.

DFM and Concurrent Engineering are proven design methodologies that works for any size company. Early consideration of manufacturing issues shortens product development time, minimizes development cost, and ensures a smooth transition into production for quick time to market.

Quality is *designed in* (Chapter 10) with concept and process simplicity, optimal tolerances, quality parts, mistake-proofing, concurrent design/selection of robust processes, and specifying quality parts to minimize the cumulative effect of part quality on product quality.

Many costs are reduced, since products can be quickly assembled from fewer parts. Products are easier to build and assemble, in less time, with better quality. Parts are designed for ease of fabrication and commonality with other designs.

Products are designed for *lean production* and *build-to-order* with aggressive standardization (Chapter 5), elimination of setup *by design,* and the concurrent engineering of versatile product and flexible processes (Chapter 4).

Companies that have applied DFM have realized substantial benefits. Total cost and time-to-market can be cut in half with significant improvements in quality, reliability, serviceability, product line breadth, delivery, customer satisfaction, growth, and profits.

1

1.1 MANUFACTURING BEFORE DFM

Before DFM, the motto was "I designed it; you build it!" Design engineers worked alone or only in the company of other design engineers in "The Engineering Department." Designs were thrown over the wall to Manufacturing, which was then placed in the dilemma of either objecting ("but it's too late to change the design!") or struggling to launch a product that was not designed well for manufacturability. Often this delayed both the product launch *and* the time to ramp up to full production, which is the only meaningful measure of time-to-market.

Poor manufacturability raises many categories of cost to pay for launch difficulties, special equipment or modifications, difficult part fabrication, inefficient assembly, excessive part proliferation, laborious procurement, numerous changes, and many other "overhead" costs. These issues not only raise cost but also delay shipments. Problem product introductions may absorb so much effort that production of stable products may suffer.

Lack of manufacturability also degrades quality which, in turn, raises cost further and delays the real time-to-market. This is because products not designed for quality are unnecessarily complex, have too many parts from too many suppliers, require more difficult manual assembly, and may not be *robust* enough for consistent processing. Further, counterproductive "cost reduction" may compromise quality, while, ironically, not lowering *total* cost.

Probably the most subtle effect (but most damaging in the long run) is that a series of problem product introductions drains resources (both people and money) away from product development and continuous improvement efforts that make product lines and factories more competitive.

Excessive proliferations of parts and products can make it harder to implement just-in-time, lean production, build-to-order and mass customization.[1]

DFM may make the difference between a competitive product line and, in the extreme, products that are not manufacturable at all.

The main causes of product failures are that costs are too high, quality is too low, introductions are too late, stable production is even later, or, in the best case scenario, production is unable to keep up with demand. *These are all manufacturability issues and therefore can be very much improved by DFM.*

What DFM is not:[2]

- DFM is not a *late* step that, once checked off, gets you through a design review or gate
- DFM is not done by the "DFM Engineer"
- DFM is not done by a "tool"
- DFM is not just done at the *parts* level; most opportunities are at the *system* level
- DFM is not an afterthought
- DFM is not to be "caught" later in design reviews
- DFM is not to be accomplished by changes

Comments from Company DFM Surveys

The following are verbatim comments from company surveys before DFM training (the use of these surveys is discussed in Section 11.2). When asked about the consequences of inadequate DFM, engineers and managers usually cite problems with quality, cost, delivery, profits, and competitiveness, which are tabulated in Section 11.2. But it is the colorful comments that convey what is like to work in a company that does not design products well for manufacturability.

The consequences of inadequate DFM with respect to delivery are:

"Line stoppers"
"Parts do not assemble correctly"
"Endless engineering change orders"
"Much pruning, grooming, and tuning to get products out the door"
"Poor yield invariably results in late delivery or 11th hour miracles"
"When a problem is encountered the production line comes to a stop"
"Emergency change orders and redlines to keep manufacturing operating"

The behavioral hurdles to good DFM are:

"Lack of DFM training" "Lack of DFM knowledge"
"Parts designed with no consideration of how it is to be built"
"'Over the Wall' syndrome: after release, no longer Engineering's problem"
"Never enough time to design parts right the first time; always enough time to do it over"

The attitude hurdles to good DFM are:

"Egos"
"Tradition"
"Designer's limited knowledge of manufacturing processes"
"Reluctance to accept suggestions from suppliers regarding design issues"
"We don't seem to allot time to design systems properly up front, but we are willing to do it over later after a product is released"

The bottom line consequences, besides profitability, include:

"Unhappy Customers"
"Sometimes problems get shipped to the field"
"Customers losing confidence in our products"
"Problems increase overall costs resulting in loss of the ability to compete"
"Low product quality leads to poor customer satisfaction, poor performance,
    and eventually to high costs"
"Post launch redesigns"

1.2 MYTHS & REALITIES OF PRODUCT DEVELOPMENT

Myths of Product Development

Resistance to DFM may come from myths about product development. Here are the most common myths, followed by corresponding realities:

Myth # 1:   To develop products **quicker**, get going soon on the detail design and software coding and then enforce deadlines to keep design release and first-customer-ship on schedule.

Myth # 2:   To achieve **quality**, find out what's wrong and fix it.

Myth # 3:   To **customize** products, take all orders, and use an *ad hoc* "fire drill" approach

Myth # 4:   **Cost** can be reduced by cost reduction efforts.

Realities of Product Development:

Fact # 1:   The most important measure of **time-to-market** is the time to stable, trouble-free production and that depends on getting the design right the first time.

Fact # 2:   The most effective way to achieve **quality** is to *design* it in and then *build* it in.

Fact # 3:   The most effective way to **customize** products is by the concurrent design of versatile product families and flexible processes. This is known as *mass customization.*[3]

Fact # 4:   **Cost** is designed into the product, especially by early concept decisions, and is difficult to remove later.

1.3 WHEN COST IS COMMITTED

Figure 1-1 shows that by the time a product is designed, 80% of the cost has been determined.[4]   And by the time a product goes into production, 95% of its cost is determined, so it will be very difficult to remove cost at that late a date.   The most profound implication for product development is that *60% of a product's cumulative lifetime cost is committed by the concept/architecture phase!*   This is why it is important to fully optimize this phase, as will be shown in Section 3.3.

PRODUCT COST vs TIME

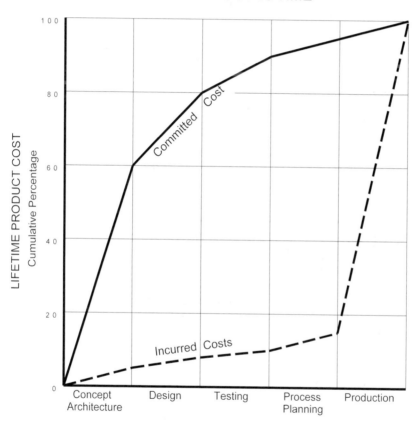

PHASE OF PRODUCT LIFE

Figure 1-1: When Costs Are Committed

The Toyota philosophy confirms this.   *"The cost of a [product] is largely determined at the planning and design stage. Not much in the way of cost improvement can be expected once full-scale production begins." "Skillful improvements at the planning and design stage are ten times more effective that at the manufacturing stage."[5]*

1.4 DESIGNING FOR LOW COST

The DFM techniques presented herein provide *proactive* ways to achieve substantially lower cost than can be achieved by *reactive* approaches like "cost reduction," the problems of which are discussed in Section 6.1. This is because of the last reality on page 4 which counters the myth that cost can be reduced by cost reduction efforts:

Cost is designed into the product, especially by early concept decisions, and is difficult to remove later.

The book, *When Lean Enterprises Collide,* studied the competition and cost practices of several lean production companies in Japan. The author, Robin *Cooper*, has also written extensively on total cost accounting. His view on product development's role in determining cost was:

"Effective cost management must start at the design stage of a product's life because once a product is designed the majority of its costs are fixed."[6]

The main cost minimization opportunity is to optimize the product architecture (Section 3.3) which determines 60% of the lifetime cumulative cost, as shown in Figure 1-1. A key part of this is optimal selection of versatile modules, (Section 4.7), previous engineering (Section 5.18), and off-the-parts (Section 5.19), which usually result in total cost savings while assuring quality and reliability because they are proven parts that can be verified by their track records. Chapter 6 shows several ways to minimize cost through design. Applying all these DFM techniques should enable companies to develop products at half the *total* cost, with special emphasis on key points discussed in Section 3.8.

Design for Cost Approaches

There are various approaches to determining the goals for costs and the pricing of products.

Cost-Based Pricing. The way this approach typically works is: engineers design the product and then add up the parts and labor costs, which is usually their only cost focus. To that the company adds overhead costs, selling costs, and profits to arrive at the selling price.

Price-based Costing (Target Costing). This approach starts with a selling price which is estimated to be competitive. From that, profits, selling costs, and overhead are subtracted to determine the *target* cost for parts and labor.[7, 8] A more advanced version would subtract profits and selling commissions from the selling price to determine the *total cost,* which would include parts, labor, and *all* overhead costs including distribution costs, which can be reduced by Build-to-Order (Chapter 4).

However, it should be kept in mind that costing/pricing policies are really *targets,* not *strategies* to design low-cost products. If product development teams do know how to really *design* low-cost products, both of these costing/pricing approaches are likely to backfire.

In the case cost-plus pricing, not knowing how to actually design low-cost products will result in higher-than-necessary costs which will then result in pricing that may be too high to be competitive. In the case of price-based costing, not knowing how to actually design low-cost products can result the following dangerous scenario:

- Engineers design the product as they usually do – for functionality. More bureaucratic companies may break down product development into subassemblies and "manage" them, but the engineers may still be designing primarily for functionality.

- Accountants add up the part/labor costs and apply the usual overhead costs.

- Management then realizes how much the part/labor costs are "over the target" and pressures the Engineering, Purchasing, and Manufacturing to "lower the cost" (of the parts and labor).

  - Design engineers and "value engineers" will find it difficult to reduce cost after design (for reasons presented in Section 6.1), so they may be tempted to do some desperate things to achieve the part/labor targets, like cutting corners, omitting features, or specifying cheaper parts. All of these incur the costs of making and documenting the changes. Moreover, cutting corners and cheaper parts will add to quality costs.

  - Purchasing might try low-bidding of parts, pressuring suppliers, or changing suppliers for a slightly better purchase cost. However, while this might *appear* to lower part cost, it will most likely raise other costs and compromise quality (Ch. 6), delivery (Ch. 4), and collaborating with suppliers to develop more manufacturable products (Ch. 2).

  - Manufacturing, under enough pressure, might do some desperate things like outsourcing and moving manufacturing to "low-labor cost" countries, which does not really save total cost on top of decreasing responsiveness.[9]

1.5 CUTTING TIME-TO-MARKET IN HALF

Define time-to-market as some big-picture measure, such as the time to target volume, quality target, productivity target, qualification, change orders completed, customer acceptance, and so forth. In order to compare to previous projects, metrics may have to be recomputed.

Define the product methodically to avoid "changes" to satisfy customers. Make sure the product requirements are complete before the engineering begins or else the requirements may be poorly formed or the project will be delayed. In one survey, 71 percent of managers said that poor product definition caused product development delays, make it the top reason for delays.[10] Another survey of 153 companies[11] concluded that the biggest cause for product failure[12] was "unclear or continuously changing product definitions" and the next most common cause of failure was "product does not meet customer or market requirements."

Ensure all specializations are available and active early to optimize all aspects of manufacturability from the very beginning.

Ensure all resources are available for immediate deployment when they are needed throughout the product development.

Begin decisively. Don't procrastinate. Don't wait for deadline pressures to get motivated.

Simplify the concept and optimize product architecture (see Section 3.3).

Raise and resolve issues early and avoid the delays of much more difficult change orders. Thoroughly resolve technical/functional challenges and issues early (see Phase 3 of Section 2.12 on raising and revolving issues).

Work together well throughout the project and "close the loop" to communicate well all through product development.

Work efficiently with the most efficient design and simulation tools and use product data management to document progress to ensure that everyone's work is based on the most current drawings/documents.

Purchase and outsource wisely, since low-bidders selected for "cost" often cause delays.[13]

Avoid "creeping elegance" to endlessly pursue unnecessary refinements and enhancements.

Avoid administrative delays for design reviews, budget hold-ups, and loss of key people, temporary or permanent, to firefights on other projects.

Design thoroughly and complete all documentation because time-to-market can be significantly delayed by design gaps and glitches and incomplete documentation. Significant, expensive launch or build delays can be prevented by up-front thoroughness, which is much more efficient in the relatively orderly design stage than in the panic mode that results when problems delay production. Design and documentation shortcomings not only delay that product but also take resources away from other products.

Don't rely on manufacturing to finish the design or documentation just to meet deadlines or budget targets.

Design for existing processes to eliminate the need to design, develop, and debug new production machinery.

Obey all the design rules for all processing to avoid delays to either correct the designs or correct the problems every time products are built.

Avoid redesigns which will take time to design, debug, *and* build, which will delay the time-to-market.

Select proven materials, parts, suppliers, and vendors. Any glitches in these can delay the market launch.

Thoroughly optimize material and part availability, including best-case sales scenarios to avoid delays to find and incorporate alternatives.

Avoid excessively long supply chains that can increase the calendar build time and are vulnerable to cumulative delays and shipping interruptions.

Proactively avoid compromising functionality, quality, cost, or manufacturability to get products out the door.

Thorough up-front work greatly shortens the *real* time-to-market and avoids wasting time and resources on revisions, iterations, and ramp problems. This is thoroughly discussed in Section 3.2 on the importance of optimizing the concept/architecture stage (the "up-front" work) citing the Lexmark model (Figure 3-1). This model graphically shows how the "concurrent" model (basically, doing everything recommended in this book) results completing the production ramp 40% sooner than the "linear" model, which rushes right through the concept/architecture stage. This graphic also appears in color as the lower graph on the back cover. The first half of Chapter 3 shows how to optimize the critical up-front work.

1.6 ROLES AND FOCUS

Optimal company performance comes from *a whole company synergy* where the whole company works together to develop products for manufacturability:

Engineering and Manufacturing currently engineer products/processes, as discussed in Chapters 2 and 3.

Marketing works together with the team from the earliest stages to define whole product families that satisfy the "voice of the customer."

Purchasing/materials groups support product development by: nurturing vendor/partner relationships instead of looking for the lowest bidders; taking pressure off product development teams by shortening procurement times; encouraging part standardization; prequalifying parts and vendors to optimize quality and delivery

Finance quantifies total cost to support relevant decision making and arranges for appropriate overhead charges for new-generation products.

Human Resource Development hires or develops very good project leaders with team leading abilities and hiring good team players.

> *"When hiring, you have to also be mindful of how well the new managers work with the rest of your existing team. Hiring a good team player is as important as hiring someone with the right expertise."* – from *Business the Sony Way.*[14]

HR should provide team leading training for managers and team building workshops for engineers.

> At Nokia, *"the focus was not just on recruiting but on 'marinating' that begins with orientation and ends with highly refined team training."*[15]

Company policy should also arrange job rotation to encourage cross-learning and informal communications, starting with placing new design engineers in manufacturing first. It can be argued that it takes new employees time just to learn their way around the company. And engineers on their first job need to learn even more. So while they are getting up to speed on how the company operates, they can be learning about the company's manufacturing practices.

"At Honda, all entry-level engineers spend their first three months in the company working on the assembly line. They're then rotated to the marketing department for the next three months. They spend the next year rotating through the engineering departments - drive train, body, chassis, and process machinery. Finally after they have been exposed to the entire range of activities involved in designing and making a car, they are ready for an assignment to an engineering specialty, perhaps in the engine department."[16]

At Samsung, *"team-building practices include frequent meetings for all individual team members along with something as simple as conversations over a drink after working hours – for the purpose of exchanging internal communications or resolving conflicts."*[17]

Nokia owns much of its success to encouraging its brightest managers to work in manufacturing. CEO Jorma Ollila says, "If you do well in manufacturing, you get a good career in Nokia."[18]

Growing departments should not be allowed to raid other departments, which may weaken critical internal functions. HR should hire design engineers with experience in manufacturing, test, field service, sales, and so forth. It should give extra consideration to potential employees who have been users or worked for customers, suppliers, or regulators. Finally, HR should arrange for training for all aspects of product development (see Chapter 11 on Implementation).

Senior management should work with HR to ensure that performance measurements encourage teamwork and support overall goals. The company should also ensure retention of talent, information, and complete teams during downturns, restructuring, and internal transfers, and strive to maximize internal continuity and minimize turnover.

DFM task force incorporates DFM steps into the product development process (Section 2.12) and creates, issues, and updates a consistent set of design rules and guidelines.

Management Role to Support DFM

View product development as an investment, not a "cost." Here are some thoughts from important studies and leading companies.

> A Battelle R&D report on product development drew the conclusion that *"the support of research and development runs the risk of being viewed as an expense and a luxury, rather than an investment, and one that can be shelved until more funds are available."*[19]

> A Deloitte study of 650 companies in North America and Europe revealed that *"while manufacturers cite launching new products and services as the No. 1 driver of revenue growth, they also view supporting product innovation as one of the least important priorities."*[20]

> When Bill George was Chairman and CEO of Medtronic, he said that *"Companies must rigorously reinvest a significant portion of their increased profits in R&D, market development, and future growth opportunities, and not let it all go to the bottom line."* In fact, Medtronic increased R&D spending from 9 percent of revenues to 12 percent, knowing that these investments would not produce any bottom-line return for five to ten years.[21] Medtronic's shareholder value increased *150 times* over a period of 18 years.[22]

> One of the key principles of innovation at Apple is *"If you believe in the future, and your future lies in R&D, don't starve R&D."*[23]

> *"Samsung believes that constant advances are the only way it can reach a sustainable competitive advantage."* Samsung *"has consistently been a first-to-market player with pioneering products – thanks in large part to its continuing investment in research and development."*[24]

Encourage innovation. Bill George, CEO Metronic, encourages *"walking through the labs and learning about creative ideas before they get killed off"* by the system, because *"a growing bureaucracy is a huge barrier to innovative ideas and dampens creativity, no matter how much it spends on research and development. Leaders committed to innovation have to work hard to offset these tendencies, giving preference to the mavericks and the innovators and protecting new business ventures while they are in the fragile, formative stage."*[25]

Plan the product portfolio *and its evolution over time* objectively to provide the greatest net profit over time as defined by *all the financial gains* minus *all the costs.*

Don't spread resources too thin by "taking all orders;" Focus on selling the *most profitable* products and rationalizing away the "losers."

Ensure resource availability so that *complete* teams can form *early.* *Don't waste product development resources trying to reduce cost* after the product is designed. *Pre-select vendors* so they can help the team design the parts they will build, which saves much more money than bidding.

Have realistic expectations compatible with product development methodology.

Encourage a high proportion of thorough up-front work through a good product definition, early issue resolution, concept simplification, and architecture optimization. Avoid early deadline pressure that thwarts thorough up-front work.

Implement total cost measurements (Chapter 7) to enable prioritizing all activities, planning product portfolios, rationalizing products by real profitability, relevant decision making.

Follow through so the team is responsible for transition into production and team stays with the project until production has stabilized in volume, productivity, and quality. Now this includes researchers. Paul Horn, who oversees research at IBM says:

> *"Everything we do is aimed at avoiding a 'handoff' – there is no 'technology transfer.' It is a bad phrase at IBM."* Research teams stay with their ideas all the way through to manufacturing.[26]

Encourage job rotation. Nokia *"encourages job rotation within the company – from Ollila's executive board to all levels of the workforce."*[27]

Empower an effective project leader to make decisions as they need to be made, thus minimizing the dependence on design reviews.

Encourage feedback and be receptive to *all* news about product developments. Create an open culture where issues can be raised and discussed early with the focus on issue resolution.

When the current Ford Americas President Mark Fields came to Ford from IBM, *he was discouraged from airing problems at meetings unless his boss approved first!*[28]

Ensure ownership so that product development teams "own" all aspects of manufacturability and is accountable for the total cost and the real time-to-market.

Implement compensation/reward systems that encourage teamwork and "big picture" goals; change sales incentives from revenue to profit.

Motorola's policy is that *"Corporate leaders must emphasize the need to partner and, as at Motorola, even overhaul how people are paid, rewarding those who promote partnering."*[29]

Focus on the activities and methodologies that lower cost and speed development, instead of relying just on goals, targets, metrics, reviews, gates, and deadlines.

It is important for product development teams to have the right focus when developing products:

- Focus on customers' needs, *not* on the company programs, competition, or technology.

- Focus on *proactive* resolution of issues early, rather than *reactive* resolution later.

- Focus on problem *avoidance*, rather than problem solving.

- Focus on eliminating Engineering Change Orders rather than streamlining the change control process.

- Focus on core competencies and new and pivotal aspects of the design instead of "reinventing the entire wheel" and diluting resources with low leverage activities.

- Focus on product and software architecture, *not* just drawings and code.

- Focus on the design process itself, *not* on project control and measurement.

- Focus how to optimize activities in the *phases,* not the gates or design reviews.

- Focus on on-demand discussions and decision-making, *not* periodic meetings and reviews.

- Focus on *product* design, *not* proofs-of-principle, breadboards, and prototypes.

- Focus on the optimizing product architecture, *not* just designing a collection of parts and subassemblies.

- Focus on rapid production ramps in real production environments, *not* pilot production by prototype technicians or engineers.

- Focus on time to stable production, *not* time to design release or first-customer-ship.

- Focus on minimizing total cost, *not* just reported costs (labor and materials).

- Focus on *designing in* and *building in* quality and reliability, *not* by testing, inspections or reacting to field problems.

- Focus on compensation systems which encourage behavior that benefits the company, *not* departments or individuals,

- Focus on what achieves *major* and *lasting* cost reduction (superior product development, lean production, quality programs, etc.) instead of questionable attempts (offshoring, low-bidding, and trying to reduce cost after the product is designed) which compromise *real* cost reduction.

- Focus on what achieves goals, *not* the goals themselves. The movie *Jerry McGuire* made famous the phrase, "Show me the money," which was chanted in the part of the movie when neither the football player (Oscar winning Cuba Gooding, Jr.) nor his agent (Tom Cruise) were being "shown" any money because they were concentrating solely on the *goal* of making money rather than *what achieved the goal*, which was playing good football. The analogies for business:

The CEO says, "Show me the profits."
The CFO says, "Show me the market value."
The V.P. of Sales says, "Show me the sales."
The V.P. of Marketing says, "Show me more market share."
The V.P. of Research says, "Show me more patents."
The V.P. of Purchasing says, "Show me less part cost"
The V.P. of Engineering says, "Show me faster developments."
The V.P. of Manufacturing says, "Show me less assembly cost."

However, none of these goals will happen unless the company has effective ways to *achieve* those goals. Dr. W. Edwards Deming said that *"A goal without a method is cruel."*

Ironically, too much pressure to *meet* departmental targets without a real way to do *achieve* them usually lead to counterproductive results, like buying cheap parts (Section 6.11), which degrades quality. Similarly, moving manufacturing to "low labor cost" areas can actually increase other costs and compromise responsiveness and product development itself, as discussed in Section 6.1.

1.7 RESISTANCE TO DFM

Despite these problems, some companies and individual designers still resist DFM. Here are the most common reasons why:

1) **Linear thinking**

"Just let me get something working now; sometime *later* we (actually someone else) will take care of manufacturability, cost, quality, reliability, serviceability, variety, et cetera, et cetera, et cetera."

2) **Misconceptions about time**

"I don't have time to worry about manufacturability now; I've got deadlines to meet."

3) **Misconceptions about constraints**

"I'm a 'blue sky' thinker; don't bother me with unnecessary constraints." "Don't limit my *design freedom.*"

4) **Misconceptions about innovation**

"I'm very creative, and don't want to be stifled even thinking about Design for . . .Whatever"

However, manufacturability problems can delay the launch, cause availability problems and shortages throughout the product life cycle, delay rapid growth if the product is a big hit, degrade the quality of the look and feel of the product, and raise the cost so much that the price has to be raised or profit lowered, all of which will result in an unsuccessful product.

Realities to Counter the Resistance

1) Linear thinking

Murphy's Law of Product Development:

*If you don't consider manufacturability early in the design,
it is very unlikely that it can be quickly and easily incorporated later.*

2) Realities about time

*If you don't have time to do DFM now,
how will you ever find the time to do it later
when it is much more difficult, maybe impossible?*

3) Realities about design constraints.

Designers may resist designing products for manufacturability if they think it limits their "design freedom." But, in reality, too few constraints will lead to the design equivalent of "writer's block." If every design decision has many open choices, the whole design will represent an overwhelming array of choices that can lead to *design paralysis.* So the designer breaks the impasse by making *arbitrary decisions.* Every arbitrary decision will make it progressively more difficult to incorporate other design considerations later. And the further the design progresses (and the more arbitrary decisions you make), the harder it will be to satisfy additional considerations. The decision-making motto for product development should be: *No arbitrary decisions.*

1.8 ARBITRARY DECISIONS

Designers may be tempted to think that fewer constraints will result in more design freedom and many may resist DFM on those grounds. But, in reality, too few constraints may lead to the design equivalent of "writers' block." If every design decision has many open choices, the whole design will represent an overwhelming array of choices that can lead to design paralysis.

So the designer breaks the impasse by making *arbitrary decisions.* Every arbitrary decision will probably make it difficult to incorporate other considerations later. And the further the design progresses (the more arbitrary decisions), the harder it will be to satisfy additional considerations.

*Not considering all the goals and constraints at the beginning
results in arbitrary decisions that eliminate solutions downstream.*

Thus, another motto for product development teams should be:

No arbitrary decisions!

Figure 1-2 graphically shows a *decision tree*. The concept of decision
trees applies to everything from product development to life itself. The
tag line in TV ads for the hit show *Touched by an Angle* was:

*In each moment, lies a choice
that can change the story of your life*

The process of developing products is a series of decisions, from
deciding which products to develop to optimizing product architecture to
designing parts. *Every* decision sends you down a certain branch of a
decision tree. Every *arbitrary* decision will probably send you down the
wrong path, which will limit subsequent choices. And more arbitrary
decisions are even more likely to send you further down the wrong path.
So instead of making *methodical* decisions to arrive at the desired point
A, *arbitrary* decisions lead you to point B. And the farther you get into
a design (and the more work is based on that path), the harder it is to
make the changes to backtrack from point B to point A.

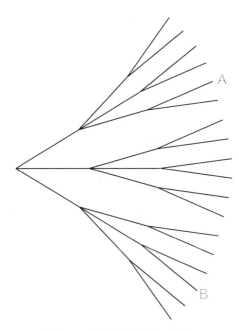

Figure 1-2: Decision Tree

The following list contains some of the common examples of arbitrary decisions that should be avoided in product development:

- **Product definition** is often arbitrary instead of systematically understanding the "voice of the customer" as shown in Section 2.11.

- **Markets in which to compete** may be chosen arbitrarily if overhead costs are averaged, thus obscuring the profitability of individual products. This may lead companies to compete and develop products in markets that, historically, may have not been the most profitable.

- **Project milestone deadlines** are often set early in an arbitrary way (for instance, based on quarterly milestones) and underemphasize crucial architecture optimization.

- **Concept/Architecture** is often based on previous/conventional concepts or the first idea to come to mind.

- **Technologies** may be chosen by "techies" that are impressed with the *advertized* functionality. However, technology decisions also need to include how proven is the technology, its track record, the *total* cost, the *real* availability, the production volume capabilities of the supplier, the financial strength of the supplier, contingency (plan B) planning, and the risks, especially if there are multiple sources of risk.

- **Manufacturing** decisions, if arbitrary, may steer the design in the wrong direction and preclude the best processes and sources.

- **Outsourcing** decisions may arbitrarily draw a line between "us and them," which can result in outsourcing all parts, even when selective internal integration would save time, money, and improve the manufacturability of the design (Section 4.8).[30]

- **Supplier decisions** may be made only on part cost and not include quality, quick turn prototype capabilities, production deliveries, and the value of assistance designing products.

- **Part selection decisions** may be based only on functional specifications and the cost of the part itself, and not include the impact of sourcing, quality, standardization, and the part's impact on total cost.

- **Order of design** may be arbitrarily from "the ground up" or starting with the most obvious or most understood aspects instead of the *most* constrained aspects first, which may be the *least* obvious.

- **Detail design decisions** are often arbitrary if designers ignore any design considerations or don't design the product as a system.

- **Tolerances** are often specified arbitrarily if designers do not understand processes, dimensional referencing, or relationships between multiple tolerances. When in doubt, many designers specify unnecessarily tight tolerances, instead of methodically specifying and dimensioning tolerances, as shown in Section 9.3.

- **Overhead allocation algorithms** usually allocate overhead arbitrarily based on labor, processing, or material costs, which does not provide relevant computations of the *total* cost (Chapter 7).

- **Styling.** Make sure that arbitrary styling decisions do not compromise manufacturability by unnecessarily complicating designs, tooling, and manufacturing operations. Don't allow anything to be thrown over the wall. Instead, the whole team should work together to create styles that both look good *and* are manufacturable.

• **Boxing the design into a corner.** Don't make so many other arbitrary decisions that make the design unnecessarily complicated.

When faced with too many open choices, seek out additional constraints. Not doing so may result in arbitrary decisions that will preclude adding them later. *When stuck,* seek out additional constraints. It may be that a solution can't be justified to solve *one* problem but can if it solves *multiple* problems.

1.9 DFM AND DESIGN TIME

Some designers may be tempted to think that considering all these constraints will take more time to complete the design. But it really takes no more time (maybe even less time) because thinking about all the constraints at once will steer the designer more quickly to the optimal design. In Chapter 12, there is a summary of ten ways that DFM saves design time.

Theoretically, the ideal number of goals and constraints would converge the designer directly to the single optimal design. Too many constraints would result in no solution. But, too few constraints would result in multiple solutions, which should be systematically evaluated. When this is not done, it is unlikely that the chosen solution will optimize manufacturability and all the other constraints.

The net result of not considering manufacturability early is a design which will be hard to incorporate DFM principles later. In order to make such a design manufacturable, it may be necessary to make changes in the design, as discussed next.

1.10 ENGINEERING CHANGE ORDERS

One of the biggest payoffs of "do-it-right-the-first-time" product developments (discussed in Chapter 1) is avoiding expensive and time-consuming engineering change orders, which are usually called *ECO's.*

Early and thorough inclusion of *all* the design considerations can do a lot to minimize the need for change orders. Methodically defining the product to satisfy customer needs (Section 2.11) will avoid changes to "satisfy the customer" – a common, but illusionary, complaint, since "changing" the design to satisfy the customer really means the product definition didn't do a thorough job of gathering the voice of the customer in the first place.

One of the most insidious aspects of change orders is that a change to fix one problem may *induce* new problems. And changes to fix those may induce even *more* problems. Further, change orders will probably negate any qualifications or certifications the product received while in its original form.

The cost of changes rises drastically as the product progresses toward production. Figure 1-3 shows how the cost *for each change* escalates during the development of a major electronics product:[31]

Time of Design Change	Cost
During design:	$1,000
During design testing:	10,000
During process planning:	100,000
During test production:	1,000,000
During final production:	10,000,000

Figure 1-3 Cost of Engineering Changes

Thus it can be concluded that a very expensive and time-consuming way to implement DFM is through Engineering Change Orders (ECOs).
And yet, that is what happens when DFM and all the other consideration are ignored in the early design steps.

1.11 DO IT RIGHT THE FIRST TIME

Do it right the first time, because you will not have the chance to do it again especially for:

- **Fast** paced projects that you *don't have time to do over*

- **Expensive** development projects that you *can't afford to do over*

- **Complex** projects, where *each change may induce other changes*

- **Regulations** or contracts that would *force re-qualification* of the product after *any* changes

And this is the case in most companies today.

Everyone that practices DFM should adopt the motto: *Do it right the first time.* This advice seems so obvious because no designer would begin a design *expecting* to redesign any part of it later. However, it is distressing how many companies routinely tolerate change orders, maybe because they always have. Some companies camouflage the process by euphemistically calling them "revisions" or even "updates." But, regardless of the label, changes, redesigns, and recalls, can have a severe impact on a product's cost and time schedule, not to mention employee morale and corporate reputation.

On the other hand, if designers use these DFM techniques to actually do-it-right-the-first-time, the new product will sail through product introduction into stable, trouble-free production with the best cost, delivery and quality to provide early customer satisfaction.

Companies' goals should be that each product is designed *once* and that the initial design can be manufactured easily as a high quality product and, of course, works properly. In many companies, the DFM program evolves from some "never again" trauma to a do-it-right-the-first-time thrust including the following strategies and methodologies.

1.12 STRATEGY TO DO IT RIGHT THE FIRST TIME

The strategy starts with multi-functional teams with *all* specialties present and active *early* and good *product definition* that eliminates engineering changes to satisfy the customer.

Throughout the product development process, the team must be raising issues (the "what if's" and the "what about's") and resolving them early through simulations, experiments, research, and early models, mock-ups, solid models, and "rapid prototypes," with statistical significance assured by Design of Experiments. Critical applications may need Failures Modes and Effects Analyses (FMEA). The MIT study, *The Machine that Changed the World,*[32] summarized that best lean projects: ". . . the project leader's job is to force the group to confront all the difficult tradeoffs [issues] they'll have to make to agree on the project."

The team must understand *lessons learned* from previous projects through summaries of lessons learned databases, investigations of lessons learned from previous projects, and presentations and feedback from previous projects, vendors, in-house production.[33]

The team needs to formulate "Plan B" contingency plans to deal with the most likely changes, setbacks, delays, shortages, or other problems regarding technology, processing, customers, markets, regulation, and so forth. For instance, products can be designed to readily accept the "Plan B" part if the "Plan A" part doesn't work out or is not available in time.

The team needs to achieve concurrence before proceeding. Another MIT study, *Made in America, Regaining the Productive Edge,* gave additional insight into Japanese product development project management:[34] "A key task of the manager is to make sure that all disagreements [issues] are aired and resolved at the outset. *Achieving consensus takes a great deal of effort,* but by skillful management at this point it is possible to gain the full commitment of all members of the program team so that *subsequent progress is very rapid.* "

The design of the product can be done right the first time by simplifying the concept and optimizing product architecture, thoroughly designing the product, focusing on new and pivotal aspects with optimal use of precious engineering, peer review and design checking, and good documentation management.

The design needs to be *conveyed* to production *unambiguously* so the product is built right the first time. And all changes, updates, and revisions, must be implemented *promptly and accurately* so that subsequent designs will be done right the first time.

Finally, fast development has the least vulnerability to changing environments with respect to changing customer preferences, markets, competitors, regulation, and trends.

1.13 COMPANY BENEFITS OF DFM

The following slogan sums up the importance of DFM:

Functionality gets us into the game;
Quality and reliability keep us in the game;
Manufacturability determines the profit.

And yet most engineers and managers focus primarily on functionality which gets a product into the game. In order to stay in the game, that product needs to be produced at high quality and reliability. And what about profits? Unless the product has a formidable head start or incredibly strong patents, the product will have to be priced competitively, which then means that profits will be determined by the cost. And, as pointed out earlier and in Section 6.1, it is very difficult to reduce cost by "cost reduction" efforts after the product is designed. Therefore, profits are determined by how well low cost can be assured *by design* – that is *designed for manufacturability.*

The benefits of DFM range from the obvious cost, quality and delivery to some important subtle benefits:

Lower production cost. Designing for simplicity, fewer parts, and easier assembly results in lower assembly cost. Lower *cost of quality* (Section 6.9) results from fewer parts and foolproof assembly. Smoother product introduction means less time spent on costly change orders and "firefighting" to deal with product introduction problems.

Higher quality. Higher quality results from more robust designs, fewer parts, foolproof assembly (Section 10.9), optimal process selection/design, the use of more standardized parts with known good quality, and designing around proven engineering, parts, modules, and processes.

Quicker time to market. DFM products fit better into existing processes and are less likely to require special equipment and procedures. The use of standard parts means most will be on hand or be easy to procure. Better DFM means fewer product introduction problems leading to a quick and smooth introduction.

Lower capital equipment cost. Designs that assemble easily need less time on assembly machinery. Less need for special equipment saves equipment capital. Designing to minimize setup (Section 4.6) and the use of standardized parts results in fewer setup changes, thus leading to greater machinery utilization.

Greater automation potential. Designing for automatic assembly maximizes the potential for automation with all its cost and quality advantages.

Production up to speed sooner. Faster development, fewer introduction problems, and less need for special equipment or procedures result in production that will be up to speed sooner.

Fewer engineering changes. Early "changes" are much easier to do than later changes that are under change control procedures. If the original design satisfies *all* the goals and constraints (Section 3.5), it will not have to be changed or redesigned for manufacturability or any of the other design considerations.

Fewer parts to purchase from fewer vendors. Having fewer parts to purchase saves purchasing expense, especially for standard parts. Dealing with fewer suppliers strengthens relations with those suppliers and results in less cost and effort to qualify parts and deal with quality problems.

Factory availability. Fewer production problems and greater machine tool utilization make factories more available for other products.

1.14 PERSONAL BENEFITS OF DFM

The above discussion cites many *corporate* justifications for DFM. The following points are used in the author's seminars[35] to motivate engineers at the *personal* level.

Why Bother to Do Anything Differently?

Many engineers think that their companies are doing fine and they are really too busy to do anything differently, especially if company success is somehow based on "technology." However, there are many compelling reasons to apply these methodologies.

1. **Assure the health of company and job security.** Very few companies are free of competitive pressures, even those with an apparent technological lead. Very few can coast along in such a turbulent and fast changing environment.

2. **World-class new product development increases fortunes** of the company *and* its employees and offers many career opportunities.

3. **Work will be more interesting** because, by using these principles, engineers will spend a higher proportion of their time doing fun design work and less time on change orders and fire fighting.

4. **The next project will be a better experience** because:

   • You won't be distracted by change orders or firefights on past projects

   • New projects can build on successful new practices and get better each time

5. **Survive, and thrive, in either growth scenario:**

   A) **Company slips:** Engineers will be under pressure to lower cost and accelerate product introductions in the face of dwindling resources.

   B) **Company grows:**

   • Production workers will be under pressure to meet demand; Engineers will have to help solve production problems that may have been tolerable in lower volumes but are "show stoppers" at peak demands.

- New opportunities will probably be more challenging, thus compounding new problems if not done right the first time.

- Since *new* engineers will be less adept at solving problems on existing products, they will probably be assigned to new designs, leaving *current* engineers to continue troubleshooting existing products.

1.15 CONCLUSIONS

DFM alone may make the difference between being competitive and not succeeding in the marketplace. Most markets are highly competitive, so slight competitive advantages (or disadvantages) can have significant impact.

DFM may make the difference between a competitive product line and, in the extreme, products that are not manufacturable at all. Products fail and go out of production because costs are too high, quality is too low, the introduction was too late, or production couldn't keep up with demand. These are all manufacturability issues and therefore very much affected by DFM.

ENDNOTES/REFERENCES

1. David M. Anderson, *Build-to-Order & Mass Customization, The Ultimate Supply Chain Management and Lean Manufacturing Strategy for Low-Cost On-Demand Production without Forecasts or Inventory,* (2004, 520 pages, CIM Press). Also see articles at www.build-to-order-consulting.com.

2. Also see Section 6.1, "How Not to Lower Cost," and Section 11.5, "Stop Counterproductive Policies."

3. Anderson, *Build-to-Order & Mass Customization;* Also see articles at www.build-to-order-consulting.com.

4. This data was generated by DataQuest and presented in the landmark article that started the Concurrent Engineering movement: "A Smarter Way to Manufacture; How `Concurrent Engineering' can invigorate American Industry," page 110, *Business Week,* April 30, 1990. In the author's in-house seminars, he presents similar data from Motorola, Ford, General Motors, Westinghouse, Rolls Royce, British Aerospace, the Allison Division of Detroit Diesel, Draper Labs, Rensselear Polytechnic

Institute, and several other published sources.

5. Satoshi Hino, *Inside the Mind of Toyota, Management Principles for Enduring Growth,* Chapter 3, "Toyota's System of Management Functions," p. 133.

6. Robin Cooper, *When Lean Enterprises Collide,* (1995, Harvard Business School Press); Part Three, "Managing the Costs of Future Products," page 131.

7. Ibid., Chapter 7, "Target Costing."

8. Yasuhiro Monden, *Cost Reduction Systems; Target Costing and Kaizen Costing,* (1995, Productivity Press).

9. See Offshoring article at www.HalfCostProducts.com/offshore_ manufacturing.htm

10. Gupta and Wileman, "Accelerating the Development of Technology-based New Products," *California Management Review,* Winter 1990.

11. Jim Brown, *The Product Portfolio Management Benchmark Report*, Achieving Maximum Product Value, August 2006, the Aberdeen Group,: http://www.aberdeen.com/link/sponsor.asp?spid=30410396&cid=3359

12. In the Aberdeen Group study, *product failure* was defined as "products that are not launched or launched products that significantly fall below revenue, market share, or profit targets,"

13. Jordan D. Lewis, *The Connected Corporation, How Leading Companies Win Through Customer-Supplier Alliances,* (New York, Free Press, 1995), page 38.

14. Shu Shin Luh, *Business the Sony Way* (2003, John Wiley & Sons), p. 195.

15. Dan Steinbock, The Nokia Revolution; The Story of an Extraordinary Company That Transformed an Industry (2001, AMACOM), p. 186.

16. James Womack, Daniel Jones, and Daniel Roos, *The Machine that Changed the World; The Story of Lean Production,* (1990, Rawson

Associates; 1991, paperback edition, Harper Perennial); pages 129- 130.

17. Lee Dongyoup, Samsung Electronics - the Global Inc. (2006, YSM Inc., Seoul, Korea), Chapter 5, "Research & Development," p. 97.

18. David Pringle, "How Nokia Thrives by Breaking the Rules," *The Wall Street Journal,* January 3, 2003.

19. John Teresko, "Recapturing R&D Leadership," *Industry Week,* August 2006, p. 29.

20. From a 2005 Deloitte study, cited in Industry Week article on Management Strategies, May 2005, p. 46

21.Bill George, *Authentic Leadership; Rediscovering the Secrets of Creating Lasting Value;* (2003, Jossey-Bass), Chapter 12, "Innovations from the Heart," p. 137

22. Ibid., p. 63

23. Jeffrey L. Cruikshank, The Apple Way (2006, McGraw-Hill); p. 26.

24. Lee Dongyoup, Samsung Electronics - the Global Inc. (2006, YSM Inc., Seoul, Korea), Chapter 4, "Research & Development," p. 83.

25. Bill George, *Authentic Leadership*, Chapter 12, "Innovations from the Heart," pp. 133-134.

26. "Out of the Dusty Labs," *The Economist,* March 3rd - 9th, 2007, pp. 74 - 76.

27. Dan Steinbock, The Nokia Revolution; The Story of an Extraordinary Company That Transformed an Industry (2001, AMACOM), p. 185.

28. "The New Heat on Ford, *Business Week*, June 4, 2007, pp. 32 - 38.

29. "Smart Partners," *Business Week;* review of "The Connected Corporation" by Jordan D. Lewis.

30. Anderson, *Build-to-Order & Mass Customization,* Chapter 6, "Outsourcing vs. Integration." Also see the article on Outsourcing at

www.HalfCostProducts.com/outsourcing.htm   and   also
www.HalfCostProducts.com/offshore_manufacturing.htm   which
discusses offshoring.

31. "A Smarter Way to Manufacture; How `Concurrent Engineering' Can
Reinvigorate American Industry," page 110, Business Week, April 30,
1990.

32. *"The Machine That Changed the World,"* Based on the MIT 5-
Million-Dollar 5-Year Study on the Future of the Automobile, by James
Womack, Daniel Jones, & Daniel Roos, published by Rawson
Associates, 1990.

33. The feedback forms in Appendix C can be used to solicit valuable
feedback from factories, vendors, and field service.

34. *"Made in America, Regaining the Productive Edge,"* from the MIT
commission on Industrial Productivity, by Dertouzos, Lester & Solow,
published by Harper Perennial, 1989.

35. For more information on customized in-house DFM seminars, see the last
page of this book or *www.design4manufacturability.com/seminars.htm.*

2

CONCURRENT ENGINEERING

Concurrent Engineering is the practice of concurrently developing products *and* their manufacturing processes. If *existing* processes are to be utilized, then the product must be design for these processes. If *new* processes are to be utilized, then the product *and* the process must be developed *concurrently.* This requires knowing a lot about manufacturing processes and one of the best ways to do this is to develop products in multifunctional teams.

The most critical factor in the success of Concurrent Engineering is the availability of resources to form multifunctional teams *with all specialties present and active early.*

2.1 RESOURCES

The most distinct contrast between advanced and primitive product development methodologies, presented in the landmark $5 million MIT study, "The Machine that Changed the World, *The Story of Lean Production,"* was on assuring that all the specialties are present and active early:[1]

> *"In the best Japanese 'lean' projects, the numbers of people involved are highest at the very outset. All the relevant specialties are present, and the project leader's job is to force the group to confront all the difficult tradeoffs they'll have to make to agree on the project."*

> *"By contrast, in many mass-produced design exercises, the number of people involved is very small at the outset but grows to a peak very close to the time of launch, as hundreds or even thousands of extra bodies are brought in to resolve problems that should have been cleared up in the beginning."*

31

This supports the philosophy of this book, which emphasizes thorough up-front work. Figure 2-1 graphically shows this "front loading" in the *Advanced Model* compared to the upper graph, which shows *Traditional Team Participation.*

The traditional product development gets off to a bad start with a vague understanding of customers' needs, with the production definition based on technological advancements, whims, or previous or competitive products. Typically, only a few people are available at the beginning, either because of resource availability problems or by choice because project management doesn't appreciate the value of complete teams. In some cases, product development begins with a small clique because of downright exclusivity or because some elite people think that "DFM starts after they are finished" (which was actually said by one physicist).

Whether or not deficiencies in the team composition are acknowledged, schedule pressures will force the "team" to make some "progress." And, a key part of making progress is making decisions. However, without the benefit of a complete team, the decisions will probably not address all the considerations discussed in Chapter 3. This problem will be even worse if there is no diversity among the people involved, for instance, if everyone works in the same department and has the same education and experiences.

Unfortunately, without a complete team, many early decisions will be *arbitrary,* which is especially problematic as these arbitrary decisions then become the basis for subsequent decisions, which in turn, will have even fewer open options. After several levels of subsequent arbitrary decision making, the product architecture becomes "cast in concrete," which makes it very hard to optimize or correct later.

Continuing to following the sequence in the top graph of Figure 2-1, what is perceived to be a "complete" team eventually forms, but it is not as complete as recommended herein. The team may proceed for a while in a state of naive contentment, but eventually there will have to be some form of redirection because of the inadequate product definition or because of the arbitrary decisions. So then more effort is expended, possible with more people added, because the project is starting to get "into trouble."

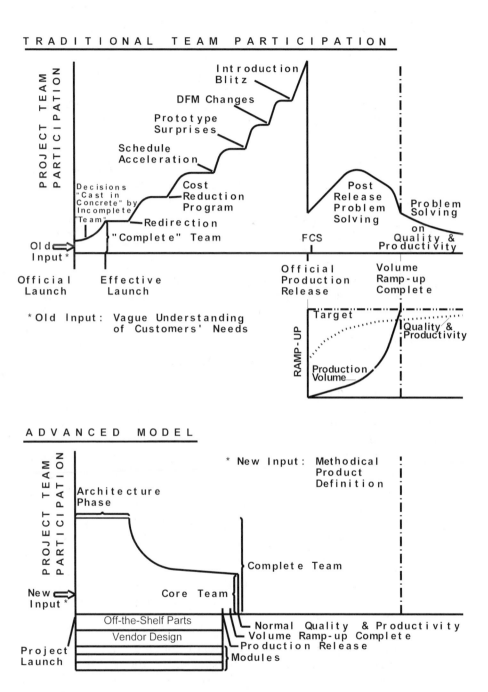

Figure 2-1 Team Participation: Traditional vs Advanced Models

By the time cost estimates are generated, word gets out that the cost is too high, so then there is a cost reduction program. But, it will be difficult to reduce cost at this stage, since 60% of cumulative cost is committed in the architecture stage, as shown in Figure 1-1.

After the above redirections and delays, the project is now behind, so the schedule needs to be "accelerated." This is so common that one product development book even has a chapter titled, "Through Money At It" based on the thinking that time is more valuable than money at this point.

Then come the *prototype surprises,* which are the inevitable consequences of an incomplete team, cumulative arbitrary decisions, and failure to address all the design considerations of Chapter 3. Work then proceeds after many fire-drills to try to correct problems and get *the* prototype to work. Of course, one prototype is not a statistical significant sample, so real life production problems could be worse indicated by a prototype.

Then the typical project starts to consider DFM only as production ramps approach. If DFM was not designed early in the product, it will probably be very difficult to make the product manufacturable through changes at this late a date (Murphy's law of product development). Faced with the formidable scope of implementing DFM by change order under intense time pressures, only the easy changes are pursued and production soon begins on a product with questionable manufacturability.

As the product goes into production, manufacturability shortcomings manifest as painfully slow ramps, sometimes taking months to reach the volume production target. Manufacturability problems also show up as poor quality and disappointing productivity which may take even longer to attain acceptable levels. Not only do these delays and shortcomings disappoint customers, but they also consume a great deal of resources – resources that should have been utilized more wisely at the proactive beginning, not the inefficient reactive end of the project. This, or course, emphasizes the importance of measuring time-to-market to the time of full stabilized production, instead of *first-customer-ship,* which is meaningless as a measure of time-to-market – the factory could build three and ship the one that works!

Does this scenario sound familiar? In fact, most of the attendees queried in the author's seminars[2] admit that many elements in this sequence are quite familiar, many painfully so.

In the Advanced Model in Figure 2-1, all the relevant specialties are present and active early. If each team member has a versatile background and can represent multiple specialties, then the team would be smaller and easier to manage. The complete team is formed at the very beginning to simplify concepts and optimize product architecture (Section 3.3). In addition to the full-time core team are vendors, consultants, and part-time specialists for specific tasks such as various analyses and regulatory compliance.

The activities start with a methodical product definition, as discussed in Section 2.11. After the Architecture Phase is thoroughly optimized, the remaining workload actually can drop off because: (a) many tasks may be completed; (b) the off-the-shelf parts selected avoid the associated design efforts; (c) vendors help design parts or actually design parts entirely; and (d) previous modules can be utilized or the design of new modules can be shared with other projects.

The result is that the volume ramp is completed quickly. Similarly, normal quality and productivity targets are reached rapidly. One important result is the ability to cut in half the *real* time-to-market as measured to stable production. The other equally important result is that the cost of engineering resources (the areas under either curve) is half compared to the traditional model.

Front-loading at Toyota

> *"Because front-loading solves problems at a root cause level early in the process, it nearly eliminates the traditional product development problem of late design changes, which are expensive, suboptional, and always degrade both product and process performance."*[3]

2.2 ENSURING RESOURCE AVAILABILITY

Resource Capability

Schedules or workloads should *never exceed the capability of design teams to develop good products.* If this is a problem, the solutions are: (a) less aggressive schedules and less ambitious workloads; (b) hiring more people, or (c) more efficient product development methodology, which results from designing products for manufacturability.

Resource Availability

The success of product development will be dependent on how complete – how *multifunctional* – the teams are and how *early* the complete team is active. Most companies understand the value of complete teams, but do not form them early because of resource availability problems. The resource situation is even more difficult when a company is converting from a back-loaded model to a front-loaded model, in which it is difficult to find enough people for a complete team when many of the people are still busy fixing the problems of the last product developments.

Resource availability issues can be solved with good prioritization of product development efforts and efficient use of team members time.

Solutions to Resource Availability Problems

Good product development methodologies can solve resource availability problems and save development cost and time with the following techniques:

- by **prioritizing product development projects** and only embarking on high return development efforts that have the most synergies with other development projects (see Section 2.3 on Product Portfolio Planning).

  The book, *Fast Innovation*,[4] presents a case study at Motorola which clearly shows how too many projects diminish the chances of project success. In 2002, Motorola's Computer Group tried to develop 120 products, but resources were spread so thin that *no products were introduced at all!* The next year they cut the development load to 22 projects and were able to introduce eight products, which took 24 to 28 months. In 2004, as they got more focused with only 20 projects, they were able to successfully launch almost twice as many products in half the time!

  During this span, *manufacturing productivity tripled, early life failures decreased by 38 times, customer satisfaction rose from 27% to 90%, revenue increased by 2.4 times, and operational earnings increased from -6% to +7%.*

  Further, the Motorola case study also correlated project success with the total number of products in the portfolio: The year when they had no products introduced, this division had 3500 products in its portfolio. After this dropped to 2,000, they launched eight products and after it dropped to 500, they were able to launch 14 products. The effect of the entire portfolio on product development effectiveness is discussed in the next point.

- by **rationalizing products** to eliminate or outsource demanding products currently in production which consume too many hours of product development resources.

  A proliferation of too many products in the portfolio means that valuable resources from Manufacturing Engineering and Purchasing, who should be helping teams develop new products, will be too busy trying to build a multitude of low-volume and unusual products with the usual firedrills to set up production, deal with the problems typically encountered with unrefined products, and find unusual parts.

Because these oddball products have such high overhead costs, they are probably losing money (or making significantly less than desired) and to pay for that loss, the *good* products will have to subsidize them – think of it as a "loser tax" on all good products.

Portfolio proliferation has a double whammy on new product development. Not only are resources drained away to build oddball products, but when the new product is launched, it *too* will have to pay this loser tax to subsidize unprofitable products, thus raising the new product's selling price, which, in turn, will make it less competitive.

The solution is to *rationalize* product lines to eliminate or outsource "loser" products to free up valuable resources to help develop "winner" products. Rationalization not only improves product development immediately (because resources are freed up whenever a company turns down a high-overhead product), but it also will improve profits immediately by eliminating the money losing products. Effective methodologies for Product Line Rationalization are presented in Appendix A.

- by **outsourcing legacy products and spare parts** production and management, unless synergistic with current production processes *and* supply chains. Legacies and spares are especially demanding when they are "revived from the dead" and haven't been built for years. *If you must build legacy products & spares, be sure to charge enough to cover <u>all</u> the costs and use that money to hire more people to build them.*

- by **outsourcing parts and subassemblies** that are hard to build, are too different, or require special skill, talent, and equipment.

- by **avoiding the practice of raiding internal resources** from critical functions. This just shifts the hiring/training burden to the critical functions, which will be weakened by both the loss of experience and the need to find and train new hires. Poorly documented companies that rely on "tribal lore" must minimize *all* forms of turnover for groups that have people that remember or know valuable knowledge and can convey that to new product development projects. *Maximize overall effectiveness by hiring for growth from the outside, unless the internal transfer results in a net gain for the company.*

- by **preserving and documenting "lessons learned"** to avoid wasting resources and time repeating past mistakes and missing out on more efficient techniques and methodologies.

- by **focusing on new and pivotal aspects of the product design**, not boilerplate and parts that could be reused or bought off-the-shelf.

- by **buying standard off-the-shelf parts** instead of designing redundant versions.

- by **reusing previously designed details, parts, and subassemblies** and software code.

- by **farming out part designs** to part vendors when appropriate.

- by **scrutinizing unusual requests for modifications/customizations** and making sure to properly estimate the total cost and resource demands.

- by **using *configurators*** to automate the processes of determining the feasibility, cost, and time to do customizations, instead of the time-consuming and less accurate manual estimating.

- by **using modular design** to use existing modules or share engineering with multiple projects.

- with **more efficient customization** using modular design and mass customization techniques.

- by **using parametric CAD** so that customizations and "new" designs can be quickly created from parametric templates.

- by **more quickly converging on the optimal design**.

- by **minimizing test development** with high enough product and process quality that can allow discarding failures instead of the developing diagnostic test needed to repair them. A six-sigma environment results in only about 3 defects/million - not worth developing diagnostic tests for.

- by **avoiding problems with factory ramp-up and productivity** targets with more thorough up-front work

- by **avoiding problems with quality and reliability** by optimizing quality/tolerances in the design stage.

- with **fewer engineering changes to write** when teams *do it right the first time.*

- by **pursuing only truly cost effective ECOs** on existing products.

- by **avoiding redesigns** for manufacturability, quality, or reliability.

- by **avoiding supply chain distractions** that keep manufacturing engineers and purchasing people from making significant contributions to product development team participation because they would be distracted by:

  - finding, qualifying, evaluating, and choosing among multiple vendor bids. As Womack, Jones, and Roos said in the book that started the lean production movement in the U.S., *in the best companies studied, vendors "are not selected on the basis of bids, but rather on the basis of past relationships and a proven record of performance."[5]*

  - finding, qualifying, or evaluating for *new low-bidders* to replace current vendors.

  - working with new low-bidders to help them up the learning curve *again.*

  - writing new contracts and change orders to accommodate new vendors with respect to material changes, different processes, translations, converting CAD drawings, generating new machine tool programming.

  - dealing with new low-bidder problems regarding quality, performance, delivery, etc.

  Part of the project leader's responsibility at Motorola is to be *"able to shield their team from distractions and people who are not actively contributing to the completion of the project."[6]*

- by selectively hiring more people to **correct critical resource shortages** that have created gaps in multifunctional teams, which all need the optimal balance of talent. Critical gaps in team participation will prevent the team from proactively avoiding the very problems that cost much more to resolve later. Thus, this hiring will represent a net savings for the company.

  Groups that support product development, like Manufacturing Engineering, should be billed to the development project, to avoid resistance to "increasing overhead costs."

Manufacturing Engineer Availability

To protect product development support from firefighting distractions and maximize their participation in product development teams, restructure Manufacturing Engineering into three subgroups that are financed and staffed differently:

- **New Product Development** support, which should be paid for by the development project. This function would be staffed with manufacturing engineers most experienced in new product introduction.

- **Process improvements** which may be on overhead, but is expected to pay back investments in process cost savings. This function would be staffed by MEs most competent in process improvement.

- **Firefighting and change orders** should ideally be paid for by the product involved, which would require total cost measurement (Chapter 7). This function should be staffed by appropriate personnel who are experienced in the ECO/firefighting process, not necessarily all degreed manufacturing or industrial engineers.

2.3 PRODUCT PORTFOLIO PLANNING

The very first step in product development is deciding what to develop. Product portfolio planning is the *proactive* determination of what products to develop.

- Prioritize product development efforts to focus resources on the *most profitable products* to maximize the ratio of total gain over total cost. Total gain includes the potential gains for all variations and derivatives over time. Total cost includes all overhead cost to be incurred by the candidates. Toyota uses *multiproject management to optimize the sharing of resources across multiple, concurrent projects.*[7]

- Prioritize customers and customer segments and focus on the ones with the best current and future opportunities for profit and growth.[8]

- Allocate resources proportional to the challenge (count and mix) for new technology, risk, cost, time, and so forth.

- Know the true profitability of all product variations to deliver the highest return from given resources.

- Develop profiles that describe the characteristics of the most profitable customers and customer segments. Use these profiles to help prioritize product development opportunities, scrutinize unusual or low-volume sales, and rationalize away high-overhead, low-profit products.

- Focus on product *families* that can benefit from synergies in product development, operations, and supply chain management. Identify opportunities where products could benefit from Build-to-Order of standard products and the Mass Customization of specials.[9] Toyota produces an average of seven different vehicles on each platform, which maximizes reliability across vehicle types. Platforms are designed to be a basis for these vehicles for up to 15 years.[10]

- Plan the portfolio around versatile products and flexible processes that can (a) easily satisfy the anticipated range of product breadth and customization, (b) have the potential to satisfy even broader ranges of customer needs, and (c) easily adapt to evolving trends and upgrade possibilities

- Plan the portfolio to avoid the commodity trap, with its inherently low profits, and evolve to innovative products designed for low cost and sold at high profit. Set aside resources and budget for *breakthroughs*[11] in *blue oceans* where innovative products would create uncontested markets. Based on analysis of 150 strategic moves spanning a hundred years and thirty industries, the *Blue Ocean Strategy* recommends using *value innovation* to pursue differentiation and low cost simultaneously,[12] a goal that is also supported by Mass Customization, which can achieve premium prices at lower cost.[13]

- Use all the above techniques to prioritize the portfolio to maximize the return from available resources. Make sure *all* approved projects will have enough resources *with the right mix of talent,* for thorough up-front work and consistently methodical work throughout the project.

- Make all product portfolio decisions rationally and objectively. Avoid temptations to base portfolio decisions on automatic upgrades, enticing market opportunities, exciting technology, whims, pet projects, competitive precedents, and so forth. Do not allow portfolio decisions to be influenced by politics, powerful backers, attachments, inertia, fears, unrealistic expectations, folklore (e.g., "I heard somewhere that . . . "), and so forth.

- Don't limit "the portfolio" to only *products*. Invest in research and module development that can benefit a broad stream of future products. At Toyota, *"managers might spend over half their time on a portfolio of ideas and projects."*[14]

- Make total cost numbers the cost basis of all product portfolio decisions, as discussed in Chapter 7.

- Relieve resource demands caused by *existing* products by planning versatile new products that can also replace hard-to-build/low-profit products that the company may not be able to rationalize away.

2.4 PARALLEL AND FUTURE PROJECTS

Each product development team should be coordinated with other *parallel* product development teams to simultaneously work together to set compatible design strategy, share engineering effort on common design features, determine common parts for use on all projects, and design modules for use on multiple projects.

Further, *future* projects should be considered to set design strategy for current *and* future projects, establish an upgrade path for current products, isolate areas most likely to change to minimize engineering on future projects, and design modules on which future projects can be based.

Management guru Peter Drucker has presented a powerful version of this principle.[15] He recommends the procedure where "a single team of engineers, scientists, marketers, and manufacturers works simultaneously on *three* levels on innovation:

1) At the lowest level, they seek incremental improvement of an existing product;

2) At the second, they try for a significant jump;

3) The third is true innovation.

The idea is to produce three new products to replace each present product, *with the same investment of time and money* - with one of the three then becoming the new market leader."

Along a similar vein, the latest "Megatrends" book, *Megatrends 2010,* reports that at Medtronics, "for each product launched, the company is working on four generations of upgrades."[16]

"At any one time, Philips Consumer Electronics is actively working on three product generations: one in production, one in final development (for which major changes are not acceptable), and one at the concept generation stage (which is where new ideas enter)."[17]

At Sony, *"from the moment the first machine was made, and before it even hit the market, Sony's engineers were already back at the design table, refining and tweaking the original blueprints to get better sound and better quality tapes to the consumers."*[18]

In all these examples, many parts and design aspects are the same while others are similar. In the first level, designers can leave hooks, connectors, and space for future features. The customers and marketing channels may be the same. While purchasing agents are getting quotes on the current models or volumes, they can easily get quotes on alternate parts and higher volumes for subsequent endeavors.

2.5 DESIGNING PRODUCTS AS A TEAM

The team should be designing the product concurrently *as a team.* In multifunctional design teams, *all members are expected to jointly design the product.*

Team members should: *not* react to drawings or prototypes; *not* give their first "input" after something has been designed or in design reviews; and *not* interact only in weekly meetings. Rather, team members should be continuously working together and calling *huddles* to resolve issues as they need to be addressed.

Major decisions should be made by the whole team, or at least all the relevant members.

Manufacturing Participation

One of the most effective ways to assure manufacturability is the early and active participation from manufacturing, including manufacturing engineers, tool designers, and whoever is experienced with problems and changes regarding assembly, throughput, quality, testing, repair, and ramping into production.

It is *much* easier to prevent these problem in the design phase instead of trying to deal with these problems when the product is going into production.

What Manufacturing people should be doing early in product development teams:

- Fully conveying the difficulties encountered, and their consequences, when products are not designed for manufacturability.

- Turning this experience into actionable proactive design recommendations and manufacturing strategies including:
  - Processing strategy, including process selection, the flows of part and products, flexible cell/line design for product families
  - Investigating the optimal use of automation and CNC operations, and, if necessary, making them flexible enough for high-mix operations (mass customization)
  - Optimizing outsourcing and internal integration decisions[19]
  - Helping the team choose and find off-the-shelf parts
  - Resupply strategy for parts and raw materials
  - Identify the supplier base for purchased parts and materials
  - The vendor strategy for custom parts, possibly part design by vendor
  - Identifying potential vendor partnerships early and arranging for early participation on the design team.
  - Strategies for quality/reliability assurance and test
  - Mistake-proofing (poka-yoke) strategies
  - Manufacturing strategy for customization, configurations, product variety, extensions, and derivatives

- Helping the team actually design the product

- Pushing back on any distracting activities that contribute less to the company's *real* profitability than new product development, such as cost reduction on existing products, building low-volume or oddball products, accepting unusual customizations, building legacy products, spare parts production, implementing big IT programs, qualifying new low-bidders and getting them up the learning curve, and dealing with quality problems from low-bidders, and so forth.

- Being an early and active team member; thoroughly raising and resolving all issues related to manufacturability; be proactive and forceful to ensure the product is designed for manufacturability.

Manufacturing Participation at Toyota

"Manufacturing and production engineers are now involved very early in the design process – working with design engineers at the concept development stage, to give input on manufacturing issues."[20]

Team Composition

The multifunctional aspect of teamwork requires representation of all relevant specialties, as discussed in greater detail in Section 2.9. Key team members may be full-time while some members may be part time (see below). The team should be led by a strong team leader, as will be discussed in Section 2.7.

In the concept/architecture phase, team staffing should consist of:

- System engineers (system architects) whose focus is simplifying concepts, optimizing product (system) architecture, system integration, off-the-shelf part decisions, and so forth.
- All the functions and specialists that are needed to optimize the product architecture (see Section 3.3)
- For critical parts, that part's designer should be an early and active participant in system engineering of the product or subassembly to help optimize the systems architecture concept that determines the part's requirements.

In the design phase, team staffing should consist of:

- Enough system engineering resources to ensure optimal system architecture and integration.
- A well coordinated group of part and subsystem designers and manufacturing people concurrently designing the parts and processing.

Team Composition at Apple

Apple *"believes that having all the experts in the same place – the mechanical, electrical, software, and industrial engineers, as well as the product designers – leads to a more holistic perspective on product development."* – The Apple Way[21]

Team Continuity at Philips

At Philips, the team *"continues from planning through design and interactive problem solving to final products being shipped. The constant makeup of the team supports easy raising of issues, shared understandings, and fast decisions. While new people occasionally enter the process, total continuity is essential during the final design iteration.* "[22]

Part-Time Participation.

Smaller companies may not have enough resources for several complete product development teams staffed exclusively with full-time personnel. In these companies, specialists (for instance: regulatory compliance, heat flow analysis, stress analysis, tolerance analysis, design of experiments, etc.) may be assigned to multiple products on a part-time basis. It is especially important that *each* team have a *complete* set of expertise early when fundamental decisions are being made. However, these part-time people must not be "spread so thin" that they cannot make meaningful contributions to all projects.

Xomed (division of Metronic) makes sure part-time team members have enough focus on all their projects:

"To assure that engineers pay close attention to projects, Xomed limits them to no more than two projects concurrently. Xomed can't afford to have time conflicts delay moving a hot new product to market." [23]

Using Outside Expertise

Consider bringing in consultants, experts, and contractors to help smooth out peak demands, enhance diversity, and add specific expertise when needed. Be careful to assure the availability of these workers when the team needs them and assure security of critical or proprietary knowledge.

"To avoid compromising either quality or time-to-market with not-invented-here issues, Xomed contracts expertise when needed." [24]

The Value of Diversity

One important benefit of having the multidisciplinary membership is to provide a variety of experience and viewpoints.

This diversity will help the team perform some of its most important tasks of raising issues, resolving issues, solving problems, and generating ideas. When Bill George was Chairman and CEO of Medtronic, he said:

"It is diversity, and the intense debates it generates, that leads to the best decisions. By calling upon the broad experiences of team members, you can avoid pitfalls and make better decisions." [25]

2.6 VENDOR/PARTNERSHIPS

Early Vendor Involvement

One of the main strengths of Concurrent Engineering is *early* and *active* participation of vendors (which is defined here as a supplier who builds your custom parts). The only way to get this is to *preselect* the vendor/partner on the basis of past relationships and a proven record of performance. They will not participate early unless they are reasonably sure paid work will follow. Implying vendors will get the business and then going out for bids will alienate vendors and ruin previous relationships.

Industry Week's "Best Plant" survey of the 25 top performing candidates found that 92% emphasize early supplier involvement in product development.[26]

"Toyota selects suppliers early in the product development program, guarantees the business, and incorporates them as part of the extended product development team."

"Teamwork at Motorola is imbedded in the firm's culture, and this is one reason for its success with supply alliances." The teams *"focus on quality (as broadly defined), speed (in terms of removing non-value-added steps), and cost reduction."*[27]

Vendor/partnerships will result in a *lower net cost* because:

- Having the vendor help design the part will greatly improve the manufacturability, quality, and lead time, thus resulting in lower manufacturing and quality costs because vendors thoroughly understand the DFM rules and guidelines for their process, in general, and for their equipment, in particular.

- Vendor/partners who work with their customers from the beginning will be able to *charge less* because they (a) understand the part requirement better, due to more thorough interactions, (b) are able work with their customer to minimize cost, and (c) won't have to add a "cushion" to deal with an unknown customer. A leading expert on supplier relations said:

  "Suppliers often add a risk premium to their pricing (thus raising the customer's cost) to cover nondisclosed or unexplored customer requirements or design flaws that may require later adjustments."[28]

- Vendors can help avoid arbitrary decisions, which unnecessarily raise cost, delay delivery, and compromise quality. One of the worst causes of arbitrary decisions is styling, especially when the designer throws a pretty shape over the wall to Engineering, which then throws it over another wall to Manufacturing, who then throws it over yet another wall to the vendor – so the tool maker is three walls away from the designer! When designers work directly with tooling engineers, the results are designs that both look good *and* are easily manufacturable.

- Vendor/partners will provide the lowest *total cost* because interacting with the customer's team results in vendors thoroughly understanding the challenges and issues, making "what if" suggestions early that will maximize manufacturability, and working with customers early to minimize total cost

- Vendor/partnerships benefit from *learning relationships* in which the customer and vendor learn from each other, thus making each job better and faster.

- After *preselecting* vendors, the team can then benefit from more participation from their own purchasing people who will now be able to help the team make the best off-the-shelf decisions, find the best balance of cost, quality, and delivery, and optimize availability for the life of the product, and so forth. At Motorola, bringing in vendors into the team has proven to be a major contributor to a project's success.[29]

Without vendor/partnerships, the design would be thrown over the wall to the vendor. And unless the customer's engineers thoroughly understand the processes, which is rare, the design will not be optimized for manufacturability and, worse, it will be hard for the vendor to make changes to make it more manufacturable because (a) there is usually no calendar time for changes, (b) there is usually no budget for changes either at the customer or the vendor, and (c) by this point, most changes will be difficult because of the reasons discussed in Section 6.11.

Vendor Selection

- Select vendors on the basis of:
  - capabilities, past relationships, and a proven record of performance, not low-bidding[30]
  - financial stability; get Dunn & Bradstreet or similar reports

- *your* business being an important share of *theirs,* especially if there are any unusual requirements or variations from typical operating procedures

- proximity; local vendors are preferred for contact and delivery

- economies of scale as standardization and modularity to get volumes up

- the ability to work well together, contribute ideas, and provide honest, candid feedback.

  "Toyota wants the suppliers to think for themselves, challenge the requirements, and provide value-added ideas to the process."[31]

  Honda's criterion for selecting suppliers is the *attitude* of their management.[32]

- Vendor/partnerships should be developed. Kiichiro Toyoda, founder of Toyota's automotive business, said:

  "First tier suppliers, in particular, must be partners in research. We don't just buy things from them. We have them make things for us."[33]

- Don't just throw a spec at a vendor and ask for a quote; work with the vendor to optimize the design for manufacturability. Explore "what if" scenarios.

- Understand the vendor's processes, sensitivities, and process capabilities. Direct interaction and visits are preferred.

- Vendors should be willing and able to do the following (HP's criteria). They must be willing and able to (1) help design the product, (2) build quick-turn prototype parts and parts for short-run projects, and (3) build production units.

- Don't change vendors as volumes rise because this adds new sources of statistical variation at the worst time for unexpected problems to occur. Similarly, don't change vendors for a "lower cost" on parts because the total cost including the cost of the change will most likely be higher. Don't dump a vendor at the first hint of disappointment; work with them to improve. In general, don't change vendors *at all* so as to preserve the "learning relationship" in which every job improves the rapport, cooperation, dialog, and feedback.

- Don't beat up vendors to lower cost. If *they* don't know how to lower cost, they will either cut corners or cut margins, neither of which is good for the OEM. Rather, work together with vendor/partners early to proactively minimize total cost.

  "Achievement of business performance by the parent company through bullying suppliers is totally alien to the spirit of the Toyota Production System." - Taichi Ohno, father of the Toyota Production System [34]

- Here is how Toyota treats suppliers. A survey of suppliers found that Toyota is rated by suppliers as "their most demanding customer" but also rated the highest: 415 out of 500 compared to GM at 114 out of 500. Toyota:

  - works with new or struggling suppliers to get up to speed

  - makes commitments to suppliers early in the product development process and makes good on promises

  - constructs contracts that are simple and for the life of the product

  - is the best at balancing a focus on cost with a focus on quality

  - honors the contracts – does not renege on them

  - treats suppliers respectively and respects the integrity of intellectual property

  - works with suppliers to achieve price targets.[35]

2.7 THE TEAM LEADER

The product development team leader is key to success and has the following characteristics:

- **Leader and project champion.** A MIT study, *Made in America, Regaining the Productive Edge,* gave additional insight into the most successful product development project management:

  "In the Japanese auto companies, each new product is assigned a program manager who: acts as the product's champion, carries great authority with the firm, and along with his staff, stays with the product from conception until well past the production launch."

- Has **respect of the team and management**

- **More than an administrator;** In fact, excess focus on budgets and schedules will stifle creativity and the crucial architecture phase optimization.

- Provide the **proper broad focus** and resist the natural temptation to think only about functionality and start designing parts prematurely.

- Understand the **importance of thorough concept/architecture, pursue that optimization, and resist temptations and pressures** from team or management to do otherwise.

- **Completes the tasks in each phase** before moving on.

The Team Leader at Toyota

The characteristics of a good team leader at Toyota[36] (called "Chief Engineer") are:

- an instinctive feel for what customers want
- exceptional engineering skills
- intuitive yet grounded in facts
- innovative yet skeptical of unproven technology
- visionary yet practical
- a hard-driven teacher, motivator, and disciplinarian, yet a patient listener
- a no-compromise attitude to achieving breakthrough targets
- an exceptional communicator
- always ready to get his or her hands dirty

"Key decisions, mentoring, lobbying for resources, building a shared vision, pushing the product to higher levels, and achieving quality, safety, cost, and timing targets all start with the chief engineer."[37]

The Team Leader at Motorola

"A good project leader's worst enemies are a chair and desk. Instead of sitting in an office, a project leader should visit the project team members at least once a day." "Project leaders have to be tenacious and want to make things happen." "They must be willing to make noise at the top and ask embarrassing questions when obstacles arise." Project leaders *"make sure that communication among team members happens on an ongoing basis."*[38]

2.8 CO-LOCATION

Concurrent Engineering works best when the product development team is in close proximity with manufacturing operations, so that the whole team can meet frequently and, *as a team,* do all the tasks recommended by this book.

Separating manufacturing people geographically from the product development team will impair the team's ability to design for manufacturability, sometimes seriously. The main issues are awareness and teamwork:

Awareness. Design engineers will not be able to frequently observe production operations first-hand and get direct face-to-face interactions with production personnel, and thus be less able to concurrently engineer products and processes.

Teamwork. The Manufacturing team members' contributions to the teamwork will be compromised if distance decreases the number of meetings and interactions. Greater distance makes face-to-face contact even less likely, thus diminishing the effectiveness of teamwork and discouraging spontaneous interactions.

Outsourcing manufacturing far away compromises Concurrent Engineering even more, because employees of other companies are less accessible in addition to the challenges of distance, time-zones, languages, and cultural differences (both between companies and countries). The effect of this separating engineering is discussed in Section 4.8 and the articles at the author's web-site www.HalfCostProducts.com on outsourcing[39] and offshoring.[40]

The Project Room (The "Great Room" or *Obeya*)

Each multifunctional team should have a *dedicated* project room (*Obeya* in Japanese) for each project to accommodate spontaneous "huddles" and display the teams' charts, graphs, drawings, experiments, samples, models, prototypes, and so forth. Not having this would discourage spontaneous discussions, simply because of the lack of availability or somewhere to meet.

In Toyota culture, *"The Obeya integrates various product development participants throughout the life of a program" facilitating meetings several times a week, which "enable fast decision making and information sharing."*[41]

The team and the team leader (chief engineer) meet almost daily in the Obeya to make decisions in real time, not waiting for periodic meetings. *"Usually, once every two days at least the whole team assembles there."*[42]

2.9 TEAM MEMBERSHIP AND ROLES

Design teams should consist of people from design engineering, manufacturing engineers, service representatives, marketing managers, customers, dealers, finance representatives, industrial designers, quality and testing personnel, purchasing representatives, suppliers, regulation compliance experts, factory workers, specialized talent, and representatives from other projects. First, this helps to ensure that all the design considerations will be covered. Second, such diversity can lead to a better design because of contributions from many perspectives. This synergy results in a better design than could result from a homogeneous "team" consisting only of design engineers or scientists.

Key tenets of Honda product development process are *trust,* which comes from teamwork and shared knowledge, and *equality,* which means to "recognize, respect and benefit from individual differences."[43] Kaj Linden, the Research Director at Nokia says, *"The common denominator of Nokia's R&D stems from concurrent engineering efforts in which product development, sales, and production units cooperate significantly."*[44]

It is very important that all team members are *present and active early* so that they will make meaningful contributions to the design team. Team members need not all be full time, but they should not be so preoccupied with other tasks that they cannot make meaningful contributions. All team members should actively participate in the product development, not waiting for "designers" to design something and then reacting to their designs. Some of the key team members are:

- **Manufacturing and Service.** Their participation is crucial to ensure that the product development team designs manufacturability and serviceability into the product. Manufacturing engineers have the responsibility of making sure that products are being designed for stable processes that are already in use or for new processes that will be *concurrently* designed as the product is designed. Manufacturing and service representatives must not wait until the stage where there are drawings to mark up. Their role is to help design the product and constantly influence the design to ensure manufacturability and serviceability. Manufacturing representatives must be isolated from the daily emergencies and "firefighting" that occur in manufacturing, since *urgent* matters usually take precedence over *important* matters.

  Problems can arise when manufacturing engineers view team participation as a career opportunity to migrate into Engineering, designing one portion of the product very well for manufacturability, while the remainder of the product has manufacturability ignored.

Valuable knowledge can be obtained from all manufacturing and service people by asking them to fill out survey forms for Factory Feedback and Field Service Feedback, which are presented in Appendix C.

- **Tooling Engineers.** When new or custom processes and tooling are required, they should be concurrently designed as the products are designed. If current manufacturing procedures are inadequate for cost, time, or quality, then new processes may need to be concurrently developed.

  Look for opportunities to create innovative tooling that replaces slow, costly, and poor-quality processing. Concurrently develop tooling and fixtures that are faster, more efficient, quick loading, more accurate, partially mechanized, or automated.

- **Purchasing and Vendors.** Purchasing agents should help design teams select parts for best balance of cost, quality, and availability. Instead of just throwing a single spec over the wall and telling Purchasing to "just buy it," engineers should provide a performance *range* so purchasing agents can look for the best price and availability within the entire range. Sometimes, a higher performance part may have a lower price and better availability if is mass-produced and is in widespread use, as shown in Figure 3-2.

  Purchasing's other role should be to set up and manage vendor/partnerships for custom parts, as discussed in Section 2.6. These partnerships should be used instead of bidding for reasons discussed in Section 6.11. The book that introduced lean production to the U.S., *The Machine That Changed the World*, recommended against bidding so that vendors should not be "selected on the basis of bids, but on the basis of *past relationships and a proven record of performance.*"[45]

- **Marketing.** Marketing is the link to the customer and must help the team define the product to so that it listens to the "voice of the customer." Product definition will be discussed in Section 2.11.

  Cooperation between Engineering and Marketing is a key determinant of product development success. A study of 289 projects found that when there was "harmony" between Engineering and Marketing, there were only 13 percent failures. On the other hand, when there was "severe disharmony," the results were the opposite: only 11 percent of those projects succeeded![46]

- **Customers.** Product development teams should be close to customers and understand how they use products. Toyota engineers spend months talking to customers and dealers to understand what customers want in new product designs.[47]

A key aspect of Guidant's product development process for surgical tools is to have engineers observe surgical procedures and get understandings and feedback directly from customers.

When Hewlett-Packard's (now Philip's) Medical Products Group develops ultrasound imaging systems, they construct full-size nonfunctional models for doctors to evaluate usability in hospitals. This gives the product development team valuable early feedback on all aspects of the user interface including how well a doctor wearing gloves can grasp probes and switches, extend and retract cords, read displays, move the system from room to room, and so forth.

On reason for Rubbermaid's early success was because its product development teams were so close to customers and products that they could minimize market testing, which dramatically reduced the time-to-market and made it harder for competitors to copy their products as "clones" or knock-offs.[48]

It is becoming more common to have customers themselves actually participating on product development teams. When Boeing developed the 777, they invited representatives of their customers, the airlines, to help design the product. At first Boeing engineers were apprehensive, but soon learned the value of hearing detailed customer input in the design stage.[49] For instance, the Boeing design team learned that their customers were having a hard time reading information displays on instruments mounted on the walls in a utility room below the floor. The reason was that the body of the person trying to read the instruments was always blocking the only light which was mounted on the ceiling. Once alerted by the customers, the engineers could easily solve the problem with a light bulb in each corner of the room.

An added value to involving customers in the design process is that it *bonds* them to the product and, thus, tends to make them more loyal customers when the new product comes out.

Industry Week's "Best Plant" survey of the 25 top performing candidates indicated that 96% of companies surveyed had customers participate in product development efforts.[50]

- **Industrial Designers.** These creative people need to be part of the design team so that product styling is not "thrown over the wall" to engineering, who must to fit everything into a pretty enclosure. It is an encouraging trend that the leading industrial design firms are evolving away from a styling emphasis to include engineering, manufacturability, and usability.[51]

- **Quality and Test.** The need for diagnostic testing is dependent on the "quality culture" of the company. If quality is *designed into* the product and then *built in* by processes that are in control, then the "fall out" will be so low that diagnostic tests may not be needed. At IBM, products that were expected to have higher than a 98.5% first-pass-accept rate could avoid diagnostic test development and the expensive ATE (Automatic Test Equipment) "bed-of-nails" testers. Above this threshold, it was more cost effective to discard defective printed circuit boards than to pay for the testers *and* test development. ATE testers cost millions of dollars and for some printed circuit boards, test development can exceed the cost and the calendar time of product development!

- **Finance.** Finance representatives can help decision making by providing relevant cost data, which does not automatically come from most accounting systems. Implementing Activity Based Cost Management, as discussed in Chapter 7, can provide data based on *total cost* considerations which will lead to much more rational decision making, for example, for tradeoff analysis of quality/diagnostics, make/buy decisions, off-the-shelf parts, quantifying quality costs, and quantifying overhead cost savings resulting from standardization and modularity.

- **Regulatory Compliance.** Every design team needs representatives who can ensure that all applicable regulations are satisfied by the *initial* product design, not by costly and time-consuming changes. Future regulations must also be considered, since regulations sometimes change faster than manufacturers can respond with another product development cycle. Some companies have legislative or environmental lawyers on the design teams to anticipate future regulations. Efficiently producing regional product variations, for instance, for many countries, is one promising application of mass customization (Section 4.3). This requires that the design team incorporate the regulations of every customer country into the design process.

- **Factory Workers** are a valuable source of input, either from actual participation on the design team or surveys, like the Factory Feedback form in Appendix C. Factory workers usually have no feedback channel for their vast amount of knowledge on past manufacturability issues. Factory worker participation in the design process may have the added benefit of improving labor relations and making the new product more easily accepted as it is launched into manufacturing.

- **Specialized Talent.** Design teams may need help from specialized talent for: automation, simulation, stress analysis, heat flow analysis, solid modeling, rapid prototyping, design of experiments, "robust" tolerancing, lab testing, safety, product liability, patent law, and so forth.

- **Other Projects.** Coordinating multiple product development projects is important to maximize synergies, share work on common module design, and standardize parts, modules, tooling, and processes.

The success of product development projects is determined by *how well* concurrent engineering is practiced: *how complete* the multi-functional team is; *how early* the entire team is active; and *how well* the team is lead. Locating people very close together, called *co-location,* also helps ensure the success of product development teams.

The largest study of corporate failures, *Why Smart Executives Fail, and What you Can Learn from their Mistakes,* emphasized the importance of multifunctional teams:

> *"Create crossfunctional teams and diverse work groups whose members will see things differently. Such heterogenous groups have been shown to be much better than homogeneous groups when it comes to developing new knowledge."* [52]

2.10 OUTSOURCING ENGINEERING

Many managers are intrigued with the prospect of outsourcing engineering as a way to "save cost" on product development with foreign engineers whose wages are a fraction of domestic engineers. Further, there is the allure of speeding up product development by keeping engineering working in three shifts a day with work passed off around the world every day.

This might work with independent activities such as call centers or insurance or loan processing, but product development should be a highly interactive and integrated team activity. Product development is most effective and efficient when products are designed by complete multifunctional teams that are "co-located" with manufacturing operations and close to customers and vendors, as discussed earlier.

Any proposals to save cost must be based on minimizing *total cost.* Chapter 6 emphasizes many the many costs that make up the total, of which product development labor cost is just one element. Some of the consequences chasing cheap *manufacturing* labor – lower labor efficiency and poorer quality – might cancel out the labor rate savings; adding in other costs could push results into a net loss.[53]

A *Business Week* article titled "The Hidden Cost of IT Outsourcing," confirmed this parallel, saying that it applies even more so for software outsourcing: "Offshoring – sending work overseas – isn't always all it's made out to be. Particularly with information technology, which can be a lot more complicated than moving traditional manufacturing operations overseas." [54]

The article also pointed out that IT quality is harder to ascertain because it required more communication and management. When total cost was taken into account, the cost was generally comparable to domestic work. Further, some experts say outsourced software has 35% to 40% more bugs and some outsourcers experienced missing code and unconnected pages, which made updating a nightmare. The article said that problems encountered are a "dirty little secret" because companies don't publicize the problems they have run into.

The best way to lower product development expenses is to *maximize the efficiency of the whole process* through concurrent engineering (with co-located teams) and design for manufacturability (with continuous interactions with manufacturing people), as discussed throughout this chapter.

A more efficient product development process consumes fewer labor hours to (a) develop new products and (b) solve problems during product launches, ramping up to volume targets, achieving quality and productivity targets, implementing engineering change orders, and all the firefighting associated with these activities, *which are really avoidable* with an efficient product development process, as discussed throughout this book.

Optimal product development practices not only minimize *engineering* costs but also can substantially reduce *product* costs, which is one of product development's primary goals. Spreading teams out geographically – with people who may not even be working at the same time – compromises that teamwork that is necessary to optimize product architecture, which determines 60% of the product's cost (Figure 1-1). Outsourcing subsystem and part design to remote engineers can produce products that may be hard to integrate, have part interaction problems, or miss out on synergistic system opportunities, as discussed in Chapter 3.

Physically integrated teamwork is even more important when products need to be designed for lean production and build-to-order. Design teams need to work closely with manufacturing people to design around standard materials and modules, design for no setup, design for CNC, and concurrently design versatile product families and flexible processes, as discussed in Chapter 4. For mass customization, engineers need to work closely with manufacturing, marketing, and the sales force to establish *parametric* CAD templates that can automatically generate CNC programs (see Chapter 4).

The transition to outsourced engineering incurs a certain cost and may cause significant consequences. It will cost money to find engineers, arrange to hire and pay them, and prepare and transfer documents, drawings, and CAD files. The effort to implement these changes will probably consume most of the available "change energy" and preclude or compromise other more valuable improvement efforts, like DFM, robust design, better CAD tools for domestic engineers, six sigma, build-to-order, and so forth.

The consequences can be even more severe if the "cost savings" from outsourcing engineering are to come from *layoffs*. In addition to the general consequences of layoffs,[55] there are special consequences for product development. Once word spreads, morale and efficiency will drop and the best engineers may leave, thus weakening engineering efforts and making product development even less efficient. Engineers who quit or are laid off will probably take with them valuable skills and knowledge, some of which may be unique and thus weaken teamwork. If documentation is less than complete, which is usually the case, departures may create serious documentation gaps. Continuity may suffer for ongoing projects. The remaining engineering capability will be less efficient with such losses. Further, teamwork will be less effective because of missing talent, knowledge, and diversity.

Which Engineering Could be Outsourced

Certain engineering tasks could be outsourced, as long as they help rather than hurt the overall product development effort. *Research* may be more suitable than *Development.* Outsourcing certain tasks could *help* new product development efforts (next paragraph). Outsourcing certain other tasks could relieve domestic engineers from distracting tasks and thus indirectly benefit new product development efforts (see following paragraph).

Tasks that support domestic new product development include: computational intensive research tasks, as long as they do not specify or imply product architecture or part design; computational intensive analysis of performance, strength, dynamics, heat flow, reliability, design of experiments, robust tolerances, etc.; materials research; structuring and adapting parametric CAD templates and CAD/CAM programs;[56] and literature or web searches in general.

Tasks that usually distract new product development efforts include the following activities on current products: engineering change order processing; changing drawings; analyses of problems on current products; cleaning up or converting documentation, drawings, or part numbers for standardization efforts or absorbing acquired products; maintenance engineering and conversions from obsolete materials for older legacy products and spare parts; cleaning up documentation for outsourcing the manufacturing of legacy, spare parts, and oddball products;[57] conversion of drawings into Geometric Dimensioning and Tolerancing (GD&T) format; or conversion of drawings to metric or dual dimensioning.

2.11 PRODUCT DEFINITION

Before product development can begin, the product must be methodically *defined* with clear and realistic goals that will satisfy customers.   Sometimes products are defined as a hodgepodge of unrealistic ambitions.

Understanding Customer Needs

Understand customer needs and develop products to satisfy customer needs rather than "build it and they will come." Offer customers *solutions* instead of just *products*. How to understand customer needs:

• Ask customers what they want with respect to functionality, cost, cost-of-ownership, reliability, and so forth. Ask customers to rank what is most important and how well your company does compared to the competition, for instance using the form shown on page 50. Plot ranked lists of customer importance vs. your competitive score as shown on page 51. Enter customer importances and grades into the QFD "House of Quality" (page 53) and compute design specs and resource prioritizations.

• Understand customer root needs well enough to predict what customers may need but don't realize it.   HP LaserJet Printer division has an *"imaginative understanding of user needs."* Proctor and Gamble recommends *"understanding your customers so well that you can predict what they want but don't know what they want."*

• Understand what customers would want if they knew what was possible: The Sony Walkman *"just wasn't an option that consumers fathomed would even be possible."[58]* Another example from Sony: *"Sony's dealers in the U.S. and some if its engineers balked at the idea of miniaturizing the transistor radio."[59]*

- Understand what customers will need in the future. Study trends and develop versatile products that can adapt to future environments.

- Understand *new potential* customer wants, which may be the basis for new markets.

- Understand what customers will need *in the future;* study trends and develop versatile products that can adapt to future environments. Understand *new potential* customer wants, which may be the basis for new markets. Understand what customers would want if they knew all the things that were possible.

Writing Product Requirements

- Make sure *all* **customer/market needs are specified** in the Product Requirements document, *never adding to it or changing it after the product development has commenced.*

- Product requirements should be specified *generically* without specifying or implying how it should be done.

- Write rational, objective, and appropriate product requirements. Avoid temptations to base product requirements on enticing market opportunities, exciting technology, whims, attachments, aversions, prejudices, competitive precedents, or the next bench syndrome (designing products for colleagues). Make sure the requirements are thoroughly written for the current products. Avoid the temptation to base the requirements on previous products or form-letter templates.

- Make sure all goals, targets, specs, and metrics are relevant to *customers.*

- Avoid feature creep and unnecessary complication. Philips Electronics found that *"at least half of returned products had nothing wrong with them. Consumers just couldn't figure out how to use them."*[60]

- Think in terms of synergistic product families (platforms) *and their evolution over time.*

Consequences of poor product definition

- Time, money, resources, and opportunities are wasted when products are developed that customers don't want.

- Product development costs and valuable resources are wasted and the project is delayed when product design requirements have to "change" to reflect what the customer really wanted in the first place.

Customer Input

First, create a list of those factors that would be important to customers. A baseline list is shown in the first column of Figure 2-2.

Second, ask customers for the relative importance of their preferences, from a low of "1" to a high of "10" (there may be more than one 10, etc.). Also ask them to grade your product (in the second column) compared to the leading competitor(s) in the third column. Use the academic scale of A (best), B (above average), C (average), D (below average) and F (worst). For plotting use F = 0 through A = 5.

Rating of Importance*	Grade**	Compared to:
Functionality		
Purchase cost		
Quality		
Reliability/durability		
Delivery/availability		
Appearance and aesthetics		
Ergonomics; ease of use		
Service, repair, maintenance		
Cost of ownership		
Technical Support		
Customizability/options		
Safety		
Environmental		
Other_____		

Figure 2-2: Customer Input Form

Third, prioritize customer preferences, which is valuable information in itself. This will help neutralize misunderstandings or internal biases toward exiting technology, markets, or "pet" features.

Forth, label each at its appropriate numerical position on the vertical scale in Figure 2-3, from a low of 1 to a high of 10. Finally, plot their positions against the competitive grade on the horizontal axis as shown in the upper graph in Figure 2-3. The graph can then be prioritized with diagonal zones (lower graph) which quickly show where to place the most effort. The first zone, with point "A," has the most opportunity since it most important to customers but our company is ranked worst. The next zone, with points "B" and "C," are the next priority, and so forth through the zones to point "P" at which our competitive grade is best on a factor that is least important to customers.

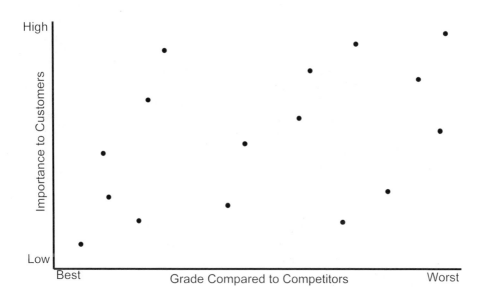

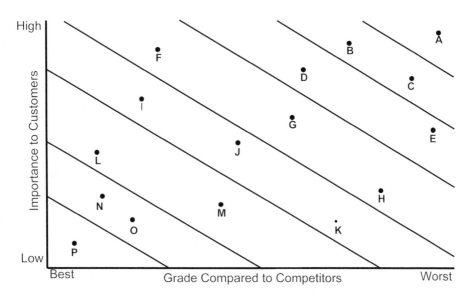

Figure 2-3: Customer Importance vs. Competitive Grade

Quality Function Deployment

Quality Function Deployment (QFD) is a tool for systematically translating the "voice of the customer" into product design specifications and resource prioritizations.[61] Its strength is to translate *objective and subjective* customer wants and needs into *objective* specifications that engineers can use to design products.

In the most general sense, the input to QFD is a set of customer preferences; the outputs are product specifications and resource prioritization (Figure 2-4). The values in the "design specifications" rows are the actual values that engineers will use to design products. The "resource prioritization" row is the percent of the design team's effort that should be spent on each aspect of the design. Using this prioritization will ensure that the design team devotes its efforts toward features that customers want the most. And, thus, they will not waste effort "polishing the ruby" more than the customer wants it polished. This can be a temptation when engineers are personally excited about certain new technologies that are being used in the product.

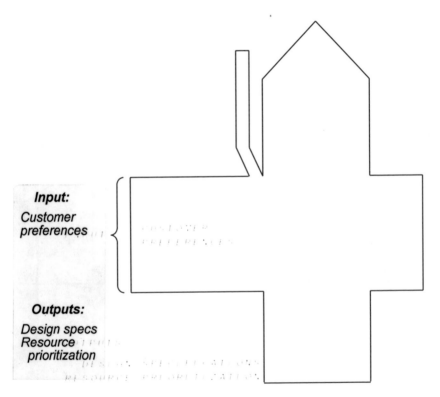

Input:
Customer
preferences

Outputs:
Design specs
Resource
prioritization

Figure 2-4: QFD Executive Overview

How QFD Works

Figure 2-5 shows the complete QFD "house of quality" chart with each area labeled according to its function in the methodology. The "customer preferences" are listed, one per row, in words that are meaningful to the customer, not in "specsmanship" jargon.

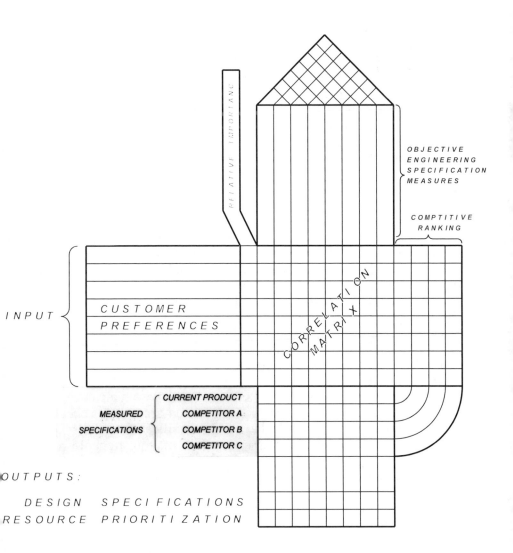

Figure 2-5: The QFD "House of Quality" Chart

Two of the most valuable aspects of QFD are obtaining customer preferences and competitive grades that can be documented in the form shown in Figure 2-2 and graphed in the format of Figure 2-3. The value of having this information can be quickly demonstrated by surveying an internal group, for instance a newly formed product development team. It is truly amazing how much the results can vary – some answers for estimated customer importance vary the entire range from one to ten! In one workshop, the team reaction was, "How can we design a product when even *we* can't agree on what's most important?" Of course, the real input will have to come from real customers themselves. The customer values (from 1 to 10) entered in the "chimney" of the house of quality and competitive rankings are entered on the right of Figure 2-5.

The full QFD procedure uses these two sets of inputs to calculate the optimal development budget allotments for various tasks. If a competitor was ranked best about something important to the customer, the company would be wise to analyze that product, using the data in the "measured specifications" section, and try to understand how it achieved customer satisfaction in this area. The things to measure would be the specifications that appear in the columns labeled "objective engineering specification measures." These contain the objective measurements that will eventually be the target numbers for discrete products or ranges for mass customized products.[62] The objective measures would be in engineering units that quantify dimensions, force, torque, energy, decibels, etc. All of those objective measurements are then actually measured for the current product and several competitors and entered in the chart under "measured specifications."

The "correlation matrix" correlates which customer preferences are affected by which engineering specifications. Symbols are placed in the square to indicate the type of correlation. Usually two to four rankings are listed: "positive" or "negative" correlation; "strong," "some" or "possible" correlation; or "strong positive," "medium positive," "medium negative," and "strong negative" correlation. Roughly half the boxed should be checked. Results become less valuable as one approaches either extreme of all boxes checked or no boxes checked.

The "conflict matrix" tabulates any specifications that might be inherently in conflict with others, to aid in making tradeoffs of one feature versus another. An example would be a more powerful car engine that may adversely affect mileage or handling because of its extra weight.

Various cells in a QFD chart are used to make calculations and normalize them to useful percentages. One of the "bottom lines" is the design target row, labeled "design specifications." The other is the "resource prioritization" which can be given in a percentage of the engineering budget or hours spent achieving the various design targets.

Defining products to satisfy the voice of the customer is one of the ways of ensuring customer satisfaction, which has an enormous effect on sales, profits, and shareholder value, according to J.D. Power's book, *Satisfaction, How Every Great Company Listens to the Voice of the Customer*[63] (some interesting quotes and results are summarized at the end of Chapter 10 of this book).

2.12 PRODUCT DEVELOPMENT PHASES

The following phases and activities are structured to ensure that important DFM steps are included early enough and thoroughly optimized. It is intended that these activities are added to a company's existing product development phases. For companies that don't utilize product development phases, these could provide the basis for implementing them.

Phase 1: Product Definition

Before product development can begin, the product must be methodically *defined* with clear and realistic goals that will satisfy customers. Identify *users* and *buyers*; if these are different, define and develop the product to satisfy both. For large customers, identify who speaks for the customer and who speaks for various divisions.

Thoroughly understand "voice of the customer" (see QFD discussion in Section 2.11). The QFD steps are to:

• Create a list of importance factors.

• Ask customers to rank importance factors on the form in Figure 2-2.

• Ask customers to rate your products compared to competition using the grading scheme shown in Figure 2-2.

• Plot customer importance vs. competitive position to get priority zones as shown in Figure 2-3. The top priority would be high customer importance *and* a weak competitive rating by your company.

• Complete QFD "house of quality" to get design specifications and resource prioritizations (see Figure 2-5).

Get early feedback on conceptual innovations and refinements customers didn't ask for. Get early feedback on hardware usability and desirability through early 3D rapid prototypes and mockups. For software, get early feedback on user interfaces that are *drawn* (without any new code) as graphics that progress from page to page to show various usage scenarios.

Select customers to participate in the product development process, especially in the product definition phase.

Phase 2A: Concept/Architecture Optimization

This phase is to be done concurrently with Phase 2B, which focuses on manufacturing and supply chain strategies. It is very important to ensure that multifunctional teams have *all* specialties actively participating early. Key tasks in this phase include:

• Form multifunctional teams with all specialties active early

• Explore many ways to achieve *design simplicity*

• Optimize product architecture

• Formulate off-the-shelf part strategy

• Optimize use of previous engineering and software code

• Formulate modular strategy

• Formulate strategies for quality, reliability, test, repair, and service

• Decide level of standardization; select or adopt standard parts lists

• Formulate strategies for part combinations and silicon integration (Section 5.12).

• Understand regulatory compliance issues and develop compliance plans

• Formulate design strategy for product family variety, configurations, customization, derivatives, and subsequent products

• Determine *design philosophy* goals and directives, such as optimizing off-the-shelf part utilization, avoiding labor intensive steps, using only proven processing and suppliers, self fixturing parts, and so forth.

Phase 2B: Manufacturing & Supply Chain Strategies

This phase is to be done concurrently with Phase 2A, concept/architecture optimization. Key steps in this phase include:

- Formulate the manufacturing strategy, including process selection, test strategy, and quality strategy

- Formulate the raw material resupply strategy: Will it be MRP-based purchase orders or automatic resupply techniques like steady flows, kanbans, min/max, or breadtruck (free stock)?[64]

- Formulate the part resupply strategy: Will it be MRP-based purchase orders or steady flows and kanban?[65]

- Identify the supplier base for materials and parts

- Optimize outsourcing and internal integration decisions[66]

- Formulate the vendor strategy for nonstandard parts and outsourcing; identify potential vendor partnerships

- Formulate manufacturing strategy for customization, configurations, product variety, extensions, and derivatives

- Structure products into synergistic families/lines/cells[67]

- Arrange for relevant overhead allocations (if not automatic through total cost accounting) to (a) prevent new products from having to pay for the overhead costs of less manufacturable products and (b) encourage behavior that further lowers overhead costs (see Chapters 6 and 7).

Phase 3: Raising & Resolving Issues

This "phase" starts at the very beginning and continues until Phase 4 with issues being raised and resolved as early as possible.

The MIT study, *The Machine that Changed the World,* which started the lean production movement in the U.S., emphasized that in the best Japanese lean product development projects, the team leader's job was to force the multi-functional team to raise and resolve all the *issues* early (see full quote in Section 2.1).

Issue analysis should address the following issues as early as possible:

- How much profit will the development generate *on a total cost basis?*

- Is there a reasonable chance of achieving the project goals in the scheduled time, given the allocated budget?

- Will the project get enough resources to accomplish its goals? Will they be allocated early enough, as recommended in Section 2.1?

- Are cost and time goals based on bottom-line metrics such as total cost and time to stable production? If goals are based on the wrong metrics, the design team may be encouraged to specify cheap parts, move production to low-labor-rate countries, not optimize product architecture, and throw the design over the wall to manufacturing "on time."

- Understand *lessons learned* from previous projects and formulate appropriate action plans. This begins with summaries of lessons learned from similar product development projects in company databases. If this information is not readily available, then the lessons learned may need to be investigated through interviews and evaluations of appropriate records. One effective way to learn from the past is to arrange for presentations from previous project members, vendors, and production or quality personnel. Another way is to survey factory workers, vendors, and field service using the feedback forms in Appendix C.
  Toyota's product development engineers are four times as productive as other companies.[68] One of the reasons is that the collective knowledge and experience of all previous projects – both successes and failures – are readily available and easily accessible to current product development teams.[69]

- All issues are raised and discussed, for instance: Are new product and process technologies proven enough and refined enough to incorporate new designs and production? Are there multiple sources of risk regarding new product technologies or new manufacturing processes? How much does success, cost, and time depend on entities and developments not under the control of the development team, such as partners, suppliers, outsourcing, regulations, etc.?

- All issues are resolved through research, experiments, experts, coordination, simulations, and risk analysis and management. For critical applications, it may be necessary to conduct the rigorous Failures Modes and Effects Analyses (FMEA).

- Proactively formulate "Plan B" contingency plans to deal with the most likely changes, setbacks, delays, shortages, or other problems regarding technology, customers, markets, regulation, corporate policies, processing, distribution, availability, economic climate, and so forth.

  Products should be designed to be versatile enough to satisfy all anticipated scenarios now or easily adapt later to these changes. For instance, products can be designed to readily accept the "plan B" part if the "plan A" part doesn't work out or is not available in time.

  Manufacturing and supply chain functions need to be prepared in case the product is a big hit. This could be the best case scenario for Marketing, but could be a challenge for Manufacturing and Supply Chain Management if not planned for. The most comprehensive study of corporate failure sited how Johnson & Johnson had much higher than the predicted success introducing the artery-expanding *stent* but couldn't follow through to satisfy demand, which lost sales and encouraged competition from Guidant.

  > *"J&J never expected the stent business to take off the way it did, and as a result corporate executives weren't prepared to make the additional investments needed to keep the franchise on top."[70]*

- Achieve concurrence before proceeding. Another MIT study, *Made in America, Regaining the Productive Edge,* gave additional insight into Japanese consensus building:[71]

  > *"A key task of the manager is to make sure that all disagreements [issues] are aired and resolved at the outset. Achieving consensus takes a great deal of effort, but by skillful management at this point it is possible to gain the full commitment of all members of the program team so that subsequent progress is very rapid."*

  The Xomed division of Metronic strives to raise and resolve issues early: *"Xomed works harder validating process at each stage of a project, which forces them to ask the right questions earlier and earlier, and wastes less overall project time by reducing the number of bad assumptions made to compensate for incomplete information."[72]*

Phase 4A: Product Design

This phase should to be done concurrently with Phase 4B, process design. Key tasks include:

- Select or adopt lists of standard parts and materials

- Select off-the-shelf parts early so that arbitrary decisions will not preclude their use; select off-the-shelf parts carefully and thoroughly with respect to function, quality, reliability, qualifications, delivery, and availability (see Section 5.19).

- Identify modular opportunities; coordinate with other projects; design modules

- Design the product as *a* system, not just a collection of parts and subassemblies to be fit together later

- Obey design guidelines for each manufacturing process

- Develop the test strategy

- Design to minimize or eliminate the need for calibration, adjustments, or tweaking

- Create parametric CAD templates for customization and variations

- Design the product to satisfy the voice of the customer, be compatible with concurrently specified processing/sourcing, and support the business model.

- Complete the design so that design decisions are not made "on the floor" by factory workers. Unambiguously document the design, processing instructions, bills of materials, and all other documentation.

Phase 4B: Process Design

This phase should be done concurrently with Phase 4A, product design. Key tasks include:

- Implement the manufacturing plan

- Set up the supply chain

- Design versatile fixtures

- Design special tooling

- Develop or modify special production equipment

- Help structure product families into flexible lines[73]

Phase 5: Launch & Production

Make designs good enough and production facilities flexible enough to run prototypes, launches, and production quantities on the same production lines, thus avoiding the cost and time delays of "pilot" production lines. The team should help launch the product, stay with it, and write all the change orders until the product is launched and production has stabilized, as defined by reaching predetermine goals (as plotted in Figure 2-1) for:

- Production volume

- Quality goals as measured by yield, first pass accept (FPA) rate, defects per million (DPM), complaints, service calls, etc.

- Productivity

ENDNOTES/REFERENCES

1. Womack, Jones, and Roos, *The Machine that Changes the World.*

2. For more information on customized in-house DFM seminars, see page 407 of this book or *www.design4manufacturability.com/seminars.htm.*

3. James Morgan & Jeffrey K. Liker, *The Toyota Product Development System* (2006, Productivity Press); Chapter 4, "Front-Load the PD Process to Explore Alternatives Thoroughly."

4. Michael L. George, et al., *Fast Innovation* (2005, McGraw-Hill), Chapter 7, "Spotlight on Conquering the Cost of Complexity," p. 167.

5. James P. Womack, Daniel T. Jones, and Daniel Roos, *The Machine That Changed the World, The Story of Lean Production* (1991, Harper Perennial), Chapter 6, "Coordinating the Supply Chain."

6. Michael McGrath, Michael Anthony, Amram Shapiro, Product Development; Success Through Product And Cycle-time Excellence (1992, Butterworth-Heinemann). Chapter 11, "Project Team Leadership."

7. Morgan & Liker, *The Toyota Product Development System,* Chapter 4: "Front-Load the PD Process to Explore Alternatives Thoroughly."

8. Richard Koch, *The 80/20 Principle; The Secret of Achieving More with Less,* (1998, Currency/Doubleday), Chapter 4, "Why your Strategy is Wrong."

9. David M. Anderson, *Build-to-Order & Mass Customization, The Ultimate Supply Chain Management and Lean Manufacturing Strategy for Low-Cost On-Demand Production without Forecasts or Inventory,* (2004, 520 pages, CIM Press). Also see articles at www.build-to-order-consulting.com.

10. Morgan & Liker, *The Toyota Product Development System,* Chapter 4: "Front-Load the PD Process to Explore Alternatives Thoroughly."

11. Mark and Barbara Stefik, *Breakthrough; Stories and Strategies for Radical Innovation;* (2004, MIT Press);

12. W. Chan Kim and Renee Mauborgne, *Blue Ocean Strategy, How to Create Uncontested Market Space and Make the Competition Irrelevant,* (2005, Harvard Business School Press).

13. Anderson, *Build-to-Order & Mass Customization,* Chapter 9.

14. Matthew E. May, *The Elegant Solution,* (2007, Free Press), p. 41.

15. Peter Drucker, quoted the cover story, "The Innovation Gap," *Fortune,* December 2, 1991, p. 58.

16. Patricia Aburdene, Megatrends 2010 (2005, Hampton Roads), page xv.

17. Jordan D. Lewis, The Connected Corporation; How Leading Companies Win Through Customer-Supplier Alliances (1995, Free Press); Chapter 5, "Cooperating for More Value," p. 92.

18. Shu Shin Luh, *Business the Sony Way* (2003, John Wiley & Sons), Chapter 3, "Stay Ahead; Feeding the Innovation Engine," p. 94.

19. Ibid., Chapter 6, "Outsourcing vs. Integration."

20. Jeffrey Liker, *The Toyota Way,* p. 62.

21. Jeffrey L. Cruikshrank, *The Apple Way*, (2006, McGraw-Hill), p. 38.

22. Jordan D. Lewis, *The Connected Corporation, How Leading Companies Win Through Customer-Supplier Alliances,* (New York, Free Press, 1995); Chapter 5, "Cooperating for More Value," p. 93.

23. Robert W. Hall, AME President, *Medtronic Xomed; Change at "People Speed,"* Target, First Issue 2004, , p. 14.

24. Ibid., p. 14.

25. Bill George, *Authentic Leadership; Rediscovering the Secrets of Creating Lasting Value;* (2003, Jossey-Bass); Chapter 7, "It's Not Just the CEO," p. 97.

26. "The Complete Guide to America's Best Plants," *Industry Week* (1995, Penton Publishing, 1995), p. 12.

27.   Jordan D. Lewis, The Connected Corporation; How Leading Companies Win Through Customer-Supplier Alliances (1995, Free Press); Chapter 13, "Successful Alliance Practitioners," p. 273.

28. Jordan D. Lewis, The Connected Corporation; How Leading Companies Win Through Customer-Supplier Alliances (1995, Free Press); Chapter 4, "Practices for Joint Creativity," p. 74.

29. Kim B. Clark and Takahiro Fujimoto, Product Development Performance (1991, Harvard Business School Press), p. 349.

30. James P. Womack, Daniel T. Jones, and Daniel Roos, *The Machine that Changes the World; The Story of Lean Production,* (1990, Harper-Perennial Division of Harper Collins), Chapter 6, "Coordinating the Supply Chain."

31. Morgan & Liker, *The Toyota Production Development System*, p. 185

32. Jeffrey Pfeffer and Robert I. Sutton, *The Knowing-Doing Gap; How Smart Companies Turn Knowledge into Action,*(2000, Harvard Business School Press), p. 23.

33.Satoshi Hino, *Inside the Mind of Toyota, Management Principles for Enduring Growth*, (2006, Productivity Press), Chapter 1, "Toyota's Genes and DNA."

34. Morgan & Liker, *The Toyota Product Development System,* Chapter 10, "Fully Integrate Suppliers into the Product Development System," opening quote.

35. Morgan & Liker, *The Toyota Product Development System*, p. 181

36. James M. Morgan & Jeffrey K Liker, *The Toyota Product Development System,* (2006, Productivity Press), Chapter 7, "Create a Chief Engineer System to Lean Product Development from Start to Finish."

37. Morgan & Liker, The Toyota Product Development System, p. 137

38. Michael McGrath, Michael Anthony, Amram Shapiro, Product Development; Success Through Product And Cycle-time Excellence (1992, Butterworth-Heinemann). Chapter 11, "Project Team Leadership."

39. See the outsourcing article at the author's web-site www.HalfCostProducts.com/outsourcing.htm.

40. See the offshoring article at the author's web-site www.HalfCostProducts.com/offshore_manufacturing.htm.

41. Morgan & Liker, *The Toyota Product Development System,* p. 308.

42. Jeffrey Liker, The Toyota Way, p. 62.

43. Micheline Maynard, *The End of Detroit, How the Big Three Lost their Grip on the American Car Market,* (2003, Currency/Doubleday), page 74 in Chapter 2 on Toyota and Honda.

44. Dan Steinbock, The Nokia Revolution; The Story of an Extraordinary Company That Transformed an Industry (2001, AMACOM), Chapter 8, "Nokia's R&D; Focusing and Globalizing," p. 209.

45. James Womack, Daniel Jones, and Daniel Roos, *The Machine that Changed the World*; *The Story of Lean Production,* (1990, Rawson Associates; 1991, paperback edition, Harper Perennial).

46. William Souder, *Managing New Products,* (1987, Lexington-MacMillan).

47. Maynard, *The End of Detroit,* page 67 in Chapter 2 on Toyota and Honda.

48. Sydney Finkelstein, *Why Smart Executives Fail, and What you Can Learn from their Mistakes,* (2003, Portfolio/Penguin Group), Chapter 3, "Innovation and Change," page 60.

49. From a speech by Boeing President, Philip M. Condit, presented May 7, 1993 at the Haas Graduate School of Business ad the University of

California at Berkeley.

50. "The Complete Guide to America's Best Plants," *Industry Week* (1995, Penton Publishing), p. 12.

51. Artemis March, "Usability: The New Dimension of Product Design," *Harvard Business Review,* (September-October, 1994), p. 144.

52. Sydney Finkelstein, *Why Smart Executives Fail, and What you Can Learn from their Mistakes,* (2003, Portfolio/Penguin Group), Chapter 7.

53. Anderson, *Build-to-Order & Mass Customization,* Chapter 6, "Outsourcing vs. Integration." Also see the article on Outsourcing at www.HalfCostProducts.com/outsourcing.htm and also www.HalfCostProducts.com/offshore_manufacturing.htm which discusses offshoring.

54. Olga Kharif, *Business Week Online,* "The Hidden Cost of IT Outsourcing; While Moving Software Development and Tech Support Offshore is all the Rage, Many Companies Find the Overall Savings Aren't That Great," October 27, 2003. The web-site URL is: http://www.businessweek.com/technology/content/oct2003/tc2003102 7_9655_tc119.htm

55. Anderson, *Build-to-Order & Mass Customization.,* Chapter 13. See the Section "Don't Lay Off People," pages 442 - 445.

56. Parametric CAD is a key tool of mass customization which allows dimensions to "float" with customized data plugged in for various product variations. Once inserted, CAD drawings can generate CNC machine tool programs through CAD/CAM software. See Chapter 8 and 9, *Build-to-Order & Mass Customization.*

57. Anderson, *Build-to-Order & Mass Customization,* Chapter 6, "Outsourcing vs. Integration." Also see the article on Outsourcing at www.HalfCostProducts.com/outsourcing.htm and also www.HalfCostProducts.com/offshore_manufacturing.htm which discusses offshoring. Also see recommendations about outsourcing unusual products to free up resources in Appendix A.

58. Shu Shin Luh, *Business the Sony Way* (2003, John Wiley & Sons), Chapter 3, "Stay Ahead; Feeding the Innovation Engine," p. 91.

59. Ibid., p. 95

60. James Surowiecki, "Feature Presentation," *The New Yorker*, 28 May 2007, p. 28

61. John Hauser and Don Clausing, "House of Quality," *Harvard Business Review,* May-June, 1988; Reprint number 88307.

62. QFD for mass customization is presented in Chapter 10 of *Build-to-Order & Mass Customization,* by David M. Anderson; pages 324 - 328.

63. Chris Denove and J. D. Powers IV, *Satisfaction; How Every Great Company Listens to the Voice of the Customer,* (Portfolio, 2006).

64. Anderson, *Build-to-Order & Mass Customization* (2003, CIM Press), Ch. 7, "Spontaneous Supply Chains."

65. Ibid.

66. Ibid., Ch. 6, "Outsourcing vs. Integration."

67. Ibid., Ch. 13, "Implementation."

68. Michael N. Kennedy, *Product Development for the Lean Enterprise,* (2003, Oaklea Press). The book is written in the format of discussions in a series of meetings, which compare current product development practices to Toyota's.

69. Ibid., page 24.

70. Sydney Finkelstein, *Why Smart Executives Fail, and What you Can Learn from their Mistakes,* (2003, Portfolio/Penguin Group), page 72.

71. Michael L. Dertouzos, Richard K. Lester, and Robert M. Solow, *"Made in America, Regaining the Productive Edge,"* from the MIT commission on Industrial Productivity, (1989, Harper Perennial).

72. Robert W. Hall, AME President, *Medtronic Xomed; Change at "People Speed,"* Target, First Issue 2004, p. 14.

73. Anderson, *Build-to-Order & Mass Customization,* Ch. 13, "Implementation."

DESIGNING THE PRODUCT

The primary focus of product development should be to *develop products,* not "project management" concerns that typically dominate product development efforts, such as:

- **deadlines,** which usually discourage thorough up-front work;

- **cost "targets,"** that can lead to much trouble if teams don't know how to meet the targets or if all costs are not included in the target;

- **development budgets,** which rarely include the costs of changes and firefighting downstream; further, budget pressures can encourage releasing unfinished or suboptimized designs to Manufacturing.

- **time-to-market,** which is usually defined as the "release" (which encourages throwing designs over the wall "on time") or defined as "first customer ship," when the first unit that works gets shipped.

If the actual product development is done right, it will naturally optimize the deadlines, total cost, development budget, and time to stable production.

No matter how many times Tom Cruise shouted "show me the money" in the title role of the movie, *Jerry McGuire,* he and his client weren't shown any money until they focused on the *activity* that achieved the goal instead of the *goal* itself.

The activity of product development that achieves the goals is *designing the product.* This is a *design* activity, so the focus must be on optimizing the *design.*

As discussed in the last chapter, the team must have early and complete participation of all the specialties and an effective team leader who can focus and lead the team to design the product to satisfy the voice of the customer and design the product for manufacturability, in the broadest sense.

In order to design a successful product that satisfies the *voice of the customer,* the focus needs to be much greater than just designing something that "works" and then later dealing with cost, quality, service, regulations, supply chain management, and customer satisfaction.

3.1 DESIGN PHILOSOPHY GOALS

In addition to the *design specification* targets generated by the product definition phase (Section 2.11 and Phase 1 in Section 2.12), design teams should establish *design philosophy* goals and strive to meet them throughout the design process. These usually focus on: making big improvements in manufacturability, quality, delivery, etc.; starting early to solve major problems at the concept/architecture level; adherence to certain rules and practices and avoiding certain parts and practices altogether; maximizing, minimizing, or otherwise optimizing certain practices.

Establishing these design philosophy goals will maximize the chance that the design team will produce a *clean,* optimized design. If these are not proactively established early, undesirable practices may slip into the design because individual engineers (a) didn't understand the importance, especially as it affects "the big picture," (b) didn't understand how their work affects other subassemblies and the product as a whole, or (c) let themselves get boxed into a corner so that the only way out is to fall back on some sub-optimal practice that compromises the product.

Design Philosophy Goal Examples:

Standard parts lists should be established or adopted early with predefined goals and expectations for adherence. These standard parts should be common across many products and readily available over the life of the product.

Designing around standard raw materials can save a lot of money and improve availability in the plant, especially for expensive or bulky raw materials. The total cost will probably be less, even if some parts get better materials than needed (see next section). For instance:

> **Sheet metal.** If sheet metal can be standardized on one type, then heavy users can buy that grade in a roll, feed it through straightening rollers, and then cut each piece on-demand on a programmable shear, thus minimizing shearing cost, material waste, handling/storing damage, and all the overhead costs to inventory and distribute many sheet metal pieces.

> **Bar stock.** If bar stock can be standardized on one type, then machine tools could be more efficient by avoiding setup delays and costs to change bar stock. A proliferation of types of stock can incur large inventory carrying costs and waste valuable space. Many different remnants (less than order size) are hard to keep track of in

inventory management, which can result in perceived shortages, unnecessary ordering of excess materials, and expensive expediting. In addition, remnants may not retain identifying grade marks which would either discourage use or risk using the wrong material.

Consolidation of expensive parts/modules will raise order volumes, increase purchasing leverage, minimize setup changes, reduce inventory for multiple versions, and arrange steady flows or kanbans of the consolidated part that will be used one way or another. Even if simpler products *appear* to get "a more expensive part" than they need, there is great potential for a net cost savings from greater economies of scale, better build efficiencies, and less material overhead cost. Total cost measurements must be used to justify consolidation or it may *appear* to raise material cost.

Consolidation may get the combined order volume over the threshold that makes available more sophisticated processes, custom silicon, and dedicated cells or lines.

Consolidation can reduce *product variety* and, in certain cases, enable easy upgrade strategies, like upgrading with software, modem commands, or keyed adjustments. This, in turn, lowers *product* variety and inventory, minimizes product obsolescence, simplifies sales and distribution, and improves order responsiveness. (See graphs on "Standardization of Expensive Parts," page 114).

Off-the-shelf part utilization strategy should be optimized *early* in Phase 2A. One of the paradoxes of product development is that:

> *Designers may have to choose the off-the-shelf parts first and literally design the products around them, or else they will probably make arbitrary decisions that will preclude their use.*

But incorporating off-the-shelf parts early into the design will greatly simplify the design and the design effort.

Proven processing should be *designed for.* If this is not done properly, then proven processing cannot be used and *special* processes will have to be concurrently developed with more cost, delays, and risk.

This may be necessary for leading-edge products – and be part of a company's competitive advantage – but it is an unnecessary waste of resources if it was needed only because designers didn't know how to design for existing processes, didn't follow the design rules for the equipment, or exceeded the equipment's capabilities.

Proven designs, parts, and modules should be specified early as a key foundation of product architecture. A high percentage of complaints, field failures, recalls, and lawsuits do *not* involve new features or new technology. Rather, they involve "boilerplate" functions that should be based on proven designs, parts, and modules.

For instance, in the automobile industry, the most serious problems and consequences involve fuel systems, seat belts, steering, suspension, tires, and so forth – all subsystems that wise companies reuse proven subassemblies for. Ironically, these are not the parts that companies are advertising or customers are clamor for, which are more likely to be things like styling, cup holders, sound systems, navigation systems, and hybrid drives.

The success of a reuse strategy will be maximized by: making reuse a key design philosophy goal; designing versatile parts, modules, and subsystems that can be used in many designs over time; encouraging receptivity to reuse and discouraging the not-invented-here syndrome; and avoiding arbitrary decisions that can exclude the use of proven design.

Arbitrary decisions should be avoided because they will very likely preclude meeting goals, satisfying the design considerations, and taking advantage of opportunities such as off-the-shelf parts and the reuse of proven designs, parts, and modules. Avoid arbitrary part choice decisions that unnecessary proliferate part variety and needlessly complicate operations and supply chain management. Avoid the practice of *independently* selecting parts for each situation, which leads to a crippling proliferation. Instead, for each situation, select the best *standard* parts that have widespread applicability.

Avoid overconstraints. Make sure there are no more *constraints* than the minimum necessary, for instance, avoiding situations where four points try to determine a plane, four linear bearings to guide precise movements, or two parts are aligned with round pins/bolts in round holes. Overconstraints are costly and can cause quality problems and compromise functionality because the design will work only if all parts fabricated to tight, maybe unrealistic, tolerances. Fortunately, overconstraints are easy to avoid in the architecture stage by specifying the exact number of constraints that will do the job (see Guideline A3). Optimize tolerances by design by:

- *choosing* the optimal tolerance, not relying on block tolerances or arbitrary assumptions

- analyzing worst case tolerance situations

- methodically specifying tolerances with Taguchi Methods™ for a robust design

- minimizing tolerance demands. Eliminate the cost, quality, and performance problems of tight tolerances by identifying tolerance sensitivities and *create designs that are not as sensitive to tolerances.* For example:

  Tolerance stacks.   When many stacked parts must mate with another part or another stack, the tolerances of all parts will be cumulative for the "stack." Solutions are: (a) Control the tolerances of all parts on both sides of the stack; (b) Eliminate parts by simplifying product architecture and combining parts in the stack(s); or (c) Drill, clamp, or spot-weld one set of mounts "at assembly," assuming that those parts do not need to be interchangeable, for instance, for structural assemblies.

System integration should be optimized *early,* not after several subassemblies have been independently designed with little regard to how they integrate and interact in the product.

Reinventing the wheel can be avoided by cooperatively designing modules and reusing or sharing previous, proven engineering.

Do it right the first time so the team will not have to make changes to correct things that should have been done right the first time. This is most likely to happen when enough time is allocated for thorough up-front work.

Avoid past mistakes by understanding *lessons learned* from previous projects. This will require an active effort to investigate, summarize, and disseminate this information as part of Phase 3.

Avoid troublesome practices entirely, like assembling with adhesives or using liquid locking compound to retain fasteners, instead of using easier and more consistent solutions. Instead use screws or nuts coated with retention compound, fasteners with deformed threads, optimal use of lockwashers. Be sure to keep in mind service needs and cycle limitations.

Develop a software debug strategy; Choices:

(a) Make imbedded software ungradable/patchable or

(b) Make software perfect using object oriented programming and basing subsequent code on previously written and debugged modules (objects).

Vendor assistance is maximized by having preselected vendors on the design team early to help the team design the product, or, when appropriate, have the vendors design the parts that they will be building.

Variety and customization strategies are developed and implemented early. Product developments will not achieve their potentials if different efforts focus only on developing single mass-produced products.

Options and upgrades are designed to be easy to add. Sometimes upgradeability can be enhanced by simple additions (that cost little more) such as extra mounting holes, signal ports, power ports, utility capacity, accessibility, and convenient mounting spaces.

Total cost is used as the basis for measuring all costs and the basis for all decisions involving cost.

Establish design practices for procedures, documentation, standards, new design guidelines, and new design practices for designing for specific processes.

Design Philosophy Goals for Electronics

Obey all design rules for printed circuit boards for component placement, spacing, and layout and proper geometries/spacing for pads, holes, vias, traces, probes, test fixtures, locating features, and stay-out zones. Violating PC board design rules either induces quality/rework problems for automatic processing or prevents automatic placement/insertion of components that then requires hand placement or soldering, which should not even be considered an option for surface mounted components.

Avoid overcrowding PC boards by identifying functional density challenges *early* and *proactively* pursing solutions at the system architecture level, such as higher levels of integration (VLSI, ASICs), more space-efficient circuitry, more compact components, removing circuitry that does not have widespread use or value to customers, spinning off configuration functions to cables, and so forth.

No hand soldering should be allowed because automatic soldering (reflow or wave soldering) is probably the most refined process in industry with many operations routinely getting *six sigma* performance (around three defects per million). Hand soldering quality is inferior by orders of magnitude; further, some hand soldered joints can pass tests in the plant and fail in the field. No hand soldering should be allowed at all for surface mount components. Component selection criteria should include the ability to be automatically soldered and survive the heat of wave/reflow soldering and cleaning processes.

Ensure automatic placement/insertion of all components possible to maximize throughput, minimize assembly cost, and minimize the chances of assembling the wrong component, wrong orientation, or bad insertions. Automatic assembly should be a criterion for component selection. No hand placement should be allowed for any surface mount components.

Avoid hand soldering on circuit boards for off-board wiring, bottom-sided leaded connectors, unusual components, etc. Instead, find auto-solderable components, combine circuit boards, or use flex layers to connect them.

Specify industry-standard form factors or vendor-compatible panels for circuit boards to simplify processing and tooling, minimize setup changes, and optimize outsourcing opportunities. At the minimum, specify company-standard form-factors and panels.

Standardize components to prevent proliferation because if component variety exceeds equipment part capacity, then boards will have to go through the machines twice with set up changes in between.

Off-the-shelf part utilization strategy optimized *early* for:

- standard off-the-shelf cabinetry. There are several suppliers with thick catalogs featuring broad selections of standard enclosures, doors, frames, partitions, rack systems, control panels, fans, and so forth.

- standard off-the-shelf card cages, which require standard form factors, as discussed above.

- standard off-the-shelf boards for processing, memory, input/output, communications, and so forth.

- an architecture based on a standard off-the-shelf power supply, which requires discipline in the demands made by the various subsystem designers.

Voltages are minimized and standardized to minimize power supply design complications and allow the use of reliable off-the-shelf power supplies or modules. The "voice of the customer" product definition will not directly specify how many voltages need to be used inside an electronic product.

However, multiple design groups working without a philosophy goal may base their module designs on many different voltages, probably chosen arbitrarily. Subassemblies may work all right and collectively satisfy the product definition, but the result of too many voltages is that the power supply will be so complex that there will be *no chance* of buying a high-quality, thoroughly debugged unit off-the-shelf.

So then a custom power supply will have to be designed and made by a supplier or, if one cannot be found, by the assembler. Keep in mind that making power supplies work reliability is considered "black magic" in that industry, so commissioning a special design and a new learning curve can incur considerable, and unnecessary, risk. The bottom line is that *customers don't by electronics products for the power supply, but if it fails, it will cause a lot of problems including ruining the reputation of the product, no matter how good the rest of it is.*

Avoid components that need to be screened, matched, calibrated or adjusted to speed throughput, lower cost, and raise quality.

Circuit board counts are minimized with higher levels of integration (VLSI) and custom silicon (ASICs). Fitting all electronics on one circuit board can eliminate card cages and interboard wiring operations

Wiring, Cables, And Harnesses. *Proactively* design wiring, cables, and harnesses as key elements of system architecture, instead of *reactively* wiring together independently designed modules later.

- **Simplify Wiring.** Constantly keep trying to simplify and optimize wiring and harnesses throughout the product concept/architecture phase and during the system architecture of key subassemblies.

- **Voltage Proliferation.** Don't let voltages proliferate to allow off-the-shelf power supplies and minimize the number of wires to transmit many voltages. A single voltage can be daisy-chained to multiple modules that need the same voltage.

- **Power bus.** Route power along a bus bar or a shared cable, not many individual routings from the power supply to every power user.

- **Off-the-shelf signal cables.** Whenever possible, route signals through standard off-the-shelf high-quality/low-cost signal cables, (e.g., DIN cables) to/from standard connectors between boxes and boards.

- **One Power Cable/One Signal Cable.** Wiring between two modules could be as simple as one power cable and one signal cable, assuming there is no signal interference.

- **Poka-Yoke.** Use polarized connectors for all polarized wiring to prevent connection mistakes.

- **Universal Harness.** Consider a single universal harness for all product variations in the family, which may have a lower *total cost* than many different harnesses, even if some harnesses have unused wires.

- Consider **creative architecture solutions,** some of which may appear to cost more for the parts, but may result in a net system cost savings, such as backplanes, LANs (local area networks), etc.

3.2 IMPORTANCE OF GOOD PRODUCT ARCHITECTURE

The process of optimizing product architecture starts with an early balance of all design considerations by a complete multifunctional team. Optimizing product architecture is the highest leverage activity in product development and has the greatest potential for ensuring success. But, as with product definition, the importance of this stage is often ignored by merely assuming that the product architecture will be the same as previous or competitive products.

One of the biggest causes of sub-optimal product architecture starts with the seemingly innocuous step of building a breadboard "just to see if it works." Breadboards are designed to prove functional feasibility and are usually built with the materials on hand (not widely-available production grade materials) in the most expedient way (not the most manufacturable way). Further, breadboards are built by prototype technicians who can usually make a single unmanufacturable unit work as a matter of pride. Product architecture optimization and manufacturability are rarely even considered at the breadboard phase based on the assumption that those tasks will be done "later." Unfortunately, once the breadboard "works" and is demonstrated to management – you guessed it – there is a strong temptation to "draw it up and get it into production." The unfortunate result is the company ends up mass producing breadboards forever! Basing production designs on breadboard architecture misses the biggest opportunities to make significant reductions in cost and development time.

As shown in Chapter 1, 60% of a product's lifetime cumulative cost is determined by the concept or architecture phase of a project (Fig. 1-1).

By the time design is completed, 80% of the lifetime cumulative cost is determined. By the time the product reaches production, only 5% of the total cost can be influenced. This is why "cost reduction" efforts can be so futile, because cost is really determined by the design itself and is very difficult to remove later.

Similarly, other important design goals, like quality, reliability, serviceability, flexibility, customizability, and regulatory compliance are most easily achieved by optimizing the product's architecture.

Thorough up-front work greatly shortens the *real* time-to-market and avoids wasting time and resources on revisions, iterations, and ramp problems, as shown by the Lexmark model in Figure 3-1.

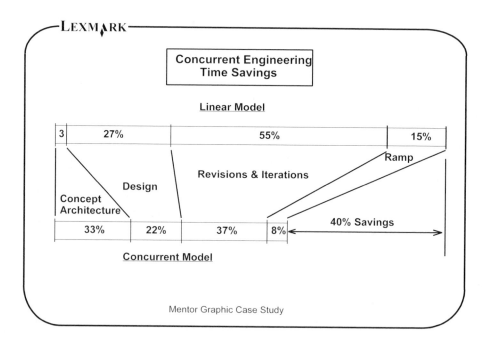

Figure 3-1: The Lexmark Model Showing True Time-to-Market
Differences Between Linear vs. Concurrent Models
(used with permission)

The projected 40% savings in the *real* time-to-market is due to early concept/architecture optimization minimizing the need for revisions and iterations and making the manufacturing ramp-up several times faster. Note that the architectural phase, labeled "conceptual design," went from 3% in the old model to 33% (of the total development time) in the new model, *an order of magnitude increase!* More thorough up-front work decreases the post-design activities (the revisions, iterations, and ramp-up) from almost three-fourths to less than a half of the product development cycle. It is more efficient to incorporate a balance of design considerations early than to implement them later with changes, revisions and iterations.

Figure 3-1 emphasizes one of the most important principles to reduce the *real* time-to-market: thorough up front work. This graphic, and its profound implications, generate much discussion in the author's in-house DFM training.[1] In fact, at one company that was high on the Fortune 500 list, we spent one hour discussing this graphic at all four seminars! In order to facilitation discussion in companies that use this book, this graphic is reproduced in color on the back cover, along with Figure 1-1.

While developing the Prius, the Toyota team avoided the temptation to jump right into detailed design:

> *"With the extreme time pressure, the temptation would be to make a very fast decision on the hybrid technology and get to work on it immediately. Instead, the team reexamined all its options with painstaking thoroughness, . . . considering 80 hybrid types and systematically . . . . narrowing it to 10 types. The team carefully considered the merits of each of these and then selected the best four. Each of these four types was then evaluated carefully through computer simulation. Based on these results, they were confident enough to propose one alternative, . . . six months later."*[2]

As engineers and managers realize the importance of thorough architecture optimization, they ask what more should be done in the order-of-magnitude increase in the "concept design" phase shown in Figure 3-1 and how this can actually reduce the final time line so much. The key elements of an optimal architecture phase are the following:

1) **Product definition,** which defines what the customer really wants and minimizes the chance that the product will be subject to change orders to reflect "new" customer needs that were really not anticipated in the beginning.

2) **Issue resolution,** which raises all the issues and then resolves them before proceeding further, thus minimizing the chances that these issues will have to be resolved later when each change is harder to implement and when each change may, in turn, induce yet more changes.

3) **Conceptual simplification,** which simplifies the overall product architecture with clever, elegant concepts, fewer parts, part

combinations, higher levels of silicon integration, modular opportunities, and so forth.

4) **Architectural optimization,** which optimizes the architecture for minimum total cost, for designed-in quality and reliability, for manufacturability and serviceability, and for flexibility and customizability.

Thorough Up-Front Work at Toyota

The 2006 book, *"The Toyota Product Development System,"*[3] emphasized the important of thorough up-front work at the company that some say is four times more efficient at product development:

"The ability to influence the success of a product development program is never greater that at the start of a project. The further into the process, the greater the constraints on decision making. As the program progresses, the design space fills, investments are made, and changing course becomes increasingly more expensive, time consuming, and detrimental to product integrity."

The book provides many details about *"bringing together your brightest, most experiences engineers from all functional disciplines to work collaboratively, thoroughly thinking through all of the critical project details, anticipating problems, applying lessons leaned, creating precise plans, and designing countermeasures from a total systems perspective . . ."*

Thorough Up-Front Work at Motorola

Motorola's most effective product development projects *"invested relatively large amounts of effort early in the initial design phase so that most, if not all, of the problems that appeared later in the implementation phases had already been considered."*[4]

3.3 OPTIMIZING ARCHITECTURE/SYSTEM DESIGN

The graph, "Product Cost vs. Time" (Figure 1-1) shows that 60% of the products lifetime cumulative cost is committed by the concept/architecture phase. Similarly this phase has the most significant effect on quality, reliability, serviceability, flexibility, customizability, etc. The graphs, Traditional vs Advanced Team Participation Models (Figure 2-1), show that thoroughly optimizing the architecture phase results in faster ramps and eliminates post-release problem solving for volume, quality, and productivity. Similarly, the Lexmark model (Figure 3-1) shows that the *real* time to market can be cut almost in half by thorough up-front work by spending 33% percent of the time line on optimizing architecture, instead of rushing through with only 3%.

Here is what to do 10 times more of to optimize product architecture:

- **Product definition.** Thoroughly understand what customers want – the "Voice of the Customer" – with optimal design specifications and resource allocations *before* starting the design process. Make sure the product definition (requirements document) is generic and does not specify, imply, or limit product architecture. Be sure to address and satisfy *all* aspects of the product requirements.

- **Team Composition/Timing.** Make sure the product development team is complete with all specialties present and active early.

- **Product Development Approach.** The team must understand and agree on the new product development approach (presented herein), especially those aspects that are different from the way things were done in the past.

- **Lessons Learned.** Thoroughly investigate and understand what worked well and what caused problems in previous projects with respect to development time/effort, functionality, quality, ramps, and so forth.

- **Technical/Functional Challenges.** If there are significant challenges for new technology, functionality, or regulatory compliance:
  - Ensure optimal manufacturability by design the first time to remove that variable so that once the technical challenges are solved, the design can go into production and won't have to be redesigned for manufacturability, cost, quality, and so forth.
  - Explore many ways to achieve the goals. Don't limit thinking to just extending conventional approaches.
  - To get breakthrough ideas, temporarily remove one constraint at a time, see if that solves the problem/challenge, and then either push back on the constraint or see if there is some way to make that idea work *within* the constraints.
  - Big leaps forward may require research projects to develop next paradigm solutions for many subsequent projects, rather than

trying to handle escalating challenges with each product development project.

- When a breakthrough may come from new or innovative components or materials, commit the time and effort to search alternatives, evaluate samples, and qualify the components.

- Thoroughly raise and resolve all relevant issues in the architecture phase. More resources can be applied early if they do not have to fight fires on other projects because *they* were not designed for manufacturability.

- Understand the challenges enough to commit enough money, resources, and time.

- Don't accept potentially naive customer or Marketing expectations for functionality, cost, and deadlines.

- Don't accept potentially naive customer expectations for functionality, cost, and deadlines. When appropriate, convey to the customer or prime contractor how minor changes in the specs could significantly lower risk, cost, and time.

- For major challenges, be sure a reasonable return can be expected based on total cost numbers and be sure to allot enough resources and calendar time.

- **Manufacturable Science.** There is temptation for scientists to "specify" *the* design or *the* process which will "work" or may have been "optimized" only for functional parameters and then throw it over the wall to the design engineers to build products or machinery that perform *the* specified process. While this is the common for experimental equipment at research labs or aerospace contractors (where equipment cost is buried in much larger research budgets), this approach will rarely result in the lowest cost and quickest development for cost-sensitive commercial products.

  Instead, scientists should: (a) understand all the issues regarding manufacturability and how problems with manufacturability affect functionality, quality, reliability, purchase cost, cost-of-ownership, and, ultimately, success; and (b) work closely with the multifunctional team members, *from the earliest stages*, to develop the practical science and robust processes that will work consistently in all anticipated environments and be easily manufacturable from readily available components and materials.

  When scientists specify *parts,* they should work with purchasing to look for a range of potential solutions and then narrow the search to the ones with the best cost, reliability, and availability (see the section on "Scale" next).

- **Scale.** A product's capacity or output should not be determined arbitrarily after which engineers specify parts for that arbitrary size. Product requirements should specify the size/scale/capacity only if it must match up with customers' equipment or operations.

- The optimal size/capacity should be determined by:

    - Ability of one *or multiple units* to satisfy most customer requirements

    - Cost and availability of the most expensive or hard-to-get purchased parts

    - Cost and availability of the most expensive or time-consuming designed/specified parts

    - Major low price anomalies in the price/performance curves of purchased parts (see Figure 3-2).

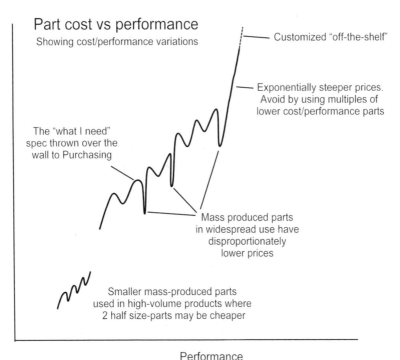

Figure 3-2: Part Cost vs Performance

When a product has dominant high-cost parts or subassemblies:

- Identify the most expensive parts or subassemblies.

- Look for the lowest cost/function (on the previous graph), for the moment disregarding the scale of the product.

- Work with scientists to scale up or down the scientific process. Look for fundamentally lower-cost design solutions and procedures.

- Work with Marketing on different scale and usage ramifications.

- **Scope.** To avoid reinventing the wheel for every project, optimize the scope of product development projects, with respect to synergies with other products:

  - At the minimum level, identify synergistic products and choose parts and processes that are common with other products in the family.

  - Develop families of products in synergistic platforms:

    - Define the product family to maximize synergies with respect to design, manufacturing, supply chain, customer base, and so forth.

    - Develop versatile, *scalable* designs that can evolve, adapt, or migrate to new features, future market needs, and broader, easier customizations. This can be accomplished by endowing current/base products with more features, capabilities, power, connectors, mounting holes, versatile circuit boards, and so forth. Any perceived "extra" cost could be more than compensated by lower total cost savings from not having to design and build many product versions. Enhanced capabilities could be enabled in subsequent versions or upgrades, perhaps with software or remote switches.

    - Identify what can be common for the family and standardize on those. Some parts or subassemblies may need to have more features or performance to satisfy the whole family, but that may result in a lower total cost for the family (see Section 5.11, "Standardization of Expensive Parts").

- Minimize engineering efforts and save time by sharing engineering amongst many products. Design products to make it quicker and easier to develop derivatives.

- Formulate modular strategy, looking for opportunities to develop modules for many products. Determine optimal modules partitions and interfaces.

- Identify the variable dimensions that account for the differences in products in the family. Establish parametric CAD templates with floating dimensions for all variable dimensions.

- Concurrently engineer flexible processes that can quickly and easily build any product in the family, ideally on product family cells or lines.

- **Metrics.** Make sure that all metrics are based on "big picture" measurements. If the project is to be compared to earlier products that were based on primitive metrics (like part/labor cost or when the design was thrown over the wall), then those projects must be recalculated based on the new metric criteria.

  - **Cost** metrics and all cost decisions must be based on total cost; all elements of selling price should be quantified to help the design team focus on minimizing all the costs (see Chapter 6).

  - **Time to Market** metrics should be based on *true* time-to-market, as measured to stable production, as shown in Figure 2-1.

  - **Efficiency** should be measured by a bottom-line metric that matters to customers, such as cost per unit of output.

    - Efficiency measured by a "percentage" of output/input can lead to a contest mentality that may exclude tradeoffs where a slight sacrifice in "efficiency" can result in large gains in manufacturability, cost reduction, reliability, etc. For instance, a design that is 10% "less efficient," and half the cost, could be 10% larger and still result in a net cost reduction of 45%.

    - Subassembly performance specs should be written to support and optimize system goals that are based on bottom-line metrics.

  - **Bragging rights.** Avoid going for bragging rights that do not benefit customers, such as efficiency, status parts, showy processing, unnecessary robotics, ambitious part combinations, inappropriate processing techniques, or award-winning parts or processes.

Concept/Architecture Design Optimization (to be done concurrently with Manufacturing and Supply Chain Strategies)

- **Design Philosophy Goals.** Establish design philosophy goals with respect design practices, such as standard parts, off-the-shelf-parts, proven processing, reuse, avoiding arbitrary decisions, doing it right the first time, avoiding past mistakes, early vendor assistance, customization, and thorough concept/architecture optimization.

- **Thoroughly optimize the concept/architecture of the** *product,* not just a collection of parts and subsystems. This phase provides the greatest opportunities for innovation, substantial cost reduction, and assuring a quick ramp to volume production.

- **Keep focusing on the architecture,** without designing a lot of detail, which may become obsolete as the architecture evolves. If necessary, keep a list of "loose ends" to finish after the architecture is optimized.

- Both engineers and managers need to **avoid the trap of trying to "wrap up" certain parts or subsystems prematurely.**

- Focus on **generating many concepts**, not making only a few detailed designs or models
  - Document all ideas: save or print with meaningful labels, file names, and layer names. For sketches, keep dated copies of all ideas. If related ideas build on the same sketch, make a dark-line copy of the sketch for the records, and then change the sketch to next idea. Repeat as necessary.

- **Don't ignore** *obvious* **aspects** of the design, since *all* aspects affect the system design

- **Don't ignore** *vague* **aspects** of the design, since *all* aspects affect the system design.

- **Build models**, when applicable, to demonstrate or compare concepts.

- **Concept Simplification/Optimization.** Explore *many* potential concepts and approaches to optimize system architecture. Use creativity (Section 3.6) and brainstorming (Section 3.7) to generate many ideas.

- Don't be limited by your current products or competitors' products.

- Don't latch onto the first idea to come along.

- Strive for *design simplicity* by minimizing the number of parts and process steps and optimizing decisions on part combinations, off-the-shelf parts, and, in general, the simplest architecture.

- Brainstorm for *many ideas*. Look for breakthrough ideas that would revolutionize the industry, even if that is not the project's stated goal.

  > *"Toyota considers a broad range of alternatives and systematically narrows the sets to a final, often superior, choice."*[5]

  > At Sony, *"thirty engineers in Ibuka's [Sony Co-Founder's] team began exploring multiple approaches to color simultaneously,"* eventually converging on three electron beams from a single gun, which became the revolutionary *Trinitron*.[6]

- Try to simultaneously optimize all the goals and satisfy all the constraints. Sometimes considering multiple goals and constraints can overcome design paralysis and avoid arbitrary decisions. This results in faster progress and better solutions than trying to solve one challenge at a time.

- If a particular idea doesn't work out:

  - Look for more ideas to *make it* work

  - If that doesn't work, go back and make the original idea better or generate a better idea.

  - The problem might be overcome by expanding the scope of the idea to simultaneously solving several problems. For instance, a solution that appears to be too expensive to solve *one* problem may be justified if it solves three.

- At Toyota, generating very many ideas presents *patterns* and *possibilities*. This provides more opportunities to combine these ideas and multiply them into bigger ones.[7] And contrary to popular belief, a steady stream of incremental innovation is what is most likely to lead to "the bid idea."

- Formulate the off-the-shelf strategy (Section 5.19) *early* because:

  - Off-the-shelf parts need to be chosen before arbitrary decision preclude their use.

  - After selecting the optimal set of off-the-shelf parts, the rest of the design will literally be designed around them.

  - Optimal off-the-shelf utilization allows the design team to focus on optimizing the architecture and designing the remaining parts.

  - Optimal off-the-shelf utilization helps the design team meet its goals for the lowest total cost, quickest development, best quality, proven reliability, and lowest risk of problems or delays.

- Formulate the strategy of what to leverage from previous designs and which designs, processes and practices to avoid. This may require some additional investigations and experiments.

- Optimize integration of parts and their assembly, interfaces, wiring, cabling and part/subsystem interactions.

- Decide the level of standardization; create or adopt standard parts lists.

- Formulate strategies for part combinations and silicon integration (VSLI, ASICs), in support of strategies for product families and standardization.

- Formulate the strategies for assuring quality, reliability, mistake-proofing, test, repair, service, and test including optimizing test points.

- Formulate the design strategy for variety, configurations, customization, derivatives, and subsequent products.

Manufacturing & Supply Chain Strategies, to be done concurrently with Concept/Architecture Design Optimization.

- Formulate processing strategy, including:

  - Process selection and the flows of part and products

  - Flexible cell/line design for product families.

- Formulate the resupply strategy for parts and raw materials: MRP based purchase orders, or steady flows, kanban, min/max, or breadtruck (free stock).[8]

- Optimize outsourcing and internal integration decisions.[9]

- Identify the supplier base for parts and materials.

- Formulate the vendor strategy for non-standard parts and outsourcing; identify potential vendor partnerships early and arrange for early participation on the design team.

- Formulate the strategies for quality/reliability assurance and test.

- Incorporate mistake-proofing (poka-yoke) into the design (to prevent manufacturing errors by design features) and the processing (to make sure manufacturing errors don't happen in fabrication or assembly).

- Formulate the manufacturing strategy for customization, configurations, product variety, extensions, and derivatives.

- Arrange for relevant overhead allocations (if not automatic through total cost accounting) to (a) prevent new products from having to pay the high overhead charged to pay for less manufacturable products and (b) encourage behavior that further lowers overhead costs.

3.4 PART DESIGN STRATEGIES

Strategies for designing parts and subassemblies (hereafter called parts) are:

- Ensure product architecture and the conceptual product design have been optimized before designing any parts.

- Thoroughly pursue off-the-shelf (Section 5.19) and modularity (Section 4.7) opportunities as explored in the architecture phase before attempting to design any parts.

- Design the most pivotal and challenging parts first. Otherwise the design of less-challenging parts may make arbitrary decisions that may compromise the most challenging designs.

- Design all parts to support the system design and work well together *by design*. Don't just design a collection of parts that may be hard to integrated later. Don't structure the project management into independent part or subassembly design efforts.

- Allocate appropriate effort to the design of various parts and subassemblies according to customer input as graphed in Figure 2-3 and calculated in the one of the bottom lines of the QFD chart (Figure 2-5).

- Understand lessons learned about similar parts including manufacturability issues and reliability track records.

- Understand the potential processes that will manufacture the parts. If multiple processes are candidates, investigate and understand all the processes; talk with appropriate vendors to help make the best decision.

- Collaboratively design parts with vendors, who know the design rules for those processes, in general, and the process capabilities of their own equipment. For vendor-assisted design to be possible, vendors must be chosen *first* based on reputations and relationships. The primitive paradigm of part bidding precludes vendor-assisted design, by definition, since the part would have to be designed *before* potential vendors are asked to bid on it (see Section 6.11 on the shortcomings of low bidding).

- Cost strategy should be focused on minimizing *total cost* of the *product or product family.* In some cases, seemingly more expensive parts may result in better quality and be more standardized, thus resulting cost-saving synergies in supply chain management and operations. Don't compare new designs to previous designs on a part-to-part basis, because that may discourage part combination strategies where, for instance, two new parts replace five old parts (Guideline S7 and Section 9.5).

- If the design of any part starts to run into trouble, *immediately* notify the rest of the team, who are still designing the rest of the product around that part. Then the team can help get that part design back on track or quickly adjust the system design to accommodate changes in that part design. Toyota's product development process emphasizes *transparency*, as summarized by a senior executive:

  > *"If you have a problem, you'd better tell somebody, because eventually you will be found out."*[10]

  Phil Condit, when he was Chairman and CEO of The Boeing Company, spoke on this problem of individual engineers running into trouble, not telling anyone, and stubbornly trying to fix it alone. The result, as Phil Condit postulated, might be that the airplane manufacture would have to go the airlines and say: "You know that plane you wanted to fly nonstop to Sydney – well, its range is going come up about 500 miles short!"[11]

• Complete all part designs and documentation. In the rush to get prototypes built, many companies use "expedient" documentation (like sketches) or no documentation at all (like verbal instructions), which can result in miscommunications and delay ramping into production when complete documentation is needed. Further, not fully completing and submitting CAD designs eliminates the opportunity to perform CAD assembly integration and error-checking, for instance, for interferences between parts. In extreme cases, some designers leave certain details "to be determined" by production workers! In one company, production line workers actually went to the local Lowe's Hardware stores to buy bolts for structural elements. Of course, this can lead to significant variations from the design intent thus resulting in performance, quality, and even product liability ramifications.

• Follow the part design guidelines in Chapter 9.

3.5 DESIGN FOR EVERYTHING

Engineers are trained to design for functionality and their CAD tool predominately design for functionality. However, really good product development comes from *designing for everything,* which is sometimes called *DFX.* Here is a list of *design considerations* for Design for Everything. The key here is to *consider all goals & constraints early*

Function. Of course the product has to work properly, but it must be kept in mind that, although function is the most obvious consideration, it is far from being the only one. A redesign to correct a purely functional problem will result in *another* product introduction and that can introduce new, unknown manufacturability problems and be an unexpected drain on manufacturing resources.

Cost. Cost has been the battleground of competition for decades now. But the lowest product cost does not result from "cost reduction" measures, *per se.* As pointed out in Chapter 1, design determines more than three fourths of a product's cost.

For example, one high tech company appointed a "cost reduction manager" for a critical new product line, who managed to reduce the *projected* cost within the goal by buying the cheapest parts. However, the parts came from 16 different countries and took nine months to deliver first articles. And, this was on a leading edge product!

Furthermore, when production began, the part quality was so poor that the plant actually ground to a halt, thus delaying delivery even further. The subject of cost will be treated in more detail in Chapter 6 on minimizing cost.

Delivery. Delivery is greatly affected by the design because the design determines how difficult the product is to build and assemble. The choice of the parts determines how hard the parts will be to procure and how vulnerable production will be to supply glitches. Standardization (Chapter 5) will affect the effectiveness of lean production which is the key to fast factory thruput (see Chapter 4).

Quality and Reliability. Like cost, quality and reliability are determined more by the design than is commonly realized. Designers specify the parts and, thus, the quality of the parts. Designers determine the number of parts and so determine the cumulative effect of *part quality* on product quality, which is especially important for complex products (Section 10.3). Designers are responsible for the tolerance sensitivity. The processes specified by the designer determine the inherent quality of the parts. Designers are responsible for ensuring that parts are designed so that they cannot be assembled wrong, which in Japan is called *poke-yoke,* or what we would call mistake-proofing (see Section 10.9). These are very much manufacturability issues since quality problems must be consistently corrected in the plant before a product can be shipped. Quality and reliability are discussed further in Chapter 10.

Ease of assembly. Ease of assembly is what comes to mind when most people think of DFM because much attention has been focused on Design for Assembly (DFA), later renamed DFMA, and software to analyze designs to look for opportunities to improve the assembly of high-volume products. The DFM techniques presented herein optimize the ease of assembly *by design,* independent of production volumes. Chapters 8 and 9 present general guidelines for designing products that can be easily assembled.

Ability to Test. Test strategy is very much affected by the company quality "culture." At companies with a good quality culture, quality is *everyone's* responsibility, including designers! The TQM philosophy is that, instead of being *tested in,* quality should be *designed in* and then *built in* using process controls. Theoretically, products need not be tested if all processes are 100% in control. However, few factories are that confident in their processes, so they may elect to conduct at least a "go/no-go" functional test. Unsophisticated factories with higher fallout (failures) producing complex products may need tests to aid in diagnostics. Designers of these products are responsible for devising a way to not only *test* the product, but also to *diagnose* it if that is needed by the factory. In complex products, test development cost can exceed product development costs and can even take more calendar time. Test guidelines are included in Chapter 8.

Ease of service and repair. Being able to repair a defective product is a manufacturability issue because any product failing any test will have to be repaired, thus consuming valuable manufacturing resources. Service and repair in the field can be more troublesome because field service centers usually have less sophisticated equipment than factories. In extreme cases, field failures may be sent back to the factory for repair, thus diluting manufacturing resources. Designers should design in ease of service and repair (see Section 8.9).

Supply Chain Management. Supply chain management can be greatly simplified by the standardization of parts and raw materials (Chapter 5), part selection based on adequate availability over time, and product line rationalization (see Appendix A) to eliminate or outsource the old, low volume, unusual products that have the most unusual parts. In many cases, this simplification, performed in product portfolio planning and product development, will be essential to the success of supply chain management initiatives as well as programs to implement lean production, build-to-order, and mass customization.

Shipping & Distribution. The distribution of products will be revolutionized by *build-to-order,*[12] which is capable of building products on-demand and shipping them directly to customers, stores, or other factories instead of the mass production tradition of building large batches and then shipping them through warehouses and distribution centers. Selling products like this from inventory has many problems: The whole system depends on forecasts, which rarely come even close to predicting customer demands, especially when markets are fast moving. Inventory costs money to *carry,* usually 25% of its value per year![13] If forecasts were too high, then inventory will have to be marked down to "move the merchandise." If forecasts were too low, then sales opportunities will be lost; sometimes manufacturers try to compensate inadequate forecasted production by expediting production, but this can be expensive and can disrupt scheduled production.

Packaging considerations should not be left until the first manufactured product reaches the shipping dock. Packaging variety and its logistics can be reduced with standard packaging that can be used for many products. Unique information can be added by printing on-demand labels or directly onto the boxes. Environmentally friendly packaging materials and recycled packages are now becoming more important.

Designing inherent shock resistance into the product can reduce the size and cost of protective packaging. Another packaging implication is that returns due to shipping damage may come back to the factory, thus adding cost, upsetting customers, and depleting manufacturing resources.

Human factors. Human factors and *ergonomics* are social considerations that should be considered at the very beginning, since ergonomic changes would be difficult to implement after the design is complete. Good human factors design (Chapter 10) of the product and process will reduce errors and accidents in use and during manufacture. In some industries (like electronics), many service calls are performed to correct customer setup and operation errors.

Appearance/style. Appearance and style should be considered an integral part of the design, not something that is added later. Sometimes, the style is dictated by an early Industrial Design study. This can really hamper incorporating DFM principles if these were not considered in the "styling" design. All factors of a design, including styling, need to be considered simultaneously throughout the design.

Safety. Safety should not be considered after the recall or first law suit. Careful design and simulations should be utilized to prevent safety problems before they manifest. If a safety issue surfaces, the root of the problem must be determined and remedied immediately. This can be a major disruption to Engineering, Manufacturing, and Sales, in addition to jeopardizing the product's and the company's reputation. Designers should make every effort to design safe products the first time as a moral and legal obligation.

Customers' needs. The ultimate goal in designing a product is to satisfy customer needs. In order to do that, designers must thoroughly identify and understand customer needs (Section 2.11) and then systematically develop the product to satisfy those needs. Engineers must beware of the "next bench syndrome" and avoid designing products for themselves or their peers.

Breadth of product line. Using the principles of lean production and build-to-order, discussed in Chapter 4, products can be designed with standard parts and be produced on flexible manufacturing lines or cells. Common parts, standard design features, modular subassemblies, and flexible manufacturing can be combined to satisfy more customers.

Product customization. Customized products can be built as quickly and efficiently as mass production if products *and* processes are designed for *mass customization.*[14] For more on mass customization, see Section 4.3.

Time-to-Market. Time-to-market is a major source of competitive advantage.[15]   In fast moving markets, being first to market can have major market share implications. Figure 3-3 shows the effect of an early product release on the revenue profile. The shaded area represents the extra *sales* due to the early introduction.   But, since the product development and tooling costs were paid for by the baseline sales profile, the shaded area is really extra *profit.*

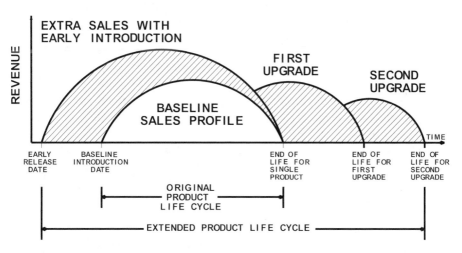

Figure 3-3: Increasing revenue with early introductions and upgrades

Expansion/upgrading. Designers should design products so that they are easy to expand or upgrade by the plant or by the customer. This capability may allow the company to increase profits by extending the life of each product. Marketing and Finance representatives should be involved early to help formulate the product upgrading strategy and calculate its value. Crunching the numbers will point out the high profit potential in the latter stages of their lifetimes after development costs are paid off, as shown in the upgrade extensions in Figure 3-3. Again, the product development and tooling costs were paid for by the baseline sales profile, so the shaded area is really extra profit.

Planning to extending a product's lifetime with easy upgrades may be a very worthwhile goal to consider in the initial phases of the product design.

Future designs. Similarly, current products should be designed so subsequent products can be based largely on current designs. This will save much time and cost in the next design if maximum use can be made of current engineering, parts, modules, and software.

Product pollution. Environmental design considerations should not be left to first time the product or its process is fired up. Problems discovered at this stage may require major changes or a redesign to correct. Designers should anticipate environmental trends and design products clean enough for *future* environmental standards.

Processing pollution. Product designers specify the process whether they realize it or not. Even specifying *the usual* process may continue a process that is causing pollution from solvents, combustion products, chemical waste, and so forth. Designers of new products have the opportunity to optimize the environmental cleanliness of the processes. This is much easier to do in the early stages of the design than later. Do not wait until environmental activists or a regulatory agency force your company to change your processes, which would result in disruptive changes in the factory, costly penalties, engineering change orders, and maybe a product redesign.

3M Corporation formulated an environmental strategy called the "3P" program: "Pollution Prevention Pays." The theme is prevention of pollution at its source. The three elements of the program are:

1) Recycling.

2) *Redesign products* and equipment for less pollution.

3) *Create products that do not pollute in the first place.*

Note that two out of three methods depend on the *design* to reduce pollution.

Ease of recycling products. Similarly, companies should be concerned about what happens to the product after its useful life is over. Can it be recycled into new products? Can it be upgraded for extended life? The company may even be able to profit in some manner from the recycling or extension of its products. If the product must be disposable, it should degrade quickly and safely without aggravating worsening solid waste disposal problems. These factors, like all the others, must be considered all through the design.

All these factors should be emphasized *early* by product development teams since redesigns or major product design changes consume a great deal of design and manufacturing resources to implement the changes. Remember that changes and redesigns consume the engineering time and money that should be invested in new product development. This leads to one of the most important design principles for design in general, not just for DFM: *The further into a design, the harder it is to start satisfying additional needs.*

It is important to design with a *balanced* set of design considerations. Do not let any considerations dominate the design or others will suffer.

Many people do not have a clear understanding of whose job is it to incorporate these considerations into the design. Some may think that assembleability comes from the Manufacturing Department. Some may think serviceability comes from the Service Department. Many think that quality is the responsibility of the Quality Department. The correct view of responsibility is a paraphrase of the motto of total quality management (TQM) programs:

> *It is* everyone's *responsibility to incorporate*
> all *considerations early into the design.*

Consequences of Not Considering Everything Early

A) You have much trouble integrating them later. The results would be delays, extra cost, and depleted resources.

or B) They are never incorporated into the design. The results would be a less competitive products, products that must be withdrawn from the market, or products that need to be redesign.

3.6 CREATIVE PRODUCT DEVELOPMENT

Inventing requires *creativity*. And designing an invention for manufacturability requires even *more* creativity. At Toyota, *"Invention without practical application is no more than a hobby. Invention becomes innovation only when stable duplication is achieved on a meaningful scale at a realistic cost."*[16] This corresponds to when the stable target volume production is achieved, as shown in the center graph in Fig. 2-1.

The prerequisite for creativity is an *open mind* and a *receptivity to ideas*. The chapter on "Innovation and Change" in the Dartmouth study on corporate success and failure stated: "Innovation is not a "thing that just happens. It's a natural outgrowth of a culture of open-mindedness."[17]

Concurrent Engineering of Innovative Designs

Tempting as it may be, innovative research must not focus only on getting something to work. The bottom line of research is products that will sell well and production that will be able to satisfy demand.

Commercial success will depend on good manufacturability, timely development, availability of parts and materials in production quantities, and compatibility with available processes. If available processes can not be used then special processes will have to be concurrently developed (see later section).

If these are not considered all along, early decisions may unknowingly choose a path that may result in functional "success" but may not be manufacturable. At that point there may not be enough time or money to backtrack and choose the path that provides both functionality *and* manufacturability. So make sure to choose that path the first time.

Investigate and understand which early arbitrary decisions may exclude the optimal processing and thus degrade performance, time-to-market, delivery, quality, reliability, etc.

Consider tradeoffs where allowing slight drops in performance or efficiency may greatly lower the cost, manufacturability, time-to-market, reliability, longevity, etc. Don't let the quest for perfection impede manufacturability.

Getting Creative Ideas

State the challenge *generically* without implying or excluding any solutions.

For new products, creative ideas should apply to all aspects of the design and manufacture. For redesigns and derivatives, the search for ideas could start with the most expensive part/subassembly or the hardest to build or any other challenges.

Identify fundamental flaws in conventional designs and then think of new concepts that are inherently not flawed.

To get good ideas, ignore what has been done before and don't be deterred by obstacles. Ignore current designs and conventional thinking. Rather, focus on what needs to be done. Pretend you are new to this industry. Ask: *what would revolutionize the industry?*

Don't limit idea generation to thinking only in one setting. Look for ideas in a wide range of situations, climates, and states-of-mind.

Generate *many* ideas to accomplish *all* the challenges and possibly more.

"The Toyota organization implements a million ideas a year."[18]

"You cannot fall in love with your first idea. You have to be able to explore openly and accept input from lots of people. It is very important to be flexible." - Frank Nuovo, VP Design, Nokia.[19]

"If you go through life convinced that your way is always best, all the new ideas in the world will pass you by." – Akio Morita, cofounder, Sony.[20]

Don't limit thinking by excluding innovative solutions, especially when previous conventional thinking says "it won't work" or "it's not possible" or it's "too risky."[21]

"If you don't take a risk on a new idea, that in itself, becomes a risk." - Tsuyoshi Kikukawa, President, Olympus

Don't limit the number of ideas by spending too much modeling or drawing each one. At the idea stage, sketching or discussing many creative ideas is more important that presentation format.

Be aware of new developments that are relevant to the project, even if they are outside your industry. Look for many relevant precedents in the field that are lower cost or higher performance and innovations outside the industry in product design, processing, etc.

When applicable, create a visual model that contains *only* the most challenging elements. This avoids limiting creativity by temporarily omitting less challenging aspects, like frames, enclosures, and so forth.

Continue to use creativity as the design progresses. *"The output from one creative process usually stimulates the need for more creativity."*[22]

Nine Keys to Creativity from *The Manger's Pocket Guide to Creativity.*[23] Here is the essence of the nine keys with a quote from each:

1) **Ask a lot of questions;** *"Most of our social institutions seem designed to limit, if not discourage, creative inquiry."*

2) **Record all ideas;** *"When you need new ideas, you can start by reexamining the old ones."*

3) **Revisit idea *and* assumptions;** *"When revisiting, you often find that assumptions are more striking than ideas"*

4) **Express ideas and follow through;** *"Most ideas are cut short by our automatic self-censorship."*

5) **Think in new ways;** *"You don't get out of the box by doing what you've always done."*

6) **Wish for more; stretch;** *"Creativity is nurtured by creative speculation."*

7) **Everyone should try to be creative;** *"Most people feel they're not creative and therefore don't try to be."*

8) **Keep trying;** *"The secret to incubation is revisiting the problem and doing so often."*

9) **Encourage creativity and ask for creative behavior all the time;** *"Most managers think" that "if you aren't visibly producing something tangible, they you're wasting the company's money."*

Creativity in a Team

For innovation, *"the real returns come from harnessing the imagination of every single employee every single day."* - Gary Hamel

Start with a creative, open-minded team which is stimulated by the challenge. The team should be diverse in knowledge as well as cultural and thinking styles.

Fire up the team.[24] Creativity is enhanced when people *really want* to invent something.

Allocate the time to be creative; hopefully, the project will realize the importance of the concept/architecture phase and allocate enough time to optimize this phase.

Put aside preconceived notions and conventional thinking and *think outside the box.* It may help to do brainstorming (next topic), possibly with an experienced facilitator, who comprehends the market and technical challenges, but can also offer an outside perspective.

To promote creative thinking, co-locate team workers close together and hold creative sessions in a permanent shared space or off site in a relaxed atmosphere away from phones and pagers; consider a site that has some relevance to the project.

Do *not* start creative product development discussing administrative issues, especially deadlines and development budgets.

Use creative solutions for follow-through and implementation activities.

The very nature of creativity and invention has many cycles of ups-and-downs, like a sinusoidal curve. Thinking of a good idea can be an exhilarating experience, which is the first "high" on the curve. Then you, or probably someone else, says, "What about . . .?" Then the curve hits the first "low," when the idea could easily die without a culture that encourages continued creativity and persistence. The down cycles are when ideas are most very vulnerable to discouragement or lack of support. To proceed back up, new ideas and solutions will be required to solve problems encountered at after each drop.

Toyota emphasizes *"The tenacity to bring ideas to fruition even in spite of initial setbacks."*[25] Toyota *"removes anything that stands in the way. That means looking at the target in a fundamentally different way. It means asking 'what's blocking perfection?' instead of what can we improve? That's what is differentiates their brand of continuous improvement from all others."*[26]

The book, *Breakthrough*, proposes *radical research* to get past obstacles and follow the problem to the root and then looks for solutions.

"In *applied research*, if there is an obstacle, the group tried to get around it. If stuck at an obstacle, the researches look for a quick fix or give up."

"In *radical research*, however, obstacles focus the research. Typically, a multidisciplinary team is deployed to find perspectives on the obstacle. As the exploration deepens, more disciplines may be brought in as needed."[27]

At Toyota, engineers are expected to "break down the problem down to its smallest definable elements and attack each one with ingenuity." And "big leaps forward are achieved not in one big swag but through the cumulative effect of multitude of much smaller hits."[28]

3.7 BRAINSTORMING

Brainstorming is a technique, normally used in groups, which can generate very many ideas. The leader can organize a formal session or just steer a spontaneous discussion into brainstorming using the following rules. The leader should make the rules clear and record everything said (but tape recorders may inhibit creativity).

Criticism and judgement are *not* allowed. Criticism discourages the generation of new ideas and inhibits everyone's responses.

Praise *all* ideas. Since judgement is not being applied, *all ideas should be praised* because the strength of a brainstorming session is to generate a lot of ideas.

Generate *many* ideas. Nobel Laureate Linus Pauling once said: "The secret to getting good ideas is to have a lot of ideas and some criterion for choosing." Further, one idea can lead to another.

Think wild. What may seem to be a ridiculous idea might trigger the thought process that ultimately leads to a useful solution. Think of the mathematical process of using imaginary numbers (the square root of negative one) to derive real answers. There are many calculations using these imaginary numbers, but in the end, a real answer appears.

<u>After</u> the Brainstorming Session:

Sort out all the candidate ideas. This is where judgement is applied. Try to prioritize the ideas to a list of leading candidates. Some ideas may seem promising but need more investigation.

Choose the final solution. Choose the best solution based on all the objectives, constraints, and resources.

After design ideas have been chosen and survived the initial follow-through analysis, they must be given a *thorough* follow-through effort to reduce the idea to practice. This must be pursued ambitiously until the design meets *all* its design goals. If the tentative design falls short, the designers should iterate the above process until the product meets all the goals. Many DFM problems are caused by dropping the manufacturability goal because the design is having problems.

3.8 HALF-COST PRODUCT DEVELOPMENT

First, companies must ensure that their policies are *not* counterproductive to the best product development practices (Section 11.5), such as outsourcing production away from Engineering (Section 4.8), attempting cost reduction after design (Section 6.1), bidding custom parts (Section 6.11), and averaging overhead costs (Chapter 7).

Prerequisites Needed for Half-Cost Development

Total Cost. The more import cost is, the more important it is to measure it properly. For ambitious cost goals, cost measurements *absolutely must* quantify *all* costs that contribute to the selling price in Figure 6-1.

Until company-wide total cost measurements are implemented, the half-cost team needs to make cost decisions on the basis of *total cost thinking,* or for important decisions, manually gather all the costs. Since a large portion of cost savings will be in *overhead*, the costing *must* ensure that new products are not burdened with the averaged overhead charges, but only the specific overhead charges that are appropriate.

Rationalization. Companies wanting to develop half-cost products will have to *immediately* rationalize their *existing* product lines to eliminate or outsource (a) demanding products that take resources away from new product development and (b) "loser" products that must be subsidized by more profitable products (Appendix A). The effects of rationalization on a Half-Cost program are to ensure that:

- resources are *always* available for multifunctional teams and not pulled away to build firedrill products or find unusual parts.

- resources are available for the *other* Half-Cost strategies.

- the new half-cost product will not have to pay the "loser tax" to subsidize less efficient products.

Designing Half-Cost Products

Half-cost product will not result just from setting an ambitious target (Section 1.4) or any other "show me the money" goal. If companies want to develop products at half the cost, *they must do everything right*, which includes implementing *all* the techniques presented in this book *and* implementing the strategies presented at *www.HalfCostProducts.com,* which presents a coordinated eight-point strategy to cut *total* cost in half or better. This book will show how to do the first point which is product development plus some of the Half-Cost strategies. The company should implement the other seven strategies to (a) help reduce the cost and (b) support product development by measuring total cost (Chapter 7), establishing vendor/partnerships (Section 2.6), standardize parts (Chapter 5), and rationalizing product to free up resources (Appendix A). Thus, a half-cost product development will consist of implementing all the recommendations of this book with special emphasis on:

Product Definition. The product definition must reflect the voice of the customer (Section 2.11) *and* yet be worded *generically* (e.g., means to _____) so as to maximize the designs possibilities. If applicable, the product requirements should *not* specify the *scale* of the product (e.g., size, output, capacity, etc.) for reasons cited in the last point below.

Lessons Learned. Thoroughly understand the total cost structure of previous or related products to identify sources of excessive waste, like defects, rework, scrap, setups, warrantee costs, and other inefficiencies.

Creative Concept/Architecture Optimization. Since 60% of cost is determined in this phase, Half-Cost product development *must* fully explore every possible way to satisfy customer needs. The multifunctional team should schedule enough time to creatively search for *many* ideas (Section 3.6) and conduct many brainstorming sessions (Section 3.7) to search for low-cost design approaches *and* manufacturing and sourcing strategies.

Tolerances. A systematic approach to tolerancing may be a key element of a Half-Cost strategy. The architecture should be optimized to eliminate the need for tolerances that have to be so tight that they add unnecessarily to the cost. Techniques to minimize tolerance costs include:

• Avoid overconstraints, as discussed in Guideline A3 in Chapter 8.

• Avoid cumulative stacks with techniques presented on page 83.

• Use concurrently designed fixtures to precisely position parts and then bolt members together or drill, pin, or spot weld "at assembly."

• Understand tolerance step functions for all contemplated processes to avoid unknowingly specifying processes that are more expensive than necessary (see Figure 9-2).

• Use Design of Experiments and Taguchi Methods™ to methodically specify tolerances for a *robust* design to achieve *"high quality at low cost,"* as practitioners say (see Guideline Q12 in Chapter 10).

• Combined parts (Guideline S7, p.282); design machined parts so all dimensions are machined in the same setup (Guideline P14, p.270).

Expensive Parts. When products have dominant high-cost parts/subassemblies:

- Identify the most expensive potential parts/subassemblies
- Look for the lowest cost/function ratio on a graph like Figure 3-2, temporarily disregarding the *scale* of the product
- Investigate ways to scale the product up or down to correspond to the lowest cost/function of the key part.
- Work with Marketing to determine the optimal scale.

ENDNOTES/REFERENCES

1. For more information on customized in-house DFM seminars, see page 407 of this book or *www.design4manufacturability.com/seminars.htm.*

2. Jeffrey K. Liker, *The Toyota Way*, (2004, McGraw-Hill); Page 57.

3. Morgan & Liker, *The Toyota Product Development System,* Chapter 4, "Front-Load the PD Process to Explore Alternatives Thoroughly."

4. Stephen B. Rosenthal, *Effective Product Design and Development,* (1992, Irwin); Chapter 9, "The Quest for Sin Sigma Quality at Motorola Corp.

5. Morgan & Liker, *The Toyota Product Development System*, "Set-Based Concurrent Engineering," p. 47.

6. John Nathan, Sony (1999, Mariner Books), p. 46.

7. Matthew E. May, *The Elegant Solution*, (2007, Free Press), p. 50.

8. David M. Anderson, *Build-to-Order & Mass Customization, The Ultimate Supply Chain Management and Lean Manufacturing Strategy for Low-Cost On-Demand Production without Forecasts or Inventory,* (2004, 520 pages, CIM Press). Chapter 7, "Spontaneous Supply Chains." Also see articles at www.build-to-order-consulting.com.

9. Ibid., Chapter 6, "Outsourcing vs. Integration."

10. Micheline Maynard, *The End of Detroit, How the Big Three Lost their Grip on the American Car Market,* (2003, Currency/Doubleday), page 62 in Chapter 2 on Toyota and Honda.

11. From a speech by Boeing Chairman and CEO, Philip M. Condit, presented May 7, 1993 at the Haas Graduate School of Business ad the

University of California at Berkeley.

12. Anderson, *Build-to-Order & Mass Customization*. Also see articles at www.build-to-order-consulting.com.

13. David M. Anderson, *Agile Product Development for Mass Customization*, (1997 McGraw-Hill), Chapter 3, "Cost of Variety."

14. Anderson, *Build-to-Order & Mass Customization*. Also see articles at www.build-to-order-consulting.com.

15. George Stalk, Jr. and Thomas M. Hout, *Competing Against Time*, (1990, Free Press).

16. Satoshi Hino, *Inside the Mind of Toyota*, Chapter 1, "Toyota's Genes and DNA," p. 3

17. Sydney Finkelstein, *Why Smart Executives Fail, and What you Can Learn from their Mistakes,* (2003, Portfolio/Penguin Group); page 73.

18. May, *The Elegant Solution,* p. xi

19. Dan Steinbock, The Nokia Revolution; The Story of an Extraordinary Company That Transformed an Industry (2001, AMACOM), p. 273.

20. Shu Shin Luh, *Business the Sony Way* (2003, Wiley), p. 103

21. Shu Shin Luh, *Business the Sony Way* (2003, Wiley), p. 103

22. *When Sparks Fly*, page 15.

23. Alexander Hiam, *The Manager's Pocket Guide to Creativity* (HRD Press, 1998, 180 pages). Excerpted in The Futurist, October 1998, pp. 30 - 34.

24. Dorothy Leonard and Walter Swap, *When Sparks Fly; Igniting Creativity in Groups,* 1999, Harvard Business School Press.

25. Satoshi Hino, *Inside the Mind of Toyota*, Chapter 1, "Toyota's Genes and DNA," p. 29.

26. May, *The Elegant Solution,* p. 42.

27. Mark and Barbara Stefik, *Breakthrough,* pages 23 and 32.

28. May, *The Elegant Solution*, Chapter 2, "The Pursuit of Perfection," p. 49.

DESIGNING FOR LEAN & BTO

In concurrent engineering, multifunctional product development teams design products for the production environment or concurrently design products and new processes. When companies embark on flexible manufacturing strategies, concurrent engineering is crucial to the success of lean production, build-to-order (BTO), and mass customization.

Products not concurrently engineered for flexible environments may impede implementations, diminish the payback, or even thwart success entirely. The product portfolio may have too many unrelated products that lack any synergy and, thus, too many different parts and processes. Even within a focused product portfolio, there may be a needless and crippling proliferation of parts and materials. The specified parts may be hard to get quickly. The products and processes may have too many setups designed in. Quality may not be designed into the product/process which results in disruptions in the flow when failures loop back for correction. The product/process design may not make optimal use of CNC (Computer Numerically Controlled) as most CNC equipment is used in a batch mode, not flexibly.

Before discussing how to design for these environments, they are briefly summarized below.

4.1 LEAN PRODUCTION

Lean production accelerates production while eliminating many types of waste such as setup, excess inventory, unnecessary handling, waiting, low equipment utilization, defects, and rework. Former MIT researchers, James P. Womack and Daniel T. Jones, authors of the definitive book on the subject, *"Lean Thinking,"* say that lean production "is *lean* because it provides a way to do more and more with less and less – less human effort, less equipment, less time, and less space – while coming closer and closer to providing customers with exactly what they want." They summarize the corporate benefits of lean production as follows:

Lean Production Benefits

"Based on years of benchmarking and observations in organizations around the globe, we have developed the following simple rules of thumb: converting a classic batch-and-queue production system to continuous flow with effective pull by the customer will:

- *double labor productivity all the way through the system (for direct, managerial, and technical workers, from raw materials to delivered product)*

- *cut production throughput times by 90 percent*

- *reduce inventories in the system by 90 percent*

- *cut in half errors reaching the customer and scrap within the production process*

- *cut in half job-related injuries*

- *cut in half time-to-market for new products*

- *offer a wider variety of products, within product families, at very modest additional cost*

- *reduce capital investments required to very modest, even negative, levels if facilities and equipment can be freed up or sold."*

"Firms having completed the radical realignment can typically double productivity again through incremental improvements within two to three years and halve again inventories, errors, and lead times during this period."[1]

Flow Manufacturing.

A key element of lean production is *flow,* sometimes called "one-piece flow." This is especially important for build-to-order and mass customization where every piece may be different.
Flow manufacturing is achieved reducing setup to the point where products can be efficiently built in a one-piece flow instead of the customary batches. A key element of flow is "dock-to-line" delivery,[2] in which parts are pulled directly to *all* points of use without the delays and cost of incoming inspection. To accomplish this, suppliers will need to be *certified* to assure quality *at the source.*
Another aspect of flow manufacturing is the dedicated *cell* or line, which may be arranged to build any variation within a product family without any setup. Each cell has a compete set of "right-sized" inexpensive machines. Utilizing older machines that have been made "obsolete" by centralized mega-machines, can be a very cost-effective way of building complete cells. It may be unlikely for contract manufacturers to commit to dedicating equipment and floor space for cellular manufacture. Thus, this can become an effective strategy for established companies to compete with "virtual manufacturing" competitors who outsource batch production.
Flexible, or agile, product development is an essential enabler of lean production which will ensure that flexible processes are concurrently designed (Chapter 2), products are designed around standard parts (Chapter 5), products are designed for easy manufacture (Chapters 8 and 9) and quality is designed into the product (Chapter 10). Specifically, products and processes must be designed to be built in a "batch size of one" by eliminating any setup delays to kit parts, find and load parts, position workpieces, adjust machine settings, change equipment programs, and find and understand instructions.

Prerequisites

In general, lean production implementations will go faster and be have greater success if companies do two prerequisites first. For companies seeking to implement cellular manufacture to flexibly build any product in the family on-demand (called *build-to-order*), these prerequisites may be required for success:

1) Rationalization products first to eliminate the most unusual products, which have the most unusual parts and procedures, as discussed in Appendix A This will provide *immediate* benefits

2) Standardize parts and materials so new products will be designed with a fraction of the part and material types. Chapter 5 shows effective ways to standardize parts and materials.

4.2 BUILD-TO-ORDER

Spontaneous Build-to-Order is the capability to quickly build standard products upon receipt of spontaneous orders without forecasts, inventory, or purchasing delays.[3] These products may be shipped directly to individual customers, to specific stores, or as a response to industrial customers' "pull signals" (signals that specific parts are needed right away for assembly).

Similarly, your suppliers may need to use spontaneous BTO to respond to *your* pull signals, which is a key element of *flow manufacturing*. And yet, if suppliers cannot actually *build* parts on-demand, then they will be tempted to meter them out from inventory, in essence, transferring *your* parts inventory to *their* finished goods inventory.

The basic strategies for implementing spontaneous BTO are supply chain simplification, concurrent design of versatile products and flexible processes, the mass customization of variety, and the development of a spontaneous supply chain.[4] Spontaneous BTO can actually build products on-demand *at less cost* than mass-produced batches, if "cost" is computed as *total cost*. Therefore, total cost measurements should also be part of this process (see Chapter 7).

Supply Chain Simplification

Although supply chain management is a much discussed topic today, most implementations fail to apply the basic lessons of Industrial Engineering 101: *"Simplify before automating or computerizing."* The simplification steps for supply chain management are standardization, automatic resupply techniques like *kanban*, and rationalization of the product line to eliminate or outsource the unusual, low-volume products that contribute to part variety way out of proportion to their profit generation ability (see Appendix A). The goal of supply chain simplification is to drastically reduce the variety of parts and raw materials with standardization to the point where these materials can be procured spontaneously by automatic and pull-based resupply techniques. Reducing the part and material variety will also shrink the vendor base, further simplifying the supply chain.

Kanban Automatic Part Resupply

Figure 4-1 shows two rows of part bins which are set up for resupply by the two-bin *kanban* system. Initial assembly starts with all bins full of parts. When any part bin nearest the worker is depleted, the full bin behind moves forward, as shown by the empty space in the illustration.

The empty part bin then is returned to its "source," which could be the machine that made the part, a subassembly workstation that assembled the part, or a supplier. The source fills the bin and returns it to this assembly workstation behind its counterpart which is now dispensing parts.

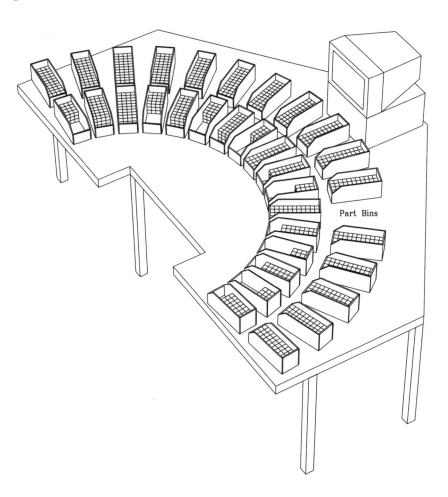

Figure 4-1: Kanban Part Resupply

The beauty of Kanban part resupply is that the system automatically ensures an uninterrupted supply of parts *without forecasts or complicated ordering procedures.* The number of parts in a bin is based on the highest expected usage rate and the longest resupply time. The sizes of the bins are determined by the bin quantity and size of the parts. For large parts, some companies use two-truck kanbans, in which parts are drawn from one truck trailer while the other trailer goes back to the supplier for more parts. Alternate systems include kanban squares marked on the floor for larger parts and a two-card system where the cards travel (or are faxed or the equivalent e-mailed) back to the source instead of the bins.

In order for Kanban systems to work, there must be enough room to dispense all parts at the points of use. This, again, emphasis the importance of part standardization, as discussed in Chapter 5.

4.3 MASS CUSTOMIZATION [5]

Mass production thrived in the bygone era of stable demand and little product variety. However today, once-stable markets are now very dynamic and product variety is increasing to the point where products need to be *mass customized* for niche markets or individual customers. Trying to satisfy this volatility and variety in the mass production mode will be a slow and costly ordeal. Since mass customization handles variety *proactively,* it is fast and cost-effective, with no extra cost or delays to handle various models, options, configurations, and customizations.

Mass customizers can use their versatile design and manufacturing capabilities to offer new, related, value-added products/services that expand the scope of their markets. These offerings may cost little extra to add, especially if they can be done in existing CNC operations. And yet, they may save customers so much time and money that they would gladly pay for the options, especially if these features are difficult for customers to make. For instance, one of the author's clients, Hoffman Engineering, built a plant in Lexington, Kentucky, which can spontaneously build-to-order a wide variety of standard or mass-customized electrical enclosures. It's high-profit value-added opportunity is to use the very same CNC laser cutters that make the boxes to make the holes and cutouts that would have cost their customers much time and money to do on their own.

There is a whole spectrum of ways that Mass Customization methodologies can benefit companies. At the most visible end of the spectrum, companies can mass customize products for individual customers. The most well known category of individual customization relates to products that people wear (clothing, shoes, glasses) as well as bicycles and pagers.

Further along the spectrum is niche market customization. For instance, a company that makes telephones has only a few customers (telephone companies) who want several dozen models in many colors all with specific phone company logos. Exporters have to deal with many niche market products, usually a different set of products for each country exported. Even if the differences are minor, the sheer variety of SKUs (stock keeping units) can have significant cost and flexibility implications. Most companies could benefit from expansion into niche markets *if* they could do it efficiently.

At the other end of the spectrum are companies that have tremendous varieties of "standard" products, for instance, industrial suppliers of valves, switches, instruments, enclosures, or any company with a catalog over a few dozen pages. As with product customization, there is a great contrast between how mass producers and mass customizers manufacture a variety of standard products. The mass-producer has the dilemma of trying to keep large enough inventory to sell a wide variety of products from stock or alternatively using the slow, reactive, costly process of ordering parts and building products in small batches after receipt of orders.

The mass-customizer can use flow manufacturing and CNC programmable machine tools to quickly and efficiently make different products in a "batch size of one" – either mass-customized products or any standard product from a large catalog.

As with lean production and build-to-order, mass customization implementation also benefits from, and may even require, the prerequisites discussed in Section 4.1: Rationalization of products to eliminate the most unusual products and their unusual parts (Appendix A) and standardization of parts and materials (Chapter 5).

4.4 DEVELOPING PRODUCTS FOR LEAN, BTO, & MC

To be successful at designing products for lean production, build-to-order, or mass customization, product development teams must proactively plan product portfolios, design products in synergistic product platforms, design around *aggressively* standardized parts and raw materials, make sure specified parts are quickly available, consolidate inflexible parts into *very versatile* standardized parts, assure quality by design with concurrently designed process controls, and *concurrently engineer* product platforms *and* flexible flow-based processes.

Further, product development teams need to eliminate setup *by design* by specifying readily available standard parts and tools (cutting tools, bending mandrels, punches, etc.), designing versatile fixtures at each workstation that eliminate setup to locate parts or change fixtures, and making sure part count does not exceed available tool capacity or space at each work station.

Finally, products must be designed to maximize the use of available programmable CNC fabrication and assembly tools, *without expensive and time-consuming setup delays.*

4.5 PORTFOLIO PLANNING FOR LEAN, BTO, & MC

For lean production, build-to-order, and mass customization, product portfolio planning (Section 2.3) must expand its focus to ensure that products are developed in synergistic families that can be produced on-demand on flexible lines.

To accomplish this, product families need to be structured so that all products use standard parts on the same flexible equipment without setup delays.

All the products within a flexible line – and possibly all the products within a flexible plant – must be compatible with respect to part standardization, raw material standardization, part/material availability, spontaneous supply chains, modularity, setup elimination, and flexible processing including CNC machine tool operation.

Older generation products may not be compatible with flexible production lines and thus may have to be dropped, outsourced, redesigned, or, at the minimum, have material substitutions. Old products worth saving may have to be redesigned or upgraded and be added to the list of potential product development projects and activities.

The evolution of product portfolios needs to be coordinated with implementation efforts for lean production, build-to-order, and mass customization. Decision making should be based on total cost and contributions to the overall business model.

4.6 DESIGNING PRODUCTS FOR LEAN, BTO, & MC

For lean production, build-to-order, and mass customization, products need to be designed so that:

- All the parts can be distributed at all points of use, which is accomplished by designing around standard parts and materials from *aggressively* standardized lists (Chapter 5). Too many parts would either clutter and confuse the work areas or force the parts to be *kitted* for a batch of products to be made, which is contrary to the one-piece flow of all the flexible paradigms. An important aspect of part standardization is fastener standardization, which is usually the easiest to do and can provide significant benefits. If screws can be standardized to one type at each work station, then *autofeed* screwdrivers can be utilized, which automatically orient screws and feed them through a flexible hose to a powered screwdriver. Of course, in order to designate a single type of fastener at each station, the design team will have to be concurrently designing the entire production flow.

- Products and processes need to be designed so that there will be no significant setup for *any* part or product in the family.[6] This includes any setup to (a) find, kit, load, or replace parts or materials; (b) change and position dies, molds, or fixtures; (c) change tools; (d) load, position, clamp, or calibrate workpieces; (e) adjust machine settings or calibrate machinery, or (f) change equipment programs.

- Equipment programs can be located and downloaded instantaneously and manual instructions can be found, displayed, and understood quickly.

- Parts and materials have been chosen so that they can be resupplied spontaneously.[7] This includes specifying readily available parts and materials, designing around aggressively standardized parts, and specifying raw materials to be cut on-demand from the same standard input stock sizes.[8]

- All parts can be pulled quickly into assembly on-demand.[9] This includes specifying suppliers who can build parts on-demand or working with in-house manufacturing to establish in-house capabilities.

Designing Around Standard Parts

Standardization of parts (Ch. 5) is the most important design contribution to the feasibility of spontaneous supply chains. *Aggressive* standardization can enable the easiest technique of the spontaneous supply chain: steady flows of very standardized parts and materials.[10] If there are too many different parts and material types, steady flows cannot be arranged because of the variety and unpredictability of demand. The total cost value of standardization and its contribution to the business model should motivate engineers and procurement organizations to implement such aggressive standardization.

Most part proliferation happens because engineers do not understand the importance to supply chains and operations and, even if they did appreciate this, do not know which parts are best to choose. The effective procedures presented in Chapter 5 show how to generate lists of standard parts and materials.

The usual operational mode in a part-proliferated environment, is to order the parts ahead based on forecasts, either for scheduled batch production or to have forecasted parts available for on-demand assembly (the Dell model). If part variety is truly unavoidable or parts are to be mass-customized, then they can be built on-demand using principles presented in the book, *Build-to-Order and Mass Customization.[11]*

Designing to Reduce Raw Material Variety

An important task in concurrent engineering is to specify not only the functional specifications of materials but also the order size and how they get cut into various parts. One company that made sheetmetal products previously ordered 600 different shapes of sheet metal, which was a logistical nightmare. The author advised them to convert to just a handful of standard types which were then cut on-demand as they were needed. Even better would be to cut sheetmetal on-demand from a coil.

Another way engineers can reduce material variety is to specify a single tolerance or grade, instead of multiple grades. As pointed out in Chapter 5, any perceived cost increase of shifting all materials to the higher grade will be more than compensated by the total cost savings and value of the business model.

Families of parts should be designed so that every CNC machine tool uses the absolute minimum of raw material types, hopefully just one so there are no setup delays to change materials.

Multiple lengths of linear materials can be obtained by ordering reels or long lengths of materials, which are then cut to length on-demand.[12]

Inflexible raw parts, like castings, extrusions, custom silicon, and bare printed circuit boards, should be *consolidated* into very versatile parts that can be used for many functions on a wide range of products (Section 5.12). Programmable chips should all be programmed using the same "blank."

Designing Around Readily Available Parts/Materials

A spontaneous supply chain depends on readily available parts and materials. Therefore, it is an important aspect of engineers' jobs to specify parts and materials that are readily available. Usually, design engineers choose parts based on functionality and hopefully quality. But for flexible operations, availability is equally important.

Parts and materials that can be obtained from multiple suppliers tend to have better available, in general, and are also more likely to be standard. On the other end of the spectrum, parts and materials available from only a single source may some day be hard to procure at all. On the lecture circuit, the author found one company whose parts had become obsolete before the product was even released!

Rapid delivery is important for flexible operations, so design teams should specify local suppliers who will be able to supply materials on-demand. Many companies preclude the ability to obtain parts and materials spontaneously by buying from supposedly "low cost" suppliers from another continent.[13] Womack and Jones, writing in *Lean Thinking*[14] summarize it succinctly: "Oceans and lean production are not compatible." They go on to say that smaller and less-automated plants close to assembly and markets will yield lower total costs, considering the cost of shipping, the inventory carrying costs, and the cost of obsolescence when products built weeks ago no longer satisfy customers.

Similarly, even local low-bidder suppliers probably are not going to be able to deliver on-demand and will most likely not have adequate quality either (see Section 6.11).

The guiding principle is to select parts and material to be readily available, delivered on-demand, and the lowest *total* cost, which includes material overhead, ordering, expediting, routing shipping, expedited shipping, incoming inspections, kitting, internal distribution, and all the costs of locating alternate sources of supply to counter availability problems.

Designing for No Setup

Part Setup. Product design has a profound effect on part setup. Excess proliferation of parts complicates internal part distribution and may make it impossible to have all parts available at all points of use. Even a moderate excess of part types will cause setup delays to distribute, find, and load parts into manual or machine bins. A greater excess of part types may make it necessary to kit parts for every batch, which is a significant setup. Part "prep" (such as cutting or bending leads on electronic components) is another setup that can be avoided by using versatile equipment or specifying parts that are already prepared properly for the product and the processing equipment.

Fixturing Setup. Designers can eliminate fixturing setup by designing parts for versatile fixturing which, if not already in place, may have to be *concurrently* designed with the parts.

Tool Setup. Designers can eliminate tool change setup by designing parts around common tools (cutting tools, bending mandrels, punches, etc.), ideally one tool that never has to be changed. If multiple tools are required, designers must keep tool variety well within tool changing capacity for the whole product line.

Instructions. Designers need to work with manufacturing engineers to concurrently develop simple assembly procedures that can be understood in a few seconds either on a computer screen or on paper instructions that can be quickly located and understood.

Parametric CAD

A wide variety of machined dimensions (for mass-customized or standard parts) can be performed quickly and cost-effectively using a combination of CNC machine tools and *parametric CAD, which stretches "floating" dimensions* and then automatically creates CNC programs as they are needed by CNC machine tools.

Universal parametric "templates" can be created ahead of time for families of parts and structured so that, when the customized dimensions are plugged in, the drawing transforms into a customized assembly drawing which automatically updates customized part drawings.

Another use of parametric CAD is to quickly show how changing a parameter impacts the system.

Designing for CNC

Computer numerically controlled machine tools (hereafter referred to as "CNC") offer vast opportunities to eliminate machining setup.[15] CNC machine tools include metal cutting equipment (mills, lathes, etc.), laser cutters, punch presses, press brakes, printed circuit board assemblers, and basically any production machine controlled by a computer. Designers need to understand enough about CNC operation to use the versatility of CNC to eliminate setup.

Grouping parts. The first step in designing for CNC is to structure compatible groups of parts to be processed in each CNC machine – this was originally labeled *group technology.*[16] Of course, this must be based on the overall manufacturing strategy and flow of parts and products. This evolves from a serious concurrent engineering activity in which the grouping and flow of parts are a key element of the design team's responsibilities. The grouping may determine the type of CNC needed, or existing machine tools may specify the grouping.

Understanding CNC. After thoroughly understanding of the range of parts to be made by each CNC, the designers will need to understand the capabilities and limitations of the equipment. This can be accomplished by studying the equipment specifications *and* talking to CNC operators. In fact, the CNC operators should actually be on the design team to optimize the design and processing plans. Of course, the ultimate understanding would come from actual CNC operational experience, either through prior work or a job rotation program.

Eliminating CNC setup. The versatility of CNC provides unique opportunities for eliminating setup if parts are designed properly. Ideally, all operations should be able to be performed on one machine in a single fixturing, as recommended in Guideline P14 in Chapter 9. Multiple machines will require extra fixturing setups. Even if multiple specialized machines have higher speed ratings, the total flow time through all operations *including setup* is what is important. The value of eliminating these setups may justify a more sophisticated CNC, compared to more setups on many cheaper machines.

In order to process parts in a single fixturing, designers need to specify a suitable *datum,* [17] from which all dimensions are referenced *and* which is suitable for clamping to a milling machine table or lathe chuck. The part also must be designed so that all the operations can be done in this fixturing. If all operations cannot, it is important that the *most* critical dimensions are cut in the same fixturing, which will routinely achieve the best tolerance of the machine tool, usually +/- .001" or better. However, removing a part to reposition for a subsequent cutting lowers accuracy of these critical dimensions because the tolerance will then depend on the accuracy of the second positioning, which is usually much worse than machine tool accuracy.

4.7 MODULAR DESIGN

Modular design is a design technique in which functions are designed in modules that can be combined into subsequent designs. A related concept is "reusable engineering" where portions of previous designs become the basis of new designs. This is easy to do in CAD by copying previous design details and transferring them to other drawings.

The benefits of reuse and modular design are: (1) less engineering effort; (2) more commonality amongst models for simpler supply chains and more flexible operations; and (3) better reliability from using proven parts and designs (Ch. 10).

When this concept is extended to manufacturing, products may actually be assembled from "building block" modules. Care should be taken in engineering to design standard interfaces for optimal flexibility. Catalog hardware often has standard interfaces, for example, for motor mounts, shaft couplings, fluid power and electrical connections, and so forth.

An effective modular design strategy would be to intentionally create portions of designs that have general usefulness for whole families of future products. For instance, machinery could have modular bases, frames, drives, gearboxes, controls, and cabinetry which could be combined with specific functional modules.

Pros and Cons of Modular Design

Time-to-market for "new" products can be quicker if existing modules have already been designed, documented, debugged, and certified. Delivery may be quicker if products can be assembled from standard modules. Modularity can lead to broader product lines and be the foundation of a proactive upgrade strategy. Further, modularity can simplify maintenance and field service when defective modules can be replace and then repaired off-line.

Modularity can lower inventory levels and overhead cost compared to several different versions of the integrated part or product. Widely-used modules have less vulnerability to lead time delays. Modularity may be a key element in a *postponement* customization strategy.[18]

Plug-together modularity may simplify some assembly and accept third-party plug-in modules, such as in personal computers. Modularity may be a key element in a *postponement* strategy. Postponement is a mass customization technique that is applicable for certain products that can have some variety postponed until just before shipping. The factory builds basic "vanilla" platforms and adds "flavors" upon receipt of order.[19]

The cost of modularity can only be determined on a total cost basis. Engineering costs will be lower if existing modules can be utilized, but may be higher if new modules and interfaces have to be designed. The cost of manufacturing the interfaces may be more than an integrated product, but using versatile modules used on many products may lower costs through economies of scale. Selecting existing modules would save the costs and delays of tested and debugging, compared to an entirely new integrated design.

Similarly, product testing may be easier if existing modules have already been tested, debugged, and certified. Diagnosis efforts may be easier with less functionality on each module. However, if all the modules in the product are new, then tests will have to be devised and all the modules will have to be tested and repaired. After the modules are tested, the entire assembly may have to be tested again.

Modularity has some drawbacks too. Modularity may not be feasible for inherently integrated products. Modular interfaces may compromise functionality by adding weight, weakening structures, or slowing down electrical signals or even causing signal interruptions at low voltage. In electronics, the extra connectors needed for modularity may cause reliability problems or degrade performance. Module interfaces may result in undesirable visual aesthetics (such as seams, joints, etc.) or undesirable acoustics (such as squeaks and rattles).

Product development expenses may be increased by the necessity to design modular interfaces. Modular interfaces may also add fabrication cost and may compromise functionality by adding weight, weakening structures, slowing down electrical signals, or even causing signal interruptions at low voltage. Sometimes the most reliable and fastest circuitry is where all electronic functions are on the same chip or circuit board.

Modular Design Principles

Module investment. Companies should invest in the design of modules that are versatile enough for *many* products. Individual projects may not have the budget or resources to develop modules for many products. Modules should be versatile enough to have general usefulness for many current and future products.

Total cost basis. Do not look at module cost at the level of one project; look only at the *total* cost of all the products that will utilize the modules.

Reusable engineering. Modular design is not limited to physical modules, but also could be reusable engineering or software code.

Standardization. For maximum usefulness, modules must have standard interfaces. Use industry-standard interfaces if available; if not, develop very versatile interfaces. Toyota engineers have a strong sense of the vehicle as a system and consequently focus a great deal of skill and energy at the design interfaces.[20]

Clean interfaces. All modular interfaces should clean and consistently easy to integrate together.

No compromises. Modularity should not compromise the product by adding excess cost, weight, or integration delays. Functionality should not be compromised by weaker structures or electrical signals that are slower or have the potential to be interrupted. Product quality should not be compromised by undesirable seams, joints, squeaks, or rattles.

Documentation. Document for modularity, with optimal CAD layer segregation, bills-of-materials, software object identification, and so forth.

Debugging. Minimizing debugging cost by using existing modules that have already been debugged. Some leading companies, like Hewlett-Packard, feel that this is the best way to produce bug-fee software. With a high percentage of reuse, debugging efforts can focus on *new* aspects.

Consistency. Resist the temptation to "improve" modules, unless the improvement is substantial and justifies the cost and time of design changes, production changes, evaluation, debugging, and recertification or requalification. Do not attempt "cost reduction" on modules unless the total cost saving *for all applications* justifies the development of a new-generation module.

4.8 OUTSOURCING AND MANUFACTURABILITY

Outsourcing manufacturing can have a significant effect on manufacturability and this is one reason why outsourcing strategy is one of the key tasks of Phase 2B (Section 2.12).

Outsourcing manufacturing usually has the unfortunate result of separating it geographically from product development engineers. This can thwart the concurrent engineering of manufacturable designs. Design teams must design products to be easy to manufacture by existing processes, which is hard to do if those manufacturing processes are far away for two reasons: (1) Most engineers are not familiar enough with manufacturing processes, so being able to observe them and talk to plant people can greatly improve the manufacturability of their designs; and (2) Multifunctional product development teams optimize manufacturability with early and active participation by manufacturing people. This is only feasible when they are working nearby in the manufacturing environment that will actually build the products being designed and, as company employees, can be assigned to actively participate on product development teams.

Design for manufacturability is even more difficult when outsourcing arrangements keep changing, ironically to try to save cost and switch to a new low-bidder. Unfortunately, the anticipated cost savings will be probably turn into a loss of both time and money because of new learning curves and lost relationships.

As pointed out in Chapter 2, design engineers may need to *concurrently* develop both products and new processes that do not already exist or may have to be modified from existing processes. In order to do this, it is imperative that design engineers work closely with manufacturing personnel and equipment developers from the earliest design activities through equipment/tooling development to product launch. Again, the best way to do this is if manufacturing operations and the appropriate people are nearby. Separation is even worse for overseas manufacturing where the time zone difference is greater than eight hours, in which engineering and manufacturing people will not be working at the same time, thus limiting communication to one round of e-mail per day.

Many companies have drawn an arbitrary line between "us" and "them," simplistically defining their companies as assemblers and their suppliers as part manufacturers. Usually these policies evolve from naive notions about core competency.[21]

However, such arbitrary demarcations can significantly raise cost by eliminating opportunities to optimize manufacturability. Outsourcing itself may require excessive modularization with more interface problems. This may preclude opportunities to fabricate monolithic structures on-site. For example, commercial airplane companies have severely compromised manufacturability by the arbitrarily deciding that they will only assembly airplanes while outsourcers will fabricate numerous structural pieces. Some of these pieces are so large that special planes, railroads, ships, and roads are needed to get them to the plant. Further, these interfaces add weight and large structural pieces can be very hard to integrate, sometimes taking months on the first articles.

Usually companies decide to outsource overseas to take advantage of low labor rates. Ironically, good DFM can reduce labor content to the point where moving to low-labor-rate areas is not needed, can't be justified, and, in fact, more money can be saved by co-locating product development teams together to take full advantage of Concurrent Engineering.

For more on outsourcing, see the author's articles at the web-site www.HalfCostProducts.com on outsourcing[22] and offshoring.[23]

4.9 THE VALUE OF LEAN, BTO, & MC[24]

Extending lean production to build-to-order and mass customization (BTO&MC) represents a business model that offers an unbeatable combination of superior responsiveness, cost, and what customers want when they want it. It enables companies to build any product on-demand without forecasts, batches, inventory, or working capital.

BTO&MC companies can grow sales *and* profits by expanding sales of standard, customized, derivative, and niche market products, while avoiding the commodity trap. BTO&MC companies are the first to market with new technologies since distribution "pipelines" do not have to be emptied first.

BTO&MC substantially simplifies supply chains – not just "managing" them – to the point where parts and materials can be spontaneously *pulled* into production without forecasts, MRP, purchasing, waiting, or warehousing.

Build-to-order is the best way to resupply stores who demand rapid replenishment, low cost, *and* high order fulfillment rates without the classic inventory dilemma: too little inventory saves cost but creates out-of-stocks, missed sales, expediting, and disappointed customers; too much inventory adds cost and costly obsolescence risks. When inventory carrying costs are taken into account, profits are completely wiped out after only five months of products siting in finished goods inventory.[25]

Mass customization can efficiently customize products for niche markets, countries, regions, industries, and individual customers.

There is a natural synergy between build-to-order and mass customization. They share the same batch-size-of-one operations and spontaneous supply chain. Build-to-order and mass customization operations are equally efficient and very compatible, unlike situations where a mass customization experiment must be run separately from the "batch-and-queue" operations of mass production. Manufacturing build-to-order and mass-customized products on the same lines will often push the combined volume over the "critical mass" threshold necessary to justify these implementations.

The following are several elements of the value of build-to-order and mass customization.

Cost Advantages of BTO&MC

BTO&MC companies enjoy substantial cost advantages, which they can use for competitive pricing, reinvestment, or enhancing profits. BTO&MC principles attack several categories of *total cost* to achieve the absolute lowest prices – or competitive enough prices at higher profits.

One of the greatest cost advantages of build-to-order is the elimination of all the costs caused by inventory: inventory carrying cost (usually 25% of value per year[26]), warehousing costs, administrative expense, obsolescence write-offs, and discounting to sell unsold or obsolete inventory. Incoming just-in-time part deliveries minimize inventory costs for parts and materials. Flow manufacturing and setup/batch reduction efforts can virtually eliminate work-in-process (WIP) inventory costs. Building to-order and shipping direct can virtually eliminate finished goods inventory costs.

Build-to-order minimizes or eliminates many other overhead costs for forecasting, MRP, purchasing, expediting, scheduling, planning, setting up production, and the extra sequence of activities required when forecasted inventory cannot satisfy demand: re-forecasting, repurchasing, re-expediting, rescheduling, re-planning, and re-setting-up production.

Building without batches eliminates the costs of setup changes, kitting, and the loss of expensive machine time and valuable resources. The rapid feedback aspect of flow production eliminates the cost of recurring defects, which are more likely to happen with large batches.[27]

Lean production eliminates many categories of waste and inefficiencies as discussed in Section 4.1.

All the inefficiencies of mass production – lower productivity, and the lack of the ability to shift production between lines – raises cost and causes the mass producer to need more overtime than the more efficient and flexible BTO&MC company.

Eliminating inventory, incoming inspection, and kitting saves much floor space cost, which can delay or eliminate the need to build more factory/warehouse space for growth.

Customization and configuration costs are less since they are proactively planned and executed efficiently, instead of the very inefficient craft production and fire-drill activities used in most companies. Learning relationships make repeat orders more efficient.[28]

Concurrent engineering products for manufacturability generally results in significant cost savings, but these are more profound for BTO&MC companies because of the greater opportunities to *design out* several categories of overhead cost.

Optimal utilization of flexible CNC automation saves labor cost. Flexible fixturing and setup reduction makes CNC even more efficient.

Distribution costs are less for BTO&MC goods because shipping is more direct, finished goods inventories are eliminated, and expediting is not needed to rectify shortages.

Finally, using product line rationalization (Appendix A) and total cost measurements to eliminate high-overhead/low-profit products eliminates the "loser tax" on cash-cow products, thus letting them to sell for less or make more profit. This advanced business model eliminates the need to discount or take low-margin sales.

Responsive Advantages of BTO&MC

BTO&MC companies build products on-demand, instead of having to forecast, order, wait, build, and stock. For phone order and web-sales, 100% of orders can promptly be shipped directly from the BTO&MC factory. One reason the "e-commerce revolution" didn't live up to its expectations is because of poor availability and delays. Poor availability is intrinsic in any system that sells from forecasted inventory, which depends on inherently unreliable forecasts. Delays will be common when shipping from inventory or trying to build "to-order" in a mass production environment.

If customers want to buy something right now off the retail shelf, BTO&MC suppliers can resupply those shelves better than anyone can from inventory, a so complete selection can always be available to customers. Stores and dealers that order frequent shelf replacements from BTO&MC suppliers will develop a good reputation for availability and eventually generate a loyal customer base that keeps coming back because they know that they will always find what they want; for example, for clothing, customers will always find the style they want in their size. Learning relationships make repeat order fulfillment quicker with each order. BTO&MC companies are the fastest to adjust to changing market conditions.

New product development and introduction can be faster when "new" products are just "variations-on-a-theme" that are easier to develop because of modularity, parametric CAD, and flexible processing. Production ramps can be faster on flexible lines that don't have to be "tooled up" for new products. A Wall Street Journal article reported that flexible automobile makers are able to release different versions of a car throughout the year instead of the traditional single release in the fall.[29]

BTO&MC companies are the first to introduce new technologies into the marketplace, since they don't have to first empty the "pipeline" of obsolete products, which usually must be discounted to clear the pipeline first. Even if that was not an issue, shorter direct distribution channels can speed new products faster to customers who can't wait for the latest and greatest.

If new product introductions result in *greater* than expected growth, the BTO&MC company can meet upsurge demands by transferring production to other flexible lines. BTO&MC implementations free up floor space which can then be used for growth. Thus, growth will be less likely to be hampered by shortages of floor space. Standard parts are available from more sources with more total capacity, so standard parts will be more readily available in times of rapid growth. Optimal responsiveness is also assured by supply chains that allow assemblers to *pull* parts quickly without lengthy hand-offs or depending on forecasted parts inventory.

Distribution is more direct, and therefore faster, for built to-order goods without delays caused by shuffling inventory from factories to warehouses to distribution centers and then to customers or stores. Eliminating inventory and many nodes in the distribution chain is not only quicker but also eliminates order aberrations and demand swings caused by the order/response lag time inherent in slow, multi-node distribution chains.

For capital equipment companies, quicker product delivery itself may be a competitive advantage. In addition, responding to RFQs (requests for quotations) will be quicker with configurators and less susceptible to subsequent delays due to order-entry errors and customer-induced changes.

Customer Satisfaction from BTO&MC

BTO&MC can provide unmatched customer satisfaction for industrial clients or the ultimate consumers. Consumers will be satisfied by products always available at the best prices. OEM and industrial clients will be satisfied by receiving parts on-demand to support *their* build-to-order efforts.

Mass customization will enable even higher levels of customer satisfaction for customers who can quickly receive high-quality/low-cost products specifically customized to their individual needs. For customized products, customers can make better choices and consider more "what if scenarios" with a good configurator. Even if individual customization is not appropriate, customer satisfaction will be enhanced when products are customized for their culture, group, country, or region.

Certain aspects of BTO&MC enhance quality from supplier relationships emphasizing quality, continuous improvement (*kaizen*), and rapid feedback that prevents recurring defects. A higher proportion of flexible CNC operations improves quality with more consistent tolerances.

Learning relationships enable the BTO&MC company to learn and adapt from each order, thus satisfying customers better on the next order and progressively developing more committed customers.

Competitive Advantages of BTO&MC

Competition now is *between business models* – the company with the best business model will be the best competitor. Ironically, the subject of several best-selling business books, *leadership* and *execution,* will only drive a company faster down the wrong path if they have the wrong business model. Dartmouth Business School Professor Sidney Finkelstein, writing in *Why Smart Executives Fail, and What You Can Learn from Their Mistakes,* concluded that "The real causes of nearly every major business breakdown are the things that put a company on the wrong course and keep it there."[30]

As a business model, build-to-order and mass customization will compete well against competitors both large and small because of a superior combination of speed, cost, and customization.

Without a superior business model, companies might have to compromise profits to enhance market share. This avoids the worst case competitive position where products revert to commodity status with purchasing decisions made solely on price.

BTO&MC company products can avoid commodity status with the differentiation aspects of build-to-order (delivery, cost, quality, etc.) and mass customizing products to better satisfy customers. Learning relationships result in greater customer loyalty with each order.

BTO&MC companies have the agility to expand business into adjacencies, niche markets, derivatives, and so forth. Finally, all the above advantages can create a reputation as a leader, which further improves sales, impresses investors, and attracts the best talent.

Bottom Line Advantages of BTO&MC

Lower total cost results in increased profits or lower selling price or both. Faster delivery, better quality, and lower cost can grow revenue and market share. Agility allows expansions into new markets. Additional value-added work offers high profit opportunities. With enough competitive advantage, premium prices may be possible.

ENDNOTES/REFERENCES

1. James P. Womack and Daniel T. Jones, *Lean Thinking; Banish Waste and Create Wealth in Your Corporation,* (1996, Simon & Schuster), p. 27.

2. "Dock-to-Line" may sometimes be referred to by the more ambiguous title of "Dock-to-Stock," which technically means part go from the dock to some form of incoming inventory "stock" area without inspection.

3. David M. Anderson, *Build-to-Order & Mass Customization, The Ultimate Supply Chain Management and Lean Manufacturing Strategy for Low-Cost On-Demand Production without Forecasts or Inventory,* (2004, 520 pages, CIM Press). Also see articles at www.build-to-order-consulting.com.

4. Ibid., Chapters 3 through 9.

5. Ibid., Ch. 9, "Mass Customization."

6. Ibid., Ch. 8, "On-Demand Lean Production," see Section on "Setup and Batch Elimination."

7. Ibid, Ch. 7, "Spontaneous Supply Chain."

8. Ibid, Ch. 7, Section on "Material cut to length"

9. Ibid, Ch. 6, "Outsourcing vs. Integration." Also see the article on Outsourcing at www.HalfCostProducts.com/outsourcing.htm and also www.HalfCostProducts.com/offshore_manufacturing.htm   which

discusses offshoring.

10. Ibid, Ch. 7, "Spontaneous Supply Chain."

11. Ibid.

12. Ibid., See Figure 8-1, "Build-to-Order & Mass Customization for Fabricated Products." This is also available in the Mass Customization article at www.build-to-order-consulting.com.

13. Ibid., Ch. 6, "Outsourcing vs. Integration." Also see the article on Outsourcing at www.HalfCostProducts.com/outsourcing.htm and also www.HalfCostProducts.com/offshore_manufacturing.htm which discusses offshoring.

14. James P. Womack and Daniel T. Jones, *Lean Thinking, Banish Waste and Create Wealth in Your Corporation* (1996, Simon & Schuster), p. 224

15. Anderson, *Build-to-Order & Mass Customization,* Ch. 8; See the section, "CNC to Eliminate Machining Setup."

16. Charles S. Snead, *Group Technology; Foundation for Competitive Manufacturing,* (1989, Van Nostrand Reinhold).

17. The *datum* concept is a key element of Geometric Dimensioning and Tolerancing (GD&T), from the ANSI Y14.5 standard.

18. Ibid., Chapter 9, "Mass Customization."

19. Ibid., Chapter 9, page 310, "Postponement."

20. Morgan & Liker, , *The Toyota Product Development System,* Chapter 4, "Front-Load the PD Process to Explore Alternatives Thoroughly."

21. Ibid., Chapter 6, "Outsourcing vs. Integration." Also see the article on Outsourcing at www.HalfCostProducts.com/outsourcing.htm and also www.HalfCostProducts.com/offshore_manufacturing.htm which discusses offshoring.

22. See the outsourcing article at the author's web-site www.HalfCostProducts.com/outsourcing.htm.

23. See the offshoring article at the author's web-site www.HalfCostProducts.com/offshore_manufacturing.htm.

24. Anderson, *Build-to-Order & Mass Customization*, Chapter 14, "The Business Case for BTO&MC." Also see articles at www.build-to-order-consulting.com.

25. Ibid., Figure 2-2, "How Inventory Erodes Profits Over Time When Selling from Finished Goods Inventory," which assumes 10% profit margin and 25% inventory carrying cost per year.

26. Ibid., Figure 2-1, "Inventory Carrying Cost from 1961 to 2002," which shows the average carrying cost at 25% of value per year.

27. Ibid., See the section in Chapter 2, "Defects by the Batch."

28. B. Joseph Pine, II, Don Peppers, and Martha Rogers, "Do You Want to Keep Your Customers Forever," *Harvard Business Review,* (March-April, 1995), p. 103.

29. Jonathan Welsh, "A New Status Symbol: Overpaying for Your Minivan; Despite Discounts, More Cards Sell Above the Sticker Price," *Wall Street Journal,* July 23, 2003, p. B1.

30. Sydney Finkelstein, *Why Smart Executives Fail and What You Can Learn from Their Mistakes,* (2003, Portfolio/Penguin), p. 138.

5

STANDARDIZATION

Standardization of parts and materials is a fundamental aspect of DFM, which can simplify product development efforts, lower the cost of parts and materials, drastically reduce material overhead costs, simplify supply chain management, improve availability and deliveries, raise quality, improve serviceability, and support lean production, build-to-order, and mass customization.

Standardization supports the fundamental precept of lean production, build-to-order and mass customization: *All parts must be available at all points of use,* not just "somewhere in the plant." This eliminates the setup to find, kit, distribute, and load parts. Standardization makes it easier for parts to be *pulled* into assembly (instead of ordering and waiting) by reducing the number of part types to the point where the *remaining few standard parts can receive the focus to allow them to be pulled spontaneously.*

This chapter presents a powerful, yet easy to implement, standardization procedure, which can reap enough benefits to be well worth the effort as a stand-alone program. As a prerequisite to lean production, build-to-order, and mass customization, its benefits are even greater.

5.1 PART PROLIFERATION

Competitive pressures are forcing manufacturers to look at all ways to lower total cost and improve flexibility. One of these thrusts is to investigate and reduce the cost of part and material variety. As a result of such an investigation, Nissan realized that, *in the one model lineup alone,* it used 110 different radiators, 300 different ashtrays, 437 dashboard meters, 1,200 floor carpet types, and 6,000 different fasteners![1] This type of variety does not add value to the customer. Of course, customers want their carpets to match interior fabrics and exterior paint, but this could be accomplished with far fewer than 1,200 carpet types.

141

An electronics company had 1,500 different types of resistors, including 120 different kinds, sizes, and tolerances of 1,000 ohm resistors.[2] That company was able to reduce the 1,500 resistor types to less than 200 actively used for manufacturing.

One of the author's clients, who made consumer products, discovered that it was using the following numbers of different part types: 1,248 wire assemblies, 152 motors, 151 screws, 74 switches, 67 relays, 65 capacitors, 37 valves, 16 transformers, 62 types of tape, and 1,399 different "standard" labels.

Every company has similar "horror stories" with regards to part proliferation. One might ask, *why?* – especially considering the facts that part proliferation raises part and overhead cost, impedes flexibility, and, as will be shown later, is really unnecessary.

5.2 THE COST OF PART PROLIFERATION

Part proliferation is expensive. A Tektronix study determined that half of all overhead costs related in some way to the number of different part numbers handled.[3] Most companies do not even know how much that cost is in dollars. A survey of several Fortune 500 manufacturing companies revealed that *not a single company or division had an accurate estimate of the cost of a part over its lifetime!*[4] According to Venkat Mohan of CADIS, Inc., who markets parts management software, "intuitive estimates range from $5,000 for a standard part to as high as $60,000 or even $100,000 per part for custom parts."[5] James Shepherd, director or research for Advanced Manufacturing Research (AMR), Boston, says that in electronics, the cost of just *entering* new purchased components is between $5,000 and $10,000 per component.[6] The Ernst & Young *Guide to Total Cost Management* states that "It is not surprising that manufacturers have estimated the annual administrative cost of each part number to be $10,000 or more."[7]

In addition to these official "materials" costs, excessive part proliferation adds cost to field service and manufacturing in important, but rarely measured, ways related to the setup, inventory, floor space, lower machinery utilization, and other flexibility issues.

Part proliferation also lowers assembly productivity. Writing about the automobile industry in a Wharton Business School report, Fisher, Jain, and MacDuffie write that "Part variety also appears to have the greatest negative impact on assembly plant productivity."[8]

5.3 WHY PART PROLIFERATION HAPPENS

Part proliferation happens for the following reasons, which are all easily avoidable:

1. **Engineers don't understand.** Most product designers do not understand the importance of part standardization, and therefore, do not attempt to design around standard parts. An example of this attitude was discovered when the author was soliciting feedback from engineers on a proposed standardization list (which was generated by techniques described below) for resistors. One electrical engineer commented *"Why are we standardizing on resistors; Aren't they cheap and aren't they in the computer?"* What this engineer did not realize is that, regardless of a part's cost and the company's ordering/tracking sophistication, *every* part must be physically delivered to the plant, possibly inspected and warehoused, and then distributed to each point of use. One solution to this perception problem would be training and education that stresses the importance of part standardization and connect it to corporate goals.

2. **"Not invented here."** Sometimes standardization is resisted because of the "not-invented-here" syndrome, but that can be countered by teamwork, training, and encouraging engineers to think "globally instead of locally."

3. **Arbitrary decisions.** Product designers make many *arbitrary decisions* when specifying parts. They may arbitrarily specify a fine pitch 5/16" bolt with a button head that is 7/16" long when a more common course-pitch 3/8" hex bolt that is ½" long could have done the job just well. Section 1.8 discusses the general problem of arbitrary decisions in product development.

    Electronic engineers at Intel's Systems Group said that for digital circuitry, they did not really need any resistor value between 1,000 ohms and 2,000 ohms. From this feedback, those values were immediately deleted from the approved parts list.

4. **Many versions of the same part to "save cost."** When product designers are pressured to lower cost, and all that is measured is part cost, they sometimes specify the cheapest version of a part for *each* application. This may appear to lower the part cost by a few pennies, but such a proliferation will generate much greater overhead costs. For example, one manufacturer of medical equipment had one printed circuit board had 11 different versions of 1K resistors on a single circuit board! The engineers thought they were saving cost by specifying the cheapest tolerance and wattage for each application.

However, not only did this practice cause rampant part proliferation, it also forced the board to be run through the assembly machine *twice* because there were more parts than bins available on the assembly machine. The standardization principles presented herein encourage using the best single version for all applications.

5. **The minimum weight fallacy.** A phenomenon that may be contributing to part proliferation is the fallacy that all parts have to be sized "just right" to have the minimum weight and be made of the minimum amount of materials. Engineers may resist standardization because the standard part may be the next-larger-size to ensure adequate strength and functionality. The following rules-of-thumb may help guide engineers get past this obstacle.

If it doesn't fly or move fast,
use the next larger size standard part.

If it isn't made of precious metals,
use the next larger size standard part.

6. **Qualifying part families.** A related cause of part proliferation is the practice of *qualifying* (for entry on approved parts lists) entire *families* of parts, like fasteners, resistors and capacitors. Intel's Systems Group discovered that out of 20,000 approved parts for printed circuit boards and computer systems, 7,000 had never been used! In other words, more than one third of the approved parts were not used on any product. And, yet, any engineer *could have* arbitrarily chosen one of those unused parts and entered a new part into the system without any approval or authorization. In this case, those unused parts were immediately deleted from the approved parts list.

7. **Contract Manufacturing.** Sometimes, a short-sighted business strategy undermines standardization efforts. Some companies, in response to downturns, respond to the pressure to "fill the factory" by, in essence, becoming a contract manufacturer. This "use-it-or-loose-it" approach may bring in some additional revenue, but, often loses money in the long run. This loss would be realized if computations included *total* cost issues such as the overhead expense to support such part diversity, and, of course, the substantial learning curve expense needed to gear up to build many new products.

8. **Mergers and acquisitions.** Another cause of excessive internal variety is the merger of dissimilar products through corporate mergers and the acquisitions of companies, products, patents, and so forth. Products that originated in different companies are likely to

have very different parts and processes. Thus, manufacturing flexibility should be added to the list of primary factors that determine such decisions.

9. **Duplicate parts.** When product designers do not know what parts exist, they will often "add" a "new" part to the database, *even when the identical part already exists.* Even if they suspect that the needed part exists, they will probably specify a new *purchased* part if it takes less time than finding an existing one. Similarly, they will probably *design* a new part if it takes less time than finding an existing one. Many times engineers find it much harder to search through awkward databases than to design new parts or purchase them.

Many companies have hundreds of incidents of duplicates, triplicates, or even several versions of the exact same part, existing under different company part numbers, plus even more situations where a *close* existing part could have been used instead of introducing a new part.

Upon the author's suggestion, one aerospace company investigated this and found that it had 900 different types of spacers! Apparently, it was easier to design number 901 than to search through all 900 existing spacers.

When a large machine tool company investigated this phenomenon, it discovered that it had 521 very similar gears. They eventually reclassified all those gears into 30 standard gears.[9] There were 17 times more gear types then necessary! Every gear had an average of 17 duplicates.

5.4 THE RESULTS OF PARTS PROLIFERATION

The net result of part proliferation is that most companies have thousands or even hundreds of thousands of different part types (unique part numbers). Such internal variety is rarely necessary, and is usually the result of this careless – often a rampant – proliferation of parts. The absence of any standardization goals or awareness allows designers to simply choose *new* parts for new designs, without any consideration of prior usage of similar parts.

Every company can investigate the extent of part proliferation by simply looking up the total number of active part numbers for all part categories. In many cases, the proliferation will seem obvious, even to the most casual observer. Another revealing investigation would be to summarize the "materials" budget for all the overhead expenses related to parts. Hopefully, these investigations will provide the motivation to eliminate existing duplicate parts and to substantially reduce part types for new designs using the very effective procedures presented next.

5.5 PART STANDARDIZATION STRATEGY

New Products

Part standardization has the most opportunities for new designs or redesigns. Usually it would cost too much to convert existing designs, part by part, and there may be issues with replacement part backwards compatibility. In addition, changing existing designs may be precluded by current qualifications of existing products.

Existing Products

The main opportunities for existing products are for "better-than" substitutions. If this is an opportunity, then the standard parts/materials lists would focus on the better grades. In most cases the overhead savings and supply chain benefits resulting from standardization would far exceed any perceived cost "increase" for better materials.

As new products with standard parts and materials are phased in, manufacturing operations and procurement will realize more benefits. When the products with the standard parts and materials reach a certain critical-mass threshold, the factory will benefit from eliminating the remaining unusual parts and materials. At this point, the old products can be redesigned around standard parts or outsourced.

5.6 EARLY STANDARDIZATION STEPS

Part Listing

Many parts lend themselves to listing in a logical order as examples shown in Figure 5-1. For these parts, simply list all existing parts in order, circulate the lists to the design community, and encourage engineers to use existing parts whenever possible. This step should be done immediately to at least stop designers from adding new parts when they could have used an existing one. A procedure will be presented below for determining *preferred* part values from these lists.

Part Type	Listing Order
Threaded fasteners	Thread diameter, pitch, length, head type, material/coating, grade
Washers/spacers	O.D., I.D., thickness, material, finish
Gears	Pitch, number of teeth, face width, material
Gearboxes	Ratio, horsepower, shaft orientations, shaft diameters
Motors	Horsepower, voltage, phase, shaft diameter, mount
Pumps	Pressure, flow rate
Power supplies	Output voltage, wattage
Resistors	Ohms
Capacitors	Microfarad
Integrated circuits	Generic numbering system

Figure 5-1 Examples of Part Type Listing Orders

For these parts, simply list all existing parts in order, circulate the lists to the design community, and encourage engineers to use existing parts whenever possible. A procedure will be presented below for determining *preferred* part values from these lists.

Clean Up Database Nomenclature

It may be necessary to clean up part and material databases before proceeding further. If every part in a category does not have consistent nomenclature, it may be hard to sort and identify duplicates. So it may be necessary to convert multiple labels to the most common or most logical label. If it is too hard to convert the official database, then extract the information and change it only for the standardization effort.

Eliminate Approved but Unused Parts

Many parts are approved in families and entered into the approved parts list *en masse*. Many of these parts have never been used. If left on the list, any engineer could add a new part into manufacturing without any approval or authorization.

So the first pre-step would be to identify approved parts that have never been used and immediately remove them from the list for new designs. A variation of this procedure would be to identify parts not used in so many years and remove them.

At Intel's Systems Group, the author's standardization task force was surprised to find that, of the 20,000 parts approved for new designs,

7,000 parts had never been used! In other words, more than one third of the approved parts were not used on any product. And, yet, any engineer *could have* arbitrarily chosen one of those unused parts and entered a new part into the system without any approval or authorization. In this case, those unused parts were immediately deleted from the approved parts list.

Eliminate Parts Not Used Recently

It would be logical to assume that parts that have not been used recently would not be good candidates for any standardization list for new designs. For the standardization effort, eliminate for consideration any part or material not ordered in the last few years – this could be two to five years depending on the product life cycles. This would not eliminate these parts from the approved parts lists, which may be needed for spare parts or infrequently build products; however, operational flexibility can be improved if these unusual products are *rationalized* to eliminate or outsource infrequently built parts and spare part production (see Appendix A).

Eliminate Duplicate Parts

The problem with multiple part numbers for the same part goes beyond the obvious extra material overhead cost of carrying extra parts. Most likely, the similar parts would be ordered separately for each product that needed the parts. This would prevent Purchasing from obtaining quantity discounts and just-in-time deliveries that would have been possible with a consolidated order. Further, the smaller order quantities increase the chances of shortages for a given part. Ironically, the missing part that delays production might be sitting in another bin under a different part number.

The problem becomes more severe for lean production, build-to-order, or mass customization, if different products are using the same part under different part numbers. Automated assembly equipment, like for printed circuit board assembly, may have to load the same part in multiple bins. Even if the machine operator notices that some of the parts *seem* similar, the operator does not have the time nor the authorization to consolidate parts on the spot. This duplication alone may prevent flexible operations if there are more parts (including duplicates) in the product family than there are bins in the equipment. If this is the case, then parts would have to be reloaded *twice* for each product, which is the type of setup that must be eliminated for flexible operations.

Using part management software, Tektronix was able to deactivate 32,000 part numbers from an active base of 150,000. Bob Vance, Tektronix VP and Chief Information Officer, summarized the return on eliminating excess parts: "There are few areas where a manufacturing company can make such a significant impact to its bottom line with so little effort. We want to invest our resources in product innovation and customer services, not carrying an overburdened parts inventory."[10]

An easy way to stop the introduction of duplicate parts is to make it easier to *find* existing parts than to release new ones, as shown in Figure 5-1.

Prioritize opportunities

Since the standardization procedure presented next must be performed for every category of parts and materials, it is important to prioritize opportunities and start with categories with the following characteristics:

• Unnecessary proliferation, which is typical for fasteners, resistors, certain raw materials, and so forth

• Excessive parts/materials inventories

• Excessive material overhead costs to procure a prolifElated variety

• Missed opportunities for automatic resupply, like kanban and breadtruck, because of the excessive variety

• Kitting parts required because there are too many parts to distribute at all points of use

• Excessive setup changes if there are more part types than bins on automatic assembly machines, for instance, for printed circuit boards

• Production delays caused by shortages

• Excessive expediting

In addition to these criteria, valuable insight can be gained simply by asking employees to rank the categories. Employees can be given a list of all major categories and asked to vote; the voting can be structured with zero for no opportunity to 10 for highest opportunity (there may be more than one 10 vote).

5.7 THE ZERO-BASED APPROACH

There is easy-to-apply approach that is more effective than *part type reduction* measures, which require tremendous efforts for their return. Reducing active part numbers, say from 20,000 to 15,000 will, in fact, lower material overhead somewhat, but it may not reach the threshold (eliminating part related setup) that would enable the plant to build products flexibly without delays and setups to get the parts, kit the parts, or change the part bins.

Instead, the most effective technique to reduce the number of different parts (part types) would be to standardize on certain *preferred* parts. This usually applies to purchased parts but it could also apply to manufactured parts and raw materials. The methodology is based on a *zero-based* principle that asks the simple question: *"What is the minimum list of part types we need to design new products?"*

Answering this question can be made easier by assuming that the company, *or a new competitor,* has just entered this product line and is deciding which parts will be needed for a whole new product line. One of the advantages of new competitors is the ability to start *fresh* without the old "baggage": too many parts. Just image a competitor simultaneously designed the *entire* product line around standard parts. Now, imagine doing the same thing internally. This is called the *zero-based approach.*

The zero-based approach, literally, starts at zero and adds only what is needed, as opposed to reducing parts from an overwhelming list. An analogous situation would be cleaning out the most cluttered drawer in a desk, a purse, or a glove compartment; removing unwanted pieces would take much effort, and still not be very effective. The more effective zero-based approach would be to empty everything, and add back only the items that are essential. The difference in these approaches is where the "clutter" ends up: still in the drawer, purse or glove compartment or in the garbage can. Similarly, parts reduction efforts have to work hard to remove the clutter (excess part variety) in the system, whereas the zero-based approach excludes the clutter from the beginning. The clutter is the unnecessary part proliferation that would have not been needed if products were designed around standard parts. Not only do these excess parts incur overhead costs to administer them, they also lower plant efficiency and machine utilization because of the setup caused by product that are designed to have more parts than can be distributed at every point of use.

This approach determines the minimum list of parts needed for *new* designs and is not intended to eliminate parts used on existing products, except when the standard parts are functionally equivalent in all respects. In this case the new standard part may be substituted as an equivalent part or a "better-than" substitution, where a standard part with a better tolerance can replace its lesser counterpart in existing products.

Even if part standardization efforts only apply to new products, remember that in these days of rapid product obsolescence and short product life cycles, all older products may be phased out in only a few years.

5.8 STANDARD PART LIST GENERATION

To determine a standard parts list, the company must achieve a consensus on the minimum number of parts necessary to design new products. It is important that all engineering groups, in particular, agree on the list because *they* will be the ones that will be designing products using the standard parts. Consensus can be reached by forming a team of key representatives from Engineering, Purchasing, Quality and Manufacturing departments.

The steps are listed as follows for each category of parts:

1.   **Determine usage histories.** Start with a baseline list based on usage history of existing products. It would be counterproductive to create a standard parts list by *adding* even more *new* parts. Usage history can be based on total quantity of all parts purchased per year or the number of products that use the parts (which can found by generating a "where used" report from MRP systems). Exclude parts used in products that are near the end of their lives and should be phased out soon anyway. The curve will always have a Pareto shape like the one shown in Figure 5-2.

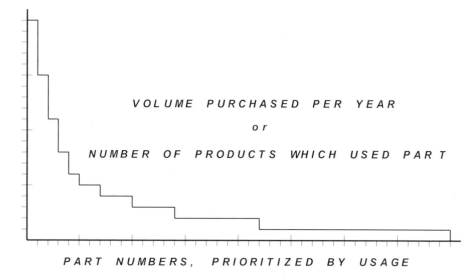

Figure 5-2: Pareto Chart of Existing Part Usage

2.   **Establish Baseline List.** The next step is to establish a *baseline list* which will be based on the inherent commonality of existing parts plotted above. Obviously, the "high runners" on the left of the curves should be part of the baseline list and the low-usage parts on the right should not. Where to draw the line (that separates common parts from the rest) will require some judgement. This judgement should come from a consensus of all engineering groups, manufacturing, purchasing and those who qualify parts and suppliers (Quality or Materials Engineering Departments). The last function would be interested because minimizing the number of part types does have a positive impact on procurement and quality activities, since fewer part types will

mean that more attention can be focused on procurement, supplier qualifications, and quality issues for the standard parts.

If the usage profile looked like Figure 5-2, the left third or forth of the parts might qualify for the baseline list. Note that, when parts proliferation has been more rampant, the low-usage and single use parts would extend much further to the right. In such a case, the standard parts may be only the top 5 or 10 percent of the parts.

In some cases, there may be anomalies, such as parts used in low volume, but used in very many products. The widespread use, in itself, may qualify that part for the list, despite the low volume. In other cases, a part may be used on only one product, but in very high volume. This may require some investigation to determine if the design team has discovered a clever use for the part that may apply to future product designs.

These parts become the baseline list, which would then be arranged in some appropriate order, as discussed earlier.

3.   **Develop Procedures to Add New Parts.** Proactively develop procedures to add new parts, for instance new generation parts, to the baseline list. Ideally, this should be done by a material qualifying group, sometimes called "materials engineering," who should also qualify the new parts *and* their suppliers. If this is not possible, new part additions should be done by consensus of researchers and engineers from "advanced" design and R&D groups, Manufacturing, Purchasing and Quality.

4   **Consolidate Duplicates.** As discussed before, many duplicates get into the system and good parts management can eliminate the exact duplicates. When companies start investigating duplications, they often discover slight differences between the duplicate parts. This presents an opportunity to select the part that could most likely replace the others. This may involve choosing the "better" part, using the procedure discussed next.

5.   **Consolidate Parallel Lines of Parts.** Next, consolidate parallel lines of parts. If whole families of parts are available in multiple tolerances, quality levels, thread pitches or material finishes, the team should consolidate them into one set of parts, even if it has to standardize on the more expensive parts. Usually, any increase in part cost, due to using the "better" parts, will be dwarfed by the overhead savings from having fewer parts overall. If the company cost accounting system cannot quantify the value of this, then the company must recognize the *qualitative* value to manufacturing flexibility and lowering material overhead costs

(see discussion below on "Standardizing on Expensive Parts"). For example, various grades of bolt strength or resistor tolerance could be consolidated, as indicated by the following example.

When the author was initiating a parts standardization program at Intel's Systems Group, there were two completely different families of resistors: 5% (tolerance) carbon resistors and 1% metal film resistors. Using this approach, they were consolidated into one line of exclusively 1% resistors, thus eliminating hundreds of part numbers for new designs. These parts were also substituted in existing products since this was considered a "better-than" substitution. A few years later in a public DFM seminar, one company reported that the purchasing leverage resulting from making all resistor purchases the same tolerance (1%) canceled out the perceived "extra" cost of raising the 5% parts to the 1% level, thus resulting in overall cost savings.

Note that consolidation based on higher quality parts may, in reality, raise product quality, even if the lower quality parts were *theoretically* adequate.

6.   **Optimize Availability.** The availability and sourcing of all parts and materials on the standard parts list should be investigated and optimized. Standard parts and materials should be selected to be readily available from multiple sources *and be available over the expected life of the products.* Investigations should include the number of sources, the technical and business strength of the sources, and the average amount available at any time.

7.   **Structure Lists.** Structure the list into appropriate order, as shown in Figure 5-1, by values of diameter, pitch, power, flow rate, voltage, ohms, microfarads, and so forth.

8.   **Review the Lists.** Review the tentative baseline lists for each type of part and feature by involving representatives of all relevant engineering departments for feedback and approval. This could be a formal process that is part of the procedures to generate standard parts lists. Or, it could be an informal process that would solicit informal feedback from some experienced engineers who could be assumed to be representative of their departments. Earlier participation of representatives of these departments on the task force should minimize surprises at this stage.

9. **Circulate the Lists.** Circulate the tentative lists to all engineers with an explanation of why the standardization is important to company goals to simplify product development efforts, lower part cost, reduce material overhead costs, simplify supply chain management, improve availability and deliveries, raise quality, improve serviceability, and support lean production, build-to-order, and mass customization. Solicit feedback about whether the tentative baseline list has the right parts for new designs. Query reviewers if any part on the list is superfluous or if any important part was wrongly omitted.

10. **Finalize the lists.** Review feedback from all those reviewing the list. Investigate promising suggestions and add or subtract appropriate items to or from the list. Finalize the lists and prepare it for implementation.

11. **Determine Scope of Implementation.** The scope of the standardization effort should be matched to implementation resources and the general company awareness of the importance and value of designing around standard parts. Some companies may choose to start with the "low hanging fruit" first, say fasteners or resistors. Success here may then be leveraged to other types of parts. As companies embrace operational flexibility, it becomes imperative to implement strong standardization efforts.

12. **Educate the Design Community.** Before standard parts lists are issued, the design community needs to be educated on the importance of using standard parts in new designs. Point out how important this is to manufacturing flexibility and lowering overhead costs. Another educational and motivational technique is the "embarrassing statistics" technique: reveal the scope of past part proliferations and discuss their causes, which are usually caused by designers who arbitrarily chose a low-usage part when a high-usage part would have worked.

    An excellent example is the company mentioned earlier that had 900 different types of spacers. Why so many spacers, when the product line really only needed a small fraction of that number? Every time engineers needed a spacer, *they just designed a new one!* The fallacy in their thinking was that spacer design appeared to be "easy," but, in reality, the documentation, procurement, manufacture, storage and distribution of 900 spacers were not "easy."

    Design engineers need to realize that *no matter how simple a part appears, every part number incurs a material overhead burden* to document, procure, store, distribute, re-supply, and, most significantly, to manufacture in low volume.

13. **Determine the Strictness of Adherence.** The strictness of adherence to the standard parts list should reflect the company's need for manufacturing flexibility, automation utilization, overhead cost reduction, and ease of service. A high volume, flexible plant with expensive automation might require 100% adherence to the standard parts list so that the equipment would not have to stop to load nonstandard parts. Lean production, build-to-order, mass customization environments may require 100% adherence for manufacturing flexibility. Companies contemplating adherence less than 100% need to analyze the effect of this *"un*commonality" on the flexibility of their operations.

Many companies just want to reduce the active parts base and encourage engineers to use parts that are already in use. For instance, General Electric Lighting has established a goal of 90% parts reuse in all new designs.[11]

14. **Issue the Standardization Lists.** Designate the parts on the standard lists officially as *standard, common,* or *preferred* parts and give them special emphasis, at least, with an asterisk or bold type on the larger approved part lists. A more effective method is to present the preferred standard parts on a separate list, perhaps in the front of the section containing that category of parts. Intel's Systems Group presented preferred parts on a gold page, followed by the existing approved parts on white paper. When standard parts are to be used exclusively, the standard parts list would be the only parts list issued to engineers.

5.9 PART STANDARDIZATION RESULTS

This part standardization approach was implemented by the author at Intel Corporation's Systems Group. Starting with 20,000 parts for printed circuit boards and computers, this standardization approach generated a preferred parts list of 500 parts! For resistors, capacitors, and diodes, 2,000 values were reduced to 35 values, one set for leaded "axials," and another set for the surface mount equivalents.

Fasteners for computer systems were standardized on one screw! This is how the standardization process worked: Service wanted a Phillips head so they, and customers, could keep using the same tools. Quality wanted a captivated "crest cup" washer to protect surface finishes and yet still have a locking effect. Engineering wanted the 6-32 size screw to be only a quarter inch long. Manufacturing recommended that the screw be three-eights of an inch long so that it would not tumble as it was feed to auto-feed screwdrivers.

Previous designs had so many different screws that Manufacturing could not use their auto-feed screwdriver at all. The next design used the standard screw in 40 locations. This, in addition to the correct screw geometry, made use of the more efficient auto-feed screwdriver practical. In order to feed the screw, it had to be one eighth of an inch longer, but this meant that the screw would protrude beyond the fastened material. This violated a workmanship standard that prohibiting such protrusions; some people even thought the standardization was doomed. But the workmanship standard was modified to allow the protrusion as long as it did not pose a safety hazard of compromise product functionality in any way.

Intel's enforcement goal was not 100%, as might be required for a totally flexible operation, but we felt that even 95% usage would result in significant material overhead savings.

In general, it should be possible to generate a preferred parts list that is 2 to 3 percent of the proliferated list. For very standard parts like fasteners or passive electronic components, it should be possible for the preferred parts list to be less than 1 percent of the current list.

5.10 RAW MATERIALS STANDARDIZATION

If raw materials can be standardized, then the processes can be flexible enough to make different products without any setup to change materials, fixturing mechanisms, or cutting tools. This is an extremely important prerequisite to build-to-order operations that strive to make any product on-demand *from standard raw materials* without having to forecast and order materials. Raw material standardization can apply to bar stock, tubing, sheet-metal, molding plastics, casting metals, protective coatings, and programmable chips.

- **Bar stock and tubing.** If raw materials can be standardized on one size of bar stock or one size of tubing, then computer controlled cutoff machines can be programmed to cut off required lengths from the same stock. This flexibility may determine the feasibility "cut-to-fit" (dimensional) customization.[12] For manual cutoff operations, material standardization would simplify instructions to the length only. This would minimize the chances for mistakes related to picking the wrong material.

- **Sheetmetal.** If sheetmetal can be standardized on one shape, thickness, and alloy, then computer controlled laser cutting machines can cut all the sheet metal parts needed without changing sheet types. Automatic sheet feeders could reload the machine as needed. This is even more important if the parts are so small that many parts could be cut from the same sheet without having to change sheets. Standardization of sheetmetal would allow heavy users to save money by ordering sheetmetal in reels, maybe directly from the mill.

- **Molding and casting.** Part of a flexible operation strategy may involve offering a wide variety of molded or cast parts. Molding and casting operations will be more cost-effective if they can standardize on the same raw material, so that many different parts could be made in the same machine without changing over the equipment for raw materials. It even may be possible to make many different parts in the same mold, thus sharing processing time and tooling expense. Standardizing materials avoids the setup of changing materials and cleaning the equipment. If molds are designed with *fixturing* standardization, they could be changed rapidly to minimize setup time. With casting material standardization, several molds could be filled with the same "pour" from a single "melt."

- **Protective coatings.** Standardizing on protective coatings simplifies processing and makes painting and coating operations more flexible by eliminating the setup to change coating materials and clean equipment. As with parts standardization, coatings could be standardized on the "better" coating. Even if that coating *appears* to cost more, the net result would be overall cost savings, considering the process value of this standardization. The logic of this concept is discussed further in Section 5.11, "Standardization of Expensive Parts," below. Coating standardization could also apply to paint if the purpose of the paint is purely functional with little aesthetic considerations, for instance, for industrial equipment or inside major appliances. In fact, many industrial and agricultural products enjoy a brand recognition because of a standard paint color. For instance, farmers immediately recognize a green tractor or combine as a John Deere product.

- **Programmable chips.** Many integrated circuits (ICs) can be programmed separately or in the product. For programmable chips, standardize on the fewest types of "blanks." This allows the flexibility to program these devices on-demand by on-line programming stations as they are assembled into the product. Ideally, each programming station would be dedicated to one blank device to avoid setup changes. Thus, programmable chip standardization minimizes the number of programming stations and, thus, may make it possible to program chips as they are inserted or placed onto circuit boards.

- **Standardization for Linear Materials.** Standardization can also be applied to material purchased by length: wire, rope, plastic tubing, cable, chain, and so forth. Linear material variety can be reduced in the following ways:

  - **Cut as Needed:** Linear materials can be standardized by *type* with only the length cut as needed. Available equipment will even cut and strip the ends of wires. This approach would require a dispensing machine at each point of use.

  - **Kanban System:** Alternatively, wire and tubing can be cut ahead of time, but, to keep overhead low, not be given individual part numbers. The following system was developed by MKS Instruments, Inc., makers of vacuum and flow measurement/control instrumentation. Instead of issuing part numbers and treating many cut lengths as many different parts, a predetermined amount (for instance, one day's worth) of wire or tubing can be cut to the needed lengths and placed in each of two adjacent *Kanban* bins at each point of use. The kanban bins are arranged one in front of the other, as shown in Figure 4-1. When the front bin is emptied, it is sent to a central dispensing machine. The label on the bin tells the machine operator the material type, length, quantity, and the bin's return destination in the factory. After filling the bin, it is returned to the point of use and placed behind its counterpart so it can be moved forward and used when the other bin is emptied. This simple approach can eliminate hundreds or thousands of part numbers from the plant, thus lowering costs, minimizing delays, improving flexibility, and encouraging flexible operations.

  - **Printing While Dispensing.** The number of types of linear materials can be reduced further by using equipment that prints on wire and tubing as it is dispensed, so that many various colors of the material need not be ordered and stocked. Printing on wire and tubing can minimize mistakes in assembly and service, since workers do not have to memorize or refer to color codes. Using words, rather than color also solves problems associated with color blindness. Examples of printing opportunities would be: Ground; +12 volts; Supply; Return; 100 psi; and so forth. For international products, these codes can be printed in multiple languages, which may reduce internal variety due to labeling

differences. Such printing/dispensing equipment could be
utilized either at each point of use or at a central location to feed
kanban bins.

5.11 STANDARDIZATION OF EXPENSIVE PARTS

Usually, standardization programs for inexpensive parts, like
fasteners, do not meet serious resistance, since the standard parts are
perceived to cost no more than nonstandard parts (in reality, they cost
less). But, as the cost of the parts increases, standardization efforts
confront more resistance because of the *perception* that specifying the
next larger (and more expensive) standard component would cost more
than one that "just satisfies" its requirements in the product. However,
considering the *total* cost of standardization can encourage
standardization, even for expensive components.

The following experience illustrates the resistance and the
opportunities involved in the standardization of expensive parts. While
training a company that manufactured heating, ventilating, and air
conditioning (HVAC) equipment, the author discovered the company
used 152 different types of motors. When he challenged the designers,
they insisted they needed every size to specify "just the right" motor for
every application. Then we asked their supplier, GE Consumer Motor
Division, "What would be the savings if those 152 motors could be
reduced to five or ten?" The one word answer was *"Massive!"* Why?
Because each of those five or ten motors would be ordered in volumes
that would be ten times their current order volumes, thus resulting in
greater economies of scale. Further, the five or ten chosen would have
been the most cost-effective in their line – the best designed motors that
they produce in high volume for other customers too.

The upper graph in Figure 5-3 shows the *apparent* implication that
the standard parts would cost more than parts that have "just enough"
performance for a given product. However, if *all* company products use
company standard parts, the cost of those parts will be less, due to
purchasing leverage and material overhead savings. Thus, there would
be a net company savings for expensive parts, as shown in the lower
graph in Figure 5-3.

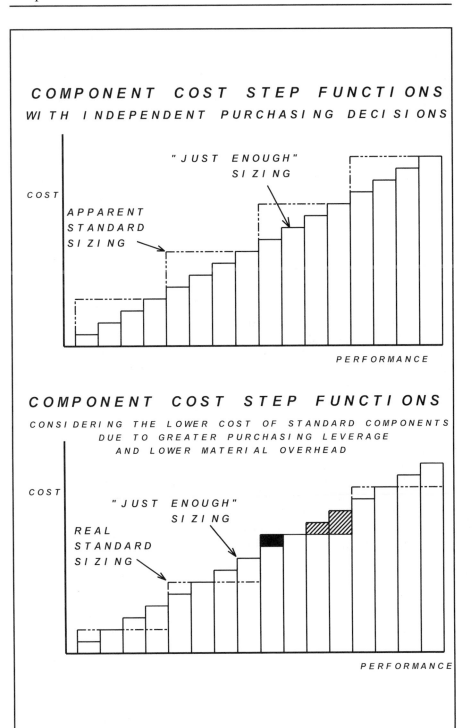

Figure 5-3: Standardization of Expensive Parts

Some products may be forced to use a more expensive part than is required (as shown for one size by black shading), but most products would be able to use less-expensive standard parts (as shown by the crosshatch shading). The result is a net cost savings for the company plus the flexibility that is essential for lean production, build-to-order, and mass customization.

Further, when a standardization task force standardizes on expensive parts, it can select the most cost-effective parts made in large enough quantities to take advantage of suppliers' economies of scale. These parts are usually the ones that have better availability and are more likely to have better quality and reliability. Design engineers, however, may not be aware of these nonlinear relationships between performance, price, availability, and quality.

5.12 CONSOLIDATION OF INFLEXIBLE PARTS

The logic of Section 5.11, "Standardization of Expensive Parts," can be applied to the *consolidation* of inflexible parts. Inflexible "raw" parts like castings, moldings, stampings, extrusions, wiring harnesses, bare circuit boards, and so forth, can be consolidated into versatile common parts that can be used on many products. The typical problem with these parts is that their processes are inherently inflexible with lengthy setups, so they are normally built in batches, which complicates supply chain management, disrupts operations with frequent setup changes, and incurs inventory carrying costs.

Several different raw parts can be consolidated in a single versatile part with enough extra metal, features, functions, "hooks," or circuitry to be useful in many applications. If this type of consolidation is done throughout the product line, substantial reduction in raw part variety can occur. This will result in greater purchasing leverage, less dependence on forecasting (with steady flows possible), less storage space needed, and simpler supply chains and internal logistics.

Figure 5-4 tabulates the costs added and costs saved from consolidation efforts.

Cost Added:
- Extra cost per part on some of the parts for extra material, wire, circuitry, etc.
- One time cost to implement the consolidation to existing products (does not apply to new product developments)

Cost Saved:
- Economy of scale savings (purchasing leverage) for ordering N times the volume at 1/Nth of the number of part types
- Tooling cost cut by a factor of N if N fewer parts result from the consolidation
- Material overhead savings on fewer parts
  - Bill-of-materials and MRP expenses
  - Ordering expenses
  - Warehousing/stocking cost for raw materials inventory
- Setup cost saved by not having to setup the eliminated parts; the cost savings include:
  - Setup labor reduction
  - Machinery utilization improvements
- WIP inventory savings from fewer types of part types
- Design cost saved by eliminating N parts in new designs
- Prototyping and debugging cost savings from fewer new parts
- Documentation and administration cost of the eliminated parts for new and existing designs
- Value of fewer work stoppages due to part shortages
- Value of the consolidation's contribution to flexible operations

Figure 5-4: Cost Tradeoffs for Part Consolidations

For example, water meter and gas regulator castings can be consolidated with extra metal included on all castings for options such as test ports. Similar logic applies to plastic moldings: all the features for many products can be molded into a few versatile plastic parts. This will have all the above advantages *plus* saving the cost of multiple molds.

Versatile "bare" printed circuit boards could have *all* the traces and holes/pads needed for several products, instead of the common practice of designing a different bare board for every product or variation. Then, steady flows of the versatile bare boards could be arranged knowing that they will be used one way or another. Printed board assembly machines are CNC machine tools and can be programmed to place or insert unique combinations of components onto versatile standard bare boards.

Automotive wiring harnesses are evolving toward this principle with a single wiring harness used regardless of the number of options ordered. In the old paradigm, many different wiring harnesses were manufactured so that a minimally optioned car would not have extra, unused wires. However, if total costs are considered, the results would conclude that the excess variety costs of manufacturing and assembling multiple wiring harnesses would greatly exceed the "cost" of the unused wires.

It may be hard to justify part consolidations if the cost system does not quantify total cost. The *extra* features will show up immediately and clearly as an *"extra"* cost. However, it may not be possible to quantify the substantial benefits in conventional cost systems. Until a total cost accounting can be implemented, the criteria presented in Figure 5-4 may help itemize the benefits of these consolidations and serve as a basis for quantification or, at least, for educated "leap of faith" decisions.

Custom Silicon Consolidation

Custom silicon can be designed to be versatile enough to be used in a wide range of products, *even if each product uses a small portion of the chip.* The increased volume for the versatile chip spreads out the NRE (non-recurring engineering) and tooling costs to encourage custom silicon even on small to medium-volume products. Figure 5-5 compares the traditional analysis for ASICs (which usually discourages their use) and the total cost analysis for widespread use.

Traditional Analysis for Independent Application

ASICs	Status Quo
High NRE charge/chip	No NRE
High tooling charge/chip	No tooling charges
High Cost per ASIC in low volume	Cost per several discrete chips
Lead time	

Analysis for Versatile ASIC with Widespread Application

Low NRE charge/chips	No NRE
Low tooling charge/chip	No tooling charges
Lower cost per ASIC in higher volume	Cost per several discrete chips
Lead time relevant only first time	

Total Cost and Other Implications

Quality improvement when dozens of discrete chips are replaced by one
  ASIC. This avoids the cumulative degradation of product quality caused
  by the quantity and quality of the parts (Ch. 10).
Eliminate the quality costs incurred when too many components are
  crowded onto PC boards
Better reliability with fewer interconnections
Higher density = fewer circuit boards, maybe one, eliminating card cages
Faster performance coming from shorter signal paths for circuits in ASICs
  and other chips brought closer together, especially if circuitry can be
  condensed onto the same circuit board
Faster factory throughput with fewer components and maybe fewer circuit
  boards
Better equipment utilization and lower equipment charges
Simplified supply chain management
Better flexibility for quicker delivery and build-to-order
Scare off competition
Thwart reverse engineering
Impress customers

Figure 5-5 Decisions for ASICs
(Application Specific Integrated Circuits)

VLSI/ASIC Consolidation

Hewlett-Packard offers a wide range of specialized calculators for many niche markets such as business analysis, engineering calculations, mathematical analysis, and so forth. In the book, *Product Juggernauts,*[13] Arthur D. Little consultants Jean-Philippe Deschamps and P. Ranganath Nayak state:

> *"Viewed in terms of functions offered, these calculators appear substantially different. However, HP has developed common architecture, subsystems, and components to an extreme degree. This strategy often means that higher grade components find their way into low-end products. In these cases, HP spends more than necessary on parts for low-end products in the interest of minimizing component diversity. The payoff comes in the efficiencies gained in production creation across the whole product line."*

Nokia designs it cellular phones with common custom silicon to gain economies of scale, spread out the design investment, simplify supply chain management, and eliminating setup changes in manufacturing.[14]

Consolidation Example

Power Supplies at Hewlett-Packard. HP's staff of Operations Research Ph.D.s used total cost analysis to prove that money could be saved by utilizing one worldwide power supply for HP Laser Printers. The part cost of the universal power supply appeared to be higher, and was resisted by engineers for that reason. But when worldwide logistic costs were figured in, the universal power supply resulted in substantial *total cost* savings.

5.13 TOOL STANDARDIZATION

A subject related to part standardization is *tool* standardization, which determines how many *different* tools are required for assembly, alignment, calibration, testing, repair, and service (fabrication tool standardization will be discussed next under *feature* standardization).

Tool standardization enhances manufacturing flexibility by eliminating the setup to locate and change tools needed in the manufacturing process. If adjustments are to be provided by dealers or users, ideally no tools should be required. But if tools are required, the product should be designed around standard tools that are easy to use and would be available to dealers or users. A single tool that performs all repairs and adjustments may be supplied with the product.

Some designs may require several lengths of screws, but if they had the same head geometry, then one screwdriver could be used for all of them. Tool standardization becomes even more important if service people have to be mobile or have to perform service in awkward situations such as clean rooms, crawl spaces, catwalks, utility poles, diving under water, "space walks," and so forth. Tool standardization can also help minimize the expense of providing repair tool kits with products (as provided with some automobiles) and enable the user to perform more repairs.

Tool standardization should be based on *standard,* readily available tools. Often *special* tools are required because tool specification was not really part of the design process. Sometimes special tools are required simply because tool access was not designed into products.

Company-wide tool standardization can be determined as follows: First, analyze tools used for existing products. Prioritize usage histories to determine the most common of existing tools. Work with people in manufacturing and service, in addition to dealers and uses, if appropriate, to determine tool preferences. Coordinate standard *tool* selection with standard *part* selection. Issue standard tool lists with standard parts lists.

5.14 FEATURE STANDARDIZATION

Features, such as drilled holes, reamed holes, punched holes, and sheet metal bend radii, require special tools, such as drills, reams, hole punch dies, and bending mandrels. Unless there is a dedicated machine for each tool, the tools will have to be changed, and this will result in a setup change every time the tool needs to be changed. Exceptions would be machines with automatic tool changing capabilities, but they are limited in the number of tools they can store.

Ironically, most sheet metal bends do not need to be any specific value within a reasonable range. But designers must enter a bend radius value to complete the drawing. Unfortunately, most designers specify an arbitrary bend radius, which often requires the shop to locate and change mandrels to bend the sheet metal to arbitrary radii. In the worse case, a special tool would have to be fabricated just for an arbitrary decision! Using feature standardization, designers would use the shop's most common bend radii. At an in-house DFM seminar[15] at Hewlett-Packard, where key vendors had been invited, the sheet-metal vendor stood up and said he could generate only four bend radii for bending sheet metal. And then he identified the *one* mandrel that was on usually on the bend brake, so if designers used that bend radius, there would be less setup delays and cost.

A more subtle, but still important, form of feature standardization is standardization around cutting tools used on machine tools such as lathes and milling machines. As with bend radii, many designers specify arbitrary fillet radii when a standard fillet radius might satisfy the needs of an entire product family. Multiple fillet radii may force a machinist to change cutting tools often or make it difficult to arrange automated machining in CNC machining centers.

When designing parts for milling, designers should specify the same standard fillet radius throughout the product family so that a single cutter or "end mill" may be used. This ensures that all parts in the family can be milled without setup changes and, thus, ensure flexibility and high machine tool utilization on expensive equipment.

To implement feature standardization, standardize features around standard production tools, making sure not to exceed the tool storage capacity. Investigating the tools used by the plant *and* by key outside vendors (whether currently used or not). A safe approach is to choose only features that can be easily built by *all* (or at least most) potential production facilities and vendors. Based on the production tool availability and capabilities, compile a feature list and issue it with the standard parts lists, hand tools, and raw materials.

5.15 PROCESSES STANDARDIZATION

Standardization of processes results from the concurrent engineering of products and processes to ensure that the processes are actually *specified* by the design team, rather than being left to chance or "to be determined later." Processes must be coordinated and common enough to ensure that all parts and products in the product families can be built without the setup changes that would undermine flexible manufacturing.

One of the processes affected by part standardization is mechanized screw fastening. The auto-feed screwdriver is a very cost-effective mechanized tool that orients and feeds a screw and then blows it down a tube to the screwdriver head, where it waits for the operator to activate the power drive by pushing down on the screwdriver handle. A preset torque-limited mechanism makes sure the screw is fastened consistently. This useful production tool can feed any style of screw (machine threads, self taping, and so forth.), but *only one size and type at a time.* Changing screw sizes is possible but would cause too much of a setup to be used in flexible operations. Thus, auto-feed screwdrivers can only be utilized effectively if there is fastener commonality.

Another concurrent engineering issue is that the screw specified must be longer than it is wide so that it will not tumble as it is blown down the feed tube. Each manufacturer has specific guidelines for specifying these dimensions. Similar devices, based on the same principle, can fasten screws automatically when mounted on robots or on assembly mechanisms specifically designed to dispense screws, such as those used in Hewlett-Packard's DeskJet factory in Vancouver, Washington.

5.16 ENCOURAGING STANDARDIZATION

Given the importance of standardization for cost, supply chain simplification, and optimizing current *or future* flexible operations, is imperative that manufacturing companies encourage standardization implementation as early as possible. This really means encouraging design engineers to design around standard parts (even ones that might appear too expensive), specify standard design features, select standard tools, base designs on standard materials, and concurrently design products to be built on standard processes. The author's experience indicates that design engineers are not naturally committed to these goals. In fact, engineers may be actually pushed the other way by poorly conceived metrics, such as emphasizing "part cost" and low bids for single products instead of *total* costs for product families and all part related expenses.

The following steps can be taken to encourage standardization. They involve "discounting" material overhead rates for standard parts, prequalifying standard parts, making samples and specifications of standard parts readily available, and emphasizing total cost thinking, preferably incorporated into total cost accounting systems. In addition to these procedural steps, managers should take every opportunity to emphasize the importance of standardization in goals, policies, directives, "pep talks," and training.

Material Overhead Rate. The procurement of standard parts and their distribution through the plant will incur less overhead burden than with the usual excessive internal variety. Therefore, the material overhead rate for standard parts should be less, to reflect the lower actual overhead. In addition to being a more accurate reflection of overhead costs, lower material overhead rates for standard parts should motivate engineers to specify standard parts.

The simplest method is to establish a two-tiered overhead rate, as done at Intel's Systems Group: a general material overhead rate and a lower rate for standard parts. This is a very logical approach since standard parts really do consume less overhead expense, because of the reasons pointed out throughout this chapter. In order to compensate for a lower material overhead rate for standard parts, the general material overhead rate may have to be raised from the previous single rate. It is also logical to assign a higher overhead rate to low-usage parts because of their higher overhead demands. Thus, if engineers choose standard parts, their design will be "rewarded" with the lower material overhead rate. Conversely, if they choose nonstandard parts, the overhead rate will be higher than even the previous single rate.

Another method of establishing overhead rates for standard parts would be a variable rate that would be inversely proportion to volume, so that a very high-usage part would have a very low material overhead rate and a very low-volume part would have a much higher overhead rate. This approach is used by the Portable Instruments Division of Tektronix as a "cost driver" to discourage engineers from using low-volume parts.[16]

Pre-Qualified Standard Parts. Companies using standard parts would be using many fewer types of parts for new designs than without standardization. Thus, these standard parts can be more thoroughly evaluated and their suppliers can be more thoroughly scrutinized than possible with many times the number of parts in the system. The standard parts can be prequalified for immediate use. This can accelerate product development, since design teams do not have to wait for this qualification.

Floor Stock. Usually, the list of standard parts is small enough to allow a *floor stock* to be kept in the engineering area, so that engineers can always have samples of the standard parts available in the design area. Having floor stock samples can help the design team visualize concepts based on standard parts, and, thus, encourage standard part usage. Floor stocks can make standard parts readily available for engineers to evaluate parts, conduct experiments, and build breadboards. Floor stocks can also be mounted on display boards in prominent places near the design team.

Personal Display Boards. For small, inexpensive parts, like fasteners, every engineer could be issued a personal display board with the standard parts mounted with labels that list the generic value plus the company part number. Hewlett-Packard, at the author's recommendation, followed the above procedure and reduced the number of fasteners for large format plotters from dozens to only seven. Samples of these seven fasteners were mounted on an aluminum plate with values and part numbers printed on paper that was affixed to the plate. These personal display boards were issued to all engineers to encourage them to use the standard fasteners.

Spec Books. Part specifications for standard parts could be reproduced and compiled into a single "spec book" or database. This would encourage engineers to use the standard parts when they can all specifications in a single reference.

Cost Metrics. If cost metrics are based on total cost for product families, they will encourage standardization. If they are based on part costs alone for single products, they may discourage standardization. If accounting systems cannot quantify total cost, then engineers should be encouraged to balance the costs that are reported with the qualitative benefits of standardization as addressed in the next section.

5.17 WHY STANDARDIZATION IS SO IMPORTANT

Implementing standardization for parts, features, tools, and materials can benefit any company, even before it embarks on operational flexibility programs like lean production, build-to-order, or mass customization. Since standardization is a prerequisite for these flexible paradigms, standardization programs are one of the first steps to implement. Since standardization generally applies only to new products, the programs should be implemented as soon as possible in order to reap the benefits as soon as possible. The following discussion presents the benefits of standardization under four categories: cost reduction, quality, flexibility, and responsiveness. The cost reduction aspects of these benefits will be discussed in more detail in Chapter 6.

Cost Reduction

*   **Purchasing costs.** Standard parts will incur much less procurement cost because fewer parts are being purchased in larger quantities. This not only results in fewer purchasing actions, but also results in better *purchasing leverage* that entitles the company to take advantage of suppliers' economies-of-scale and get quantity discounts and better delivery. Ordering fewer types of standard parts in large quantities is the key to arranging just-in-time deliveries, which is important for flexible operations. The cost of expediting unusual or hard-to-get parts can also be eliminated.

*   **Inventory cost reduction.** Part standardization can, directly or indirectly, reduce all three categories of inventory (raw materials, WIP, finished goods) and their significant carrying costs. Use of standard parts and materials results in fewer types of parts in incoming parts inventory and fewer types of materials in raw materials inventory. Part and feature standardization help eliminate setup which supports lean production, which, in turn, reduce WIP

inventory. Standardization makes parts available for build-to-order, which reduces finished-goods inventory.

- **Floor space reduction.** Reducing inventory and eliminating kitting can significantly reduce floor space requirements. Floor space can also be saved by eliminating the fork lift aisles needed to move large bins of parts, since flow manufacturing moves single parts between work stations. Reducing floor space needs can be a very attractive alternative to expanding buildings or moving to larger facilities. This issue may be a real "sleeper" until the company needs to expand facilities or move to where more floor space will be available. If floor space reduction was part of a continuous improvement program, the need to expand facilities or move may be postponed or averted entirely.

- **Overhead cost reduction.** In addition to purchasing, inventory reduction, and floor space reduction, standardization also reduces the other costs that constitute "materials" overhead, including the documentation, administration, qualification and distribution of parts. Feature standardization lowers tooling costs by minimizing the number of tools needed to fabricate features like punched holes and sheetmetal bends.

Quality

- **Product quality.** Having fewer part types in the plant means that there will be less likelihood of using the wrong part. A manufacturer of semiconductor processing equipment had so many different screws that the wrong screw, one that was too long, was used to fasten the cover to a case that housed light-sensitive sensors. Since the screws were too long, they "bottomed out" in the blind tapped holes and, thus, did not adequately seal the case from extraneous light. This caused the equipment to malfunction when placed in service. The company and its customer wasted much time on the diagnostic effort, first checking the sensors and related circuitry, before discovering the light leak caused by the wrong screws.

- **Continuous Improvement.** In addition to the enormous cost savings of eliminating WIP inventory, discussed earlier, inventory reduction is also a key element to *continuous improvement* programs.[17] Inventory hides many problems; eliminating the inventory exposes the problems and, thus, forces solutions.[18]

- **Supplier reduction.** Standardization programs reduce the number of suppliers because fewer parts usually come from fewer sources. Dealing with fewer suppliers can strengthen ties with those suppliers, thus resulting in the very desirable *supplier partnership* relationship. Having fewer suppliers means that the company can do a better job qualifying each supplier, and also, do a better job evaluating each part.

Flexibility

- **Steady Flows.** If parts and materials can be standardized to the point where there is only one version (or a predictable proportion among multiple versions), then delivery can be arranged in steady flows where "ordering" is as easy as matching the tonnage *in* to the tonnage *out*.

- **Eliminating setup.** If the number of parts used in manufacturing is small enough, those standard parts can be permanently loaded on assembly machines or in the manual assembly pick bins. This allows all the products to be built by the same process without having to change the setup for different parts.

- **Inventory reduction.** Inventory can be significantly reduced with fewer types of parts to stock and distribute. This will, obviously, reduce incoming or "raw" parts inventory. Parts standardization and setup elimination also encourage lean production that can drastically reduce work-in-process (WIP) inventory expense and floor space.

- **Internal material logistics.** The flow of parts within the plant will improve with fewer parts to order, receive, log in, stock, issue, load, assemble, test, and reorder. Having so few parts that they can all be distributed at their points of use will avoid the space and expense of kitting parts.

- **Breadtruck deliveries.** High-usage, low-cost standard parts can be delivered directly to all the points of use *without any overhead costs* for purchasing or internal distribution. Arrangements can be made with suppliers of low-cost parts who will simply keep the bins full of standard parts at all the points of use, much like *breadtruck* deliveries keep the shelves stocked with bread in markets. The supplier simply bills the company for each month's usage. This is a very attractive approach for low-cost standard parts like fasteners, washers, and other hardware items. In addition to the obvious cost savings, this procurement methodology is much less likely to cause part shortages, which can stop production, even for lack of a one cent washer.

• **Supports Lean Production, BTO, and Mass Customization.** Eliminating setup changes allows products to be built in any size batch. With setup reduced to zero, any quantity of any product in the family can be built. This flexibility is the key to building products to order that allows companies to build-to-order and mass customize orders.

Responsiveness

• **Build-to-Order.** Build-to-order can eliminate finished goods inventory and let the plant build only the products that will ship immediately (for which it has orders). Another important benefit of build-to-order is that scarce parts are only consumed in products that go immediately to customers. Further, expensive parts are consumed closer to the time of the sale, thus lowering interest expenses.

• **Parts availability.** In general, fewer part types used in greater quantity will mean less chance of running out of parts and delaying production. Further, standard parts are available from more sources with more total capacity (this should be a standardization criteria), so standard parts will be more readily available, which is especially important for rapid growth situations.

There are special availability considerations when mass customized products are built-to-order. Consider, for a moment, the situation when products are built to forecast: the forecast provides the information that MRP systems use to order parts in advance, so that they can be shipped to the plant before they are needed. Build-to-order environments have much less forecasting information to use for ordering parts. Stocking all parts for all possible orders would theoretically work, but would incur too much inventory expense and space. This dilemma can be solved with parts standardization in one of three ways: Kanban resupply can be arranged for the high-volume standard parts. Breadtruck suppliers can keep bins full for inexpensive high-usage parts. The remaining standard parts could either have a steady flow arranged or be stocked, since each stocked part could be used for many different order scenarios in a flexible environment.

- **Quicker deliveries from suppliers.** Standardization of parts and materials can accelerate deliveries from suppliers if they have fewer types of parts to order and stock. Parts designed around standard raw material sizes will be quicker to order and may even be in the supplier's own raw materials stock. Suppliers will not need to order special tools if products were designed around the standard tools that they already have.

- **Stronger suppliers.** Standardization of parts helps part suppliers *rationalize*[19] their product lines and allow them to simplify their supply chain management, improve their operational flexibility, resulting in better delivery, reduce their overhead costs and cross-subsidies, which allows them to be more cost competitive and free valuable resources to improve operations and quality, implement better product development practices, and introduce new flexible capabilities.

5.18 REUSING DESIGNS, PARTS, AND MODULES

How to avoid reinventing the wheel

The most obvious way to make parts more common is to use parts that already are in production. In addition to the automatic standardization benefits, existing parts have gone through the learning curve and have been debugged and stabilized in production. Thus, products designed around existing parts can have fewer introduction problems.

A key quality principle from Chapter 10 is reusing proven designs, parts, modules, and process to minimize risk and assure quality, especially on critical aspects of the design (Guidelines Q19 and Q20). This was one of the *design philosophy* goals presented in Section 3.1.

To product designers, one benefit of using existing parts is the time saved from not having to "re-invent the wheel." Before using previously designed parts, the designer should check if they are still in production, how easy they are to manufacture, and how well they perform in use.

If the exact part or design cannot be found, existing designs can be modified to produce a new design with less effort than would be necessary starting from zero. Previous designs can be copied and modified easier using Computer-Aided Design, which is easier if various details were drawn on unique "layers" or "views."

In addition to the checking part history, designers should also perform enough analysis, as with any design, to ensure that the design will satisfy all its design objectives.

In order to use existing parts, designers will need to know what has already been designed. Comprehensive coding and classification schemes have been devised by some companies, but such schemes are not generally available. However, most parts can be listed in some logical order as discussed in Section 5.6.

Obstacles to Reusable Engineering

Some engineers resist using previous engineering because of the "not-invented-here" (NIH) syndrome. Others want to start with a "clean sheet of paper" or a clear computer screen. Sometimes poor documentation discourages reusing previous designs. Incomplete documentation is bad enough, but incorrect documentation is even worse.

The NIH syndrome might be overcome by team training or more selective hiring. Documentation issues can be corrected by insisting on good documentation as part of every project team's responsibilities.

Reuse Studies

A survey of 53 companies that were group technology users indicated the following results: *The need for designing new parts was down by 50%:*

- 20% of their needs could be satisfied by an existing part.

- 18% required only slight modification of an existing part.

- 12% required extensive modification.

One aerospace company discovered that a virtually identical part had been designed independently five times. Parts had been purchased from five suppliers *at prices ranging from 22 cents to $7.50 each!*

5.19 OFF-THE-SHELF PARTS

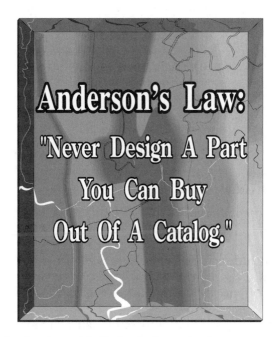

For *standard* parts with little variety, designers can greatly reduce development time and cost in addition to reducing product cost by *never designing a part that is available out of a catalog.* Rarely can anyone save any money or time by designing and building parts that are available from catalogs.

Many designers are often misled by their own accounting systems into thinking that internally produced parts can be designed and built less expensively than off-the-shelf hardware. Accounting systems rarely report the *total* cost of parts (see Chapters 6 and 7). Usually when designers look up part "cost" in an accounting database, they are only provided the material cost and labor cost with very little "burden" (overhead). Considering the enormous overhead in some companies, "part" costs may be understated substantially.

Using off-the-shelf parts has an inherent standardizing effect on a company's parts list because many catalog parts are used broadly enough to become *de facto* standards.

Paradoxically, designers may have to choose the off-the-shelf parts *first* and design the product *around* them, or else they may make arbitrary decisions that may preclude their use. But incorporating off-the-shelf parts early into the design will greatly simplify the design and the design effort.

Off-the-shelf parts are less expensive to design considering the cost of design, documentation, prototyping, testing, debugging, in addition to the overhead cost of purchasing all the constituent parts and the cost of non-core-competency manufacturing.

Off-the-shelf parts save time considering the time to design, document, administer, and build, test, and fix prototype designs.

Suppliers of off-the-shelf parts are more efficient at their specialty, because they are more experienced on their products, continuously improve quality, have proven track records on reliability, design parts better for DFM, have dedicate production facilities, offer standardized parts, and sometimes pick up warrantee/service costs.

Off-the-shelf part utilization helps internal resources focus on their *real* missions which are designing products and building products.

When to Use Off-the-Shelf Parts

Designers should specify off-the-shelf parts when the following conditions exist:

- **Parts are standard.** Off-the-shelf parts are especially applicable when they are *de facto* standards, always available, and can be purchased from multiple suppliers.

- **Volumes are high.** Standard parts can be manufactured in high volumes. Even companies with small order quantities can benefit from suppliers' economies of scale. Very high volume parts may be mass produced on dedicated lines, which further lowers cost and improves quality.

- **Quality/reliability are important.** Good suppliers will be able to focus more on their products and thus achieve higher quality levels than occasional production at an assembler's plant, especially when suppliers have been making them for a long time and are already "up the learning curve." Parts that have been produced for a while will have track records that can be used to predict and assure reliability targets will be met.

- **Specialized skill, expertise, or costly equipment.** Suppliers may have specialized skill and expertise that may be hard to equal in-house. High-volume suppliers may have costly equipment that can make parts faster, at lower cost, and at higher quality.

- **Different processing.** If certain parts require different processing than can be efficiently done in-house, it will be better to get those parts from off-the-shelf suppliers.

- **Growth or constrained capacity.** If in-house capacity is limited or growth is anticipated, off-the-shelf parts can relieve capacity constraints and make that capacity available for product growth.

- **Lowest total cost.** Off-the-shelf standard parts will usually have a lower total cost, even through in some applications, standard parts may *appear* to cost more than the "just right" sizing in Figure 5-3. But when the effects of purchasing leverage and material overhead are included, the standard parts will be the lowest cost solution for the company.

When *Not* to Use Off-the-Shelf Parts

In-house production of parts would be warranted under the following conditions:

- If they are used in significantly different ways than intended.

- If they were designed and used predominantly in other industries with different demands and lifespans.

- If you are a very small part of the suppliers business which may make it hard to get help with the application or develop modified or custom versions or may result in undependable delivery when bigger customers "pull rank."

- If the supplier acts like a monopolist, charges high profits, won't help with the application, gives poor service, or may not be counted on for on-time delivery.

- If the supplier has not designed the product well for manufacturability and missed opportunities to lower cost and improve performance and quality. This is more like for complex parts or subassemblies made in low volume.

- If you or your vendor/partners can manufacture it better: more consistently, at higher quality, and at a lower *total* cost

- When you want propriety control over manufacture, trade secrets, or intellectual property.

Finding Off-the-Shelf Parts

The first task in finding off-the-shelf parts is to search of all the potential sources for the type of part needed. A common shortcoming here is to make a superficial search and then conclude that no one makes the needed parts. Then the designer feels justified in designing and building the part.

There are many directories and other sources that can show engineers where to find off-the-shelf parts including the Thomas Register, trade journal annual "directory issues," the yellow pages, internet searches, and trade shows.

Catalogs of off-the-shelf parts can be obtained from company headquarters, local representatives, reader service cards ("bingo cards") in trade journals, trade shows, company libraries, and peers' private collections. Many web-sites contain complete catalogs on-line, but if the site is too cumbersome to navigate, the complete printed catalog may be better at showing the range of parts available.

There is a wealth of information in catalogs including specifications, selection guidelines, design guidelines, cross-references to other brands, listings of local reps, and policies on specials or custom parts.

Prices have generally not been published in catalogs for years. Usually prices are obtained on specific parts by asking the headquarters or local rep. Price lists for the entire line are more useful for doing "what if" analyses. They *can* be obtained with enough persistence. One method is to inform the supplier that in the "pricing stage" of the design, you use the catalog that has a price list and that these tentatively chosen parts often end up in the final design.

Designers can get some indications of relative availability by cross referencing other brands to reveal which sizes or models are supplied by the most suppliers. These are likely to be the most standard parts with greater availability than parts only available from one or two sources. The best indication of availability is to find "quantity in stock" data. The size or model with the highest quantity in stock will probably be the most standard and have the best availability, not to mention the best pricing.

After the needed part is located in a catalog, the designer will want to evaluate the actual part. The quickest way to get a part for evaluation is to ask for a *sample.* Samples are usually sent out immediately without charge unless the parts are very expensive or semi-custom in nature. This is quicker than purchasing and actually saves administrative expense at both ends. To maximize success in obtaining samples, be sure to mention yearly or lifetime projected consumption of the parts being considered.

5.20 STANDARDIZATION IMPLEMENTATION

Standardization can be implemented by forming a standardization task force, which would include key people from Engineering, Manufacturing, Purchasing, Quality, Finance, plus appropriate managers and implementers. A key member of this effort would be a "database wizard" – a designated person who has the skill and availability to quickly extract data and generate many Pareto plots from various IT systems. The standardization steps are:

• Generate interest in standardization by creating an overall Pareto chart showing the periodic consumption of *all* parts (on the vertical axis) in descending order, with only the ascending count on the horizontal axis (with no part numbers).

• Arrange training on standardization methodologies (or, at least, have all implementers read this chapter) followed by workshops to standardize *each* category of parts and materials.

• Discuss any Pareto charts previously generated, including any anecdotal and documented consequences of standardization shortcomings.

• Start with the early steps: list existing parts to immediately stop the proliferation, clean up database nomenclature (e.g., for the many labels for bolts and screws), eliminate approved but unused parts, eliminate parts not used recently, and eliminate duplicate parts (Section 5.6).

• Prioritize opportunities of what categories of parts to standardize first and start from the top of the list creating standard parts lists using the procedures presented in Sections 5.7 and 5.8.

• Similarly, standardize raw materials (Section 5.10), tools (Section 5.13), features (Section 5.14), and processes (Section 5.15).

• Determine related investigative tasks to identify standardization issues, like backward compatibility, "copy-exact" policies, implications of lean/cellular manufacture.

• Start the process of developing standardization implementation procedures. Discuss and assign tasks to change procedures or policies that may hinder standardization.

• Assign tasks to generate more Pareto plots.

- Designate people to do the above.

- Subsequent sessions would analyze new Pareto plots, specify additional investigations, start creating lists of standard parts/materials, obtain approvals, and issue the lists.

- For the standardization of expensive parts (Section 5.11), quantify the benefits of the standardization (in the format of Figure 5-3) for specific cases, and, in general, start the process of creating a financial model to help quantify the overall cost savings and overcome resistance to some products getting what appears to be a "better" standard part.

- Issue the standardization lists (Section 5.8, point 14) and incorporate into subsequent DFM training

- Encourage standardization through appropriate material overhead rates, prequalified standard parts, floor stock, personal display boards, spec books, and cost metrics (Section 5.16).

- Perform *product line rationalization,* ideally as a first step if time permits, to eliminate or outsource the most unusual *products* that usually have the most unusual *parts* (see Appendix A).

ENDNOTES/REFERENCES

1. Clay Chandler and Michael Williams, "A Slump in Car Sales Forces Nissan to Start Cutting Swollen Costs." *The Wall Street Journal,* March 3, 1993.

2. Brian H. Maskell, *Software and the Agile Manufacturer,* (1994, Productivity Press), p. 335.

3. Robin Cooper and Peter B. B. Turney, "Internally Focused Activity-Based Cost Systems," *Measures of Manufacturing Excellence,* edited by Robert S. Kaplan (1990, Harvard Business School Press), p. 293.

4. Tim Stevens, "Prolific Parts Pilfer Profits," *Industry Week,* v244, n11 (July 5, 1995), pp. 59-62.

5. Source: Venkat Mohan, President and COO, CADIS Inc., Boulder, Colorado.

6. George Taninecz, "Faster in, Faster out," *Industry Week,* v 224, n 10 (May 15, 1995), pp. 27-30.

7. Michael R. Ostrenga, Terrence R. Ozan, Robert D. McIlhattan, Marcus D. Harwood, *The Ernst & Young Guide to Total Cost Management,* (1992, John Wiley & Sons), p.150.

8. Marshall Fisher, Anjani Jain, and John Paul MacDuffie, "Strategies for Product Variety, Lessons From the Auto Industry," The Wharton School, University of Pennsylvania, October 9, 1992, Revised January 16, 1994.

9. Eric Teicholz and Joel N. Orr, *Computer Integrated Manufacturing Handbook,* (New York, McGraw-Hill, 1987), p. 96.

10. Tim Stevens, "Prolific Parts Pilfer Profits," *Industry Week,* v 244, n 11, June 5, 1995, pp. 59-62.

11. Source: CADIS case study, CADIS, Inc., Boulder, Colorado.

12. Anderson, *Build-to-Order & Mass Customization,* Ch. 9, "Mass Customization," presents three ways to customize products: (1) modules or building-blocks, (2) adjustments or configurations, and (3) dimensional customization which involves a *permanent* cutting-to-fit, mixing, or tailoring. See articles at www.build-to-order-consulting.com.

13. Jean-Phillippe Deschamps and P. Ranganath Nayak, *Product Juggernauts, How Companies Mobilize to Generate a Stream of Market Winners,* (1995, Harvard Business School Press), pp. 35-36.

14. David Pringle, "How Nokia Thrives by Breaking the Rules," *The Wall Street Journal,* Jan. 3, 2003.

15. For more information on customized in-house DFM seminars, see page 407 of this book or *www.design4manufacturability.com/seminars.htm.*

16. Robin Cooper and Peter B. B. Turney, *Measures for Manufacturing Excellence,* edited by Robert S. Kaplan (1990, Harvard Business School Press), page 293.

17. Kiyoshi Suzaki, *The New Manufacturing Challenge, Techniques for Continuous Improvement,* (1987, The Free Press).

18. Richard J. Schonberger, *Japanese Manufacturing Techniques; Nine Hidden Lessons in Simplicity* (1982, The Free Press); and *World Class Manufacturing; The Lessons of Simplicity Applied* (1986, The Free Press).

19. See Appendix A on "Product Line Rationalization"

MINIMIZING COST BY DESIGN

Cost must be *designed* out of the product and production processes, as it is very difficult to remove cost *after* the product has been designed through "cost reduction" measures. Many cost "reduction" efforts may not even pay off the expense of the cost reduction effort!

The key to achieving the lowest product cost is to base all thinking and decisions on a *total cost* perspective, as will be discussed further in Chapter 7. Unfortunately, the typical company cost system reports only material and labor costs. All other costs are called *overhead,* which is spread over corporate activities according to some arbitrary allocation (averaging) algorithm, for instance, proportional to material, labor, or processing cost. And yet, all products do not have the same overhead demands. In fact, much can be done to lower overhead costs by design.

This chapter will discuss two categories of cost: "reported costs," such as labor and materials, and "overhead" costs. It will show how to use advanced design techniques to design low-cost products for minimum labor and materials costs, and then build them very efficiently for the minimum overhead cost.

This chapter has the goal of presenting several ways to minimize cost by design. Chapter 7 will show how to *think* in terms of total cost and *measure* total cost so that product development teams will make the best cost decisions to minimize total cost.

6.1 HOW *NOT* TO ACHIEVE LOW COST[1]

First, let's look at cost reduction as Dysfunctional Engineering Inc.:

So let's look at what is wrong with this very common picture. The first shortcoming of this approach is leaving cost reduction until *after* the product is designed and already in production. In their haste to rush early production units to market, many companies defer cost concerns until later with "cost reduction" efforts. The first problem with this strategy is that it probably will not happen because of competing priorities, and thus, costs remain high for the life of the product. The second problem is that cost reduction simply cannot be very effective at all!

Cost-Cutting Doesn't Work

Mercer Management Consulting analyzed 800 companies from 1987 to 1992. They identified 120 of these companies as "cost cutters." Of those cost-cutting companies, "68% did not go on to achieve profitable revenue during the next five years."[2]

There are also intangible impacts of an excessive focus on cost reduction: it absorbs effort and talent that could be applied to more productive activities, like developing better *new* products and improving operations. One division of a large international company did not have time for the author's training on low-cost product development because they were too busy with 31 cost reduction efforts!

Why Cost Is Hard to Remove After Design

Cost reduction after the product is designed an ineffective way to lower cost because:

- Cost is designed into the product and is hard to remove later; 80% of cumulative lifetime cost is committed by design and by the time it gets to manufacturing, only 5% is left, as shown in Figure 1-1.

- So much is cast in concrete, *systematic* cost reduction will be almost impossible.

- Cost reduction efforts on one product will not have the time or bandwidth to reduce any overhead costs which may be more then half the cost. Besides, overhead costs are not quantified unless the company has a total cost program.

- So the focus usually shifts to specifying cheaper parts, cutting corners, omitting features, beating up suppliers, switching to a new low-bidder, or chasing cheap labor around the world.

- The changes will cost money, which may not be paid back within the life of the product.

- The changes will cost time, especially if *requalifications* are required, which may delay the time-to-market.

- Changes may induce *more* problems, thus needing *yet more changes*, thus expending more hours, calendar time, and money to do the subsequent changes and possibly compromising functionality, quality, and reliability.

- In addition to the above, cost reduction can't be counted on because it may just not happen due to competing priorities, like mandatory changes and designing *new* products.

- Committing valuable resources to do cost reduction after design takes them away from other more-effective efforts in product development, quality, lean production, etc.

- If too many resources are committed to cost reduction, then:

   a) There will not be enough available for *real* cost reduction through new product development. If this continues over time, the result will be little, if any, *real* reduction in cost, while such a drain of resources will impede new product development efforts.

b) It will prevent the transition from back-loaded efforts to the more-effective front-loaded methodology that uses complete multifunctional teams to design low-cost products right the first time.

c) The company will be lured into *thinking* it is doing all it can to lower cost, when, in fact, costs are not really being reduced and opportunities for real cost reduction are not being pursued.

Finally, "cost reduction" attempts, coupled with incomplete cost data, may discourage innovative ways to lower cost, maybe even thwarting promising attempts. While teaching DFM to companies, the author often suggests innovative ways to lower cost by design, only to be countered by a chorus of "we looked into that, but it didn't work out." However, it is hard to be innovative when so much is cast in concrete that there are very few opportunities available.

6.2 COST MEASUREMENTS

Usual definition of cost. Traditional cost systems provide the cost breakdown shown in the upper pie chart of Figure 6-1 and encourage product development teams to focus only on material, labor and tooling costs. Considering only these costs gives a limited perspective and might lead to short-sighted conclusions that 80% of the product's cost consists of parts (and tooling). Therefore, "cost reduction" measures often focus only on minimizing parts costs, usually by buying cheaper parts. However, the following slogan shows what is really important to customers: You don't compete on *cost;* You compete on *price.* Customers don't care about *your* cost; They only care about *their total cost* which is *your price.* There, the only relevant pie chart is selling price.

Selling Price Breakdown. Total cost measurements enable the creation of the selling price breakdown chart (shown in the lower pie chart in Figure 6-1 for an integrated company) and encourages everyone to make the best decisions that will minimize the total cost while maximizing profits.

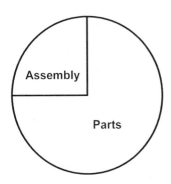

USUAL COST BREAKDOWN

However, you don't compete on *cost;* you compete on *price.*

Customers don't care about *your* cost;
They only care about *their* cost which is *your price.*

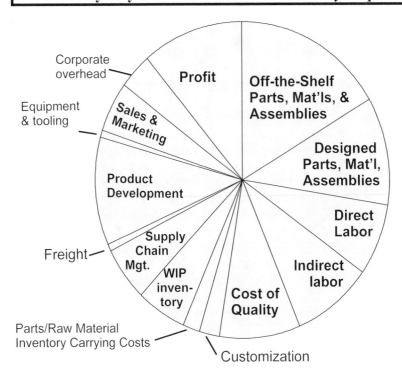

SELLING PRICE BREAKDOWN

Figure 6-1: Cost Without Overhead vs. Selling Price Breakdown

Selling Price Breakdown for an Outsourced Company

Unlike an integrated company (previous chart), heavily outsourced companies buy a lot of parts (like the left chart below) and therefore don't think that they have to consider overhead costs. However, each OEM's part is a supplier's *product,* which, in turn, has parts that are *its* suppliers' products, so the net result is a collection of pie charts (at the right), all with the same proportion of overhead costs of an integrated company. For the OEM to have visibility and control of the overhead costs throughout an outsourced supply chain, it must have very good vendor relationships.

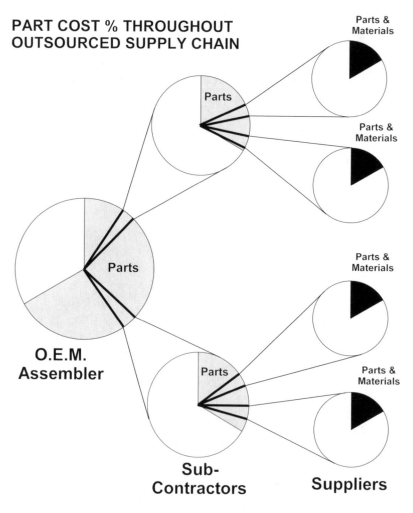

Figure 6-2: Part Cost % Throughout Outsourced Supply Chain

6.3 OVERHEAD COST MINIMIZATION STRATEGY

Total cost can be minimized by addressing all the costs that contribute to the selling price. Figure 6-3 shows the overall strategy with design for manufacturability and lean production efficiencies minimizing direct labor, indirect labor, and quality costs. Concurrent Engineering, standardization, and product family synergies minimize material overhead, product development, shipping, and sales and marketing costs. Build-to-order and mass customization techniques, working with on-demand lean production (Ch. 4), can virtually eliminate setup changeover costs, customization costs, raw material inventory, work-in-process (WIP) inventory, and finished goods (FG) inventory both at the factory and in the distribution channels.

The remainder of this chapter discusses specific cost minimization opportunities for the various elements of total cost.

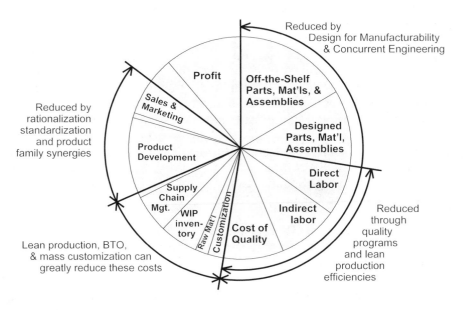

Figure 6-3: Programs That Reduce Specific Costs

Strategy to Cut Total Cost in Half

The author's book-length web-site, *www.HalfCostProducts.com*, presents a comprehensive cost reduction strategy consisting of the following eight strategies, each of which can offer significant returns as a stand-alone program. When combined, these coordinated cost saving strategies support each other synergistically for a whole-is-better-than-its-parts effect, instead of the more common, but ineffective, parts/labor focused initiatives that can raise other costs, compete for resources, and compromise longer-term cost reductions. The site has the equivalent of a 250 page book and 700 hyperlinks. The text after this summary discusses cost reduction opportunities that relate to product development.

1. Cost Reduction by Design. Product development determines 80% of product cost (Figure 1-1). The concept/architecture phase alone determines 60% of cost! Other strategies are enhanced by designing for quality, designing for Lean production and Build-to-Order, Concurrent Engineering with vendors, which saves more than bidding, and designing around standard parts, which simplifies supply chain management.

2. Lean Production Cost Reduction. Lean production benefits include eliminating many forms of waste and the ability to double labor productivity, cut production throughput times by 90 percent, reduce inventories by 90 percent, cut errors and scrap in half, thus lowering other costs of quality, procurement, and inventory (see Chapter 4).

3. Overhead Cost Reduction. Build-to-Order can build standard products to-order without forecasts of inventory, which costs 25% of its value to carry per year. Specials can be quickly and easily built by Mass Customization[3] (See Chapter 4).

4. Standardization Cost Reduction. Standard part lists can be 50 times less than proliferated lists, thus generating purchasing leverage, lowering material overhead and inventory costs, and improving quality (Ch. 5).

5. Product Line Rationalization. Eliminating or outsourcing unusual, high-overhead, low-volume products and options can lower total cost immediately and free up valuable resources for other cost strategies. It eliminates the "loser tax" on cash-cows to subsidize products that have low-margins or are really losing money (see Appendix A).

6. Supply Chain Management Cost Reduction. Supply chain resources can be most effective in reducing cost by supporting product development teams, establishing vendor/partnerships, buying high-quality parts, driving and encouraging standardization, rationalizing products (since the most unusual products have the most unusual parts and materials), supporting lean efforts and automatic resupply of parts (that eliminates forecasts, purchase orders, inventory, and expediting costs), and keeping control of local in-house manufacturing that supports product development, lean production, build-to-order, inventory reduction, and quality programs.

7. Quality Cost Reduction. The Cost of Quality can be a significant proportion of revenue or selling price. Improvements are supported by designing for quality, lean production, and rationalization because rationalizing away unusual products raises net factory quality and avoids wasting quality resources on inherently lower quality products (see Section A-9 on how rationalization improves quality).

8. Total Cost Measurement to support, justify, and quantify the savings of all cost reduction strategies. Until total cost can be quantified, everyone should make decisions based on *total cost thinking* (See Chapter 7).

6.4 MINIMIZING COST THROUGH DESIGN

As shown in Figure 1-1, 80% of the lifetime cumulative cost of a product is determined by the product's design. An even more important fact is that 60% of a product's cost is determined by product *architecture*. Low-cost product design is based on the premise that cost is designed *into* the product, especially by early concept decisions.

Tools like design for manufacturability can help design products that are easier, and thus less costly, to build. Concurrent Engineering can ensure the lowest cost processing since the processes were concurrently designed with the product. Quality can be designed into the product with *robust* design techniques (Taguchi Methods,[TM] based on design of experiments) and then built into the product with process controls instead of the more expensive inspection paradigm. Maximum utilization of catalog hardware can minimize part cost. Involving suppliers early can result in lower cost outsourced parts. Total cost accounting data (Chapter 7) can lead to decisions that result in the lowest total cost. Applying all these DFM techniques should enable companies to develop products at half the *total* cost, with special emphasis on key points discussed in Section 3.8.

Optimizing Architecture. The highest leverage opportunities for minimizing cost are in the architecture stage, which generally determines 60% (or more) of a product's lifetime cumulative cost. And yet, this high leverage opportunity is virtually ignored in many product development projects, when designers make snap decisions or just assume that the product will have the same architecture as previous or competitive products. The architecture phase of product development abounds with opportunities to greatly lower cost through creative concept simplifications.

6.5 MINIMIZING OVERHEAD COSTS

Engineers, purchasing agents, and "cost reduction" managers often spend much effort trying to reduce reported costs, like labor and materials. They precisely calculate these costs, *and then multiply by three of four* to get the selling price. Yet they rarely challenge the overhead "burden" rate.

Product development can have significant effects on overhead costs by *designing* to minimize them. Overhead costs can be reduced by design by minimizing product development expense, the "cost of quality," inventory and other factory overhead costs, and material overhead (see subsequent sections).

Overhead cost can be significantly lowered with concurrent product/process design, parts and processes standardization, reuse of engineering and software code, modular design, designing quality into the product, designing it right the first time, and designing to optimize manufacturing flexibility.

6.6 MINIMIZING PRODUCT DEVELOPMENT EXPENSES

Advanced product development can significantly reduce product development and related expenses with:

Product Portfolio Planning. Total cost is a key element of product portfolio planning. Before anyone can decide in which market segments to compete, they should understand the *true* profitability of their existing products. The *reported profitability* of existing products is only as meaningful as the *reported costs*. As will be discussed in Chapter 7, typical cost reporting systems are too "aggregated" to distinguish the real cost differences between products, thus distorting product costing. Distorted product costing leads to distorted perceptions of profitability and, thus, to distorted decision making on which products to develop. Developing products for *truly* profitable market segments will result in the most efficient utilization of product development resources. Developing products for market segments that are *thought to be* making money, but are really marginal or losing money, is a waste of product development resources.

Multifunctional Design teams. To minimize product development expense, product development teams must be efficient. They must "do it right the first time" because engineering change orders are expensive and redesigns are even more expensive. Designing products right the first time required good product development methodologies.

Using multifunctional teams to raise and resolve issues early will save the considerable expense of trying to do this later, after things are "cast under several layers of concrete."

Multifunctional teams can concurrently design and select the optimal processes and suppliers for the lowest total cost. With manufacturing and suppliers involved the team will be better able to make rational decisions regarding tooling and automation.

Product development expense can be minimized by utilizing the most efficient designers, which may not always be in-house engineering working alone. The multifunctional team *with active manufacturing or supplier assistance* would be more efficient than an isolated group of engineers working alone. The suppliers who make the parts may be the most efficient at designing them, and will probably design lower cost parts, too.

And remember, the most efficient part design effort is none at all! This is accomplished with optimal use of off-the-shelf hardware.

Methodical Product Definition. Similarly, product development expenses can also be minimized by *defining* it right the first time because it is very expensive to make product definition iterations at the prototype stage when the customer says, "that's not what I wanted." Designing in unwanted features would have wasted product development resources and would cause the product to be overpriced.

Total Cost Decision Making. All decisions must consciously be based on a total cost *focus,* even if total cost cannot be quantified. The product development culture must support decisions that "just make sense" from a total cost perspective, even if they cannot be justified quantitatively by the current cost system.

Arbitrary decisions must be avoided. Making arbitrary decisions assumes that all choices have the same cost impact, which is rarely the case.

On the other hand, "cost" concerns can have a counterproductive effect if decision makers are giving too much focus on *reported costs,* like labor and materials, and not enough focus on *total costs.* Sometimes product development teams limit their opportunities by making major decisions based on rough estimates of reported costs, instead of using good cost models based on *total* costs for *multiple approaches, ideas, and scenarios.*

"Reinventing the wheel" can be avoided in product development with maximum use of off-the-shelf parts, reusable engineering, and versatile modules. There is a common tendency for product development projects to ignore previous work and completely start over, when they could be more efficient by leveraging previous work. This can be facilitated by proper CAD practices: a good *layer* convention will segregate designs into well defined layers, so that subsequent development projects can easily find and reuse pervious engineering. Modular design can allow new products to be derived from standard modules.

Basing designs on catalog parts can eliminate the cost of designing those parts and, at the same time, lower part cost and quality costs for those parts (see "Anderson's Law" in Chapter 5).

Extending product life can be accomplished through upgrades rather than redesigns. Products can be *designed* to be easy to extend the product life with upgrades. Modular design can facilitate upgrading if anticipated changes can be confined to the fewest number of modules. Many common functions of a product can be reused for many iterations of the product.

Minimizing debugging cost can be accomplished by using existing modules that have already been debugged. Some leading companies, like Hewlett-Packard, feel that this is the best way to produce bug-fee software. With a high percentage of reuse, development *and* debugging efforts can focus on *new* aspects.

Diagnostic test development can be avoided by designing quality into the product and building it in with process controls. In such a quality environment, failures would be so low that diagnostic test development could be avoided, because the cost of discarding failed parts would be less than the cost of test development, test equipment, and repair efforts. At IBM, printed circuit boards that were expected to have higher than a 98.5% first-pass-accept rate could avoid diagnostic testing entirely. This eliminated time-consuming test development and the expensive ATE (Automatic Test Equipment) "bed-of-nails" equipment. Above this threshold, it was more cost-effective to discard defective printed circuit boards than to pay for the testers, the test development, and the repairs. Avoiding diagnostic tests can have a significant effect on product cost since diagnostic test equipment for circuit boards can cost up to two million dollars and, for some products, diagnostic test development can exceed the cost of product development!

Development expenses would be paid off sooner because of quicker product development cycles. This lowers the interest or "opportunity" cost of the money invested in product development. Similar logic applies to research expenses for technology development and tooling expenses. **More efficient development costs less.** Advanced product development methodologies are more efficient because the product is well defined and the architecture is simplified around optimal concepts. This thorough early development work means fewer false starts, "looping back" to do things over, fewer changes, and redesigns.

Faster Developments Have Less Obsolescence Risk. Shorter product development cycles result in less chance of market shifts and technical obsolescence by the time the product reaches the market, thus resulting in fewer changes and redesigns.

6.7 COST SAVINGS OF OFF-THE-SHELF PARTS

Specifying off-the-shelf parts, subassemblies, and modules (Section 5.19) offers several ways to minimize cost in product development, purchasing, manufacturing, quality, and reliability.

Off-the-shelf parts are less expensive to design considering the cost of design, documentation, prototyping, testing, debugging, and, if necessary, change orders or redesign.

Purchasing one off-the-shelf subassembly is one purchasing action, which incurs less material overhead than the effort to purchase all the constituent parts.

The cost of off-the-shelf parts will be less because suppliers of off-the-shelf parts are usually more efficient at their specialty since they are more experienced on their products, continuously improve quality, design parts better for DFM, and may dedicate production lines. Further, they are far up on the learning curve, so they don't have to incur costs and delays to learn how to make good parts.

Quality costs will less, often much less, because good suppliers are already up the learning curve and have processes under control, with the best suppliers utilizing statistical process controls and six-sigma quality techniques. Many suppliers make parts routinely at six-sigma levels (about 3 defects per million). Suppliers who have dedicated product lines can ensure higher quality than lower-volume lines that have to keep changing over lines for different products.

Reliability costs can be lower, especially if a supplier's part have been in production long enough to get feedback from the field and implement corrective action. Some suppliers will even pick up warrantee/service costs.

6.8 MINIMIZING ENGINEERING CHANGE ORDER COST

Advanced product development methodologies result in more products designed right the first time and, thus, fewer engineering change orders (ECOs). Better product definition results in fewer changes to satisfy customers. Early "changes" in the planning stage are less expense than late changes at the hardware stage. Reused engineering and modules have fewer "bugs" because of their widespread usage over time and across many product lines.

Well-designed products can minimize a substantial overhead expense that is not always included in ECO cost reporting: "firefighting" or problem solving. This is the often considerable effort expended to solve production problems, which is usually intense when a new product is launched into production.

The cost of changes rises drastically as the product progresses toward production. Figure 1-3 is repeated here as Figure 6-4 to reiterate how the cost of changes escalates as product development progresses:

Time of Design Change	Cost
During design:	$1,000
During design testing:	10,000
During process planning:	100,000
During test production:	1,000,000
During final production:	10,000,000

Figure 6-4 Cost of Engineering Changes[4]

6.9 MINIMIZING COST OF QUALITY

The "cost of quality" is really the cost of *poor* quality: the cost of finding and repairing defects. Companies without strong Total Quality Management programs can have quality costs equal to 15% to 40% of revenue.[5] Advanced product development can *design in* quality. Concurrently engineered processes that are in control can *build in* quality. This dual approach to quality can substantially reduce both the internal and external cost of quality, which are defined as follows:

Internal cost of quality includes the cost of non-value-added activities such as testing, diagnostics, rework, scrap, waste, etc. It also includes the cost of test development, which, for some products can exceed the cost of product development, and millions of dollars for test equipment. Designing in quality and designing well-controlled processes can produce products with such a low failure rate that diagnostic test development would not be required.

External cost of quality includes the cost of field failures, warranty expenses, legal liabilities, and hard to quantify costs, such as bad publicity, that damages a product's reputation.

Companies can have poor internal quality but, with a good "test screen" can keep defects within the factory, and, thus, have a high external quality. Achieving external quality totally by testing and rework is very expensive, and such a company would have a high cost of quality. Many luxury products, such as non-Japanese luxury automobiles enjoy a quality reputation, but are very expensive because quality is achieved at a high cost. Before TQM spread to this industry, some luxury automobiles require several times more labor effort to *fix* than a well-designed car requires to *build*.[6]

Another cost of quality is the "defects by the batch" effect in which large batches of parts are made with recurring defects and this is not noticed until the batches have traveled through many more work stations. By the time the defects have been spotted in final inspection, hundreds or thousands of defective parts would have been made, which would then have to be reworked or scrapped. In lean production, parts are made in a *one-piece flow* with immediate feedback after each "handoff," so there should be very little chance of recurring defects being produced.

Continuous improvement, or *kaizen* in Japanese, is an effective technique to keep driving costs down with incremental improvements that can have significant cumulative effects. Continuous improvement can be performed spontaneously by in-house workers,[7] as a part of quality programs,[8] or in cooperative efforts with suppliers. [9, 10]

6.10 RATIONAL SELECTION OF LOWEST COST SUPPLIER

The rational selection of the lowest cost supplier encompasses both the make/buy decision and supplier selection. These decisions must be made rationally on a total cost basis. As discussed throughout this chapter, conventional cost systems can mislead decision makers if they only report labor and materials. Not quantifying and including all the overhead costs for in-house manufacture creates a bias toward that option, since purchases include all costs, by definition, and in-house production does not.

Regarding supplier selection, total costs can actually increase as a result of choosing the supposedly "low-bidder" if purchase cost is emphasized over such subtle, but important, characteristics such as quality, delivery, flexibility, and help with product development (see discussion on low-bidding below). Jordan Lewis, in his book about customer-supplier alliances, *The Connected Corporation*,[11] commented about the effects of General Motor's 1992 demands for double-digit price cuts from suppliers, which were instituted by the now infamous J. Ignacio Lopez De Arriortua:

> *"By emphasizing price alone with its suppliers GM won immediate savings – and ignored total cost. At GM's plant in Arlington, Texas, an ill-fitting ashtray from a new, substandard supplier caused a six-week shutdown of Buick Roadmaster production."*

Another GM plant saved 5 percent going with a low bidder; when the parts were delivered, one-half failed quality tests. The other supplier, who lost the bid, had to gear up production in four days and fly parts to GM by chartered plane. The second supplier commented that "My guess is that their 5 percent savings turned into a 15 percent loss."

Peter Drucker, writing in *Managing in a Time of Great Change*,[12] encourages lowering total cost by minimizing "interstitial" costs between suppliers and manufacturers or between manufacturer and distributer:

> *"But the costs that matter are the costs of the entire economic process in which the individual manufacturer, bank, or hospital is only a link in a chain. The costs of the entire process are what the ultimate customer (or the taxpayer) pays and what determines whether a product, a service, an industry, or an economy is competitive.*

> *"The cost advantage of the Japanese derives in considerable measure from their control of these costs within a keiretsu, the 'family' of suppliers and distributors clustered around a manufacturer. Treating the keiretsu as one cost stream led, for instance, to 'just-in-time' parts delivery. It also enabled the keiretsu to shift operations to where they are most cost-effective."*

Early and *active* participation of vendors will result in a lower net cost because having the vendor help design the part will *greatly improve the manufacturability*, quality, and lead time, thus resulting in lower manufacturing, quality and supply chain costs. Further, vendor/partners who work with their customers from the beginning will be able to *charge less* because they: (a) understand the part requirement better, (b) are able work with their customer to minimize cost, and (c) won't have to add a "cushion" to deal with an unknown customer.

6.11 LOW-BIDDING

Going for the low-bidding is something we management consultants have been trying to discourage for years, but now it has seen a resurgence just because it is easy to do on the internet. This comes at a time when many purchasing functions are under heavy pressure to "use the net" and "get into e-commerce."[13]

Bidding for the cheapest parts is not only an ineffective way to achieve *real* cost reduction, but it can substantially raise less-obvious costs and compromise other important goals like quality and delivery. Quality usually takes a back seat when buying decisions are focused on purchase cost, especially in bidding situations. Some say that quality "standards" can be set for all bidders, but it is a dangerously naive assumption to believe that quality can be assured simply by setting a metric. Further, focusing cost reduction efforts on part bidding distracts attention from *real* cost reduction opportunities, which are addressed throughout this book.

Dick Hunter, Vice President of Fulfillment and Supply Chain Management for Dell Computer says that on-line auctions are no "silver bullet:"

"Auctions and exchanges have fueled the thinking that price is everything. But there is more to procurement of materials than just price. Quality, service, responsiveness, and the willingness to improve common processes also are very critical to driving down the total cost of materials."[14]

The Cost Reduction Illusion. In old-paradigm companies, "cost reduction" efforts are focused primarily on parts and materials (hereafter called parts) because that is all that most cost systems are able to quantify, besides labor. Many manufacturers, especially in the automobile business, beat up their part suppliers for repeated cost reductions. And now B2B internet web-sites are able to conduct competitive bidding auctions to offer the "lowest cost" parts.

But before manufacturers fall for a magic elixir, they should consider how part costs really would be lowered under such pressure. One assumption is that either purchasing agents have naively offered to pay too much or that cavalier part makers have been gouging their customers. While this may have been true in sleepy industries of the past, it is rarely true in today's dynamic marketplaces.

Another assumption is that inefficiencies can be corrected by pressure after a supplier "wins" a contract at a lower-than-usual price. However, soon after a supplier wins a bid, it is expected to deliver the goods, and there will not be time to implement any meaningful cost reduction program, as presented throughout this book. Thus, without a real means to lower costs, the supplier will either have to cut its margins (which will be resisted from the corner office all the way to Wall Street), cut corners, or do the same to thing to *its* suppliers, who may have the same difficulty achieving real cost reductions. Further, if suppliers are either making disappointing profits or struggling to reduce costs, they will not be very receptive or cooperative with build-to-order assemblers' needs for on-demand part delivery.

In some cases, suppliers will temporarily lose money to "buy into the business" with the expectation of raising costs later, once they are "in." And there are even suppliers out there whose strategy is to bid jobs at zero profit and plan to make all their money on the expected change orders.

In other cases, low-bidders "win" because they don't understand the problem and then are ultimately unable to deliver at all. In other cases, winning bidders are "vapor" companies, whose goal is keep bidding down until they win, and then patch together a "virtual" network of alliances to somehow fulfill the order. This phenomenon came out at an in-house seminar,[15] when the discussion topic was if anyone had noticed any problems with on-line competitive bidding. Within seconds, the purchasing manager was jumping up and down waving both hands in the air. They discovered that one low-bidder was working out of an apartment and its strategy was to win the auction and then figure out later how to deliver the goods! He also said that a corporate dictate to do part bidding was alienating their valued suppliers with whom they had good relationships.

The Cost of Bidding

Bidding keeps Purchasing so busy managing the bidding process that they will not be able to help their teams develop products, assure availability, and set up vendor/partnerships. The *Toyota Product Development System* book sums up the cost and wasted resources of bidding as follows:

> *"Searching the globe for the lowest cost means managing very large numbers of suppliers as well as introducing a steady stream of new suppliers into your system. These suppliers are unfamiliar with your requirements and demand a great deal of attention to get up and running. While administering complex contracts, managing global bidding wars, and overseeing the constant introduction of new suppliers into the process, U.S. automakers must maintain mammoth purchasing organization, deal with incredibly cumbersome and slow sourcing processes, and live with constant variation of supplier performance in the development process."[16]* – all to "save cost!"

Even after all that effort, problems often arise because low-bidders may not understand the problem or may be cutting corners, which raises other costs such as quality, expediting, delayed launches, warranty costs, or the costs of recalls. The biggest cost of bidding may be value of the resources it takes away from product development to support bidding (at both the customer and vendor), to: first, update/change documentation, CAD files, materials, tooling, and processing; second, complete transfers; and, third, deal with new or ongoing problems related to ramps, delivery, quality, or getting up the learning curve, sometimes through many iterations. All the above problems are much worse when offshoring to another continent.

Pressuring Suppliers for Lower Cost. Pressuring suppliers for drastic part cost reduction is what Lopez tried at GM, which not only failed to generate real, lasting cost savings, but also alienated its supplier base and drove the best suppliers to its competitors. The suppliers that remained put their best people on Ford and Chrysler projects and withheld their newest developments from GM, since Lopez was using proprietary supplier information to press all suppliers for lower prices. Further, the so-called "savings" in purchasing cost caused severe cost to be incurred elsewhere.

> The "cost-cutting campaign of Lopez, whose heavy-handedness drove away many of the company's best suppliers – and, perversely, may have helped raise GM's total costs."[17]

When Rubbermaid first encountered cost pressures from powerful retailers, like Wal-Mart, its first response as a "leading" company was to make sure customers understood the necessity of price *increases!* When they realized that they really had to reduce prices, they tried what didn't work for Lopez and got the same alienation of the supply base, according to the largest research project ever devoted to corporate failures, *Why Smart Executives Fail, and What You Can Learn from Their Mistakes:*

> "With little talent in cutting costs in-house, Rubbermaid looked to shift responsibility elsewhere. Suppliers were prodded to knock down their own prices, alienating some of the best, low-cost vendors in the process."[18]

Bidding creates a standoffish relationship between buyers and sellers that inhibits cooperative cost reduction, which is the key to *real* cost reduction. An extensive study that analyzed deficiencies in the American automobile industry concluded this about the effects of bidding on supplier relations:

> "A key feature of market-based bidding is that suppliers share only a single piece of information with the assembler: the bid price per

part. Otherwise, suppliers jealously guard information about their operations, even when they are divisions of the assembly company. By holding back information on how they plan to make the part and on their internal efficiency, they believe they are maximizing their ability to hide profits from the assembler." [19]

The Value of Relationships for Cost Reduction. Another common assumption is that if suppliers know they will have to bid, they will implement effective long-term cost reduction efforts. However, the most successful real progress in cost reduction has come from long-term relationships where manufacturers work together with suppliers.[20, 21]

The book that launched the lean production movement in the U.S., *The Machine That Changed the World,* notes that in lean production companies, suppliers "are not selected on the basis of bids, but rather on the basis of past relationships and a proven record of performance."[22] Honda's criterion for selecting suppliers is the *attitudes* of their management.[23] As a philosophy-driven company, Honda feels it is easier to *teach* product and process knowledge than to find a technically-capable supplier with the right attitudes, motivation, responsiveness, and overall competence.[24]

Much of the real cost reduction opportunities are not just at the assembler or at the supplier, but rather *in their relationship.* In a thorough study of Japanese lean manufacturers, *When Lean Enterprises Collide,* Robin Cooper states that "it is no longer sufficient to be the most efficient firm; it is necessary to be part of the most efficient supplier chain." The key to accomplishing this is inter-company cooperation, summarized by Cooper as follows:

"The blurring of organizational boundaries becomes critical as competition intensifies because it not only reduces the time it takes the entire supplier chain to bring out new products with increased functionality but also allows quality to be improved while reducing cost."

Cooper recommends partner companies "create relationships that share organizational resources, including information that helps improve the efficiency of the interfirm activities." [25]

Such inter-company cooperation offers significant cost reduction opportunities, especially if suppliers can build parts on-demand for build-to-order assemblers.[26] Then *both* avoid all the cost and risk of parts inventory in addition to minimizing many categories of overhead for procurement, material overhead, expediting, warehousing, internal distribution, and so forth.

However, switching suppliers every time a competitor drops its price is incompatible with this strategy and can jeopardize ongoing relationships. A Fortune magazine analysis of dot-com failures summarized the failure of an on-line bidding site:

"For the bulk of spending, corporations have long been moving in precisely in the opposite direction, establishing deep relationships with a few favored suppliers in a 'total cost' approach. Under this approach, price is but one of a host of criteria, which include quality, cycle time, service, and geography." [27]

The same article also revealed some realities about the purchasing process that question how welcome bidding would be for typical buyers:

"In retrospect, say analysts, most B2B efforts betrayed pronounced cluelessness about how industrial buying actually works. Start with the supposition that purchasing managers would be thrilled to take bids online from dozens if not hundreds of suppliers each vying to be the lowest bidder."

Another article that proclaimed B2B auction sites as "yesterday's darlings," said that:

"Many companies just weren't willing to dump the networks of suppliers they had built up over the years and do all their buying through a new, unfamiliar medium." [28]

Cheap Parts – Save Now; Pay Later. Actually, this phrase should be, more precisely: *save a little now, pay a lot later.* Many times trying to save money on purchase cost has the unintended effect of driving up other costs many times the assumed savings, like the old English adage: *penny wise, pound foolish,* or the more colloquial *"you get what you pay for."*

Cheap parts are usually just that – *cheap parts* that usually earn the stereotypical image of poor quality, which will add significant cost in the plant and cost even more if bad products get out, not to mention hazards to life and limb and loss of corporate reputations. A Wall Street Journal article published in 2001 had the headline: "Ford Says Last Years Quality Snafus Took Big Toll – Over $1 Billion in Profit." [29]

Even though quality disasters may look like infrequent anomalies, these costs must be included in the company's cost of quality metric, not just considered a one time "charge." Programs that aim to improve quality should be justified on their ability to prevent *all* quality costs, from an accumulation of many to "the big one."

Ford's enormous problem with tires is not surprising coming from an industry historically obsessed with bidding on part cost and later enthralled with on-line bidding. An Industry Week article described the procurement process for tires at Ford. Although the millions of recalled Firestone tires may have been made before these on-line auctions, the low-bidder paradigm has been prevalent in Detroit since before the time of Lopez. Here is a description of the tire bidding process in early 2000:

> *". . . five tire manufacturers participated in an auction earlier this year in which an initial bid was set by Ford and the tire suppliers then reverse bid downward to capture the business. 'Twelve hours later they were still bidding,' says Brian Buersmeyer, Ford's e-business planning manager. 'The suppliers kept lowering the cost. The market tension that created was dramatically different than the traditional buying processes.' "* [30]

In the 1990 J.D. Power rating of automobile reliability, Mercedes-Benz received the top rating. But by 2003, Mercedes' rank slipped to 26 out of 37 cars ranked.[31] One of the reasons for the drop in quality was cited by European analysts:

> *"Executives of what then was Daimler-Benz grew worried about escalating production costs in the early 90's. Executives then made a policy decision to start trimming costs by notching down specifications for many components."* [32]

Reduce Total Cost Instead of Focusing on Cheap Parts. In addition to the cost ineffectiveness of part bidding and its detrimental effects on relationships, there is the compelling argument that *other* cost categories provide much greater opportunities for real cost reduction, as is emphasized throughout this book. This presents many ways to minimize *total* cost; Chapter 7 presents easy ways to quantify total cost.

One of the cover stories of an Industry Week issue on B2B exchanges pointed out the disappointments of auction-based exchanges and how they distracted focus away from programs that promise real promise:

> *"Meanwhile, executives looking for big-time cost reductions could be in for major disappointments. Perhaps worse, the infatuation with auction-based first-generation exchanges threatens to sidetrack supply-chain management initiatives that offer the greatest promise for long-term results."* [33]

There are enormous opportunities to reduce total cost throughout the supply chain, without any negative consequences, by designing for manufacturability, specifying off-the-shelf parts, eliminating the costs of setup, inventory, and obsolescence and substantially reduce the costs of quality, distribution, and material overhead.

The Value of High Quality Parts. Receiving high quality parts is especially important to lean and build-to-order operations because:

(1) Dock-to-line deliveries count on "quality assured at the source" so that incoming inspections are not necessary and parts can go straight to all the points of use. This not only saves on the cost of incoming inspections, but also enables spontaneous resupply techniques.[34]

(2) One-piece-flow operations are more sensitive to failed parts "looping" back and disrupting the flow.

(3) Testing large batches of identical parts is not compatible with flexible operations.

(4) Having part quality assured at the source plus the continuous quality feedback of one-piece flow will enable lean plants to assure quality by process controls rather than expensive and time-consuming testing – or risky low-bidding.

(5) Raising the quality of *parts* improves *product* quality exponentially (Section 10.3).

Of course, there are suppliers that practice *kaizen* continuous improvement and *can* provide both high quality products at a low price. But because of their cooperative nature and "big picture" orientation, these companies would naturally align with customers who value long-term relationships instead of participating in the bidding process.

Another related trend is becoming apparent: The best suppliers are shunning B2B auctions. Philip L. Carter, professor of purchasing at Arizona State University, Temple, and executive director of the Center for Advanced Purchasing Studies (CAPS) concludes that: *"Manufacturers that are tempted to source key parts and materials through a trading exchange may find it difficult to connect with the most innovative, quality conscious vendors, since many likely will boycott the auction bidding process, viewing it 'as a margin-squeezing play,' "* [35]

6.12 MAXIMIZING FACTORY EFFICIENCY

Rapid product development can more quickly phase out older, more costly products with new generation cost-effective products. The older, less efficient products, in addition to having higher direct costs for labor and materials, have higher overhead demands for ECOs and firefighting. More efficient production, from better designed products, can result in more output from existing plants and equipment. For growing companies, this extra output might spare the company, or at least defer, the expense of adding new equipment or expanding facilities.

6.13 LOWERING OVERHEAD COSTS WITH FLEXIBILITY

Flexibility can reduce overhead costs significantly. There are some interesting parallels between flexibility and quality. Twenty years ago, it was commonly believed that quality cost more. Then Philip Crosby wrote the book, *Quality is Free,* and showed that the gains from lowering the cost of quality would pay for quality, thus making it free. Similarly, the financial gains derived from flexible operations can more than pay for the effort to make operations flexible. These gains will become a source of competitive advantage over competitors that do not embrace lean production, build-to-order, and mass customization.

There is a lot of *working capital* tied up in various forms of inventory: raw materials and parts inventory; Work-in-Process (WIP) inventory; and finished goods inventory in factory warehouses, at distributers, and at the dealers. Fortune Magazine estimates that, for Fortune 500 companies, working capital averages an amount equal to 20% of sales.[36]

Ironically, inventory shows up on the balance sheet as an *asset* when, in fact, inventory is really a *liability* to the operation of any manufacturing plant, especially those needing to be flexible. This point was one of the revelations presented in Eli Goldratt's *The Goal* when managers of the fictional plant, faced with extinction, realized that they had to focus on *the goal* (making money) instead of letting their behavior be dictated by irrelevant cost accounting metrics.[37]

One progressive materials manager of a processing equipment company told the author that after much successful work to reduce inventory, he got a call from the company Controller, who was having trouble preparing the annual report because the inventory had been reduced so much that it was "lowering company assets," according to their traditional accounting rules. Companies must make sure they are pursuing the real "goal" instead of irrelevant metrics.[38]

The following discussion presents several opportunities to lower the costs of inventory and other overhead costs by designing flexibility into products and plants.

6.14 MINIMIZING CUSTOMIZATION/CONFIGURATION COSTS

Many companies offer customized goods, but do not do it cost-effectively. By *mass* customizing products, the customization process is built into the system – the product design and the manufacturing operation. For more on mass customization, read the book, *Agile Product Development for Mass Customization.*[39]

Thus, the mass-customizer has cost advantage over companies that are inefficient at customization and configuration. Two under reported costs related to customization are custom engineering and changing/modifying standard designs and processes. Both of these activities usually cost much more than are indicated by current cost systems. Many companies do not even keep track of engineering costs by project. In addition, engineers often try to get a lot of "free" help from many support people who are "just on overhead."

The extra manufacturing cost to do *ad hoc* customization and configuration reactively is much more than it would be for mass customized products. These customization costs often include extra tooling, lengthy setups for small runs, inefficient production control, low equipment utilization, special programming, slow and frequent "learning curves," special tests and inspections, and lots of "fire drills" to shove customized products through mass production factories. Further, these low-volume customized products may disrupt the manufacturer of the standard products, thus increasing *their* cost. Thus, it is often the case, in companies with traditional accounting systems, that custom products are really being *subsidized* by the standard products.

6.15 MINIMIZING THE COST OF VARIETY

A large part of working capital is tied up in the cost of variety, which is discussed in depth in Chapter 3 of *Agile Product Development for Mass Customization*.[40] Eliminating setup and reducing the batch size to one eliminates most of the cost of variety.

The key element of lean production is set-up elimination. If setup could be eliminated, then operations would be flexible, meaning that every product could be different and, yet, still reap "mass production" efficiencies. In low-volume operations, setup could be caused by any effort to do something "different," for instance, to get parts, change dies and fixtures, download programs, find instructions, or any kind of manual measurement, adjustment, or positioning of parts or fixtures.

Work-in-Process inventory can be virtually eliminated by set-up reduction, JIT, and design commonality of parts and processes. WIP inventory costs rise proportional to batch size, except when the batch size is one, in which case WIP inventory can be virtually eliminated. WIP inventory carrying cost could be 25% of its value per year. Thus, eliminating WIP inventory could result in substantial savings.

Floor space can be reduced because of reduced inventories, elimination of the fork lift aisles necessary to move large batches of parts, elimination of kitting, and higher utilization of machinery and people. Appreciation of the cost or value of floor space varies according to the need to expand manufacturing. But floor space reduction should be constantly pursued. The cost of expanding manufacturing space is a very large step function that may force a company to move away from an area that is too crowded or expensive. Floor space reduction can provide an attractive alternative to expansion or relocation. Further, floor space requirements can be reduced faster than new facilities can be built. The lead time for physical plant expansion is so large that such plans must be started well ahead of the anticipated need, often based on inaccurate long-range marketing projections. Between 1991 and 1994, Compaq Computer quintupled production without increasing factory space by implementing programs like WIP inventory reduction.[41]

Internal transportation costs, such as fork lift activity, can be reduced. This can be eliminated when parts and products flow individually, between adjacent work stations, instead of in large, heavy bins between distant work stations.

Utilization is improved with less setup, thus reducing equipment cost, a very big cost savings potential for expensive equipment, like CNC machining centers, surface mount printed circuit assembly equipment, or expensive testers. Machine tool utilization can be as low as 10%, which means the equipment is only producing parts 10% of the time the machine is available for work; the remainder is setup or waiting. It is important to realize that *doubling the utilization rate will double output.* If production equipment had utilization of 30%, output could be *doubled* by raising the utilization to 60% and another 1.5 times by raising utilization to 90%. Utilization improvement is a cost-effective way to increase production, *and* it is quicker, considering the lead time to procure and install new production equipment.

Set-up labor expenses can be eliminated including the labor cost to change machine set-ups and to retrieve parts, tools, and drawings.

Flexibility can improve the balance of labor and machinery utilization in sequential operations such as assembly lines. Products built in flexible lines can be optimally ordered (product with high demands on the A process and low demands on the B process followed by product with low A and high B) to offset imbalances in the workloads of adjacent machinery or people, using a concept known as *product complementarity.*[42]

Production can quickly adapt to changing market conditions by building all the products on the same flexible line. Inflexible operations are always faced with a dilemma when the demand for "model A" has exceeded capacity while "model B" is having a sales slump. Manufacturing may have adequate overall capacity, but the model A line or plant will not be able to satisfy demand while the model B line or plant is partly idle or laying off people. A slightly more flexible approach would be to be able to move people from the "B" line to the "A" line, but that assumes adequate equipment capacity on line "A." Flexible operations would simply pull more model A products, and fewer model B products, through the flexible line(s).

Operational flexibility can allow companies to transfer production from one flexible line or plant to another to respond to changing market conditions, rather than the more expensive alternatives of overtime, rapidly bringing contract labor up to speed, and spontaneous outsourcing to ease production bottlenecks for the product that is in demand. Similarly, by transferring production, companies can avoid layoffs at plants making products in low demand. Mazda resolved such a dilemma by moving production of the popular Miata from its Hiroshima plant to the Hofu plant which was underutilized with Mazda 626 production. Because of manufacturing flexibility, Mazda could combine production of a niche sports car with a family sedan in the same plant to balance output at these two plants.[43]

Kitting cost and space can be eliminated. Without flexibility, there will be labor costs and space requirements to gather all the parts for a batch, "kit" them together and deliver them to manufacturing.

6.16 MINIMIZING MATERIALS MANAGEMENT COSTS

Purchasing costs can be reduced if there are fewer purchasing actions for fewer part types. Standardized parts will cost less because of the greater purchasing leverage of higher volume parts. Further, the "bread-truck" concept can be used where a supplier is responsible for keeping the bins full for common inexpensive parts, much like a bread truck keeps the shelves full in a grocery store.

Supplier fabrication and assembly are more feasible, and thus quicker and less costly, if parts are well designed *and* documented, especially if the supplier was part of the design team. Sometimes it may be more cost-effective to have the supplier design the parts, as is common now days in the automobile industry.

Fewer part numbers means less material overhead for raw materials and parts inventories, documentation, controls, etc. There will also be less expediting cost for seldom-used parts that are difficult to obtain. Pareto's law (the "80/20" rule) applied to inflexible plants would say that 80% of the material overhead costs would be consumed on low-usage parts that may only represent 20% of total part volume (see Appendix A on product line rationalization).

Spare parts logistics and field service can be greatly simplified, and thus cost less, with part standardization and modular design. Products designed around common parts have smaller spare parts kits. This could lower the effective product "price" for customers who add the cost of spare parts kits to the product's list price. Part standardization can also result in less downtime due to part shortages. Service costs can be reduced if failed modules can be quickly replaced and repaired in more efficient facilities.

6.17 MINIMIZING MARKETING COSTS

When manufacturers keep listening to customers' wants and needs and keep designing and manufacturing products to satisfy these evolving needs, this results in *learning relationships* which result in the ability to *keep customers forever.*[44] Not only is this good for generating revenue, but it also saves the considerable cost of acquiring new customers to meet growth objectives. Studies, such as one done by the Technical Assistance Resource Project for the U.S. Office of Consumer Affairs, show that the price of acquiring new customers is five times greater than the cost of keeping old ones.[45]

6.18 MINIMIZING SALES/DISTRIBUTION COSTS

There are considerable cost reduction opportunities in the warehousing and distribution of products. The physical distribution system accounted for 9.8 percent of the Gross National Product in 1994.[46]

Designing modular products and concurrently engineering products and production systems to build products on demand can save a lot of money with respect to the way products are configured, packaged, shipped, distributed, and sold. In fact, build-to-order can eliminate most of the distribution chain as we know it. Being able to build-to-order and ship from the plant eliminates warehousing and associated distribution costs from the plant to the customer.

In industries where product variety is considerable, like blue-jeans and shoes, this cost can be enormous, considering the number of sizes and styles. Sung Park, founder of Custom Clothing Technology Corporation in Newton, Mass., which developed the technology that Levi Strauss is using for its customized Personal Pair™ line, said, "You've got to look at the whole value chain. Zero inventory. No markdown. No distribution-centered costs. The product doesn't sit in the warehouse."[47]

6.19 MINIMIZING SUPPLY CHAIN COSTS

Supply chain management has become a strategic competitive advantage, especially for companies like for Hewlett-Packard.[48]

Peter Drucker points out the opportunities of minimizing cost in the supply chain: "Process-costing from the machine in the supplier's plant to the checkout counter in the store also underlies the phenomenal rise of Wal-Mart. It resulted in the elimination of a whole slew of warehouses and reams of paperwork, which slashed costs by a third."[49]

6.20 MINIMIZING LIFE CYCLE COSTS

An often neglected part of total costs is *life cycle* costs, which are those costs that are incurred over time, such as service, repair, maintenance, field failures, warrantee claims, legal liabilities, changes over the life of the product, and subsequent product developments. Products can be designed to minimize life cycle costs. The cost of changes can be minimized by a methodical product definition and thorough product development. Change costs and subsequent product development costs can be minimized with modular product architecture, where many modules can remain unchanged as other modules are updated or redesigned.

Designing for reliability can minimize many costs related to product reliability. There are several techniques that can be used to maximize reliability, which are presented in Chapter 10.

6.21 SAVING COST WITH BUILD-TO-ORDER

If products and production processes can be designed to build products to-order, then many costs can be saved:

Factory finished goods inventory can be eliminated by building products to order, instead of building to forecast and then holding products in a warehouse until ordered by distributers or customers. Like WIP inventory, finished goods inventory may cost the same to "carry" except that finished goods are completed and therefore are more valuable. Using 25% of value per year, $10 million worth of finished goods in inventory would cost $2.5 million per year to carry. Build-to-order can eliminate factory finished goods inventory and, thus, save its yearly inventory carrying cost.

Dealer finished goods inventory can be almost eliminated if resupply orders can be quickly filled and delivered to the customer. As with factory inventory, dealer inventory has a carrying cost. Even if the dealer/distributer is separate from the manufacturer, the carrying cost will have to be paid, ultimately by the customer. For example, an automobile dealer with 200 vehicles "in stock" with an average value of $20,000 each would represent $4 million worth of inventory. Using a yearly carrying cost of 25%, the carrying cost would be $1 million per year.

When new car prices exceed customers' ability to afford them, customers buy more used cars as a cost-effective alternative.[50] Built-to-order new automobiles could compete well against used cars, with lower prices, since the new cars could avoid dealer inventory expenses, whereas used cars must be stocked in inventory by definition.

Supply chain inventory can be minimized since build-to-order products do not need to be stocked at various warehouses along the supply chain: at distributers, consolidators, forwarders, etc. Similarly, a build-to-order system "pulls" parts from suppliers on a just-in-time basis, thus eliminating parts inventory along the supply chain. Regardless of who "pays" for this inventory, the customer ultimately must pay a higher price. Eliminating excessive supply chain inventory costs will allow customers to pay less for equivalent products.

Companies known for rapid deliveries, like Federal Express, are providing companies with "inventory-less" direct deliveries of parts and products to and from factories. After National Semiconductor commissioned Federal Express to run National's storage, sorting, and shipping activities, delivery time was reduced from 45 days to four days with an ultimate goal of 72 hours. At the same time, distribution costs have been reduced from 2.6% of revenue to 1.9%.[51] Adding the value of increased sales from customer satisfaction would make inventory-less distribution even more attractive.

Less interest expense will be incurred for expensive components in products that sell sooner because of the quicker throughput of flexible plants and the elimination of finished goods inventory.

Inventory write-offs can be eliminated because there would be no products in inventory that could deteriorate, or incur damage, or become obsolete. If there is a substantial finished goods inventory of an expensive product at the end of that product's life, the obsolescence write-off can be enormous.

Quicker transitions to new technology are possible if there are no older technology products waiting in inventory that must be sold first. Rosendo G. Parra, Group Vice President of Dell Computer Corporation, summarized the advantage of built-to-order for Dell: "We were probably the first vendor to transition into the new Pentium FPU processor, simply because we didn't have a hundred and some days of inventory out in distribution that we had to move first."[52]

BOM/MRP expenses could be minimized. Build-to-order could minimize overhead expenses with respect to generating bills-of-materials (BOMs) and translating forecasts into materials ordering requirements with MRP (Materials Requirement Planning) systems.

6.22 EFFECT OF COUNTERPRODUCTIVE "COST REDUCTION"

Companies will have a hard time achieving *real* cost reduction if they are trying "cost reduction" attempts that are, in fact, counterproductive:

- Manufacturing companies that offshore their manufacturing will have a hard time implementing Concurrent Engineering when there are no manufacturing people there to be "concurrent" with. In many offshoring situations, people in engineering and manufacturing are not even working at the same time. For more, see Section 2.8 (Co-Location), Section 4.8 (Outsourcing), and the articles on outsourcing[53] and offshoring.[54] at www.HalfCostProducts.com.

- Manufacturing companies that try to take cost out after the product is designed will find it difficult and a waste of resources, for reasons discussed in discussed in Section 6.1.

- Manufacturing companies who insisting on bidding custom parts, are, in effect, precluding vendor/partnerships and, thus, preventing those vendors from helping the company design the parts. The benefits of vender/partnerships are discussed in Section 2.6.

In companies that practice all three of the above, a very high percentage of product development resources will spend most of their time: making change orders to try to implement DFM (because it couldn't be done with Concurrent Engineering); trying to take cost out after the product is designed with change orders; converting documentation for outsourcing; getting outsourcer up to speed; dealing with quality and delivery problems; and so forth. In his travels, the author has encountered several companies that spend *two-thirds of product development resources* on the above three activities (which are cited at the bottom of the home page of www.HalfCostProducts.com under the heading "How Not to Lower Cost"), which really puts their future in doubt if that future depends on new product development.

ENDNOTES/REFERENCES

1. See "How Not to Lower Cost" (and the linked articles) on the bottom of the home page at www.HalfCostProducts.com.

2. Robert G. Atkins and Adrian J. Slywotzky, "You Can Profit From a Recession," *Wall Street Journal,* February 5, 2001, p. A22.

3. David M. Anderson, *Build-to-Order & Mass Customization,* (2004, 520 pages, CIM Press). See articles at www.build-to-order-consulting.com.

4. "A Smarter Way to Manufacture; How 'Concurrent Engineering' Can Reinvigorate American Industry," *Business Week,* April 30, 1990.

5. Phillip Crosby, *Quality is Free* (1979, Mentor Books).

6. James Womack, Daniel Jones, and Daniel Roos, *The Machine That Changed the World; The Story of Lean Production,* (1990, Rawson Associates; paperback: 1991, Harper Perennial,).

7. Kiyoshi Suzaki, *The New Manufacturing Challenge, Techniques for Continuous Improvement*, (New York, Free Press, 1987).

8. James H. Saylor, *TQM Field Manual,* (1992, McGraw-Hill), Chapters 3 (Continuous Improvement) and Chapter 4 (Continuous Improvement System).

9. Jordan D. Lewis, *The Connected Corporation, How Leading Companies Win Through Customer-Supplier Alliances,* (1995, Free Press), Ch. 8.

10. Womack, Jones, and Roos, *The Machine That Changed the World,* Ch. 6, "Coordinating the Supply Chain."

11. Lewis, *The Connected Corporation,* p. 38.

12. Peter F. Drucker, *Managing in a Time of Great Change,* (1995, Truman Talley Books/Dutton), p. 117.

13. Philip L. Carter, professor of purchasing at Arizona State University, Tempe, and executive director of the Center for Advanced Purchasing Studies, was cited in *Industry Week* (February 12, 2001, p. 43) as observing that "Many purchasing organization are under heavy pressure form the corporate brass to implement some form of e-commerce."

14. John H. Sheridan, 'Proceed with Caution," *Industry Week,* February 12, 2001, pages 38 - 44. One of the cover stories on Manufacturing Exchanges.

15. For more information on customized in-house DFM seminars, see page 407 of this book or *www.design4manufacturability.com/seminars.htm.*

16. Morgan & Liker, The Toyota Product Development System, Chapter 10, "Fully Integrate Suppliers into the Product Development System, , p. 200

17. "Smart Partner," *Business Week*; review of *The Connected Corporation* by Jordan D. Lewis.

18. Sydney Finkelstein, *Why Smart Executives Fail and What You Can Learn from Their Mistakes,* (2003, Portfolio/Penguin), p. 62.

19. Womack, Jones, & Roos, *The Machine that Changed the World, The Story of Lean Production,* 1990, Harper Perennial, p. 142.

20. Yasuhiro Monden, *The Toyota Production System*, Second Edition (1993, Institute of Industrial Engineers).

21. Womack, Jones, & Roos, *The Machine that Changed the World*, (1990, Harper Perennial), Chapter 6, "Coordinating the Supply Chain."

22. Ibid., p. 146.

23. Jeffrey Pfeffer and Robert I. Sutton, *The Knowing-Doing Gap; How Smart Companies Turn Knowledge into Action,* (2000, Harvard Business School Press), p. 23.

24. John Paul MacDuffie and Susan Helper, "Creating Lean Suppliers: Diffusing Lean Production through the Supply Chain," *California Management Review,* Summer 1997, pp. 118-150.

25. Robin Cooper, *When Lean Enterprises Collide,* (1995, Harvard Business Press), Chapter 9, "Interorganizational Cost Management Systems."

26. Anderson, *"Build-to-Order & Mass Customization."* See articles at www.build-to-order-consulting.com.

27. Jerry Useem, "Dot-Coms: What Have We Learned?" cover story, *Fortune,* October 30, 2000, p. 92.

28. "Lessons from the Dot-Com Crash," cover story, *Fortune,* October 30, 2000, p. R8

29. Gregory L. White, "Ford Says Last Years Quality Snafus Took Big Tool – Over $1 Billion in Profit," *Wall Street Journal,* January 12, 2001, p. A3.

30. *Industry Week*, August 21, 2000, p. 39.

31. Lee Hawkins, Jr. "Finding a Car That's Build to Last," *Wall Street Journal,* July 9, 2003, page D1.

32. John O'Dell, "Even Mercedes Hits a Few Speed Bumps," *Los Angeles Times,* July 13, 2003, pages C1 and C4.

33. John Sheridan, "Proceed with Caution," *Industry Week,* February 12, 2001, p. 38.

34. Anderson, *Build-to-Order & Mass Customization,* Chapter 7, "Spontaneous Supply Chain."

35. Ibid., p. 43.

36. Shawn Tully, "Raiding a Company's Hidden Cash," *Fortune Magazine,* August 22, 1994, page 82.

37. Eliyahu M. Goldratt, *The Goal,* (1992, North River Press, second revised edition), Ch. 33, p. 268.

38. Eli Goldratt's, *The Goal,* makes this point often about the need to do "what makes sense" to achieve "the goal" rather than basing decisions and actions on attempts to satisfy arbitrary performance metrics and cost

measurements that only make a small part of the system *appear* to look productive or cost-effective.

39. Anderson, *Build-to-Order & Mass Customization.* See articles at www.build-to-order-consulting.com

40. David M. Anderson, with an introduction by B. Joseph Pine II, *Agile Product Development for Mass Customization* (1997, McGraw-Hill), Ch. 3, Cost of Variety.

41. Ronald Henkoff, "Delivering the Goods," *Fortune,* November 28, 1994, p. 62

42. Marshall Fisher, Anjani Jain, and John Paul MacDuffie, "Strategies for Product Variety: Lessons From the Automobile Industry," Working paper from the Wharton School, University of Pennsylvania; page 26; January 16, 1994, p. 26

43. Ibid., page 31.

44. B. Joseph Pine, II, Don Peppers, and Martha Rogers, "Do You Want to Keep Your Customers Forever," *Harvard Business Review,* (March-April, 1995), p. 103.

45. Wilton Woods, "After All You've Done for Your Customers, Why Are They Still Not Happy," *Fortune,* (December 11, 1995), p. 180.

46. Robert V. Delaney, *Sixth Annual State of Logistics Report,* (St. Louis, MO, Cass Information Systems, June 5, 1995), Figure #8.

47. Niklas von Daehne, "Database Revolution," *Success,* v42, n4 (May, 1995), pp. 38-42.

48. Dr. Corey Billington, "Strategic Supply Chain Management," *OR/MS Today,* April 1994, pp. 20-27.

49. Peter F. Drucker, *Managing in a Time of Great Change,* (New York, Truman Talley Books/Dutton, 1995), p. 117.

50. Douglas Lavin, "Stiff Showroom Prices Drive More Americans to Purchase Used Cars," *Wall Street Journal,* November 1, 1994, page 1.

51. Ronald Henkoff, "Delivering the Goods," *Fortune,* Nov. 28, 1994, p. 64.

52. Niklas von Daehne, "Database Revolution," *Success,* v42, n4 (May 1995), pp. 38-42.

53. See the outsourcing article at the author's web-site www.HalfCostProducts.com/outsourcing.htm.

54. See the offshoring article at the author's web-site www.HalfCostProducts.com/offshore_manufacturing.htm.

7

TOTAL COST

7.1 TOTAL COST MEASUREMENT

In order to appreciate all of the cost savings and revenue enhancements cited in Chapter 6, it would be highly advantageous to be able to *quantify all costs*. If costs were tracked on a *total cost* basis, then the cost saving potential of well-designed products could be known, and products could be given appropriate overhead charges and thus competitive prices. However, if total cost is not tracked, then well-designed products may be assigned the same overhead as "loser" products, which is an unfair burden and may ultimately compromise the well-designed product's success.

Most companies have such inadequate cost systems that it actually hinders good product development and distorts product development decisions. Merely reporting labor and material costs encourages (sometimes forces) engineers to specify cheap parts and low-bidders to achieve "cost targets" and move manufacturing offshore, away from engineering, "to save cost," which, in reality, thwarts Concurrent Engineering.

Products with too much setup, inventory, "firefighting," engineering change orders, excessive parts variety, low equipment utilization, and high quality costs *should have* a higher overhead rate. Products that are designed, using the methodologies presented herein, for quick and easy manufacture should have a much lower overhead rate. Overhead *rates* should be proportional to overhead *demands*, which vary by product.

The ability to quantify total cost is one of the infrastructures that are important for Design for Manufacturability.

Let us consider the proverbial "Model-T plant" – a plant with only one product and no variations. The *Ernst & Young Guide to Total Cost Management*[1] discusses the cost management implications of a single product plant:

219

"If product variety were absent, the business environment would be simple . . . In a world like this, you could do product costing literally on the back of an envelop. You would simply divide the total production costs by the total production volume to calculate a unit cost."

However, as Cooper and Kaplan[2] pointed out in an article with the profound title, *How Cost Accounting Distorts Product Costs,* overhead costs "vary with the diversity and complexity of the product line." And, product diversity and complexity have gotten out of hand as companies keep *adding* products but *don't rationalize any away,* as discussed in Appendix A. Thus, it is important to quantify overhead costs, since they can be much greater than the typically reported costs of labor and materials.

7.2 QUANTIFYING OVERHEAD COSTS

There are four steps involved in quantifying overhead. The first is to acknowledge deficiencies in current product costing practices. The second step is to estimate the degree of cost distortions. The third step is to understand the value of total cost measurements. The final step is to implement total cost measurements.

A. Acknowledge Deficiencies of Traditional Accounting

The first step in quantifying overhead is to acknowledge the deficiencies in the current cost system, which is the central theme of Johnson and Kaplan's pivotal book, *Relevance Lot, The Rise and Fall of Management Accounting.*[3] Traditional cost accounting systems were designed to present operational results and the financial position of the organization *as a whole* for investors and for agencies that tax or regulate. On the other hand, managers and engineers need *relevant* cost information to make good decisions. Typical problems caused by conventional cost systems are:

Distortions in product costing, which is discussed at length in the Cooper and Kaplan reference cited above. Johnson and Kaplan concur:

"The management accounting system fails to provide accurate product costs. Costs get distributed to products by simplistic measures, usually direct-labor based, that do not represent the demands made by each product on the firm's resources."

The *Guide to Total Cost Management* asserts that product costs "are distorted because each product typically includes an assignment of overhead that was allocated on some arbitrary basis such as direct labor, sales dollars, machine hours, material cost, units of production, or some other volume measure." [4]

Distorted product costing results in distorted pricing that can underprice some products so low that they actually lose money and overprice other products to the point where they are uncompetitive.[5] Distorted product costing results in a distorted perception of the profitability of all the company's products. This distorted view of profitability can cause managers to "feed the problems and starve the opportunities" with detrimental effects on product development priorities. Understanding *the real* profitability will allow companies to drop unprofitable products and focus on profitable ones.

Cross subsidies, where high-volume products subsidize low-volume products and standard products subsidize custom products. Johnson and Kaplan state unequivocally:

> *"The standard product cost systems, which are typical of most organizations, usually lead to enormous cross-subsidies across products,"* [6]

Cooper, Kaplan, et. al., in their Institute of Management Accountants sponsored study, summarized what their eight case study manufacturing organizations discovered after they implemented total cost measurements:

> *"The manufacturing companies generally found, as expected, that low-volume, complex products tended to be much more expensive than had been calculated by the existing standard cost system."* [7]

One of the most dangerous consequences of cross-subsidies is penalizing new generation DFM products and programs like build-to-order and mass customization by making them pay the same overhead charges that should have been paid only by the products that have the high overhead demands. Such unfair charges could ultimately thwart new generation products and programs.

Relevant decision making. Good decisions are the keys to success in any business venture, and this especially applies to product development. Unfortunately, many managers and engineers try to make decisions by the numbers, when the numbers are misleading or even irrelevant. Again quoting Johnson and Kaplan:

"Ironically, as management accounting systems became less relevant and less representative of the organization's operations and strategy, many companies became dominated by senior executives who believed they could run the firm 'by the numbers'." [8]

Again quoting the Ernst and Young Guide:

"If the costs are wrong, then all decisions about pricing, product mix, and promotion could be undermining long-term profitability."

Johnson and Kaplan state that accurate, relevant numbers, based on total cost, can lead to much better decision making:

"The management accounting system also needs to report accurate product costs so that pricing decisions, introductions of new products, abandonments of obsolete products, and responses to the appearance of rival products can be made with the best possible information on product resource demands." ". . . An ineffective management accounting system can undermine even the best efforts in product development, process improvement, and marketing policy." [10]

Cost Management. Since one of the major challenges of Design for Manufacturability is to produce products at low cost despite the other challenges of speed and quality, cost management takes on a new level of importance. But conventional cost management systems are of little help here:

"Management accounting reports are of little help to operating managers attempting to reduce cost and improve productivity." [11]

Downward spirals. Cost accounting distortions can cause "reinforcing" behavior (reinforcing loops) that can cause a business to "spiral down." The concept of reinforcing loops was presented by Peter Senge in his book, *The Fifth Discipline.*[12] Companies making both high-volume and low-volume products, as pointed out by the above cost management references, really do have different overhead demands. However, if overhead is spread "like peanut butter," then the following spiral will occur, as shown in Figure 7-1.

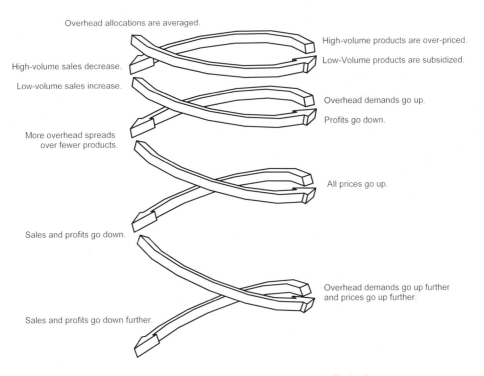

Overhead allocations are averaged.

High-volume products are over-priced.

High-volume sales decrease.

Low-Volume products are subsidized.

Low-volume sales increase.

Overhead demands go up.

Profits go down.

More overhead spreads
over fewer products.

All prices go up.

Sales and profits go down.

Overhead demands go up further
and prices go up further.

Sales and profits go down further.

Figure 7-1: Cost Distortion Downward Spiral

Thus, the loop reinforces and the company continues to "spiral down." This may drag a company down to the point of unprofitability, or weaken an otherwise strong company.

B. Estimate the degree of cost distortions

- Subjectively draw conclusions about how much cost distortion is probably occurring when overhead is spread "like peanut butter."

- Conduct a pilot investigation to quantify one worst case product cost distortion. Choose a low volume or seldom built product suggested by the product line rationalization (Appendix A). Use polls and surveys to narrow the search by asking manufacturing people to *vote* on a candidate.

C. Understand the value of total cost measurements

Total cost measurements can be extremely valuable for the following:

- It is essential to know the relative profitability of existing products in order to identify:
    - The most profitable products and market segments, which should be the basis for product development prioritization and resource allocations.
    - The least profitable products to rationalize away (Appendix A).
- Decisions to redesign a product to lower cost.
- A basis for sales incentives based on profitability instead of volume or sales.
- Standardization: justifying, encouraging, and quantifying total cost savings.
- Decisions on designing parts or buying then off-the-shelf.
- Integration of silicon (VLSI, ASICs) and structures (part combinations).
- Knowing the total cost of "cost reduction" efforts which may then free up resources so they can save more money through product development, lean production, quality improvement programs, and so forth.
- Justifying design tools, training, and overhead reduction programs.
- Justifying automation and CNC machine tools.
- Decisions on local integration or outsourcing/offshoring.
- How to best handle variety, configuration, and customization.
- Investing now in the development of hardware and software modules that will benefit future product developments.
- Identify products that are losing money or have very low margins, which will encourage more objective pricing and greatly help rationalization efforts (Appendix A).

7.3 RESISTANCE TO TOTAL COST ACCOUNTING

Despite the deficiencies pointed out earlier about traditional cost systems and case study testimonials, like the one cited above, many managers resist company-wide ABC implementation. This stems from a general resistance to change based on the following misconceptions. Many managers:

1) **Do not accept the deficiencies** in the current system. This was the topic of the first section of this discussion on total cost accounting. Many of the books referenced in this section make thorough arguments about this point, especially Johnson and Kaplan's *Relevance Lost, The Rise and Fall of Management Accounting.* [13]

2) **Underestimate the benefit.** This chapter and Chapter 6 reinforce the value of relevant cost numbers as a basis for good decision making, in general, and, specifically for decisions governing product line rationalization, standardization efforts, implementing manufacturing flexibility, and many aspects of product development.

3) **Overestimate the effort** to make any improvements. Sometimes resistance comes from horror stories that some formal "Activity Based Costing" programs have been so cumbersome that they have died under their own weight. However, the low-hanging-fruit approach, presented in Section 7.8, quickly generate benefits without consuming a lot of time and resources.

7.4 TOTAL COST THINKING

Even before any formal total cost accounting programs are implemented, companies can improve some decisions subjectively by using *total cost thinking.* The principles presented in this chapter can help individuals make better subjective decisions by correcting many misconceptions about cost and instilling the proper attitudes and beliefs.

But, in order for this to happen, the corporate culture must encourage this. Management policies can either encourage or discourage this. If all proposals must meet strict criteria for payback and ROI (return on investment), this will govern the decision making process. If the criteria are based on traditional cost accounting, then the decisions will tend to be governed by irrelevant numbers (mentioned above) and many truly good proposals will fail to win approval, because much of their benefit comes from benefits that are not quantifiable by the current system. If companies rigidly adhere to criteria based on incomplete costs, then attempts to inject subjective total cost decision making will fail, even if it is in the best interest of the company and its customers.

One subjective approach to this dilemma was proposed by Robert Kaplan in the article about justifying Computer Integrated Manufacture (CIM): *Must CIM be Justified by Faith Alone?*[14] Kaplan's technique to "work around" deficiencies in accounting systems was to:

1) compute how much the proposal fell short of the objective criteria: the *shortfall*

2) summarize the "intangible" benefits (all the benefits that could not be quantified)

3) pose the question, "Is it worth the shortfall to gain all these intangible benefits?"

One of the examples of part standardization, cited in Chapter 5, was the author's effort to standardize all resistors to 1% tolerance to replace the previous duplication of resistors in both 1% and 5% tolerance versions. There were no numbers available to justify the change. But it "just made sense" to cut in half the number of resistors in all three factories. Subsequently, the author has learned of people who did the same part consolidation and concluded quantitatively that the purchasing power of the combined orders offset the "cost" of the higher tolerance. Thus, all the variety cost savings would go straight to the bottom line.

Sometimes, subjective decisions must be made *in spite of the numbers*. One of the author's clients, who makes water meters, consolidated seven raw castings into three by adding extra brass (for test ports) to every product whether or not they needed the optional tapped holes. This extra material appeared to add cost to some of the raw castings because of the extra brass was not needed for test ports. In fact, the person who did the change felt like he would be "beat up" for raising the "standard cost." But, company management supported the change, knowing subjectively that it would lower the cost of variety enough to be a net gain and make operations more flexible.

Management policies can encourage total cost thinking by *empowering* product development team leaders to make the best decisions, in their judgement, instead of trying to *limit bad decisions* by making them pass some predetermined threshold based on irrelevant numbers. Empowerment is part of the team approach to product development.

7.5 IMPLEMENTING TOTAL COST ACCOUNTING

Total cost accounting focuses on the *activities* performed to produce products so formal programs were called *Activity Based Costing*, although much easier techniques are now available, as presented in Section 7.8. Costs are either assigned directly to products or to activities, which are then assigned to products based on how much of these activity costs were incurred by each product.

Total cost measurement systems are *not* intended to replace the existing finance system. In most cases, these implementations create independent decision making models. In the study that Cooper, Kaplan, et. al. did for the Institute of Management Accountants, this was the case:

"No modifications to existing financial systems were required, and companies continued to run all their existing systems in parallel with their new ABC model." "The activity-based model was treated as a management information system, not as part of the accounting system."[15]

The numbers from this model were more useful than that available form the existing cost system:

"Managers found the numbers generated from the activity-based analysis more credible and relevant than the numbers generated from the official costing system."

7.6 COST DRIVERS

In any change process, there is always some "low-hanging fruit," which is always a good place to start to get some early results with little effort. Success in these high-leverage areas can then generate more interest and support for more ambitious efforts. The low-hanging fruit approach is also a good way to start the change process if there is a lack of widespread support.

In ABC implementation, the low-hanging fruit is the identification and implementation of simple *cost drivers* that make cost accounting more accurate and relevant and encourage behavior to lower these costs. Cost drivers are defined as the *root causes* of a cost – the things that "drive" cost. Identifying cost drivers makes the root causes visible and this has two important consequences.

1) Total cost can be measured

2) The behavior that actually lowers total cost can be encouraged

The cost driver approach identifies key drivers of cost that should be quantified instead of lumped in with all other overhead. The cost driver approach is easy to implement and starts with the most important overhead costs that need to be quantified. New data collection efforts are focused on only a few key cost drivers. Cost drivers can be based on estimates, as long as there is universal consensus. Cost drivers can provide a more rational basis for performance measures.

For example, the *activities* that incur the following costs could be analyzed for significant ranges beyond the averages that usually are the basis for overhead allocation.

- Engineering Change Order costs

- Material overhead

- Quality costs, scrap, rework, and other non-value-added activities

- Inventory costs and inventory related costs

- Setup costs

- Equipment utilization

- Process yields, scrap, rework, etc.

- Costs of field service, repairs, warrantees, claims, litigation, etc.

The activities that cause these costs should be analyzed to find out what is causing the variation. Experience managers will probably be able to identify the key cost drivers that are *driving* difference in these activities, for instance:

- Volume: high volume or low volume

- Degree of customization: standard or custom

- Part standardization: approved or preferred

- Part destination: for production products or spare parts for products that are out of production

- Distribution costs: direct or through channels

- Product age: launching, stabilized, or aging (experiencing processing incompatibilities with newer products and/or availability challenges for parts and raw materials)

- Market niches: commercial, OEM, military, medical, and nuclear markets have varying demands for quality, paperwork, proposals, reports, certifications, traceability, etc.

Those activities that incur difference costs from the variations in these cost drivers should be investigated. The costs of these activities should be charged accordingly. For instance, if low-volume products do incur more cost than high-volume products, then this should be reflected in the overhead allocation. If standard parts do incur less material overhead, then they should be charged a lower overhead, as will be shown in the next examples. If certain operations incur more overhead than others, then the cost drivers should reflect this, as will be shown in the following examples.

Intel's Systems Group. When the author implemented a parts standardization effort, using the procedure described in Chapter 5, the result was that 500 "commonality" parts were identified as being preferred for new designs. These common parts really did deserve lower material overhead than the 13, 000 remaining "approved" parts because they were purchased in higher quantities. And the standardization program wanted to encourage engineers to use these parts. To accomplish both these goals, the Accounting Department structured material overhead into a two tiered system: one rate for the 13,000 approved parts and a lower rate for the 500 commonality parts. This reflected greater "material world" efficiencies and encouraged usage.

Tektronix Portable Instruments Division. To encourage part commonality and assign accurate material overhead, Tektronix assigned a material rate that was inversely proportional to volume. Thus, a high volume part had a very low overhead rate; conversely, a "low runner" was assigned a very high rate.[16]

HP Roseville Network Division (RND). HP RND formerly had only two cost drivers for its printed circuit board assembly: direct labor hours and the number of insertions. A special survey showed that axial insertions were about one-third the cost of DIP insertions; manual insertion was three times as expensive as automation; and "low availability" parts had an additional cost of ten times their materials cost. So they implemented the following nine unit-based cost drivers.[17]

1. Axial insertions   6. Solder joints
2. Radial insertions   7. Boards count
3. DIP insertions   8. Part count
4. Manual insertions   9. Number of slots
5. Test hours

HP Boise Surface Mount Center (BSMC) implemented the following ten cost drivers for surface mount printed circuit board manufacture.[18] Note driver number seven which encourages part commonality.

<u>Cost Pools</u>	<u>Drivers</u>
1. Panel Operations	Percent of a whole panel; if one panel contains four individual boards, then each board is charged 25% of the panel rate
2. Small component placement	Number of "small" components placed
3. Medium component placement	Number of "medium" components placed
4. Large component placement	Number of "large" components placed
5. Thru-hole component insertion	Number of leaded components inserted
6. Hand load component placement	Minutes required to place all components that must be hand loaded rather than automatically placed on the board
7. Material procurement & handling	Number of unique parts in the board
8. Scheduling	Number of scheduling hours during a six-month period
9. Assembly setup	Number of minutes of setup time during a six-month period
10. Test & rework	Number of "yielded" minutes of test & rework time per board

Figure 7-2 shows the changes in product costing after implementing these cost drivers. Note that one-third of the products had their costs go down and two-thirds had their costs go up, with one product doubling in cost!

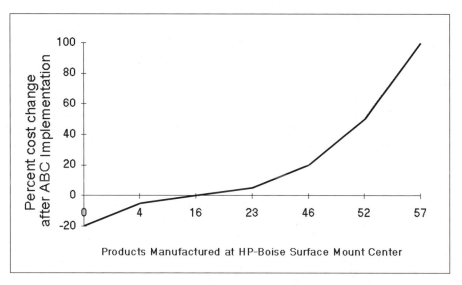

Figure 7-2: Changes in Cost after Implementing ABC

Results: "Accountants now provide important inputs into product design and development decisions. Under the prior cost system, all overhead was applied as a percent of direct material cost, and it was difficult to understand how changing a board's design would change manufacturing costs. Also, designers had little motivation to optimize the board for efficient production. With ABC, however, the cost system attempts to mirror the manufacturing process, so that engineers and production managers easily can see how design changes will affect cost."[19]

7.7 TRACKING PRODUCT DEVELOPMENT EXPENSES

Some companies fail to collect important information, such as tracking product development expense, since they feel that they cannot ask engineers to keep track of which projects they work on. Many engineers do, in fact, resist such rigor. But such information is extremely important for making good decisions about product development and product costing. In fact, engineering labor accountability may be the biggest gap in total cost accounting program. The solution to this apparent dilemma is as follows:

1) **Emphasize the importance** of the information, using all the reasoning presented herein and in the references. Some experts in the field argue that "an organization's cost accounting system can actually make or break an otherwise sound business." [20]

2) **Make it easy** to keep track of engineering time. It is better to have an approximate accountability than nothing at all. One division of Hewlett-Packard used the "bowling score" method to track engineering effort. The engineers are provided a form with lines for all the projects they may be working on. At the right of each line, there is a square box. An engineer, who worked all day on one project, would enter the bowling mark for a "strike." An engineer, who worked on two or more projects, would enter the symbol for "spare" on each of them. Here is how the system worked in practice: Engineers agreed to cooperate because the system was easy. But, since engineers are inherently precise, they eventually "corrected" the impreciseness of the system and voluntarily began to fill in more precise entries like hours or percent time worked.

3) **Make it required.** Total cost measurements depend on adequate data input. If senior management decides this is an important initiative, then everyone in the company will have to participate. Emphasizing the importance and making it easy will certainly make any mandates more easily implemented and ultimately more effective.

7.8 "abc" – The *Low Hanging Fruit* Approach

An excellent "how-to" book oriented toward cost-effective ABC implementations is Douglas Hicks' *Activity-Based costing for Small and Mid-Sized Businesses.* It is based on the valid premise that *it is better to be approximately correct than to be precisely wrong; accuracy is preferable to precision.*[21] Said another way, it would be better to be *approximately right* than *precisely wrong!* Knowing that a product has a negative profit margin between -55% and -65% is more valuable than *thinking* it has a positive profit margin of exactly 10.89%. Hicks claims that the false pursuit of precision in product costing is unrealistic: "No cost accounting system provides an organization with precision. *All* product costing is approximate. *All* cost systems contain too many estimates and allocations to be precise." [22]

With this focus on relevancy over precision, it is easier to implement this approach than the "full-blown" ABC, especially for smaller companies. Hicks calls this "activity based costing" with the lower case acronym, "abc," which he describes as follows:[23]

"In abc, activities are defined as *groups of related processes or procedures that together meet a particular work need of the organization. Under this definition, the activities of the Accounts Payable department would most likely be Accounts Payable. Period."*

Hicks makes similar arguments for treating the entire purchasing function as an activity, instead of identifying all the activities in purchasing. Many purchasing costs are avoided by *kanban* and "bread truck" deliveries. In addition fewer types of parts ordered in larger quantities reduces purchasing costs and increases purchasing leverage. The study published in *Just-in-Time Purchasing* reported that JIT users expected to cut expediting effort by a factor of three.[24]

If good quantitative data is lacking, it would be preferable to implement some of the following shortcuts than to continue with grossly inaccurate allocations. One of these shortcuts is to *estimate* the percentage of an activity's cost caused by a particular cost driver, for instance, high-volume products compared to low-volume products. Thus, instead of averaging the cost allocation where all products get the same charge, the low-volume products would be charged, say, 80% and the high-volume products 20% (for the typical Pareto effect).

Hicks presents a simplified approach to implementing abc, with the emphasis on accuracy and relevance rather than precision. He proposes an abc cost model in a format suitable for spreadsheets, like Excel.

An alternative to creating a model on a spreadsheet would be software specifically developed for ABC analysis. The eight case studies, cited in the Institute of Management Accountants ABC study, all used such software packages on PCs.[25]

Implementing "abc"

Understand the importance of total cost measurements for relevant costing, pricing, and decision making. For any "cost reduction" program, the measurement of cost is just as important than the steps to reduce cost because total cost measurements:

- helps the company make the right strategic decisions that will be most effective

- keeps directing behavior that will continually reduce cost

- quantifies the real cost savings (or losses), which then affect subsequent decisions

The drive for implementing abc should come from the most *motivated* group while the implementation could be by the most *willing and able* group, which may or may not be the Finance Department.

Approach and label the program in a way that mitigates resistance and generates support. If "Activity Based Costing" is not an appropriate label, it could be called something like a "Costing" or "Decision Making" model.

Identify the *cost drivers* of activities that should be quantified instead of lumped in with other overhead.

Roll the quantified cost driver data into the total cost model. Keep it up to date.

Make sure the total cost information is readily accessible, easily understood, used for all cost-based reporting, and the basis for decision-making.

7.9 IMPLEMENTATION EFFORTS

Most companies do not need a system as complex as would be needed for the multinational mega-corporation, despite misconceptions to the contrary. Implementing some degree of total cost measurements can be achieved with modest resources. Of the eight companies that implemented ABC in the Institute of Management Accounts study, the companies that used "medium involvement" of outside consultants took an average 6.5 months by 2.1 FTEs (full-time equivalent workers) to implement the ABC model. Companies that used "active involvement" of consultants took an average of three months by 1.6 FTEs.[26]

One practitioner reported that efforts to implement basic ABC have "ranged from 80 hours for a small commercial printer to 500 hours for a large automotive supplier with very poor historical financial and operating records."[27]

The implementation chapter (11) has a section summarizing "Total Cost Measurement Implementation," Section 11.10.

7.10 TYPICAL RESULTS OF TOTAL COST IMPLEMENTATIONS

When ABC is implemented, companies start to see the real picture about product cost, which is often surprising. Cooper, Kaplan, et. al. refer to the "typical ABC pattern," where several offerings are shown to be highly profitable, most at or near breakeven profitability, and a few highly unprofitable.[28] A Schrader-Bellows case study[29] showed that, out of seven products originally thought to be profitable, three actually were, one was barely breaking even, and three were unprofitable, with one highly unprofitable. And the plant could not eliminate that unprofitable product until the costing changed (see Section A-6).

Total cost analyses often adjust manufacturing costs up for most products, while lowering them only for a few "deserving" products. After HP implementing the nine cost drivers cited above, they found that 72% of the products were really costing more than assumed, as shown in Figure7-2. Cost adjustments ranged from slightly lower to double![30]

ENDNOTES/REFERENCES

1. Michael R. Ostrenga, Terrence R. Ozan, Robert D. McIlhattan, and Marcus D. Harwood, *The Ernst & Young Guide to Total Cost Management*, (1992, John Wiley & Sons).

2. Robin Cooper and Robert S. Kaplan, "How Cost Accounting Distorts Product Costs," *Management Accounting*, April, 1988.

3. H. Thomas Johnson & Robert Kaplan, *Relevance Lost, The Rise and Fall of Management Accounting,"* (1991, Harvard Business School Press).

4. Ostrenga, Ozan, McIlhattan, and Harwood, *The Ernst & Young Guide to Total Cost Management.*

5. Douglas T. Hicks, *Activity-Based Costing for Small and Mid-Sized Businesses, An Implementation Guide,* (1992, John Wiley), p. 20. Note that a second edition of this book was published in 1998, *Activity Based Costing; Making it Work for Small and Mid-Size Businesses.*

6. Johnson and Kaplan, *Relevance Lost.*

7. Robin Cooper, Robert S. Kaplan, Lawrence S. Maisel, Eileen Morrissey, Ronald M. Oehm, *Implementing Activity-Based Cost Management,* (1992, Institute of Management Accounts, Montvale, NJ), p. 4.

8. Johnson and Kaplan, *Relevance Lost.*

9. Ostrenga, Ozan, McIlhattan, and Harwood, *The Ernst & Young Guide to Total Cost Management*, p. 146.

10. Johnson and Kaplan, *Relevance Lost.*

11. Ibid.

12. Peter M. Senge, *The Fifth Discipline, The Art and Practice of The Learning Organization,* (1990, Doubleday/Currency).

13. Johnson and Kaplan, *Relevance Lost.*

14. Robert S. Kaplan, "Must CIM be justified by Faith Alone?" *Harvard Business Review,* (March-April, 1986), p. 87.

15. Cooper, Kaplan, Maisel, Morrissey, Oehm, *Implementing Activity-Based Cost Management,* p. 7.

16. Robin Cooper and Peter B. B. Turney, "Internally Focused Activity-Based Costing Systems," *Measures of Manufacturing Excellence,* edited by Robert S. Kaplan (1990, Harvard Business School Press), pp. 292 - 293.

17. Ibid., pp. 294-296.

18. Mike Merz, Professor of Accounting at Boise State University, and Arlene Harding, Finance Supervisor at HP BSMC, "ABC Puts Accountants on Design Team at HP," *Management Accounting,* (September 1993), pp. 22 - 27.

19.Ibid., pp. 22 - 27.

20. Hicks, *Activity-Based Costing for Small and Mid-Size Businesses*, p. 14.

21. Ibid., p. 7.

22. Ibid., p. 8

23. Ibid., p. 35.

24. A. Ansari and B. Modarress, *Just-In-Time Purchasing,* (New York, Free Press, 1990), p. 44.

25. Cooper, Kaplan, Morrissey, and Oehm, *Implementing Activity-Based Cost Management,* pp. 6, 25, and 256.

26. Ibid., p. 296.

27. Hicks, *Activity-Based Costing for Small and Mid-Sized Business,* p. 9.

28. Cooper, Kaplan, Morrissey, and Oehm, *Implementing Activity-Based Cost Management,* p. 5.

29. The Schrader-Bellows case study is described in Harvard Business School Case Series 9-186-272; A summary of the findings appears in "How Cost Accounting Distorts Product Costs," by Robin Cooper and Robert S. Kaplan, *Management Accounting,* (April, 1988).

30. Merz and Hardy, "ABC Puts Accountants on Design Team at HP," *Management Accounting,* September 1993, pp. 22 - 27.

DFM GUIDELINES FOR PRODUCT DESIGN

This chapter lists some general guidelines for *product* design strategy and deals with assembly strategy, fastening strategy, assembly motions and test strategy. These guidelines should be considered in the *earliest* checklist when using checklists grouped by phases or review events.

8.1 GUIDELINE NUMBERING SYSTEM

Guidelines throughout this book will use the following guideline numbering system for instructional clarity. Each company is encouraged to develop the numbering system optimal for its operations. Several categories of guidelines allow adding new guidelines to the appropriate category rather than at the end of a single list. If new guidelines are added next to related ones, they will be considered together when the designer is dealing with that subject. In this way newer guidelines will be less likely to be overlooked than if they were just added to the end of one list of guidelines.

Prefix   Category

A   Assembly strategy

F   Fastening

M   Motions of assembly

T   Test

S   Standardization

P   Part shape

H   Handling by automation

Q   Quality and reliability

R   Repair and Maintenance

If guidelines are to be used in checklists, they should be worded to optimize usefulness as checklists. Guidelines should then ask if the guideline has been obeyed or how much the product deviates from a certain goal, say, zero or 100%.

8.2 ASSEMBLY GUIDELINES

A1) Understand manufacturing problems/issues of current/past/related products

In order to learn from the past and not repeat past mistakes, it is important to understand all problems and issues with current and past products with respect to manufacturability, introduction into production, quality, repairability, serviceability, regulatory test performance, and so forth. This is especially true if previous engineering is being "leveraged" into new designs.

A2) Design for easy fabrication, processing, and assembly

Designing for easy parts fabrication, material processing, and product assembly is a primary design consideration. Even if labor "cost" is reported to be a small percentage of the selling price, problems in fabrication, processing, and assembly can generate enormous costs, cause production delays, and demand the time of precious resources.

A3) Eliminate overconstraints to minimize tolerance demands

An overconstraint happens whenever there are more constraints than the minimum necessary, for instance, joining two rigid frames with four bolts, guiding a rigid platform on four rigidly mounted bearings, or trying to precisely align two parts with multiple round pins inserted into round holes (the solutions for both are shown below).

Overconstraints are costly and can cause quality problems and compromise functionality because the design will work only if all parts are fabricated to tight, maybe unrealistic, tolerances.

Fortunately, overconstraints are easy to avoid by specifying the exact number of constraints that will do the job: not enough constraints will result in an extra degree-of-freedom (something is loose); too many constraints will result in troublesome overconstraints. Here are some solutions:

- **Mount bearing housings or rigid members to each other on *three points, not four.*** Unless the tolerances are perfect for a four-point mount, three will determine the position and the fourth will try to warp both structures.

- **For critical alignment of parts use round/diamond pins.** Use pairs of inexpensive but tight-tolerance dowel pins to locate critical parts. Matching tight-tolerance hole diameters can be made easily with reamers. To eliminate the tolerance match problem between holes, use one round pin to locate in "x" and "y" dimensions and a *diamond* pin to locate the angle from the round pin. The diamond is precision ground to locate in the angle direction, but is relieved in the direction of the hole spacing. Although this technique was developed to locate tooling, it can be also useful for aligning parts for assembly as shown in Figure 8-1.

ROUND PIN   DIAMOND PIN

Figure 8-1: Alignment Using Round and Diamond Pins

A4)   Provide unobstructed access for parts *and* tools

Each part must not only be designed to fit in its destination location, but also must have an assembly path for entry into the product. This motion must not risk damage to the part or product and, of course, must not endanger workers.

Equally important is access for *tools and the tool operator* whether that is a worker or robot arm, which usually requires more access room than a worker's hand. Access may be needed for screwdrivers, wrenches, welding torches, electronic probes, and so forth. Remember that workers may be assembling these products all day long and having to go through awkward contortions to assemble each product can lead to worker fatigue, slow throughput, poor product quality, and even worker injury.

Access is also needed for field repair where the tools may be simpler and, maybe bulkier.

A5)   Make parts independently replaceable

Products with independently replaceable parts are easier to repair because the parts can be replaced without having to remove other parts first. The order of assembly would be more flexible since parts can be added in any order. This could be a valuable asset in times of shortages, in which case the rest of the product could be built and the hard-to-get part added when it arrives.

A6)   Order assembly so the most reliable goes in first; the most likely to fail go in last

If parts must be added sequentially, make sure that the most likely to fail are the easiest to remove. This is important for both factory assembly *and* field repair.

A7)   Make sure options can be added easily

Another advantage of independently replaceable parts is the ease of adding options later, either in the factory or in the field. Future options should be *anticipated* and the product should be designed to accept these options. Considerations include allowing space for added parts, mounting holes, part access, tool access, software reconfiguration, and, of course, the safety of those performing the upgrade.

A8)   Ensure the product's life can be extended with future upgrades

Early consideration of the product upgrading strategy could be crucial to extending the life of a product. Advances in technology should be anticipated so the product can be upgraded without a complete redesign. Modular design concepts can be used to allow modules that are prone to obsolescence to be replaced with upgraded ones. Extending product life through upgrading allows products generate even more profit after the development and introduction costs have been paid off. Figure 3-3 shows the value of upgrades.

A9)   Structure the product into modules and subassemblies, as appropriate

The use of subassemblies can streamline manufacturing since subassemblies can be built *and* tested separately. Subassemblies could be built in specialized departments, which is especially advantageous if those processes are different from those of the product, for instance, clean room assembly (assembly in a dust-free room).

If the entire product consists of a collection of pretested subassemblies, product testing may be eliminated or reduced to only a final go/no-go test before product shipment. In designs where potential quality problems are concentrated in one subassembly, test and diagnostic attention could be focused there. The remainder of the product may then rely on process controls.

Products built from subassemblies are easier to repair in the factory and in the field by simply replacing the defective subassembly, which can be then sent back to its specialized assembly area for repairs.   See the discussion on modular design in Section 4.7.

A10)   Use adhesives as a last resort

If justified, make a thorough selection, be sure to optimize part alignment and repair strategy, standardize on one adhesive per workstation (to avoid picking the wrong one), and standardize on the same application procedure (to avoid procedural errors).

A11)   Use press fits as a last resort

Press fits add tolerance challenges to both parts; this is a high potential for things going wrong; successful assembly and operation may be sensitive to temperature, cleanliness, procedures, etc.; and parts can't be successfully taken apart for service or recycling.

The first design step is to thoroughly pursue alternatives first. If justified: plan for the optimal alignment, guidance, pressing forces, etc.; ensure mating parts do not scrape, gouge, or bind; assure engaging surfaces are free of contaminants; specify only one fixture and procedure per workstation; optimize interference/tolerance design; and assure tolerances of mating parts

More assembly guidelines (on error prevention) are presented in Chapter 10.

8.3 FASTENING GUIDELINES

F1)   Use the minimum number of total fasteners

Fasteners may represent only about 5% of the products *direct material cost*, but all the associated labor costs can reach 75% of total assembly costs.[1] Parts must be aligned before fastening, fasteners must be found and positioned, the tool has to be positioned, torque has to be applied *properly,* and the tool may need to be changed for the next job. Further, fasteners have to be ordered and delivered to the point of use. The fasteners themselves may need to be assembled (e.g., bolts to washers). In some cases, assembling with fasteners may be difficult or impossible for robots or other automation.

F2)   Use fewer large fasteners rather than many small fasteners

To help accomplish the objective of Guideline F1, designers can specify fewer large fasteners instead of several small ones. Since each fastener takes roughly the same effort to supply and install, fewer larger fasteners could be a cost-effective way to reduce assembly cost. Of course, designers must make sure that strength and function will be adequate and that damage will not result from the greater gripping force possible with larger fasteners.

F3)   Maximize fastener standardization with respect to:

• fastener part numbers

• fastener tools

• fastener torque settings

Fastener standardization is easy to implement and has enormous benefits to manufacturing: fewer parts to order, receive, log in, stock, issue, load, assemble, and reorder. Purchasing costs will be reduced and the increased order quantities of the standard fasteners will result in quantity discounts and better deliveries. The supplier can act like a "bread truck" and simply keeps all the factory bins full.[2]

Regardless of the delivery system, standard fasteners are much less likely to run out and delay production. Further, standard fasteners are much easier to stock in the field and they require fewer tools to service, an important consideration when repairing complex products on the road.

The most effective technique for applying fastener standardization is simply *discipline.* The author redesigned a food processing machine that had evolved over many years with 150 different *types* of fasteners. The tool box for field repair was quite cumbersome. The redesigned machine had no nuts and *only two bolt types: large and small.*

Careful selection of bolts encourages widespread use. Multiple grades (for strength or corrosion) could be consolidated into the better grade that could serve well for all applications. The difference in fastener cost would small compared to the benefits from part standardization.

If the product is assembled with one predominant fastener, it will be much easier to justify automatic assembly or, at least, semiautomatic auto-feed power screwdrivers, which can only handle *one* type of screw at a time (see the next guideline).

F4) Make sure screws are standardized and have the correct geometry so that auto-feed screwdrivers can be used

A special version of the powered screwdriver feeds screws automatically from a hopper through a hose so that they are positioned under the screwdriver bit. When the screwdriver is positioned over the hole and activated, the screw is advanced into the hole and torque is applied up to a preset limit.

Auto-feed screwdrivers are inexpensive and improve productivity greatly. For automatic fastening, they can be mounted on a robot or special automation machinery.

Auto-feed screwdrivers are somewhat bulky so designers must plan for tool access as in Guideline A4. The geometry of the screws must meet the specifications of the equipment. Usually the screw length below the head must be greater than the diameter of the head by a margin specified by the equipment manufacturer.

Auto-feed screwdrivers can only feed one type of screw. But they are too bulky to allow more then one per workstation. Therefore, screws should be standardized on one size for each workstation. So the development team will have to practice concurrent engineering and specify standard screws as they are structuring the flow of the work and laying out each workstation.

F5) Design screw assembly for downward motion

Screws are easier to apply from above, especially if downward force is needed to keep the tool bit engaged with the screw. For manual operations, applying this force from above is less fatiguing. Many robots can only traverse in a horizontal plane and apply force vertically.

F6)   Minimize use of separate nuts

Separate nuts usually require a worker to position the nut while engaging the bolt. This will slow down manual assembly especially if the nut location is hard to see or find. Semiautomatic operation of auto-feed screwdrivers will be far from optimal if the worker has to position a nut while activating the screwdriver. Robots are not advised for positioning both bolt and nut because of the expense of installing two robots. Separate nuts can be eliminated by using threaded holes, self tapping screws, or captive nuts that are retained on the part to be fastened (see next guideline).

F7)   Consider captive fasteners when applicable

Captive fasteners are retained in some way on the part by pressing into the part (for captive nuts or studs), by forming around the part (for threaded rivets) or by welding to the part (for weld nuts or studs). They are available to function as threaded holes (nuts) or as male threads (studs). Captive nuts or weld nuts function like thread holes in the part but they *must* be applied on the *opposite* side from the bolt. There are hundreds of types of standard captive, riveted and welded fasteners available from catalogs

F8)   Avoid separate washers

Separate washers increase the number of parts to order, deliver, and assemble. If forgotten, they can cause quantity problems. They are often difficult for workers to apply with the nut and they are virtually impossible for automation to install. The washer can be captivated on the bolt or nut so it can still spin with respect to the fastener. Or the washer surface can be an integral part of a one piece bolt or nut.

F9)   Avoid separate lockwashers

The same arguments against separate washers apply to lockwashers. There are many solutions to fastener retention that do not rely on separate lockwashers. Captivated lockwashers are available with the lockwasher attached to the nut but free to spin. Locking ribs on the surface of the nut or bolt are also available. Fastener suppliers use many thread locking techniques that include: deformed threads, plastic plugs or rings that bear on the threads, chemical locking agents, and part of the nut that pinches against the thread while seating. There are hundreds of different *self-locking* fasteners available from catalogs. Be sure to coordinate fastener selection with repair strategy because some self-locking fasteners cannot be reused safely.

F10) Use slotted nuts only when necessary

A common technique in the aerospace industry for critical fastening situations is to use "castle," slotted, or drilled nuts (and sometimes bolts too). These fasteners are secured with a cotter pin or wire which goes through the nut slot (or hole) or a hole drilled through the bolt. These are very secure *if done properly* but are labor intensive, hard to automate, and prone to service omissions (forgetting the wire or the cotter pin). Thus, slotted nuts with cotter pins or wire should be used only when necessary for safety and reliability with rigorous quality standards in place.

F11) Use self tapping screws when applicable

Self tapping screws form or cut their own threads and, thus, do not require tapped threads or nuts. With the right geometry, they can be fed to auto-feed power screwdrivers. When tapping screws form their own thread, they may exert tensile stresses on the surrounding material, so they should not be used on brittle material, like printed circuit boards. Reuse may be limited because of wear in the base material. Self-cutting screws in metal holes should not be used for electronics because the metal chips could cause shorts.

F12) Eliminate fasteners by combining parts

Every interface between two parts must not only be fastened together but also involves *two sets of dimensions and their tolerances.* If the interface is eliminated, so is the cost of fabricating the interface shapes, aligning the interfaces, and fastening them together. The cost of fastened interfaces is a large, but often overlooked, cost. See Section 9.5 for the criteria for combining parts.

F13) Consider snap together features

One part can be attached to another without fasteners at all. The assembly strategy of the product could be that the part shapes allow the parts to simply snap together. This is a common practice on many consumer products which are carefully designed for manufacturability. Plastic molded parts lend themselves especially well to the incorporation of snap together features. Be sure to consider repair implications: Will the consumer be servicing the product and be able to open the product for routine service? Is service only to be performed by trained service personnel who can use special "unsnapping" tools? Safety regulations require certain types of products *must* be opened *only* with a tool.

F14) Consider fasteners that push or snap on

Retaining rings (snap rings) are a very compact way to fasten parts (like bearings) to shafts and holes. Retaining rings can be used to form a shoulder on a shaft instead of machining. They do require special tools and so they might frustrate user repair attempts. But, with the right procedures, they can be installed quickly. Care must be taken that the retaining rings are properly inserted into their slots for critical applications.

There are also a wide variety of snap-on and push-on fasteners that can snap or slip onto shafts or special studs. "Spring nuts" clip onto sheet metal and provide enough threads for screws to attach to.

F15) Specify proper tolerances for press fits

Mating parts for press (interference) fits and shrink fits *must* have proper dimensions and tolerances.[3] Fits that are too loose will not "hold" under all service conditions; fits that are too tight may not be able to be assembled or disassembled (see general discussion on tolerancing in Section 9.3). Make sure press fits will not impair servicing.

Press fit tolerances can be loosened by using "elastic" pins that are made by rolling spring steel sheet metal into a "C" shape or spiral wound cylinder.

8.4 ASSEMBLY MOTION GUIDELINES

M1) Design for easy, foolproof, and reliable alignment of parts to be assembled, in order of most desirable first:

- No alignment needed, using symmetry, *Poka-yoke* (mistake-proofing) as discussed in Chapter 10, and other means

- Self jigging parts, using clever geometries align parts and hold them in place for fastening, pressing, or soldering

- Part features allow alignment by simple fixtures or automatic equipment

- Easy manual alignment with hands free assembly allows air presses to be used.

Avoid scenarios where parts must be positioned and held by hand during press operations.

M2) Products should not need any tweaking or any mechanical or electrical adjustments unless required for customer use

Products should be designed so that there is no tweaking or adjustments required in assembly. Adjustments slow down the assembly process and can cause quality problems if not performed correctly. Zero adjustments should be a goal for the product design and the design team should use all the creativity at its disposal to achieve that goal. If adjustments are required for customer use, there should be a "default" setting that is easy to set during manufacture, for instance, at a detent or clear mark.

M3) If adjustments are really necessary, make sure they are independent and easy to make

Make sure necessary adjustments are independent of other adjustments and are easy to make consistently.

M4) Eliminate the need for calibration in manufacture; if not possible, design for easy calibration

Calibration is a form of adjustment that is time consuming and usually requires special equipment and trained personnel. Often calibration can only take place after the product is fully assembled making correction more difficult. If calibration is really necessary, make sure that it is easy to perform consistently.

M5) Design for easy independent test/certification

Design modules/subassemblies and their processing for independent test and certification, to isolate corrective procedures at the lowest level. Final product certification may be avoided if modules can be designed so that if the modules pass certification, then the assembled product will be considered certified.

M6) Minimize electrical cables; plug electrical subassemblies directly together

Electrical cable assemblies are time consuming for workers to build and install and almost impossible for automation to deal with. A better alternative for assembly is to plug electrical subassemblies directly together with the appropriate connectors designed into each part.

M7) Minimize the number of *types* of cables and wire harnesses

If cables must be used, minimize the number of pin types, lengths, and connector body styles. Standardize on wire harnesses with enough wires for many products, even if some applications have unused wires. Standardize on a few common lengths even if some applications have more length than needed. Standardizing on connector body types will also minimize the number of tools used for cable assembly.

8.5 TEST GUIDELINES

T1) Product can be tested to ensure desired quality

If confidence in process control is not high enough to ship products without testing, the product will need to be tested. The product will have to be designed in such a way to allow efficient testing. Tests may have to be developed to include diagnostics for complex products. But this could be avoided with high enough process quality (Section 8.6).

T2) Subassemblies and modules are structured to allow independent testing

Guideline A10 encourages the use of modules and subassemblies to streamline manufacturing. They should be structured to allow them to be tested separately prior to assembly. The interaction between subassemblies should be predictable enough to count on the product working properly if all the subassemblies work separately. It may also be useful to be able to test subassemblies separately after assembly into the product.

T3) Testing can be performed by standard test instruments

Tests should be designed to be accomplished quickly by *standard* test instruments, which are easier to obtain and do not need to be designed, modified, or debugged, as may be necessary with custom test instruments. Further, field repairs will be easier for the customer to perform with standard test instruments which the customer may own and know how to use.

T4)   Test instruments have adequate access

Just as parts and tools need adequate access, as specified in Guideline A4, test instruments need to have adequate access. On electronic products, special test "ports" may be incorporated that are accessible even when the product is assembled. Test instrument access needs to be planned ahead if modules and subassemblies are to be tested separately in the product.

T5)   Minimize the test effort spent on product testing consistent with quality goals

Since test, itself, is not a value-added activity, product quality goals should be achieved with the minimum test effort. Process controls may dispense with much testing. If the quality "fall out" is low enough, simple go/no-go tests may suffice without the need for testing with diagnostics (Section 8.6). Subassembly testing may reduce testing requirements of the assembled product.

T6)   Tests should give adequate diagnostics to minimize repair time

If test "fall out" is high, the test should aid in diagnostics to minimize repair time. If the product is complex, test diagnostics may be necessary to make any repairs at all. However, manufacturing companies should strive to have their processes so well controlled that diagnostics are not needed. In fact, if the fall out is low enough, it actually may be feasible to *discard* products that do not pass the final go/no-go test and spare the expense of diagnostic test development and the testing and repair itself, as discussed next.

8.6 TESTING IN QUALITY vs. BUILDING IN QUALITY

Testing in Quality with Diagnostic Tests

Diagnostic testing, for instance using ATE (Automatic Test Equipment) for printed circuit boards, would be necessary if test fallout is high and many boards need to be repaired. Diagnostic tests can pinpoint the problem component and instruct rework people to replace it. However:

- ATE test equipment is expensive, with equipment costing millions of dollars plus significant costs in training, tooling (test fixtures) and infrastructure.

- Multiple plants require the same equipment and infrastructure, just to be complete, even if they are not needed for capacity. Thus, million dollar testers would be needed in every plant building that type of product.

- Test development, in many cases, can equal or exceed the cost and calendar time of circuit board development. Those engineers could benefit the company more by *designing* new products.

Building in Quality to Eliminate Diagnostic Tests

Quality should be assured by robust design, by process controls, and by assuring part quality at the source, in which case functional test yields can reach a breakeven point where the total cost of diagnostic testing exceeds that of discarding failed products.

For printed circuit boards, IBM figured that
if first pass yields were above 98.5%,
it could dispense with diagnostic tests
and discard failed circuit boards.

If product testing is still required and diagnostic tests are not used, then go/no-go functional tests and built-in self test (BIST) would be need to test all functions used in service.

8.7 DESIGN FOR REPAIR AND MAINTENANCE

The more the product will need to be repaired in the factory *or* in the field, the more important it will be to design for repair. Part of a repair strategy may be to simply replace parts or modules which are, themselves, either repaired, discarded, or recycled.

The need for ease of maintenance depends on the reliability of the product and demands for "uptime" (how much time the product needs to be available for use).

Designing for ease of *field* repair may be more challenging than for factory repair, because field repair may not have the use of test and repair equipment that is as sophisticated as the factory's.

8.8 REPAIR DESIGN GUIDELINES

R1)   Provide ability for tests to diagnose problems

The need for a consistent method of providing diagnostic information is proportional to product complexity and the probability of product failure in the factory or in the field. Products with a high "fall out" after test can bog down a manufacturing plant if they are difficult to repair. Diagnostic information can specify where the problem is and recommend repair actions.

The need for building diagnostic capability into the tests is proportional to the inherent difficultly of diagnosing problems independently. Some complex products may take hours to diagnose with normal diagnostic tools (meters, oscilloscopes, etc.) and may need the advanced diagnostic capability available from advanced testing technology.

R2)   Make sure the most likely repair tasks are easy to perform

Anticipate the most likely repair tasks and plan for ease of repair. This applies to part removal, part reinstallation, tools needed, and skill required. Ease of repair is especially important if customers perform repairs.

R3)   Ensure repair tasks use the *fewest* tools

If fastener commonality has been designed into the product, this should have provided an inherent tool commonality also. When fasteners are selected, make sure the *minimum* number of *common* tools is specified. Repairability may be important to customers and common tools may be part of their purchase criteria.

Avoid the need for special tools, unless the user needs to be precluded from repair for skill requirement or safety reasons. Special tools increase the number of tools that have to be supplied to repair facilities. In addition, users may be frustrated if repairs cannot be made with common tools. Users and even factory workers might not have the special tools and be tempted to use the closest common tool even if it damages a part or results in incomplete re-assembly.

A small repair tool set may be important if field repairs need to be made in remote sites where it would be difficult to bring a large number of tools.

R4)   Use quick disconnect features

If part replacement is likely and must be done quickly, provide quick-disconnect features to facilitate quick removal, for example, quarter-turn fasteners. Electrical connectors and fluid power quick disconnect fittings can be provided where quick separation is likely to be needed.

R5)   Ensure that failure or wear prone parts are easy to replace with disposable replacements

If some parts are likely to fail or wear out during the useful life of the product, they should be easy to replace with disposable (or rebuildable) replacements. If an area is subjected to wear, cover it with a replaceable wear strip or sheet. Automobile brakes shoes and pads are common examples of this principle, although ease of replacement varies from car to car.

R6)   Provide inexpensive spare parts in the product

Spare parts that are expected to be needed, lost, or wear out can actually be included in the product. This practice may not cost much for inexpensive parts, but it may provide a major benefit to users. Examples of the practice are extra buttons sewn on clothing, extra nozzles on spray paint cans, and extra light bulbs in flash lights, automobile tail light assemblies, and overhead projectors. In fact, some overhead projectors even allow lamp assemblies to be changed by moving an exterior lever.

High-wear parts are candidates for inclusion in products, for instance, extra knife blades in retractable knives. The same principle can be applied to non-wearing parts like extra tool bits in screwdriver handles.

If the spare parts themselves cannot be included, at least provide a place to hold spare parts that can be supplied by the user.

R7)   Ensure availability of spare parts

Make sure that spare parts are readily available. It may be a risky business strategy to try to monopolizing the spare parts business, or *inadvertently so* by designing in parts that are hard to find. Using industry standard parts greatly improves the repairability. Customers will appreciate being able to get parts in a hurry from local sources of supply.

For parts that are only available from the product manufacturer, recommend that the customer buy a "spare parts kit" for situations when downtime is intolerable.

R8) Use modular design to allow replacement of modules

One of the advantages of modular design is that it allows replacement of modules as a repair strategy. Modules can then be returned to a repair facility or the factory for repair.

Modular repair is especially applicable for modules which need specialized facilities for repair. It also removes the actual repair function from the site of use, which is significant if the entire product is too large to move and is in a place that precludes easy repair.

R9) Ensure modules can be tested, diagnosed and adjusted while in the product

Testing modules or subassemblies *while still in the product* will save time and prevent handling damage. Ideally, modules should be able to be tested from the controls or from software commands. If necessary, the module could be disconnected (if this is safe) and still be tested in the product. If modules need to be adjusted, make sure adjustments can be made while the module is in the product, preferably from the product's controls. Make sure adjustments are independent and do not affect other functions.

R10) Sensitive adjustments should be protected from accidental change

All adjustments should be protected from accidental change during servicing, repair, or maintenance. Adjustments and settings should be locked in position. Dial adjustments could stop at detents or be covered to prevent accidental change.

R11) The product should be protected from repair damage

The product should be protected from repair damage from workers, their tools, and the removal of other parts. Partitions and barriers may help protect parts. Subassemblies may need feet or guards to prevent handling damage. Removal aids may also help (see next guideline).

R12) Provide part removal aids for speed and damage prevention

If it is likely that parts, modules or subassemblies will be removed, make it easy by providing removal aids like tracks, slides, guides, hooks, handles, and so forth. Many automobile engines have hooks installed over the center of gravity to aid in factory assembly *and* removal for repair. Inexpensive handles can be added where they would be most useful for removal. Many standard slide assemblies are available for mounting subassemblies so that they may slide out for easy servicing. This is common for many electronic systems. All of these measures not only make it easier to remove parts but also make the removal process quicker and safer for the repairer and the equipment.

R13) Protect parts with fuses and overloads

Some repair can actually be *eliminated* by protecting parts with fuses and overloads. Electrical fuses are common devices for protecting electrical equipment. Mechanical overload devices are available to protect mechanical machinery. In many applications, these devices may be necessary for safety.

R14) Ensure any module or subassembly can be accessed through one door or panel

For larger systems, repair will be easier if any subassembly can be accessed through one door or panel. Subassembly removal should be possible through the single door.

R15) Access covers which are not removable should be self supporting in the open position

If the system has access covers or doors, they should be self supporting in the open position like most car doors, hoods and trunk lids.

R16) Connections to modules or subassemblies should be accessible and easy to disconnect

If subassemblies need to be removed or disconnected, make sure that connections are accessible (for tools and workers), easy to disconnect, and easy to reconnect.

R17) Make sure repair, service or maintenance tasks pose no safety hazards

Anticipate *all* possible repair, servicing and maintenance tasks and make sure workers will not be exposed to any hazards from electrical shock, heat, sharp edges, moving parts, chemical contamination, and so forth. Anticipate the possibility of untrained users attempting service. Use warning signs and interlocks that cut off power when doors are opened. If unauthorized servicing may pose a safety hazard, prevent unauthorized access with locks or special tools.

For large products and production equipment, it is common practice for repair personnel to use their own paddle lock on special "lock-out" switches (that are designed into the equipment) so no one can turn on the machinery while repairs are underway. If multiple people are working on the machinery, then each repair person will lock out the switch with his or her own paddle lock; all paddle locks will have to be cleared for the machine to be turned on.

R18) Make sure subassembly orientation is obvious or clearly marked

If modules or subassemblies need to be removed for service, make sure that orientation is obvious for correct reinstallation. Markings could be molded in or signs applied that indicate which end is up or which side mates with which other parts. Use *polarized* electrical connectors to avoid incorrect reconnection.

R19) Provide means to locate subassemblies before fastening

As recommended in Guideline M1 for fasteners, reinstallation of modules and subassemblies will be easier and more precise if the subassemblies can be located before fastening with guides, pins, tracks, stops, and so forth. This is especially important where correct orientation is difficult to see.

Relevant guidelines, repeated from *Assembly Guidelines,* **Section 8.2**

A4)   Provide unobstructed access for parts *and* tools

Each part must not only be designed to fit in its destination location, but also must have an assembly path for entry into the product. This motion must not risk damage to the part or product and, of course, must not endanger workers.

Equally important is access for *tools and the tool operator* whether that is a worker or robot arm, which usually requires more access room than a worker's hand. Access may be needed for screwdrivers, wrenches, welding torches, electronic probes, and so forth. Remember that workers may be assembling these products all day long and having to go through awkward contortions to assemble each product can lead to worker fatigue, slow throughput, poor product quality, and even worker injury.

Access is also needed for field repair where the tools may be simpler and, maybe bulkier.

A5)   Make parts independently replaceable

Products with independently replaceable parts are easier to repair because the parts can be replaced without having to remove other parts first. The order of assembly would be more flexible since parts can be added in any order. This could be a valuable asset in times of shortages, in which case the rest of the product could be built and the hard-to-get part added when it arrives.

A6)   Order assembly so the most reliable part goes in first; the most likely to fail goes in last

If parts must be added sequentially, make sure that the most likely to fail are the easiest to remove. This is important for both factory assembly *and* field repair.

8.9 DESIGN FOR SERVICE AND REPAIR

• Understand the lessons learned about serviceability from current and past products including what design features worked well and what design features impeded service.

• Avoid "ignorance is bliss" (giving not enough attention to service).

• Avoid "management by folklore" (focusing on well-circulated, but not statistical-based, service tales).

• Quantify the cost of service, repairs, warrantees, legal and related costs; estimate how much of that could been prevented by good design for service.

• Look up customer importance rating and competitive grade of reliability/serviceability (on Figure 2-2) to ascertain how much effort to apply to various issues of design for service.

• Gather service data and plot a priority chart, in the format of Figure 2-3, that plots service frequency vs severity, as shown in Figure 8-2:

PLOTTING SERVICE FREQUENCY vs SEVERITY

with priority zones of importance

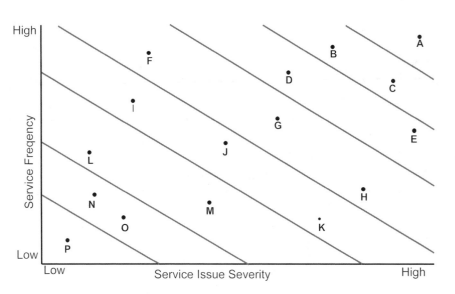

Figure 8-2: Service Frequency vs Severity

- Optimize the product concept/architecture to minimize service needs with high enough quality and reliability designed in.

- Make sure people knowledgeable about service (yours, users, customers, and third parties) are early and active participants on product development teams.

- Focus efforts on the highest priority zones in the priority plot.

- Identify the highest priority service tasks and make them easy to do by design including: architecture designed for ease of service; helpful diagnostics that either avoid service or aid in subsequent service; easy to open or disassemble quickly; easy to repair or swap defective parts; minimize or eliminate recalibration after service; and quick, easy, and foolproof closure or re-assembly.

- Consider modularity as part of a service strategy, to allow replacement of defective modules in the field.

- Consider build in self test to quickly ascertain product status and service/repair approach.

- Consider remote diagnostics to remotely ascertain product status and make good decisions about service calls.

8.10 MAINTENANCE

Maintenance can either be performed after something fails (unscheduled maintenance) or at scheduled intervals to replace parts before they are likely to fail (preventive maintenance).

- **Unscheduled maintenance:** restoring operation after a failure. Designing for ease of repair (above) will greatly improve the ease of maintenance in general.

- **Preventive or scheduled maintenance.** If it is important to avoid downtime, then preventive maintenance can be scheduled to replace parts *before* they are *expected* to fail. The scheduling of such maintenance needs to be based on projected or measured failure histories of suspected parts. Useful data may be available on many purchased parts from historical performance. Critical applications require reliable parts and maintenance programs need good reliability data.

8.11 MAINTENANCE MEASUREMENTS

Mean Time To Repair

The measurement of repair time is the *Mean Time To Repair* or MTTR. This represents the mean time it takes to repair the product. In reality, it may take some time for repair personnel to respond before repairs can begin, which is called the Mean Response Time (MRT). Adding the MTTR to the Mean Response Time (MRT) equals the "downtime" during which the product is not available for use.

Availability

Availability is the measure of time that the product is available in an operative state. This is called the "uptime."

$$\text{Availability} = \frac{\text{Uptime}}{\text{Total time}} = \frac{\text{Uptime}}{\text{Uptime} + \text{Downtime}}$$

Uptime is measured by the Mean Time Between Failures (MTBF)

$$\text{Uptime} = \text{MTBF}$$

Downtime is measured by the Mean Time To Repair (MTTR) plus the Mean Response Time (MRT)

$$\text{Downtime} = \text{MTTR} + \text{MRT}$$

$$\text{Availability} = \frac{\text{MTBF}}{\text{MTBF} + (\text{MTTR} + \text{MRT})}$$

8.12 DESIGNING FOR MAINTENANCE GUIDELINES

Maintenance strategy is not something to be left until after the product has been designed. Ease of maintenance should be designed into the product as one of the early design goals. Reliability studies should predict part failure modes and frequencies and, of course, be a criterion for part selection. The usage environment should be identified early. These are some if the inputs that help develop a product maintenance strategy.

R20) Design products for minimum maintenance

Design the need for maintenance out of the product. Parts should be carefully selected for optimal reliability. Automobiles have made great strides lately in designing for minimum maintenance by extending the maintenance periods, like for oil changes. Designs should have conservative *factors-of-safety* so that part will not be over stressed, even in worst case conditions.

R21) Design self correction capabilities into products

Design products with capabilities to correction problems they sense. Critical applications, like in aerospace, use design features that can automatically switch to backup systems.

R22) Design products with self-test capability

Design the product to have the capability to run its own "built-in-self-test" (BIST) to aid in diagnostics and repair. Self-test data should be stored in some form so it is available to repair personnel.

R23) Design products with test ports

Design the product with a *test port* which could make key electrical test points easily available. This is especially useful if access to test points is difficult.

R24) Design in counters and timers to aid preventive maintenance

Products designed for ease of preventive maintenance should have counters and timers built in to determine when maintenance should be performed.

R25) Specify key measurements for preventive maintenance programs

Designers should be in the best position to know product weaknesses and so should be able to specify key measurements to determine wear or deterioration. Key parts, like drive belts, should be measured periodically and replace as necessary. Mechanically complex products can be analyzed by measuring their frequencies and amplitude of the noise they emit (their "sound signatures") which may predict when parts are approaching failure.

R26) Include warning devices to indicate failures.

The Mean Response Time (MRT) can be minimized by signals (like red lights or buzzers) and other warning devices so that repair can begin quicker. In sophisticated factories, central control panels show machine status and can instantly know when a machine is "down." Self-diagnostics capability will also minimize the response time.

As mentioned before, plug-in modules can greatly benefit field maintenance and allow modules to be repaired off-line where there are better repair and diagnostic facilities.

The maintenance strategy may determine the order of assembly, as specified in Guideline A6, which states that the most likely parts to fail should be the easiest to remove.

ENDNOTES/REFERENCES

1. "The Best Engineered Part is No Part at All," *Business Week,* May 8, 1989.

2. David M. Anderson, *Build-to-Order & Mass Customization, The Ultimate Supply Chain Management and Lean Manufacturing Strategy for Low-Cost On-Demand Production without Forecasts or Inventory* (2004, 520 pages, CIM Press). See articles at www.build-to-order-consultig.com.

3. For tables of press fits (also called forced or interference fits), see the section "Allowances and Tolerances for Fits" in the Chapter "Dimensioning, Gaging, and Measuring," in the *Machinery's Handbook,* published by Industrial Press Inc. A revised edition has been published every few years since 1914.

DFM GUIDELINES FOR PART DESIGN

This chapter lists some general guidelines for *part* design including fabrication, part standardization, symmetry, tolerances, part shapes and combining parts and functions.

Designing Parts for Manufacturability

• For critical parts, the part designer should be an early and active participant in system engineering of the product or subassembly to help optimize the systems architecture concept that determines the part's requirements.

• Understand the purpose of the part, how it fits in, how it relates to the whole, and the relative importance of function/performance, cost, rigidity, weight, and tolerances, especially stacks it is a part of.

> *"Toyota's process does not focus on the speedy completion of individual component designs in isolation, but instead looks at how individual designs will interact within a system before the design is complete. In other words, they focus on system compatibility before individual design completion."[1]*

• Investigate past/similar parts to learn from their good or bad histories with respect to function, quality, cost, manufacturability, ramps, etc.

• First consider off-the-shelf parts. Thoroughly search for and investigate available candidates.

• Explore all the ways to design and make the part. Don't just jump at the first idea that comes to mind. Choose the optimal design approach.

• Keep thinking about how the part is to be made throughout the design process.

• If the systems engineering has not been optimized, recommend ways that better system engineering/integration could improve the part's design and the manufacturability of the product overall. This especially applies to the rational apportionment of tolerances in stacks.

• Understand *all* the candidate processes well enough to *choose* the best process for the optimal cost, tolerance control, quality/consistency, ramps, delivery time, compatibility with company operations and supply chains, equipment/vendor availability, tooling cost and lead time, setup time, appearance/finish.

   If you *don't* understand all candidate processes, find colleagues who do, bring in outside experts, or call in the appropriate vendor(s), being careful to explain the nature of the inquiry.

• Decide if the vendor should design the part under careful supervision and coordination.

• Research and understand the specific design guidelines for the part and its chosen processes to optimize the function, cost, quality, and manufacturability in general.

• Work with the vendor, who should be pre-selected, to collaboratively design the part.

• Design the part keeping in mind the optimal balance of design considerations: e.g. function, performance, cost, quality, manufacturability, etc.

• For large or complex structures, optimize partitioning into multiple parts so that all dimensions can be made in the same operation (Guideline P14) and multiple parts can be accurately aligned (Guideline A3).

• Follow the part design guidelines (next).

9.1 PART DESIGN GUIDELINES

P1) Adhere to specific process design guidelines

It is very important to use specific design guidelines for parts to be produced by specific processes such as welding, casting, forging, extruding, forming, stamping, turning, milling, grinding, powdered metallurgy (sintering), plastic molding, and so forth. A good summary of design guidelines of several processes would be well over a thousand pages and is thus beyond the scope of a general book on DFM. Some reference books are available that give a summary of design guidelines for many specific processes.[2,3,4,5] Many specialized books are available devoted to single processes.[6]

Industrial organizations and suppliers of specific processes often, at no cost, furnish designers with design guidelines for their process.[7]

P2)   Avoid right/left hand parts; Use "paired parts" for top & bottom, front & back, etc.

Avoid designing right or left-hand (mirror-image) parts. Design the product so the same part can function in both right or left-hand modes. If parts cannot now perform both functions, add features to both right and left-hand parts to make them the same. Another way of saying this is to use "paired" parts instead of right and left-hand parts. Purchasing of right/left parts or paired parts (plus all the internal material supply functions) is for *twice* the quantity and *half* the number of types of parts. For pairs of molded parts, this principle can *cut tooling costs in half.*

At one time or another, everyone has opened a brief case or suit case upside down because the top looks like the bottom. The reason for this is that top and bottom parts are identical parts used in pairs.

Consolidate *similar* parts to be the *same* part results in a fraction of the part types and several times the purchasing leverage.

P3)   Design parts with symmetry

Design each part to be symmetrical from every possible "view" (in a drafting sense) so that the part does not have to be oriented for assembly. In manual assembly, symmetrical parts cannot be installed backwards, which can be a major potential quality problem for manual assembly. In automatic assembly, symmetrical parts do not require special sensors or mechanisms to orient them correctly. The extra cost of making the part symmetrical (the extra holes or whatever other feature is necessary) will probably be saved many times over by not having to develop complex orienting mechanisms and by avoiding quality problems.

It is a little known fact that in felt-tipped pens, the felt is pointed on both ends so that automatic assembly machines do not have to orient the felt.

P4) If part symmetry is not possible, make parts very asymmetrical; polarize all connectors

The best part for assembly is one that is symmetrical in all views. The *worst* part is one that is *slightly* asymmetrical which may be installed wrong because the worker or robot could not notice the asymmetry. Or worse, the part may be *forced* in the wrong orientation by a worker (that thinks the tolerance is off) or by a robot (that doesn't know any better).

So, if symmetry cannot be achieved, make the parts *very* asymmetrical. Then workers will less likely *install* the part wrong because it will not *fit* wrong. Automation machinery may be able to orient the part with less expensive sensors and intelligence.

In fact, very asymmetrical parts may can even be oriented by simple stationary guides over conveyor belts.

P5) Design for fixturing; concurrently design fixtures

Understand the manufacturing process well enough to be able to design parts *and* dimension them for fixturing. Flexible operations require that whole families of parts be positioned in a common fixture without any setup changes.[8] Parts designed for automation or mechanization need registration features for fixturing. Machine tools, assembly stations, automatic transfers, and automatic assembly equipment need to be able to grip or fixture the part *in a known position* for each operation. This requires *registration* locations (e.g., tooling pins) on which the part will be gripped or fixtured while part is being transferred, machined, processed or assembled.

When appropriate, concurrently design versatile fixtures for welding, assembly, and other processing steps to improve cost, time, cost, and quality of *both* the parts being fixtured *and* the subsequent assembly. Fixtures could be discrete (for a mass-produced part). For families of products, fixtures should be versatile to accept any part or assembly in the family. Versatile fixtures could be adjustable and set by detents or gauge blocks or programmable with positioning adjusted by servo mechanisms.

P6) Minimize tooling complexity by concurrently designing tooling

Use *concurrent engineering* of parts *and* tooling to minimize tooling complexity, cost, delivery lead time and maximize throughput, quality and flexibility.

P7) Make part differences very obvious

Different materials or internal features may not be obvious to workers. If parts cannot be identical, make sure their differences are obvious. This is especially important in rapid assembly situations where workers handle many different parts. To distinguish different parts, use markings, labels, color, or different packaging if they come individually packaged. One company uses different (but functionally equivalent) platings to distinguish metric from English fasteners.

P8) Specify optimal tolerances for a Robust Design

Design of Experiments can be used to determine the effect of variations in all tolerances on part or system quality. The result is that all tolerances can be optimized to provide a *robust* design to provide *high quality at low cost.*[9] See the next section for more on tolerancing.

P9) Specify quality parts from reliable sources

The "rule of ten" specifies that it costs 10 times more to find and repair a defect at the next stage of assembly. Thus, it costs 10 times more cost to find a part defect at a subassembly; 10 times more to find a subassembly defect at final assembly; 10 times more in the distribution channel; and so forth. All parts should have reliable sources that can deliver consistent quality over time in the volumes required.

The Rule of 10

Level of completion	Cost to find & repair defect
the part itself	X
at subassembly	10 X
at final assembly	100 X
at the dealer/distributer	1,000 X
at the customer	10,000 X

9.2 DFM FOR FABRICATED PARTS

P10) Choose the optimal processing

Use concurrent engineering to proactively *choose* the optimal processes (casting, forming, machining, and so forth.) for the minimum total cost and throughput time. Versatile primary processes can eliminate or minimize certain secondary operations, thus saving cost and throughput time. Design to avoid unnecessary operations. Understand how fabrication processes work and their capabilities and limitations.

P11) Design for quick, secure, and consistent work holding

Design parts for quick, secure, and consistent work holding for clamps, collets, arbors, vises, chucks, centers, jigs, and fixtures. Provide consistent parallel, conical, or circular clamping surfaces. Design parts to be rigid enough to withstand cutting tool *and* work holding forces without distortion or damage. Do not plan to clamp on parting lines or other uneven and inconsistent surfaces. Provide access room for cutting tools, clamps, and clamping tools.

P12) Use stock dimensions whenever possible

Design parts so that non-critical dimensions can be provided by stock dimensions of *standard* raw material, instead of requiring machining for these non-critical dimensions.

P13) Optimize dimensions and raw material stock choices

Specify dimensions and select the raw material for the best balance of fabricating efficiency and raw material standardization for the lowest total cost. Raw material standardization needs to be even more aggressive for build-to-order and mass customization, as discussed in Chapter 4.

P14)   Design machined parts to be made in one setup (chucking)

Having to reposition parts or move to another machine: increases cost for setups and machine time charges; increases the chance of errors for extra setups and repositionings; lowers accuracy, compared to the precision of locating all cuts on the same chucking; disrupts lean flow and complicates machine scheduling; and takes more time to processing hours, labor hours, and calendar time. To take advantage of this, designers must:

- Make all dimensions from the most logical datum, which corresponds to the fixture, machine bed, or clamping surface

- Concurrently design fixtures, locating features, clamping geometry, etc.

- Design geometries to minimize the number of cutting tools, ideally one

- Use total cost measurements to justify one 5-axis operation instead of multiple 3-axis operations by including all costs for setup, loading, zeroing, machine time, error correction, scrap, and so forth.

Single setup machining is an effective way to achieve tight tolerances between many features at low cost.

Figure 9-1 shows how the author's consulting[10] improved the manufacturability of a robot bearing holder. In the original design, the bearing mount holes had to be machined from each end after repositioning the part, so it was hard to align the bearing bores to the +/- .001" concentricity tolerance. Further, it was also hard to grind the bore to the exact diameter needed for the bearing mounts. The new part was redesigned it so that the critical bearing bores could be made in one operation, which guaranteed alignment and made it easy to grind a tight-tolerance diameter.

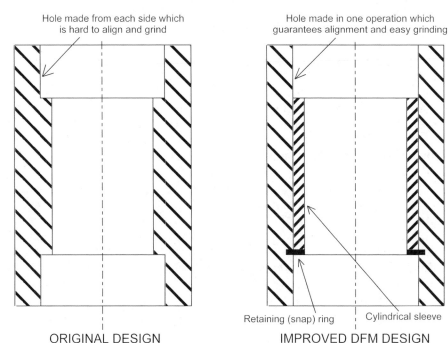

Figure 9-1: Improved design for easier and better machining

P15) Minimize cutting tools for machined parts

For machined parts, minimize cost and throughput by designing parts to be machined with the minimum number of standard cutting tools that cut standard features, like end mill radii. Avoid tool/proliferation and arbitrary decisions. Keep tool variety within the capability of the tool changer.

P16) Avoid arbitrary decisions that require special tools and thus slow processing and add cost unnecessarily

Designers should avoid arbitrary decisions when specifying dimensions that require unique tools like bend mandrels, hole punches, and cutting tool bits for machine tools. Find out what are the most common tools in the shop and design around them instead of arbitrarily requiring tools that may not be readily available.

P17) Choose materials to minimize total cost with respect to post-processing

Optimal selection of materials can minimize cost of, and possibly eliminate, post-processing steps for strengthening, hardening, deburring, painting, surface coating, and so forth. Materials that *appear* to cost more may actually have a lower total cost if all post-processing costs are considered. For instance, choosing stainless steel can avoid painting costs and rusting problems of inferior metals.

P18) Design parts for quick, cost-effective, and quality heat treating

It is the responsibility of the designer to specify the quickest, highest quality, and most cost-effective (from a total cost perspective) post-processing for heat treating and any other post-processing step. Work with manufacturing and vendors to consider all the possible scenarios and then systematically choose the best one.

P19) Design and utilize versatile fixtures

Design families machined parts to be processed in the same versatile fixture. If multiple fixtures are to be used in the same machine tool, design the fixtures to have standardized mounts. Flexible fixtures can speed loading and can minimize setup changes for different parts, thus improving flexibility while lowing cost. New flexible fixtures should be *concurrently engineered* as the product is designed (Chapter 3).

P20) Avoid interrupted cuts and complex tapers and contours

Interrupted cuts occur when cutting tools encounter holes or other gaps in the workpiece, which results in vibrations, excessive tool wear, and inferior dimensions and surface finish. Complex tapers and contours may be difficult to manufacture and inspect.

P22) Minimize shoulders, undercuts, hard-to-machine materials, specially ground cutters, and part projections that interfere with cutter overruns

Designers should avoid features that are difficult to machine. Specially ground cutters may not yield consistent results. Although machinists are taught to grind their own cutting tools in training classes, this practice should be discouraged in production to avoid inconsistency from tool to tool.

P23) Understand tolerance step functions

Understand tolerance step functions and specify tolerances wisely. The type of process depends on the tolerance. Each process has a practical limit regarding how close a tolerance can be held for a given skill level on the production line. If the tolerance is tighter than the limit, the next most precise (and expensive) process must be used. Designers must understand these step functions so that do not arbitrarily specify a tolerance that inadvertently bumps up the next more expensive process (see the graph on the next page).

9.3 TOLERANCING

Properly specifying tolerances is one the most important steps to making designs manufacturable. Tolerances that are unnecessarily too tight often force the use of a more precise process which results in more cost and delays. Designers must understand fabrication processes so they will know the effect of tolerancing on processing.

The type of process depends on the tolerance. Each process has its practical limit to how close a tolerance could be held for a given skill level on the production line. If the tolerance is tighter than the limit, the next most precise – and expensive – process must be used. Designers must understand these *step functions* and know the tolerance limit for each process (Figure 9-2).

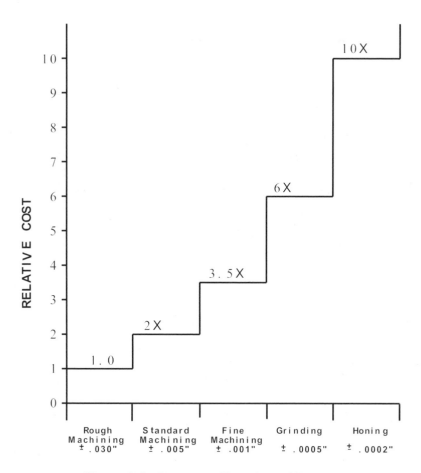

Figure 9-2: Cost as a Function of Process

Excessive tolerances

If tolerances are *perceived* by manufacturing as excessively tight, many undesirable things can happen. Manufacturing people who challenge the tight tolerances may question why they are needed and if they really do warrant a more expensive process. If they bring the concern to Engineering, the designer who specified the tolerance should welcome the input and adjust the tolerance accordingly. The worst thing that can happen would be to act too busy or stubborn and refuse to act when changes are warranted.

Unfortunately, what happens too often in industry is that manufacturing receives a verbal tolerance change *without* documenting the change for the next build or for similar products. This only ensures that the problem will recur and implies to manufacturing that the tight tolerance was not really necessary, thus eroding the credibility of tolerances in general.

In other cases, manufacturing people "interpret" tolerances because of a perceived low credibility of the tolerances. This risky procedure can backfire if some parts are made with inadequate tolerances on some really critical dimensions. The tolerance problem is intensified when parts are sent out to suppliers who do not have an understanding of which tolerances must be held precisely and which can be changed. The supplier will (and should) bid on the basis of the stated tolerances on the drawing. The unfortunate result of the "double standard" on tolerance "hedging" might be an improperly biased make/buy decisions in favor of internal manufacture.

If tolerances are specified (or interpreted) too loose, the product may fail functional tests, encounter "random" difficulty at assembly, have quality problems, wear out prematurely, and pose a safety hazard in use.

Worst case tolerancing

A related problem is tolerance "stack-up" and "worst case" tolerancing. Tolerance stack-up refers to the cumulative effect of all the tolerances in a "string" of dimensions (the combination of which affects the same overall dimension). Worst case tolerancing refers to combining the "worst" of all the tolerances to analyze what the net effect will be. For instance, to do a worst case analysis on the clearance between a shaft and a hole, one would consider the *largest* possible shaft in the *smallest* possible hole *and* the *smallest* possible shaft in the *largest* possible hole. This analysis will yield the extremes in clearance which should conform to design requirements. The product must be able to function reliably and safely with *all* worst case tolerance situations. Tolerance stack-up analysis should be done adequately on relevant part stacks, modules, and subassemblies *and* on the product itself.

When several dimensions combine to determine an overall dimension (which has *its* own desired tolerance), the tolerances of all the elements should be *apportioned* rationally based on the lowest *total* cost for all holding *all* dimensions in the chain. If there is not a planned apportionment of tolerances, the result may be that the last part designed ends up with excessively tight tolerances because previously designed (and maybe built) part tolerances have already been set.

Tolerance strategy

The goal should be to optimize tolerances for a *balance* of function, quality, safety, *and* manufacturability. Tolerances should have enough credibility to be respected *as specified* so manufacturing can then concentrate on meeting them. All tolerances specified need to be carefully thought out with respect to the processes. Working with manufacturing engineers very early in the design will help, but the best approach is for the designers to be thoroughly familiar with the processes and their limitations. Tolerances that are changed on one build should be immediately documented for future builds.

Tolerance philosophy

One secret of how *continuous improvement* (kaizen) manufacturers earned such outstanding reputations for quality lies in their treatment of tolerances. Where the traditional custom is to hold dimensions "within spec" (merely within the tolerance range specified), kaizen manufacturers strive to make parts to the *target* dimension. For example, the conventional approach to a dimension of 1.000" ± .005" would that any part within .995" and 1.005" would be acceptable, as shown in Figure 10-1. The kaizen approach would be to aim for the target of 1.000" (as shown in Figure 10-2) and continuously strive to get closer through continuous improvement activities.[11] See Guideline Q12 - "Continuously improve the product."

Block tolerances

Another problem is the block (or blanket) tolerance printed on the drawing: for instance ± .005" for linear dimensions and 63 RMS for surface finish "on everything not otherwise specified." This often results in many tolerances that are tighter than necessary, and, if strictly enforced, would prohibit the use of standard stock, say ½" stock, for a ½" dimension. Block tolerances technically could even apply to chamfers and radii which are only needed for clearance, appearance, or safety.

If a company *must* use a tolerance block, it should specify *several* blanket tolerances for different needs, for instance:

.XXX dimensions to indicate a ± .005" tolerance;

.XX to indicate a ± .015" or ± .020" tolerance;

fractions to indicate a ± 1/32" tolerance.

Each company should determine *its* most common tolerances and specify them in the tolerance block. Designers will need to realize that a two-digit dimension of five eights of an inch will have to be specified as .62 or .63, not .625.

Using Taguchi Methods for Robust Design

The Taguchi Method™ for Robust Design is a systematic way to optimize tolerances to achieve *high quality at low cost.*[12] It does this by using Design of Experiments to analyze the effect of all tolerances on functionality, quality, and manufacturability to:

- Analyze tolerance "stacks" and "worse case" situations.

- Identify critical dimensions that need tight tolerances and precision parts; then specify those tolerances methodically.

Identify low demand dimensions that can have looser tolerances and cheaper parts; then specify those tolerances accordingly.

Such a design would be considered *robust* if it could be manufactured predictably with consistently high quality and perform adequately in all anticipated usage environments. Without a methodical way to determine tolerances, the alternatives would be:

- Make all tolerances tight "just to be sure," which is expensive. Tolerances that *appear* to be overly tight may have credibility problems and invite interpretation.

- Inadvertently (or deliberately) make tolerances too loose, leading to manufacturability and quality problems. Performance, quality, and manufacturability problems may be inconsistent and thus hard to troubleshoot and rectify.

P24) Specify the widest tolerances consistent with needs for functionality, quality, reliability, and so forth. Avoid "choosing" tolerances arbitrarily or by overly tight tolerance blocks

P 25) Be careful about too many operations in one part, especially if the part must pass through multiple machines, to decrease the cost and delays of setup or machining mistakes

P 26) Concurrently engineer the part and processes for the best manufacturability, cost, quality, and throughput time

P 27) Avoid sharp internal corners that require sharp cutting tools which can easily break

P28) Proactively deal with burr removal and provide room for burrs and their removal tools

P29) Specify 45 degree bevels instead of round external corners, to avoid special/unusual tools and tool changes

P30) Don't overspecify surface finishes. Use "comparitors" which are gauges that show the look and feel of various surface finishes for machined, molded, and cast surfaces

P31) Reference each dimension to the best datum for the optimal:

- Tolerance control

- Clearly and unambiguously conveying the *design intent*

- Ability to make all key dimensions in the same setup on the same machine

- Ease of CNC programing

- Ability to inspect first articles on Coordinate Measuring Machines

DFM for Castings

P32) Obey all the guidelines for design of castings and molds using handbook guidelines or, preferably with the help of the casting vendor working with the team.

P33) Standardize cast parts to minimize the number of parts and the number and cost of the molds/dies.

P 34) Design *versatile* raw castings that have all the shapes and features for all versions of the casting to minimize the number of raw castings. The cost of the extra metal will probably be saved many times over in mold/die cost, setup costs, and inventory management for multiple raw castings.

P35) Capitalize on opportunities to avoid machining with "as cast" shapes whenever possible. The comparitors mentioned in Guideline P30 will help ascertain when this is feasible.

P36) Carefully plan out the sequence of machining castings starting with the machining reference points so that the raw castings are properly positioned in the machine tool.

DFM for Plastics

Understand that plastic molding is an *inflexible* process where every different shape requires a different mold and thus encourages *versatile* standard shapes. On the other hand, metal fabrication is a *flexible* process where CNC machine tools can machine many different shapes.

P37) Obey all the guidelines for part design and mold design using handbook guidelines or, preferably with the help of the molding vendor working with the team. Optimize draft angles, surface finish, wall thickness, thickness transitions, ribbing, features, holes, corners, parting planes, mold filling, sprue/riser locations, ejection, cooling times, and so forth while minimizing the effect of shrinkage, warpage, and surface variations.

P38) Standardize molded parts to minimize the number of parts and the number and cost of the molds/dies.

P39) Design *versatile* molded parts that have all the shapes and features for all versions to minimize the number of designs and tooling. The cost of any extra plastic will probably be saved many times over in mold/die cost, setup costs, and inventory management for multiple plastic parts.

P40) Standardize raw materials for all parts, or at least all parts in a product family. Even if it appears that some parts may be getting better material than needed, the total cost to the company will be less because of:

• purchasing leverage (economies of scale)

• lower material overhead with fewer types of materials to procure

• fewer setup changes at the molder to change raw materials

In addition, delivery will be faster without setup changes and procurement for multiple types.

P41) Choose raw materials commonly used, especially at the chosen vendor, to eliminate extra procurement cost and setup changes. Try to choose common materials used throughout the vendor base. Be sure these cost savings are factored into the vendor's cost.

P42) Don't limit thinking to one-for-one replacements, when substituting plastics for other materials.

P43) Optimize the number of functions in each part. Optimize decisions between part/mold complexity and the total cost savings in assembly and supply chain management.

- **Mold complexity/cost.** Compare cost of one complex mold to several simpler molds.

- **Assembly labor.** Compare assembly cost of multiple parts to one monolithic part.

- **Material overhead.** Compare purchasing and logistics costs of one vs. multiple parts.

- **Vendor base.** Complex molds and unusual processing may limit the vendor base.

- **Tolerance control.** Monolithic parts control tolerances between features and avoid tolerance stacks. On the other hand, precise part alignment techniques (Guideline A3) may be able to ensure alignment tolerances between multiple parts.

- **Appearance.** Monolithic parts eliminate seams. However, clever styling could mitigate this problem.

P44) Methodically *choose* tolerances for molded parts. Avoid unnecessarily tight tolerances and finishes. Understand tolerance step functions (Guideline P23). Specify optimal tolerances for a "robust design" using the Taguchi Method™ for Robust Design (Guideline Q12 in the Quality Section).

9.4 STANDARDIZATION GUIDELINES

These are the guideline versions of standardization, which was discussed in Chapter 5.

S1) Use standard parts

Select parts from the company standard parts list. Reuse parts that are prevalent in previous designs. Use off-the-shelf hardware produced in volume by several suppliers.

S2) Standardize design features

Standardize on design features like drilled hole sizes, punched hole shapes, thread types, bend radii, and so forth. Each size of these requires the factory to have a unique tool in stock and to set it up for each usage. This guideline is based on Section 5.14 on feature standardization.

S3) Minimize the number of part types

Use standard parts throughout the design, like very few fastener types for the whole product. The use of common parts means fewer parts to design, document, test, debug, order, and supply to the factory floor. Fewer part types means greater purchasing leverage which results in lower cost and better delivery.

S4) Minimize the number of total parts

In addition to minimizing the number of *types* of parts, designers should strive to minimize the *total number* of parts in a design. Simplicity of design can result in inherently fewer parts. Remember that *every* part, no matter how small, incurs significant overhead costs because of the cost of ordering, stocking, delivering to all points of use, reordering, and supplying to field service.

The number of parts can also be minimized by combining multiple parts into a single part (Guideline S7). Part fabrication cost might be slightly more, but assembly cost will be greatly reduced by combining parts.

S5) Standardize on *types* of linear materials; cut & mark as needed

Material that can be supplied by length (wire, cable, rope, chain, and plastic tubing) should be standardized by *type* with the length cut on-demand. For ease of service, some linear material can have codes (ground, return, etc.) printed on them *as they are dispensed.*

S6) Consider prefinished material

Manufacturing operations can be eliminated by ordering prefinished material that is prepainted, preplated, embossed, expanded, anodized, or clad with a different surface alloy. Painting operations for sheet metal can be eliminated by switching to stainless sheet metal. This might be justifiable if the *total* cost of painting is considered. Prefinished material can be ordered with the finished side protected by adhesive backed paper that can be peeled off after assembly.

S7) Combine parts

Every part combination eliminates the need to manufacture the interface features, hold their tolerances, and the time and cost of assembly. It may be possible to fabricate combined parts on a single machine tool in a single setup. Examples are: many parts combined into a monolithic plastic or machined part; many integrated circuits combined into VLSI or ASICs; and multiple circuit boards combined into one, thus eliminating card cages and inter-board wiring operations

9.5 CRITERIA FOR COMBINING PARTS

Parts should be combined whenever possible as a means of reducing the part count and simplifying manufacture. The criteria for combining parts involves asking for following three questions:

1) When the product is in operation, do adjacent parts move with respect to each other?

2) *Must* adjacent parts be made of different materials?

3) *Must* adjacent parts be able to separate for assembly or service?

If all three answers are no, consider combining the parts into one. It is important to remember that every interface between parts requires geometrical features to be designed and manufactured plus all interface tolerances need to be held.

Eliminating interfaces eliminates the need to create interface features and hold their tolerances.

9.6 DESIGNING FOR AUTOMATION

Don't assume that all *labor-intensive* processes can be easily automated. Don't assume that all *quality-sensitive* processes can be easily automated.

Simplify the concept/architecture to combine, consolidate, or eliminate assembly steps.

Understand the spectrum from fixtures through various forms of automation (below), which must be concurrently designed as the product is designed by the design team itself, local specialist contractors working closely with the design team.

Remote contractors may not be able to provide adequate interaction on product/process optimization.

Product design and automation equipment design are so interrelated that preselected vendor/partners should work with teams early. *Do not send assembly drawings out and ask for bids on automation projects.*

Analyze opportunities and justify cost/benefit analysis based on total cost data. Justification should include not only labor savings but also quality, speed, flexibility, etc.

Choose the optimal candidates for various fabrication or assembly tasks. If a clear "winner" emerges, design for that one. If multiple candidates are still in the running, design for all.

Design for the chosen automated process(es) making sure to understand and obey the design rules for every aspect of the process: part singulating, part feeding, alignment, the operation(s), ejection, possibly inspecting, and conveying to next operation.

Make lines flexible to allow new products to ramp up on existing production lines. Select parts suitable for automated handling (see Section 9.7).

Automated and Mechanized Processes

- **Jigs & Fixtures,** to enable easy, consistent fabrication/assembly and hold tolerances. High-volume fixtures can be dedicated for one part or operation with *jig* features that guide cutting tools, e.g., drill guides. Flexible fixtures can be designed to easily position and clamp a family of parts.

- **Dies and molds,** for moldings, castings, extrusions, stampings, etc.

- **Mechanization,** which will aid manual assembly, especially for critical operations. Simple mechanisms can be designed to guide pieces together, load/remove pieces from machine tools, position pieces for subsequent operations, etc. The mechanisms could be human powered or the worker could switch on a powered actuator with appropriate safeguards.

- **Semi-automated processes** assisted by people for non-critical steps like loading, starting, unloading, etc.

- **CNC machine tools,** where standard machine tools can be programmed to perform many automated steps, and, as necessary, quickly change programs for other parts/products. If designers obey design rules for the equipment, standard CNC machinery can be a low-cost way to achieve accuracy and speed. The inherently versatile equipment can be designed to process a wide range of operations on a wide range of parts if changeover setups are eliminated and the following steps can be done quickly:

  - Part positioning

  - Tool or part loading/changing

  - Changing already-written CNC programs. For a large variety, programs can be generated automatically when predetermined parametric CAD templates accept unique dimensions from order entry databases and plug numbers into "floating" dimensions or altered parametric designs then go through CAD/CAM program generators that automatically create CNC programs "on the fly."

- **Robots,** where the motions can be performed programmably by off-the-shelf robots, but custom end-effectors (e.g., grippers) may have to be designed and built. A rule of thumb is that the robot itself represents half the system cost. Robots can be structured into flexible cells if:

  - All workpieces can be quickly loaded, positioned, and unloaded, which could be done manually if appropriate safeguards are in place.

  - End-effectors are adaptable or can be quickly changed, which could be done manually with appropriate safeguards are in place

  - Stored programs can be quickly loaded or automatically generated.

- **Special *flexible* automation,** which is concurrently designed by the team and can be versatile enough for a range of parts or operations.

- **Special *fixed* automation,** which is concurrently designed by the team to efficiently perform repetitive tasks on a single part or subassembly. The automated operations themselves will provide the most benefit to cost, quality, flow, and time. Feeding and unloading automated equipment may have less benefit and may unnecessarily increase the scope, resources, and time for the automation project. It could be added later if justified if allowed for in the initial design. There are many guidelines for feeding part to automation (see next section).

9.7 HANDLING BY AUTOMATION

For automated assembly, product assembly and part shapes need to be optimized for singulating, orienting, feeding, presenting, gripping and installing.

H1) Design products so that parts are assembled from above or from the minimum number of directions

Assembling parts from above is easier for workers and automation equipment. Products must be design for vertical assembly to use "SCARA" robots, whose arms move in a horizontal plane with the gripper moving only up and down. Assembling parts from the bottom may require turning the product over, or worse, forcing workers or robots to work underneath the product.

H2) Design and select parts that can be oriented by automation

Make sure parts can be oriented by automation. The best way, of course, is to design parts so they do not *need* orientation as recommended in Guideline P3 (design for symmetry). If the part is not symmetrical, then provide some features on the parts that will allow easy orientation. The ease of orientation can have a significant impact on automation costs. The right geometry may permit passive orientation like stationary guides over a moving conveyor belt. To orient from visual features would require vision systems and possibly some artificial intelligence.

Vibratory bowl feeders singulate and orient small parts by vibrating a bowl lined with a spiral/helical track in such a way that the parts creep up the track to a "gate" which passes properly oriented parts and dumps misoriented parts back in the bowl. References are available on designing parts and gates for vibratory bowl feeders.[13] Suppliers of vibratory feeders offer a standard line of bowls and most will design special tracks and gates as part of the sale.

In order to know which features to specify for the least cost automation equipment, the designer will have to know something about automatic orientation and work with manufacturing engineers and equipment suppliers.

H3) Design parts to easily maintain orientation

A basic principle of automated assembly is that *once a part is oriented, that orientation should be maintained through the entire process.* Design part shapes so that orientation is easy to maintain. Design parts for easy stacking, nesting, or movement in other transport devices (Guideline H8).

Avoid part shapes that can only be shipped in bulk unless the part shape is extremely easy to orient by part feeders.

H4) Use parts that will not tangle when handled in bulk

If parts *must* be shipped in bulk, make sure they will not *tangle.* An example of tangling is a box of the wire hooks used to hang Christmas tree ornaments. To avoid tangling, parts must not have any features that could hook into (or allow being hooked by) another part. Ring shaped or cylindrical parts should close all the way. Springs should be ordered with *closed* ends.

H5) Use parts that will not shingle when fed end to end

It is common in automatic parts handling to transport parts along some form of linear conveyance like an enclosed track. The parts are touching end-to-end and are propelled by gravity or some powered means. The parts must have flat enough surfaces where they touch or they will "shingle" on top of each other, thus jamming the conveyor. Thin disks or any wedge shaped features are prone to shingling.

H6) Use parts that do not adhere to each other or the track

Similarly, when parts are fed end-to-end, they must not adhere to each other or the track because of any tackiness on their surfaces. Be sure that tackiness does not develop with age, heat, light, and so forth.

H7) Specify tolerances tight enough for automatic handling

Automatic handling may place special tolerance requirements on parts for sorting, orienting, transferring, and the assembly itself. Fixed automation (even robots without adaptive capability) may not be able to adjust to dimensional variations beyond a certain tolerance.

H8) Avoid flexible parts which are hard for automation to handle

Flexible parts like cables are very hard for automation to transfer or assemble. Instead, use a rigid equivalent or eliminate the need for the flexible part.

H9) Make sure parts can be presented to automation

Every part that is automatically assembled must be able to be presented *accurately in a known position*. This may require fixturing locations (as specified in Guideline P5) and also special "parts presenters" to be devised by automation engineers. Parts presenters consist of a means of *transporting* or *feeding* the parts (after they are singulated and oriented), *presenting* or *positioning* the parts in a known location, and *releasing* the parts at the right time when picked up. Often, singulation/orientation mechanism (e.g., vibratory bowl feeder) suppliers may also furnish the part presentation mechanisms.

To avoid designing or buying custom parts presenters, design parts to be presented in semi-standard part presenters like trays. Many robots can be programmed to pick parts from a tray if they are arranged in some regular pattern; the robot can advance through the entire pattern and then stop or signal when finished.

Parts can also be presented on "tape and reel" where parts are temporarily captivated between *tapes* which are rolled up on a *reel*. Leaded resistors and capacitors have been routinely presented suspended between two parallel tapes which are discarded after the part is cut off by the insertion machine. There are semi-custom presenters available that can accurately present many small part shapes "sandwiched" between two tapes. The lower tape has index holes which the machine uses to index the part each time a part is picked. The upper tape is peeled away after each pick to expose the next part.

H10) Make sure parts can be gripped by automation

The most common universal gripper is the parallel jaw type which requires parallel surfaces *in an accessible area* of the part. Even if the part does not need accessible parallel surfaces for function, consider adding them for gripping. Special grippers can be devised to grip any *single* shape but the robot may have to change grippers each time that part is to be picked. This may be all right for a dedicated part line, but would be too cumbersome for a flexible work cell.

H11) Make sure parts are within machine gripper span

Automation machinery and robot grippers have limited *spans* (how wide they can open). Special grippers may force the robot to change grippers. Gripper extenders may limit the minimum grip or add too much bulk to the gripper and impede access into tight spaces.

H12) Make sure parts are within automation load capacity

Most robots have limited load capacities, which may be reduced to just a few pounds of *load* capacity after deducting the weight of the grippers themselves. Gripper changers add even more weight to the arm and thus decrease payload capacity even further. Keep part weight below the *net load capacity* available from the planned automation.

H13) Make sure parting lines, sprues, gating or any flash do not interfere with gripping

Grippers need predictable surfaces (usually flat or round) to grip reliably. Be sure that parting lines, sprues, gating or flash do not protrude from castings or moldings and interfere with gripping.

ENDNOTES/REFERENCES

1. Morgan & Liker, *The Toyota Product Development System,* Chapter 4, "Front-Load the PD Process to Explore Alternatives Thoroughly."

2. James G. Bralla, Editor, *Design for Manufacturability Handbook* (1998, McGraw-Hill), 1344 pages, 1292 illustrations.

3. *Tool and Manufacturing Engineers Handbook, Volume 6, Design for Manufacturability,* (1992, Society of Manufacturing Engineers, Dearborn, MI).

4. H.E. Trucks, *Designing for Economical Production,* 2nd edition (1987, Society of Manufacturing Engineers), 366 pages.

5. G. Pahl and W. Beitz, *Engineering Design; A Systematic Approach,* (1988, Springer-Verlag), translated from German; 400 pages with 50 on DFM..

6. Omer W. Blodgett, *Design of Welded Structures,* published by the Lincoln Arc Welding Foundation.

7. Charles W. Briggs, Editor, *Steel Castings Handbook*; published by the Steel Founders' Society of America; 950 pages.

8. David M. Anderson, *Build-to-Order & Mass Customization; The Ultimate Supply Chain Management and Lean Manufacturing Strategy for Low-Cost On-Demand Production without Forecasts or Inventory*, (2004; 520 pages; CIM Press). See articles at www.build-to-order-consulting.com.

9. Lance Ealey, *Quality by Design*, (1998, ASI Press, Dearborn MI).

10. For more on DFM consulting and design studies, see page 408 or visit the *Consulting* page at www.design4manufacturability.com.

11. Kiyoshi Suzaki, *The New Manufacturing Challenge; Techniques for Continuous Improvement*, (1987, The Free Press).

12. Ealey, *Quality by Design.*

13. Geoffrey Boothroyd, *Handbook of Feeding and Orienting Techniques for Small Parts*, published by , Boothroyd Dewhurst, Inc. 30 Holley Street, Wakefield, RI 02879.

10

DESIGN FOR QUALITY

10.1 EFFECT OF DESIGN ON QUALITY

Design is more responsible for quality than most people realize. Long ago, Dr. Joseph Juran,[1] the quality control guru, concluded that *"One-third of all quality-control problems originate in the product's design."*
Designers determine the number of parts, decide which are purchased off-the-shelf, select the purchased parts, design the rest of the parts (indirectly specifying how they will be made), determine how the parts must be assembled, and specify how the parts function together. The product's design really determines the factory processes, whether or not the designers realize it. If designers realized this they might be more inclined to work with Manufacturing as a team and simultaneously design the product and process.

Manufacturing is often held solely responsible for quality. To be sure, manufacturing has definite responsibilities to do everything *it* can to ensure quality.

Manufacturing may expend substantial effort to *try to* ensure high quality to compensate for insufficient attention devoted to the *inherent* quality of the design. If diligent, the factory may be successful at keeping quality problems from escaping the plant, but the company may be incurring a high *cost of quality* as discussed in Chapter 6. Manufacturing, and often Product Development, can be seriously disrupted by diagnostics, rework, excess inventory, firefighting, and quality control efforts.

Merely talking up quality or having a quality program is not enough if the product is not designed well for quality and there is a lack of understanding how customers value quality.

On the other hand, if the steps presented here are not followed and the product has quality problems in manufacturing or in the field, engineering resources will be depleted by excessive change orders and

291

factory troubleshooting. In the worse cases, quality problems can force a redesign, the ultimate drain on engineering resources.

As pointed out in Chapter 1, 80% of a product's lifetime costs are determined by the first 8% which is the design. And no matter how hard the factory tries, it can only affect the remaining 20%. Similarly, a large percentage of the products quality is determined by design.

10.2 QUALITY DESIGN GUIDELINES

The following is a list of proactive guidelines, procedures, and cultural perspectives that product development teams can use to design quality into products.

Q1) Establish a quality culture

Establish a quality culture where "quality is everyone's responsibility," not just the Quality Department. Understand that quality starts with product development.

Q2) Understand past quality problems and issues

Thoroughly understand the root causes of quality problems on current and past products to prevent new product development from repeating past mistakes. This includes part selection, design aspects, processing, supplier selection, and so forth. It may be useful to have Manufacturing, Quality, and Field Service people make presentations to newly formed product development teams showing, hopefully with some real life examples, some of the past problems that can be avoided in new designs.

Q3) Methodically define the product

Methodically define the product so it will meet the customer's needs with Quality Function Deployment (QFD) discussed in Chapter 3. This ensures that the first design will satisfy the "voice of the customer" without the cost and risk of changing the design.

Q4) Make quality a primary design goal

Proactively design in quality by making sure that quality is a primary design goal as important as functionality, manufacturability, and all the considerations discussed in Chapter 2. In older reactive product development cultures, quality issues were only dealt with only after problems surfaced in manufacturing, or worse, in the field.

Q5)   Use Multifunctional teamwork

Break down the walls between departments with multifunctional design teams (Deming's 9th point) to ensure that *all* quality issues are raised and resolved early and that quality is indeed treated as a primary design goal.

Q6)   Simplify the design and processing

Simplify the concept/architecture with the fewest parts, interfaces, and process steps. Elegantly simple designs and uncomplicated processing result in *inherently* high quality products.

Q7)   Chose parts for quality

Too often parts are selected for only functionality and cost. However, to ensure quality by design, parts must also be selected for quality. If part "cost" goals seem to be at odds with quality goals, then cost is probably not being computed on a total cost basis (Chapter 7), which would include quality costs, as discussed in Chapter 6. When total cost is taken into account, leading product development teams would never choose the proverbial "lowest-bid" part, despite the faddish popularity of on-line internet part bidding. Select parts and suppliers on a total cost criterion that includes quality is Deming's 4th point.

Q8)   Optimizing processing
\

Select or concurrently engineer manufacturing processes to ensure the highest quality production. Be careful to be sure that new processes are robust enough to ensure high quality products *in production quantities from production environments*. Design within process capabilities; design for processes that are in control and can reliably produce quality parts.

Q9)   Minimize Cumulative Effects

Understand the cumulative effect of part quality on product quality, as discussed below. Product quality degrades *exponentially as part count increases* (see Section 10.3).

Q10) Thoroughly Design the Product Right the First Time

Use the techniques presented in Chapter 1 to ensure that the product is design right the first time. If quality is not assured by the initial design, then expensive change orders (Section 1.10) will have to be carried out, wasting valuable engineering resources and possibly inducing further quality problems in the process. Be sure to be able to comfortably satisfy all the design goals and constraints without having to compromise the product just to get it out the door.

Q11) Mistake-proof the Design with Poka-Yoke

Proactively prevent defects in manufacture and repair with *Poka-Yoke*, which is Japanese for mistake-proofing or "idiot-proofing." This is discussed in Section 10.9.

Q12) Optimize tolerances for a *robust* design that are compatible with manufacturing processes

Specify optimal tolerances for a "robust design" to ensure the high quality by design. The Taguchi Method^{TM} for Robust Design is a systematic way to optimize tolerances to achieve *high quality at low cost.*[2] It does this by using Design of Experiments to analyze the effect of all tolerances on functionality, quality, and manufacturability to analyze tolerance "stacks" and "worse case" situations. The procedure can identify critical dimensions that need tight tolerances and precision parts, which can then be toleranced methodically. The unique strength of this approach is that it can minimize cost while assuring high quality by identifying low demand dimensions that can have looser tolerances and cheaper parts.

Such a design would be considered *robust* so that it could be manufactured predictably with consistently high quality and perform adequately in all anticipated usage environments. Without a methodical way to determine tolerances, the alternatives would be: (1) make all tolerances tight "just to be sure," which is expensive. Tolerances that *appear* to be overly tight may have credibility problems and invite interpretation or (2) inadvertently (or deliberately) make tolerances too loose, leading to manufacturability and quality problems. Performance, quality, and manufacturability problems may be inconsistent and thus hard to troubleshoot and rectify.

Q13) Continuously improve the product

Use continuous improvement, or *kaizen,* to make incremental improvements to the product and processing. The old paradigm for tolerances was that quality would be assured if each dimension was made "within spec" or within the specified tolerance band. This not only costs more because parts outside the band must be scrapped but also this can become problematic when many parts are rejected outside the acceptable tolerance range; when this happens, it means that the parts that *do* pass will have a high percentage of parts at either extreme of the tolerance range, as shown in Figure 10-1. This could result in problems when they are combined with other mating parts that are skewed toward the "worst case" combinations.

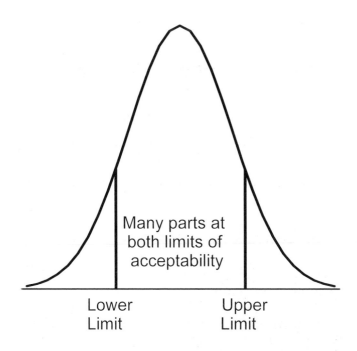

Many parts at both limits of acceptability

Lower   Upper
Limit   Limit

Figure 10-1: Parts Within Spec, but Many at Tolerance Extreme

Continuous improvement programs, on the other hand, strive to continuously tighten the accuracy of manufactured parts, so that the dimensions become closer and closer to the target, as shown in Figure 10-2. This results in the population of parts being closer to the center with few, if any, parts near the original limits.

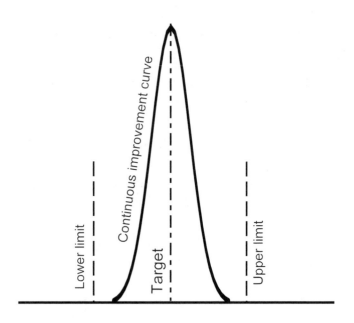

Figure 10-2: Continuous Improvement Curve Approaches Target

Q14)   Document thoroughly

In the rush to develop products, many designers fail to document every aspect of the design thoroughly. Drawings sent to the manufacturing or vendors need to convey the design *unambiguously* for manufacture, tooling, *and* inspection. Imprecise drawings invite misunderstandings and interpretation, which add cost, waste time, and may compromise quality.

Geometric Dimensioning and Tolerancing (GD&T) is an unambiguous methodology that can clearly convey the design. In GD&T, each dimension is dimensioned from the most logical and precise *datum*. For instance, several holes to be machined in a piece of metal would be dimensioned from a single datum rather than from each other (which would cause a cumulative error) or from various edges (in which the edge tolerance would affect the hole spacing).

GD&T optimizes dimensioning for (1) function, ensure the parts are made as intended, (2) manufacturing, to optimize processing and fixturing and (3) inspection, allowing the use of Coordinate Measurement Machines. Proper datum referencing also allows the maximum number of operations to be done in the same setup without repositioning the part (Guideline P10 - "Design machined parts to be made in the same setup").

Q15) Implement incentives that reward quality

In many organizations, individuals do what they are *rewarded* to do. If they are rewarded for releasing a design "on time," they will, effectively, *throw it over the wall on time, ready of not!* If they are rewarded for achieving "cost targets" without total cost accounting, they will do so by buying the cheapest parts available, probably without concern for part quality. So reward systems must be structured to include quality metrics.

In addition to these quality guidelines, there are also several "human factors" guidelines that affect quality, which are presented later.

10.3 CUMULATIVE EFFECTS ON PRODUCT QUALITY

It is very important to understand the *cumulative* effect of the number and quality of parts. Computations will be based on the assumption that any single part failure will cause the product to fail. This is valid unless the product has redundancy or backup features that are used in critical applications (like aerospace).

Statistically, this situation is similar to a *series reliability model* which states that the reliability of the system is computed by *multiplying* the individual reliabilities of *all* the parts of the system assuming any single failure causes a system failure (in series):

$$R_s = R_1 \cdot R_2 \cdot R_3 \cdot R_4 \cdots R_n = \prod_{I=1}^{n} R_i$$

where $R_s =$ the reliability of the system

  $R_n =$ the reliability of component n

The equivalent formula for product quality would represent the probability of the product functioning properly or having no defects given the individual probabilities of the parts being free from defects:

$$Q_p = Q_1 \cdot Q_2 \cdot Q_3 \cdot Q_4 \cdots Q_n = \prod_{I=1}^{n} Q_i$$

where $Q_p =$ the quality level of the product measured as the probability of proper function or being defect-free

  $Q_n =$ the quality level of part n.

The quality level of parts is easily measured in percent that are defect-free. Quality levels have been rising so much that the "percent good" is becoming a cumbersome number, for instance, 99.95%. In these cases the quality level is expressed in *defects per million (DPM)* which, for 99.95% would be 500 DPM, a more manageable number. The DPM measurement psychologically fits in better with "zero defect" programs since the goal is zero DPM. When making these calculations, be sure to convert to the decimal equivalent of percent, for instance .9995 to represent 99.95%.

Product quality can be approximated by the *average* quality level of the parts using the formula:

$$Q_p = (Q_a)^n$$

where Q_p = Quality level of the product

Q_a = Average quality level of parts

n = Number of parts

Example

A product consists of 25 parts that are all 99% good, which some suppliers might contend is adequate:

$$Q_p = (Q_a)^n = (.99)^{25} = .78$$

This means that *only 78% of products will be good because 25 parts are only 99% good!* And *this assumes perfect processing quality.* Factory quality problems will lower product quality even further.

Graphical Effects of Part Quantity and Quality

Figure 10-3 graphically shows how product quality varies with part quality and part quantities. The lines are plots of the equation,

$$Q_p = (Q_a)^n$$

for varying part quality levels. Note that each line represents *twice* as "bad" a part as the one above it.

Printed circuit boards are built with several hundred components covering the whole range of lines on the graph. All designers should carefully use these formulas to predict product quality degradation just from the number of components.

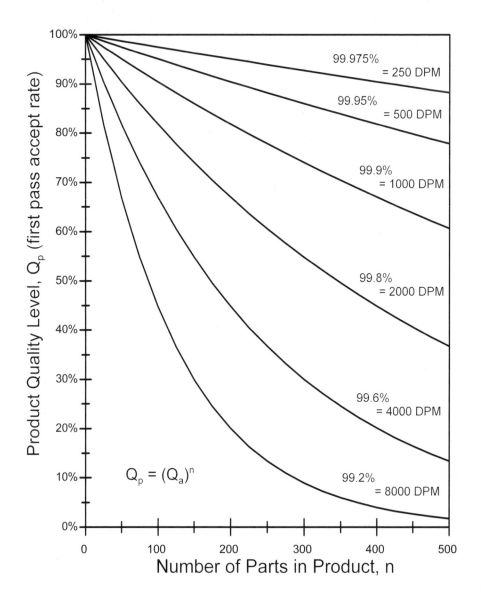

Plotted lines are for average part quality levels, Q_a
cited as percent good and DPM (Defects/Million)

Figure 10-3: Quality as a Function of Part Count
For Average Part Quality Levels

Predictive Quality Model

For products with groups of parts with different quality levels, the formula, say for four, would be:

$$Q_p = Q_{a1}^{n1} \cdot Q_{a2}^{n2} \cdot Q_{a3}^{n3} \cdot Q_{a4}^{n4} \ldots \text{ and so forth}$$

where Q_p = Quality level of the product

Q_{a1} = Quality level of the first group

$n1$ = Number of parts in the first group

This formula is an extremely powerful tool that can be used as a *predictive model* to estimate product quality based on a parts list, which is usually available early in the design process. This formula can easily be incorporated into a spreadsheet so that various "what if" scenarios can be calculated.

It is important to realize the following conclusions about these formulas: Mathematically, any number less than 1.0 (perfection) raised to any positive integer exponent (1 or more) will lower the resultant product quality *exponentially!* Thus, unless part quality levels are very high, *an excessive number of components will have an exponential degradation on product quality!*

10.4 QUALITY STRATEGIES FOR PRODUCTS

Given the above part quality issues affecting product quality, the following strategies can be developed.

Maximize: $(Q_a)^n$ by:

a) Maximizing the average part quality level, Q_a

b) Minimizing the number of parts, n

c) Optimize both of the above.

Designers should continually think in terms of maximizing $(Q_a)^n$. When doing a trade off analysis on competing designs, they should choose the solution with the highest $(Q_a)^n$.

If the product trend is toward more complexity, *and thus higher part count,* and the part quality is the same, then the cumulative exponential effective of part quality will cause the *product* quality to suffer. Senior managers may be puzzled why product quality is dropping when the incoming part quality is the same.

Part of the solution involves *continuous improvement[3]* of part quality and factory process quality to compensate for this increase in complexity. Another solution is to keep trying to *decrease* the part count, despite increasing product complexity. Designers of complex electronics circuitry have the option of combining dozens of small integrated circuits into a single standard VLSI chip or custom ASIC (Application Specific Integrated Circuit) device with a higher quality level than any of the chips replaced! This type of option can make a major improvement in product quality, or, in some cases, may be the only way to achieve an acceptable level of product quality.

10.5 RELIABILITY DESIGN GUIDELINES

Reliability can be defined as *quality in the time dimension.* A product with good reliability has *freedom from failure in use.* The classical definition is *the probability of a product will perform satisfactorily for a specified period of time under a stated set of use conditions.* The elements of reliability include probability, performance, time, and usage conditions. Here are some guidelines for optimizing reliability by design:

Q16) Simplify the concept

Concept simplicity is the key to *inherent* reliability, although this rarely is mentioned in statistically oriented reliability handbooks. Significantly reducing the number of parts, interfaces, connectors, interactions, and complexity, in general, will greatly improve product reliability.

Q17) Make reliability a primary design goal

Proactively design in reliability by making sure that reliability is a primary design goal as important as functionality, manufacturability, and all the considerations discussed in Chapter 2. In older reactive product development cultures, reliability issues were only dealt with only after problems surfaced in the field.

Q18) Understand past reliability problems

Thoroughly understand the root causes of reliability problems on current and past products to prevent new product development from repeating past mistakes. This includes part selection, design aspects, processing, supplier selection, usage conditions, and so forth. It may be useful to have Manufacturing, Reliability, and Field Service personnel make presentations to newly formed product development teams showing, hopefully with some real life examples, some of the past reliability problems that can be avoided in new designs.

Q19) Simulate early

Use simulations & computer models to simulate and optimize reliability early to optimize early design decisions, which are much easier and more effective to incorporate than any changes that would be implemented later based on data from the field. Conduct *Failure Mode and Effects Analysis* (FMEA) early to predict most likely failure modes and develop strategies to minimize failures and their consequences. When early units are available, utilize accelerated stress tests.

Q20) Optimize part selection on the basis of substantiated reliability data

Select parts on the basis of *substantiated* reliability data, not just advertised claims. The lack of substantiated reliability data, which is more common for new parts, may encourage greater use of proven parts (see next guideline).

Q21) Use proven parts and design features

Use *proven* standard parts and design features that have been used successfully before and would be most likely to provide reliable service. Past performance data can steer designers quickly to the best parts and design features to help them maximize reliability. A key goal of design teams should be to reuse proven designs, parts, and modules. As mentioned in Section 3.1, a high percentage of complaints, field failures, recalls, and lawsuits do *not* involve new features or new technology. Rather, they involve "boilerplate" functions that should be based on proven designs, parts, and modules. For instance, in electronics, many problems arise from the mundane power supply. In the automobile industry, the most serious problems and consequences involve fuel systems, seat belts, steering, suspension, tires, and so forth. These are not the parts that companies are advertising or customers are clamor for, which are more likely to be things like styling, cup holders, stereos, and navigation systems.

Q22) Use proven manufacturing processes

Use proven manufacturing processes that are in control and have a history of producing reliable parts. This can avoid the added variables introduced when new processes are utilized. Ironically, some products cannot utilize existing proven processes because they are not designed well enough for manufacturability for those specific processes.

Q23) Use pre-certified modules

Use proven, pre-certified modules that can be individually certified. If the product's architecture was optimized for this, then it may be possible to consider the product certified if all the modules were pre-certified.

Q24) Design to minimize errors with Poka-Yoke

Design to proactively minimize errors in fabrication, assembly, installation, maintenance, and repair with *Poka-Yoke,* discussed in Section 10.9, which is Japanese for mistake-proofing or "idiot-proofing" and Section 10.10 on Designing to Minimize Errors.

Q25) Design to minimize degradation during shipping, installation, or repair

Design products *and* packaging so that products do not suffer any damage during shipping. Specify the installation process so that reliability is not degraded by all the steps involved in installation or repair.

To maximize reliability in electronics:

Q26) Minimize mechanical electrical connections

Minimize mechanical electrical connections, especially for low voltage. A common illustration of this problem is the automatic reflex that we all shake flashlights when they do not come on right away. Some specific solutions to avoid low-voltage connectors are:

- Combine circuit boards to eliminate cables and connectors

- Use a means of connections with the minimum mechanical connections such as *flex cable,* which can connect different circuit boards with flexible traces (the conductors in circuit boards) that are soldered to components on both circuit boards.

- Minimize use of sockets

Q27) Eliminate all hand soldering

Hand soldering is the least reliable way to make electrical connections. Some companies have discovered disturbing data that hand soldered joints can pass tests in the factory and fail later in the field. In contrast, automatic soldering of circuit boards (reflow or wave solder) is about the most refined industrial process, with plants routinely achieving "Six Sigma" quality levels (about 3 defects per million). Hand soldered joints can be avoided by two strategies:

a) Design out of the products the need for hand soldered joints by combining circuit boards, using flex cable, and proper use of connectors and cables.

b) Design within the DFM guidelines for printed circuit boards so that component location rule violations will not force components to be soldered by hand to circuit boards.

Q28) Establish repair limits for circuit boards

Most companies do not have repair limits on the number of times components can be desoldered and replaced. Excessive hand soldering can damage the circuit board pads or holes and possibly adjacent components. Ray Prasad, author of "Surface Mount Technology," recommends a maximum of two repairs to prevent internal thermal damaged to printed circuit boards.[4]

Q29) Use burn-in wisely

Use *burn-in* or *run-in* to induce early failures until the problem can be isolated. Then use this information to eliminate the causes of the problems.

10.6 MEASUREMENT OF RELIABILITY

The measure of reliability is the *mean time between failures* or MTBF = $1/\lambda$

where λ = the *failure rate,*

What this measure means is that, on the average, one failure in operation can be expected to occur after a period of time equal to the MTBF.

The reliability of a product can be numerically expressed as:

$$R(t) = e^{-\lambda t}$$

where t = time

10.7 RELIABILITY PHASES

There are three phases in which products experience different reliability behavior: the *infant mortality, useful life,* and *wearout* phases, shown in Figure 10-4:

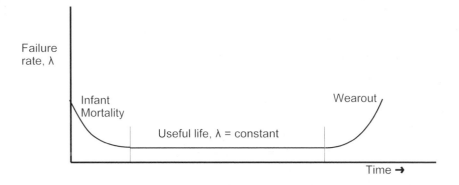

Figure 10-4: Reliability Phases

The following discussion lists causes of reliability failures in the infant mortality and wearout phases. Note that many of these causes can be prevented proactively by optimal design of products and processes.

Infant mortality phase

This phase characterized by early failures due to:

• Built in flaws from processing:
  • Poor welds or seals
  • Cracks in castings
  • Poor solder joints
  • Surface contamination
  • Chemical impurities
  • Handling or static damage
  • Incorrect positioning of parts

- Transportation damage:
  - Physical damage to parts
  - Shock sensitive parts overstressed
  - Parts loosened during shipping
- Installation and set-up errors:
  - Factory errors
  - Customer errors

Wearout phase

The wearout phase is when the product failure rate begins to rise from deterioration. Causes include:

- Frictional wear
- Fatigue
- Creep
- Corrosion or oxidation
- Chemical changes
- Insulation breakdown
- Shrinkage or cracking in plastics

10.8 HUMAN FACTORS AND DFM

Human factors considerations focus on the interactions of human beings with products, equipment, facilities, procedures and work environments.[5] Human factors are some of the many constraints to be considered along with function, cost, quality, manufacturability and repairability.

Human factors affect the level of skills needed to build products, the amount of human errors that can occur in production, and the effectiveness of manual inspections. Product designers should keep human factors in mind to optimize the human elements of product manufacture and user acceptance.

10.9 POKA-YOKE (MISTAKE-PROOFING)

"Poka-Yoke" is a Japanese concept that originally evolved to prevent mistakes in manufacturing.[6] *Poka-Yoke* can be used as a *design* methodology to "mistake-proof" the design so parts cannot be assembled wrong or products manufactured incorrectly. Clever design features need only be designed once, but these features go on to prevent mistakes in manufacturing for the life of the product. The following discussion presents the general principles of poka-yoke applied to product development. After that, there are several guidelines to minimize errors.

With parts standardization, there are fewer *types* of parts and, thus, less chance of choosing the wrong part. Symmetrical parts cannot go in backwards. Non-symmetrical parts with exaggerated asymmetry will not be assembled wrong or forced into a wrong orientation; this avoids one of the most effort-prone parts – one that is almost square. Non-symmetrical parts should have polarized connectors or mounts.

If different parts have different installation geometries, then the product can be designed so that the wrong parts cannot be installed, such as unique shafts with unique diameters, unique gears with unique bores, unique fasteners or valves with unique threads.

Avoid choosing the wrong part by indicating or presenting only the correct part and by minimizing the number of part types with standardization, ideally with only one of each type of part at each workstation.

Features can be added to prevent incorrect assembly, such as alignment pins or tabs, unique geometries and shapes, and markings to indicate correct assembly and aid in inspection.

Potentially confusing assembly can be avoided entirely by conceptual simplification like combining parts or eliminating them entirely.

10.10 DESIGNING TO MINIMIZE ERRORS

The following guidelines are grouped into four categories of errors, oriented toward manufacturing:

• Errors of *commission*

• Errors of *omission*

• *Sequence* errors

• *Timing* errors

Errors of Commission

Generally, these errors involve installing a part in the wrong position, installing the wrong part, installing the part in the wrong orientation, or damaging the part or assembly. The following guidelines (some are repeated here for completeness) are designed to prevent human factors errors:

S1) Use standard parts.

This guideline is repeated from Chapter 9 and discussed in depth in Chapter 5 on standardization. The chance of an assembler picking the wrong part is lower if there are *fewer different parts* in the assembly. Standardization programs encourage widespread use of the fewest types of parts throughout the assembly.

P3) Design parts with symmetry.

The possibility that an assembler will insert a part backwards can be *eliminated* if that part is symmetrical.

P4) If part symmetry is not possible, make parts very asymmetrical.

The best part for assembly is one that is symmetrical in all views. The *worst* part is one that is *slightly* asymmetrical which may be installed wrong because the worker or robot could not notice the asymmetry. Or worse, the part may be *forced* in the wrong orientation by a worker (that thinks the tolerance is off) or by a robot (that doesn't know any better).

So, if symmetry cannot be achieved, make the parts *very* asymmetrical. Then workers will less likely *install* the part wrong because it will not *fit* wrong.

P7) Make part differences very obvious.

Different materials or internal features may not be obvious to workers. If parts cannot be identical, make sure their differences are obvious. This is especially important in rapid assembly situations where workers handle many different parts. To distinguish different parts, use markings, labels, color, or different packaging if they come individually packaged. Intel's Systems Group uses different (but functionally equivalent) platings to distinguish metric from English fasteners.

P14) Design machined parts to be made in one setup

For machined parts, ensure accuracy by designing parts and fixturing them so all key dimensions are all cut in one setup (chucking). Removing the part to reposition for subsequent cutting can result in mistakes and lowers accuracy relative to cuts made in the original position. Single setup machining is less expensive too.

A12)   Make sure the *wrong part* cannot go in the intended position.

Make sure that, even if the wrong part *is* picked up, that it physically cannot go into the intended position. Design the product with foolproof assembly geometries so that the wrong part cannot physically fit into intended position. The physical shape of the part could be such that only the correct part fits into its proper destination. Tabs or obstacles could be added that would prevent the wrong part from being assembled. The obstacles can be on the installed part or where the part goes.

A13)   Make sure the part cannot go into the *wrong position.*

Again, use foolproof geometries so that a part physically cannot be installed in the wrong position. Use tabs or other protrusions to preclude the part from being assembled in the wrong position. The obstacles can be on the installed part or in the area where the part is to go.

A14)   Design so parts cannot be installed in the wrong orientation.

First, make parts symmetrical (Guideline P3) so that orientation is not an issue. If parts cannot be made symmetrical, make them *very* asymmetrical (Guideline P4) so that they cannot physically be installed in the wrong orientation. Special obstacles or features can be added to prevent incorrect orientation. The obstacles can be on the installed part or in the area where the part is to go. If wrong orientation cannot be *prevented*, it can be minimized by markings, labels, arrows or color to identify correct orientation. The part shape can be molded in or printed in the correct orientation on the area where the part is to be installed.

A15) Revisions (changes) to the product design are *clearly* **conveyed to manufacturing and implemented.**

If the design has been changed after release, be sure the change is *clearly* conveyed to manufacturing and implemented as intended in a timely manner. Make sure the change itself does not induce the need for other changes.

Errors of Omission

Generally, these errors involve leaving out parts or forgetting operation steps or changes.

A16) Design so that omissions cannot happen.

Design products with special features that can prevent one part from being assembled if the previous part is missing. Design geometries so that the next part will either not go in at all or go all the way through to the other side if the previous part is missing. The special features can be on the part, on adjacent parts, or somewhere in the area where the part is to be installed. For instance, if a pulley was missing, the belt could not be installed.

A17) Design so that subsequent part installation will sense previous part omission.

Design products so that if a part is missing, the worker can sense this when installing the next part. For instance, when installing a gear in a gear train, workers should be expected to make sure the gear cannot spin freely, indicating a missing gear in the gear train.

A18) Design so that omissions would be visually obvious.

Add markings or colors so that an omission would be visually obvious. Part outlines can show when a part is missing, just like the common tool outlines that show that tools are missing in a shop.

A19) Design so that omissions would be easy to see during inspection.

Provide visual access to critical assembly areas so inspectors, or subsequent operators, can tell if parts are missing.

A20)   Eliminate process steps that depend on operators' memory.

Make assembly steps so simple, obvious, and consistent that quality does not depend on workers' memories.

A21)   Revisions and changes *do* get documented and implemented.

Make sure that revisions and changes *actually do* get implemented in a timely manner to *everyone* who needs to know.

Sequence Errors

Generally, sequence errors involve tasks performed out of sequence, parts installed in the wrong order, or process steps performed in the wrong order.

A22)   Design so assembly or process sequence doesn't matter.

Design so that parts are independently replaceable, as recommended in Guideline A5, so that assembly order is not important. Design so process steps can be performed in any order.

A23)   Design so assembly steps cannot happen in the wrong order.

Use foolproof mechanisms or part features so that assembly steps physically cannot happen in the wrong order. For instance, a nesting set of different size kitchen bowls cannot be "assembled" in the wrong order. Parts mounted *on top of each other* could prevent incorrect assembly with the right geometries; but make sure this does not complicate repair.

A24)   Design so assembly or process sequence is intuitively obvious.

If assembly or processing must be done in a required sequence, make sure the sequence is intuitively obvious, for instance, parts installed in order of increasing (or decreasing) part size. Parts can be marked with sequence markings.

A25)   Clearly specify assembly or process order.

If the sequence is not intuitively obvious, provide clear directions on the parts, products, or work areas with arrows, marks, written instructions, or on-line instructions. Policies and procedures should be clearly presented to workers.

Timing Errors

Generally, timing errors involve process operations performed too short or too long.

A26)   Design without the need for timed processes.

If there are no timed processes, then process timing will not be a source of errors.

A27)   Eliminate operator timed processes.

If timed processes are required, make them automatic or computer controlled so that workers will not have to do the timing.

A28)   Make all timed operations the same.

If all timed processes are the same, there is less chance that one process timing will be confused with another process.

A29)   Make different timings *very* different.

If processes timing must be different, make them very different to avoid confusion.

Solutions to Error Prevention After Design

If error prevention is *not* addressed in the design, the factory will have to compensate by hiring more skilled (and more expensive) workers, training them more, and exercising constant vigilance with procedures and inspections.

Design happens once. But hiring and training must
be repeated as new people become part of the system.
And, vigilance must be constant.

10.11 STRATEGY TO DESIGN IN QUALITY

The methodologies of this book can be used to proactive assure high quality and reliability *by design* using the following techniques:

• Understand past quality problems through "lessons learned" databases, research, and presentations from related project people.

• Quality design guidelines Q1 through Q29.

• Quality Function Deployment (QFD) to define products to *capture the voice of the customer.* QFD is one of the techniques in the collection of tools known as "Design for Six Sigma."

• Use multifunctional teamwork (Deming's 9th point) to ensure that quality is a primary design consideration and that *all* quality issues are raised and resolved early and quality is proactively designed in.

• Thorough up-front work to implement all the above early and avoid significantly greater quality and ramp problems later.

• Simplify the design for inherently high quality and reliability.

• Minimize the exponential cumulative effect of part quality and quantity by specifying high-quality parts and simplifying the design with fewer parts.

• Select the highest quality processing. Automated processing produces better and more consistent quality than manual labor.

• Raise and resolve issues early by: learning from past quality problems; early research, experiments, and models; generate plan-B contingency plans; and proactively devising and implementing plans to resolve all issues early (Phase 3).

• Optimize tolerances for a robust design using Taguchi Methods™ (guideline Q11). Robust design is one of the techniques in the collection of tools known as "Design for Six Sigma."

• Chose materials for quality (Deming's 4th point) not from auctions, low-bidding, or switching suppliers for price.

• *Poka-Yoke* principles applied to product design to prevent mistakes by design in addition to concurrently engineered manufacturing procedures to prevent incorrect manufacture.

- Reuse proven designs, parts, modules, and processes to minimize risk and assure quality, especially on critical aspects of the design.

- Rationalize product lines to raise corporate quality by eliminating the unusual, low-volume products which usually have the lowest quality (see Section A-9).

- "Big picture" metrics and compensation to reward actions that assure quality and avoid compromising quality with cheap materials to save "cost," chasing cheap labor, or throwing a sub-optimal design over the wall "on time."

- Total cost, including the cost of quality, is the basis for all part and processing decisions; all elements of cost of quality are quantified.

Designing for quality is what gets quality from 5 sigma to 6 sigma.[7]

Design for Six Sigma

Design for six sigma (DFSS) is the product development element of the six sigma quality program.[8] *Six sigma* is a management approach aimed at eliminating mistakes, rework, and waste. The goal of DFSS is to prevent defects by *designing* quality into the product.

Design for six sigma supports DFM quality strategies, presented above, by offering in-depth treatments of rigorous computational and statistical-based methodologies such as using QFD to capture the *voice of the customer,* Taguchi Methods™ to optimize robust parameter and tolerances, the theory of inventive problem solving (TRIZ) to generate ideas, and Failure Modes and Effects Analysis (FMEA) .

Customer Satisfaction.

Designing for quality is a key element of providing customer satisfaction as is Quality Function Deployment (Section 2.11). The book, *Satisfaction, How Every Great Company Listens to the Voice of the Customer,* from J.D. Power,[9] shows how good customer satisfaction dramatically improves sales, profits, and shareholder value:

> *"Garner a reputation for providing great customer satisfaction and you can charge a price premium that goes straight to the bottom line.*

> *"Saddle yourself with a reputation for marginal customer satisfaction and the only way to build market share will be through discounts and other incentives that will wreak havoc on your bottom line."*

J.D. Power has correlated customer satisfaction with sales and shareholder value. For automobiles, those brands with low satisfaction, sales dropped 4% over a five year period, while *high satisfaction resulted in a 44% rise in sales!* Over the same period, companies with a drop in customer satisfaction experienced a 28% decline in shareholder value, whereas, for companies with improved satisfaction rankings, *shareholder value rose 52%![10]*

ENDNOTES/REFERENCES

1. Seth Godin and Chip Conley, *Business Rules of Thumb,*(1987, Warner Books).

2. Lance A. Ealey, *Quality by Design; Taguchi Methods and US Industry,* (1998, ASI Press).

3. Kiyoshi Suzaki, *The New Manufacturing Challenge; Techniques for Continuous Improvement,* (1987, The Free Press).

4. Ray P. Prasad, *Surface Mount Technology, Principles and Practice,* (1989, Van Nostrand Reinhold), p. 547.

5. Wesley E. Woodson, *Human Factors Design Handbook; Information and Guidelines for the Design of Systems, Facilities, Equipment, and Products for Human Use* (1981, McGraw-Hill), 1047 pages.

6. *Poka-Yoke: Improving Product Quality by Preventing Defects* (1989, Productivity Inc.), 295 pages with 240 examples.

7. Subir Chowdhury, *"Design for Six Sigma,"* (2002, Dearborn Trade Publishing).

8. Subir Chowdhury, *Design for Six Sigma,* (2002, Dearborn Trade Publishing).

9. Chris Denove and J. D. Powers IV, *Satisfaction; How Every Great Company Listens to the Voice of the Customer*, (Portfolio, 2006).

10. Denove and Powers, *Satisfaction,* Chapter 1, "Show Me the Money."

11

IMPLEMENTING DFM

To paraphrase the punch line of the entertaining IBM commercials, *There is no magic tool to implement DFM* – no magic software, no magic shrink-wrapped solution, no magic "models" with trademarked names. To say this in a different way, *you can't buy DFM.*

Nor can companies simply *manage* their way to great product development. Project management techniques may allow management to track progress and feel that things are "on schedule," but these measures could be counterproductive without an understanding how products should be developed, in general, and designed for manufacturability, in particular. For instance, if intermediate deadlines are set arbitrarily or without knowing the importance of thorough up-front work, they may force engineers to rush prematurely into part design and miss the greatest opportunities to simplify concepts, optimize product architecture, and raise and resolve issues early. The concept/architecture stage is when 60% of cost is committed (Figure 1-1) and is the key to the quickest time to stable production (Figure 3-1).

Another popular way of *managing* product development is to "measure performance," but that, too, can produce counterproductive results if the measures are not based on total cost and the time to stable production. If teams are measured, judged, and evaluated on "cost," but all that is quantified is part and labor costs, then they may be driven to specify cheap parts, move production to "low-labor-cost" areas, and resist standardization, modularity, and off-the-shelf parts because of the false belief that they will "raise cost." Similarly, if engineers are measured, judged, and evaluated on meeting deadlines, then they will just *throw it over the wall on time* with less regard as to whether the essential tasks have been accomplished in a way that will allow the design to satisfy all its goals and constraints.

DFM is not a stage – it is *the way engineers should be designing* for manufacturability *throughout* the design process. Good DFM does not come from turning the proverbial crank on some "tool," "model," or "procedure" – somewhere in all those grandiose models, a team has to creatively design for manufacturability. Good DFM does not focus on "hitting numbers" that are poorly defined – it focuses on actually *designing* products for the lowest total cost, the best quality, and the fastest time to stable production.

Successful DFM comes from a combination of education, teamwork, diversity, leadership, commitment, creativity, "big picture" metrics, understanding customer needs, understanding manufacturing processes, and management support and encouragement of all of that, as summarized in Figure 12-1. This rest of this chapter shows how to successfully implement DFM.

11.1 CHANGE

Before implementing any changes, companies need to understand the *need* to change and the *benefits* of changing. At this point, it might be a good idea to read Section 1.1 again about the consequences of not having products designed for manufacturability and the survey comments describing what is it like to work in a company that doesn't practice DFM. Identify how many of these points are routinely experienced. But before changes can begin, the most common objections must be overcome:

"Things aren't so bad – There is no need to change." This head-in-the-sand approach ignores many realities about changes in markets, customers, technology, workers, competition, and other changing trends. The largest study ever conducted on business failures found that:

> *"There is one blind spot that appears somewhere near the center of almost every major business disaster: a seriously inaccurate perception of reality among executives."*[1]

Dr. Deming said that companies are reluctant to change unless there is a crisis. However, deferring change until a crisis hits is a poor strategy since meaningful change will be much more difficult to implement in the face of dwindling sales, falling stock prices, shrinking market share, more demanding customers, threatening competition, changing regulation, negative publicity, credit downgrades, or quality problems flaring up. "Crisis management" usually tries to band-aid the immediate *symptoms* rather identify root causes and implement systematic *solutions.* Product development can be either the *cause* or the *solution* to many of these problems. But since product development is a long-term endeavor, companies in crises will have to live with the shortcomings of products designs until they can be redesigned. To prevent such a predicament, companies should start *now* to develop good products and, as necessary, change the ways products are developed, built, sourced, and distributed.

"I don't understand it." Although no one would admit it, many people don't understand or comprehend the challenges going on in product development. And if they don't understand the problems, they probably won't understand solutions like DFM, standardization, quality assurance, and designing products for lean production, build-to-order, and total cost accounting.

"We're already doing it." A combination of the first two objections would be believing that the company is already doing a proposed solution. One company was heard to confidently say, "We practice Concurrent Engineering." However, upon further investigation, it was discovered that what they meant was that a manufacturing engineer was invited to the design release review!

"We've always done it this way." Even if some vague need to change is perceived, many companies run into the brick wall of historical inertia. But consider the following slogan:

If you do what you have always done,
you will get what you always got.

In stable markets without competition, the *status quo* may be hard to knock, but that is rare these days. Usually, companies have many challenges related to profits, sales, cost, changing markets, advancing technologies, and product developments that need to be better and faster.

At Honda, managers are encouraged to respect sound theories but not hesitate to challenge old habits with new ideas. Company literature encourages proceeding with *"ambition and youthfulness, seeking out challenges with fresh, open-minded passion for learning."[2]*

"We've never done it that way." Change is often resisted because the solutions are new. This can be overcome by understanding new ways and learning how to implement them through books, articles, classes, seminars, and bringing in outside experts to help. Many companies (see the list after the title page) circulate multiple copies of this book to familiarize decision makers with solutions.

"We've tried it; didn't work." Specific solutions may be shot down because of *perceptions* about earlier unsuccessful experiences. However, earlier attempts may have "failed" from insufficient commitment, support, time, or efforts. Or the wrong solution was attempted or it was applied in the wrong way.

Another variation of this is "management by folklore" where undocumented tales circulate about previous "failures" without any facts or understanding about the incident. This can temporarily block inside innovators or outside consultants in the short term – until the facts are revealed.

Reluctance to use off-the-shelf parts is justified by the common excuse, "we looked, but couldn't find any." But this is based on either half-hearted superficial attempts or perceptions that previous searched were unsuccessful. However, Section 5.19 presents many reasons to commit serious efforts to look for off-the-shelf parts.

A corollary of this objection is that *someone else* tried it and it didn't work.

The main shortcoming of this objection is the verb "tried." Real change doesn't come from *trying;* it comes from *doing.*

"We don't have time or resources." The companies that use this excuse are probably spending most of their engineers' time and efforts correcting deficiencies in the product/process design, as shown in the top graph in Figure 2-1 and the top bar in Figure 3-1.

In the distant past, many people believed that quality would cost more, until Philip Crosby wrote the book, *Quality is Free,* which said that the returns from better quality would more than pay back the effort to achieve quality.[3] Similarly, the "cost" of implementing concurrent engineering and DFM will be more than paid back by better products with cost designed out, quality designed in, and rapid ramps into production as shown in the lower graph in Figure 2-1 and the lower bar in Figure 3-1.

"We'll just change the goals." As pointed out in Section 1.6 on *focus,* real change cannot be achieved simply by applying more pressure or more ambitious goals. Many companies ignore the truism:

> *Trying to get much better results*
> *by doing things the same way*
> *– definition of insanity[4]*

"Do something – anything." If decision makers realize some kind of "change" is in order, but don't understand the problems or the solutions, they may jump at whatever *appears* to be a solution. This could happen at staff meetings (when members present pet projects) or at slick sales presentation for some "cure all" shrink-wrapped solution. Many companies think they have responded to change by bringing in some packaged "program" or "throwing software at it."

The degree of the challenge dictates the degree of the changes needed. Ambitious goals may require some fundamentally different ways of doing things.

> *Ambitious results require ambitious changes.*

Change at Leading Companies

"Although new behaviors always provoke opposition, those who are complacent will be left behind and ultimately defeated." - Sakichi Toyoda (1867 - 1930), patriarch of the Toyota dynasty[5]

At Medtronic, *"The entire organization is now embracing change and innovation as a way of life and as a competitive advantage. These innovations have been a key factor in changing Medtronic's image from the pacemaker company of the 1980's to the innovative, high-growth leader in medical technology for the twenty-first century."*[6] - Bill George, Chairman/CEO Medtronic

At Xomed, *"upper management stressed culture change – no swift transformation, but a gradual increase in empowerment to those doing the work making change fun, not a threat."*[7]

11.2 PRELIMINARY INVESTIGATIONS

Conduct Surveys

The first implementation step should be to understand how well the current product development systems works – or understand its shortcomings. Conduct anonymous surveys of everyone in product development and ask questions like:

- How do you rate our products for manufacturability compared to competitors, the industry, and the best know in any industry?
- What are *good examples* of DFM?
- What are *inadequate examples* of DFM?
- What are the *consequences* of inadequate DFM?
- What are the *hurdles* to good DFM?
- What are the *opportunities* for good DFM?

The author has been conducting this poll for 15 years before his in-house seminars[8] and has found that this information is a valuable starting point for implementation – hearing candid comments about the product development culture and its performance. This information is also very useful for customizing training. Further, presenting the results is a good way to kick off DFM seminars and get people discussing the issues raised. Survey comments have a special impact since they refer to actual company products and procedures.

The following is a summary of the top eight responses of 650 responses from 10 companies in several industries: two consumer products; two OEM suppliers; two scientific instruments; two processing equipment; and two aerospace.

Consequences	Hurdles	Opportunities
Quality, 33%	Time, 19%	CE teams, 23%
Assembly hard, 18%	Lack, teamwork, 17%	Methodology, 13%
Cost problems, 12%	Attitudes, 12%	General, 9%
Time/ramps, 8%	Cultural, 12%	Vendor relations, 8%
Changes, 7%	Communications, 7%	Quality, 6%
Service/ repair, 5%	Resist change, 5%	Cultural changes, 6%
Inflexible, 4%	Changes, 5%	Resources/tools, 5%
Not competitive, 4%	Discipline, 4%	Profit/success, 5%

Estimate Improvements from DFM

Next, summarize measures of corporate "bottom line" performance, such as profits, revenue, growth, and stock price. Then identify the *drivers* for those measures, in other words, the activities and programs that would *drive* their achievement, for instance cost reduction, shorter time-to-market, better quality, and better customer satisfaction.

Ascertain how well the product development process is performing and what are management's goals for improvement. Estimate how corporate performance could be improved by DFM.

To estimate cost reduction, look at all the cost reduction techniques of Chapter 6 and estimate how much could be saved with DFM in relevant categories such as assembly, quality, change orders, inventory, material overhead, and so forth. Scrutinize existing products to see how excess costs may have been *committed* in the concept/architecture phase in the same way the type of data in Figure 1-1 was generated.[9]

Ask assembly supervisors how much labor cost and assembly steps could be saved by better DFM. Ask the Manage of Purchasing how much material overhead could be saved it new products were predominately designed around standard parts. Talk to operations people to find out how designing products for lean environments could reduce setup costs and improve flow and machine tool utilization. Find out how much the budget of Engineering and Manufacturing is spent on firefighting and change orders. Estimate how much of that cost could be saved by better design for manufacturability. Analyze completed feedback forms presented in Appendix C.

To estimate quality gains, ascertain the main causes of quality problems and recommend design solutions such as better parts, fewer parts (as shown in Figure 10-3), mistake-proofing, optimal tolerances, vendor partnerships, and concurrent process design and selection.

To estimate time-to-market gains, analyze past product development projects for their *real* time-to-market after all the revisions, iterations, and ramp-up in Figure 3-1 and after targets have been reached for volume, quality, and productivity, as graphed in Figure 2-1.

Get Management Buy-in

To implement DFM formally, structure and propose a DFM program. Present the program to management with the intent of getting management support and buy-in for the program. Chapter 12 contains many summarizes of key DFM principles, which can be presented to management. Use the above estimates of improvements and any other qualitative benefits, like the ones presented at the end of Chapter 12. Such a program may include a DFM implementation task force that would carry out the steps recommended herein.

Less formal DFM implementations can be started at any level, for instance, by individuals or product development teams practicing the DFM principles presented in this book or in DFM training. Early successes can be leveraged to other projects and more formal programs.

11.3 DFM TRAINING

The Need for DFM Training

Companies need to provide DFM training because DFM is only taught in a few colleges.[10] Engineers are almost exclusively taught to design for functionality. Further, engineering tools primarily help engineers design for functionality. And years of work may have turned this focus into a habit.

So product designers need to be *taught* to design for manufacturability. Further, besides the obvious learning benefits, offering DFM training can be a catalyst to change behavior. Many companies use DFM training to kick off DFM programs.

Customize Training to Products

Schedule training for all product development personnel in DFM principles. DFM training should be customized to the company's product line and culture. Beware of bringing in training that is based only on generic principle or "canned" presentations; an easy way to spot inflexible canned presentations is if they have been *named,* or worse, if the name has been trademarked. Don't limit training to only procedures or project management techniques. Be suspicious of "training" that may really be trying to sell software.

Ask prospective trainers how much they will be customizing the material, on what will they will base such customization (like surveys or interviews), and how much relevant experience the *actual presenter* has with your type of products – not just having similar products on the client list of the training company. Beware of high-powered sales presentations by experience people, who will send less experienced people to do the actual training.

Don't Do Training "on the Cheap"

Don't try to do DFM training "on the cheap," because *you only get one chance at DFM training.* If the training is bad, it will give the message, or even confirm preconceived notions, that DFM is useless and therefore engineers should continue to design only for function. If that happens, it will be hard to get engineers to attend a better class later, not to mention all the opportunities lost in the intervening time.

Trainer Qualifications

DFM training should be presented by someone thoroughly familiar with DFM principles and with enough experience to answer questions and engage the audience in discussions on how to apply these principles in your company and how other companies did. Experience in both design and manufacture will enable the trainer to talk from the perspective of designers (with personal design examples) and manufacturing (relating personal experiences with manufacturable and *un*manufacturable designs).

DFM training by in-house personnel is a possibility, but only if the trainer thoroughly understands DFM principles and has enough experience and facilitation skills to answer questions, encourage discussions, and convey all the important principles. This book could be used as a textbook for the course.[11] Keep in mind that the copyright policy of this book permits copying a limited amount of material for internal presentations, meetings, and internal reports, but does not allow extensive reproductions for training. If this book is used as the textbook in classes and seminars, then presenters may project material from this book in such classes.

With in-house trainers, position and title can be an asset or a liability. DFM training from manufacturing people might appear to be "preachy," whereas training from design people might not fully understand manufacturability issues. Senior managers would carry more authority than "worker bees," but usually senior managers don't have the time or bandwidth to adequately prepare and present the training. Further, inside trainers may not have as much credibility as "outside experts." In fact, a common experience of outside trainers is the appreciation from insiders who have been trying to emphasize similar points, but with little success, because they lack the outside expert's credibility and experience.

DFM Training Agenda

An excellent way to kick off a DFM seminar is start with some rousing opening comments by the President, Vice President of Engineering, or division General Manager. These comments are important to convey management support and motivate everyone to learn the principles and then be *expected* to put them into practice. Motivation emphases can range from stressing opportunities to "we gotta do this for survival."

One President kicked off a DFM seminar relating the experience when they shipped a million dollar processing machine to a semiconductor fabrication plant and no one could understand why it wouldn't work, until they figured out that a light-sensitive enclosure was not sealed properly because someone grabbed the wrong screw from a proliferated selection.

The kick off executive should also introduce the trainer along with a brief bio-sketch and then hopefully stay for at least the high-level topics, which roughly correspond to the first three chapters of this book in addition to Chapter 6.

An effective opening topic is to review and discuss the results of the survey, described above, which says in the attendees own words what is wrong with the current product development culture and what are the opportunities for improvement.

The recommended training order is to start with "the big picture" topics so that senior managers can attend the first morning session, which focuses on the importance and implementation of:

- Product line planning (Section 2.3), prioritizing, and rationalization (Appendix A)

- Clear product definition to satisfy the "voice of the customer" (Section 2.11)

- Thorough optimization of the crucial concept/architecture stage, which determines 60% of a products cumulative lifetime cost (Sections 1.3 and 3.3)

- Cutting the real time-to-market in half thorough up-front optimization and design work (Sections 3.3)

- Resource availability to ensure the formation of compete teams with *all* specializations active *early* (Sections 2.2 and 3.3)

- Preselection of vendor/partners who can help develop products (Section 2.6)

- An effective team leader (Section 2.7)

- Ensuring teams have the proper focus (Section 1.6).

- Activities and deliverables for phases (Section 2.12)

- Raising and resolving issues early (Section 2.12, Phase III)

- Decision making, costing, product pricing, and performance measures based on total cost accounting (Chapter 7)

The remaining sessions should teach the following to engineers and managers:

- Motivation and overcoming resistance for DFM (Sections 1.7 and 11.1)

- Understanding manufacturing through experience and teamwork (Section 11.8)

- Optimizing product design by satisfying all design considerations (Section 3.5)

- Avoiding arbitrary decisions (Section 1.8)

- Creative product development (Section 3.6) and brainstorming (Section 3.7)

- Do it right the first time (Section 1.11) to minimize the costs and delays of changes (Section 6.6)

- Considering off-the-shelf parts early (Section 5.19)

- Designing around standard parts (Ch. 5)

- Designing for lean, build-to-order, and mass customization (Ch. 4)

- Follow appropriate design guidelines for products (Ch. 8) and parts (Ch. 9)

- Design in quality and reliability (Ch. 10) to eliminate the cost of quality (Section 6.9)

- Total cost minimization (Ch. 6) and measurement (Ch. 7)

- Change (Section 11.1)

- DFM implementation (Ch. 11)

- The importance and benefits of DFM (Sections 1.13, 1.14, and 12.9)

As an example, the author's baseline agenda for his in-house DFM seminars is shown in the *Resource* Appendix on page 407.

"What Happens Next?"

As a last event in the training, poll the audience and ask "What should happen next?" The answers can be very helpful for formulating implementation strategies. For example, after in-house DFM seminars, the author writes all the answers on several flip charts, draws a line between each response, and then has the audience vote what they think is the most important. The easiest way to arrange for voting is to issue each attendee eight votes, in the form of round sticky-back dots, which everyone can affix to the zones for each point (the rules are only one vote per point). Experience has shown that this is an invigorating way to wrap up the seminar, since most people hang around to see the voting results unfold. The DFM "champion" should then prioritize the results and distribute to all attendees, management, and any DFM task forces.

The following is a summary of the top 11 responses, representing 80% of 3622 votes cast over the last few years of the author's seminars:

556   Teamwork and thorough up-front work

355   Standardization

323   Total Cost

266   Product Portfolio Planning

252   Updating product development processes and procedures

207   Lessons Learned

206   Vendor/partnerships

203   Resource availability

181   Management buy-in and support

159   Product definition, product requirements, and QFD

150   Training and management education

Many of these desired changes will require some degree of *stopping bad habits*, which will be discussed in Section 11.5.

Training Attendance

Attendance for DFM training should include everyone involved in product development so training is not just be "preaching to the choir" of manufacturing engineers or "DFM engineers" who, after training, would attend design team meetings in the hopes of steering the team to more manufacturable designs. That goes against the main principle of this book, which is that DFM is *designed* into the product by the *entire team*. Thus, all team members need to be trained in DFM.

Nor should DFM training be limited to engineers. Managers should attend with the engineers. Senior manages should either attend an "executive education" session or attend the first day of the seminar, which focuses on higher-level topics. Lack of management attendance has two negative consequences: management doesn't learn their critical role in assuring DFM success (Section 12.7, I); worse, attendees interpret lack of attendance as lack of management support.

DFM training benefits from a diverse audience, beyond the usual design engineers and manufacturing engineers, so include purchasing agents, materials managers, vendors, and key people from Quality, Field Service, and so forth.

11.4 DFM TASK FORCE

DFM can be implemented at many levels including individual actions, product development teams, and implementation task forces. A new product development effort can apply new DFM principles from the beginning. For the first DFM application, choose an appropriate product, consistent with product portfolio planning. The product should have many open opportunities but not be an overwhelming challenge.

A more widespread implementation strategy would be to create a DFM implementation task force, with the charter to implement DFM in general, and specifically to:

• Form the task force with representatives from appropriate engineering groups, Manufacturing Engineering, Supply Chain Management, quality, management, and so forth. Multidivisional companies may have a joint task force or corporate headquarters efforts. If the members are well respected, especially the leader, the results will be more likely to be endorsed by management and followed by design teams.

• Summarize how well the current product development culture is working based on the pre-seminar survey and other investigations.

• Estimate improvements that will come from implementing DFM (Section 11.2).

• Get management buy-in, support, and resources to implement DFM.

• Arrange DFM training; prioritize and circulate the post-seminar voting (Section 11.3)

• As a team is just beginning to develop each product (after DFM training), arrange a product-specific workshop, led by an experienced facilitator, to implement DFM on that specific product development project. This is an effective way to get a new product development project "off on the right foot" and ensure that the team will design in manufacturability, low-cost, flexibility, quality, and reliability. The agenda would consist of a series of planned brainstorming sessions to encourage the team to explore many ways to implement the DFM principles. These exercises themselves would be the start of many actual tasks, which would be continued after the workshop.

• Enhance or implement the development of vendor/partnerships ahead of time so that vendors will be willing to participate on product development teams and help the team design the parts to be made in the vendors' shops.

- For product development methodologies and processes, decide what to keep, what to modify, what to discard, and what to add.

- If product development phases do not exist, then create them based on the phases delineated in Section 2.12. If phases or stages already exist, merge the phase activities and focus topics of Chapter 2 into existing company stages. Make sure that phase timing emphasizes thorough work in the concept/architecture phase to exert maximum influence on the 60% of the cost that is committed then (Figure 1-1) and ensure the design is good enough to avoid 70% of the time-line consumed in revisions, iterations, and ramp-up (Figure 3-1).

- Compile relevant DFM guidelines for all relevant processes. A starting point can be the 165 general design guidelines presented in Chapters 8, 9, and 10, which are listed without discussion in Appendix B. Companies may also want to convert certain DFM principles (which are summarized in Chapter 12) into guidelines.

- Convert design rules and guidelines into checklists, if desired. Checklists can remind design teams of all the things that need to be done at various stages of the design process. Checklists also provide a quantitative way to measure compliance and rate products for manufacturability, part count, and utilization of standard parts. Checklists can also ensure and monitor that *rules* are not broken and, if so, proper exception procedures are followed.

    However, care must be taken not to let checklists become the primary focus of the product development process. Quantitative tools like project management software and checklists can easily *become* the product development process and draw attention away from "softer" qualitative aspects like simplifying concepts and optimizing product architecture (Chapters 1, 2, and 3).

11.5 STOP COUNTERPRODUCTIVE POLICIES

In a DFM seminar, someone asked how long it would take to go from the primitive *linear* timeline to the more advanced *concurrent* timeline in the Lexmark model (Figure 3-1). The short answer is, "How long will it take to stop the bad habits?" Consider the scenario where a well financed startup venture begins with DFM training supported by management and the venture capitalists – the startup should then *immediately* be able to apply all the principles presented in this book.

Half the challenge to implement new methodologies may be getting rid of existing counterproductive policies. For product development, here are some of the worst. Corrective actions are cited by Section:

- Don't bite off more than Engineering can chew when planning product portfolios, as Motorola learned (Section 2.2). Prioritize the portfolio based on potential profitability (Section 2.3). Be sure to hire enough resources when the portfolio *must* expand.

- Don't allow, or, worse, encourage, the Sales force to "take all orders" and pollute operations with low-volume, hard-to-build products that drain resources away from product development and other improvement programs. Rationalize Product Lines (Appendix A).

- Don't "manage" product development to death with arbitrary early intermediate deadlines that compromise the critical up-front work (Section 3.2) just for the *illusion* of "early progress."

- Don't quantify only labor and part cost and then allocate (average) all other cost (overhead) over all products, good or bad (Ch. 7).

- Don't offshore manufacturing, which makes it hard to do Concurrent Engineering when there are *no manufacturing people around to be "concurrent" with*. In many offshoring situations, people in engineering and manufacturing are not even working at the same time. For more, see Section 2.8 (Co-Location), Section 4.8 (Outsourcing), and the articles on outsourcing[12] and offshoring.[13] at www.HalfCostProducts.com.

- Don't try to take cost out after the product is designed, which is so hard to do that is a waste of resources, as shown in Section 6.1.

- Don't go for the low bidder on custom parts, which precludes *vendor/partnerships* and, thus, prevents those vendors from helping the company design the parts, for reasons presented in Section 2.6.

As pointed out in Section 6.22, companies that practice the above three will have to devote a very high percentage of product development resources of their time to: make change orders to try to implement DFM (because it couldn't be done with Concurrent Engineering); try to take cost out after the product is designed with change orders; convert documentation for outsourcing; get outsourcers up to speed; deal with quality and delivery problems; and so forth. In his travels, the author has encountered several companies that spend *two-thirds of product development resources* on the above three activities which really puts their future in doubt if that future depends on new product development. Ironically, these attempts *thwart six of the eight Half-Cost strategies*, for reasons presented at www.HalfCostProducts.com/outsourcing.htm.[14]

11.6 TEAM IMPLEMENTATION

Each *team* should develop products according to the principles of this book, even if they have not yet been implemented company-wide. Regardless of the level of implementation, be sure do the following:

- Get lessons learned from databases, investigations, or presentations
- Hold discussions to thoroughly raise and resolve all issues early
- Ensure availability of all specialties early. The team leader may have to lobby for these.*
- Push back on team member distractions and resource drains*
- Ensure access and availability for meaningful contributions from Manufacturing, Purchasing, Quality, Service, etc.*
- Ensure enough time for thorough up-front work; push back on early deadlines as necessary*
- Secure concurrence for setting up vendor/partnerships*
- Work with Purchasing to arrange specific vendor/partnerships
- Find space for a dedicated project room (Obeya)*
- Make all decisions based on total cost data; if not available:
  - use total cost *thinking,* seeking exceptions to metrics if the metrics (cost, profit, etc.) are not based on total cost*
  - campaign for relevant overhead allocations*
- Focus on minimizing cost by design; resist pressures for counterproductive policies (offshoring, bidding, cost-reduction after design and others discussed in Section 11.5)*

---

* When these are not automatically forthcoming, use the following approaches:

1) Summarize principles and justifications from the seminars, books, articles, and experiences, both within and outside the company.

2) If necessary, use the following argument: *"The only way we can achieve the goals of this project is for us to have _____ (fill in the blank). "*

3) If what is needed is still not forthcoming, say: *"OK, lets talk about how to scale back the project goals"* (deadlines, functionality, feature sets, and so forth). *"*

11.7 INDIVIDUAL IMPLEMENTATION

There are many things that individual engineers can do before DFM is implemented company-wide:

- Implement whatever methodologies you can personally to improve manufacturability within your sphere of influence.

- Keep thinking about how to optimize the *product*, not just your *parts*.

- Work interactively with other team members on whatever relates to your work.

- Initiate dialog with Manufacturing, Purchasing, Quality, Service, and others early on *each* design decision that affects manufacturability.

- Concurrently develop tooling and manufacturing and supply chain strategies for your parts.

- Remember the messages of this book, as you work your way up and gain more influence.

Either individuals or their teams can take the initiative on the following:

- **Use feedback forms** to understand the manufacturability of your products (see appendix C for forms to use with your plant, your vendors, and field service)

- **Interact frequently** with people in manufacturing, purchasing, quality, and service on an ongoing basis.

- **Observe frequently** manufacturing and vendors' operations. Taiichi Ohno, the father of the Toyota Production System, drew a circle on the factory floor (the "Ohno circle") and made people stand in it all day to watch and questioning the process. His thinking was that new thoughts and ideas come from observing and understanding the processes.[15]

- **Arrange shop demonstrations** at your plant or at your vendors, who would undoubtedly welcome the opportunity to show design engineers how various design practices make it easier or harder to make parts.

11.8 DFM FOR STUDENTS AND JOB SEEKERS

Knowing how to design products for manufacturability is a valuable skill that should be appreciated by hiring companies. So do a good job at the following and be sure to mention these things in résumés and job interviews:

Books. Read this book thoroughly along with others listed at the end of each chapter and the "Book" section of Appendix B on Resources. The best company-based book is *"The Toyota Product Development System,"[16]* which corresponds very well to the principles of the book you are reading.

Classes. Prospective employers value relevant courses ranging from specific college courses to extension or continuing education seminars throughout your career. Relevant courses should be listed on your résumé. Early planning should map out which of these courses to take to support your overall career goals. Students should find out which CAD programs are used in your target industry and take classes to learn that program(s). Most CAD software suppliers offer student/academic discounts to help students learn how to use their programs.

Industry Events. Students and working engineers can learn a lot about manufacturing by attending conferences, trade shows, and exhibitions. And working engineers usually get paid to attend. Some conferences have student discounts and many exhibitions are free or charge only a nominal fee. Students can learn much about the latest design and manufacturing techniques by going to presentations at conferences and seeing equipment and demonstrations at the exhibitions.

Experience. Most job experiences may be valuable in the next job. Career paths should be planned to accumulate experience that ultimately supports a strategic career goal. Job seekers should (a) look for jobs where their previous experiences will be valued by prospective employers and (b) emphasize this previous experience in résumés and job interviews. Students can build up some experience through summer jobs and internships. *Any* job in a given industry will count as, at least, exposure to that industry. For instance, the author worked his way through college as a mechanic in a cannery, which help him get a job later designing food processing machinery. When joining a new company, design engineers can request manufacturing experience before design assignments if the company does not already have this a policy, which was recommended in Section 1.6.

Learn the trades of the process that makes what you are designing or want to design, for instance: machining, CNC programming, welding, and so forth. Working designers can learn these skills by taking night courses at local community colleges. Engineering students should take these courses in their engineering schools, or, if not available, enroll in nearby community college courses. These shop courses are taught by practical instructors and give students "hands on" experience. Usually, one general course in each skill would be sufficient.

Companies should encourage their engineers to take these by paying course fees and giving time off for the classes. Companies with in-house shops could hold shop classes for designers on-site. They could be taught by teachers from community colleges or by factory workers.

For students, saying that "I am a machinist," "I am a welder," or "I can program a CNC machine," should be valuable to manufacturing companies that machine or weld parts. While in the Engineering program the University of California at Berkeley, the author took community college courses in welding and machining.

Even relevant hobbies count. The skills learned in, for instance, a welding class could turn into a fun hobby that may impress interviewer even if you welded artwork with an easily affordable oxyacetylene gas welder or basic arc welder. Experience with a used home version of a programmable plasma cutter or prototype milling machine may be relevant experience for companies that use CNC machine tools.

The recommendations of Section 1.6, which advises companies to hire design engineers with experience in manufacturing, would apply to both work experience and trade skills.

Profiles. The fifth bullet point in Product Portfolio Planning (Section 2.3) recommends that companies develop *profiles* to identify the best opportunities. Similarly, anyone who wants to apply DFM in a new job should develop a profile of favorable company characteristics, such as:

• use of multifunctional teamwork.

• strategies to achieve low cost and quality *by design.*

• manufacture most of their products at the same site, co-located with Engineering.

• utilize vendor/partnerships so that vendors will be willing and able to help them design the products where both the vendor and manufacturer will learn from each engagement.

• measure total cost for the reasons cited in Chapters 6 and 7.

• investment in product development where management encourages and supports innovation.

Conversely, profiles indicating a company will have a hard time implementing DFM would include the companies who try counterproductive "cost reduction" attempts mentioned in Sections 6.22 and 11.5.

11.9 STANDARDIZATION IMPLEMENTATION

Standardization can be implemented by forming a standardization task force, which could be the same as, or a subgroup of, the DFM task force. The best choice of a leader would be someone from the "materials" organization (Purchasing or Supply Chain Management), which could logically *own* standardization after implementation.

- Begin procedures to create standard part lists for new designs (Chapter 5) for all relevant categories of parts and materials.

- Arrange training on standardization procedures (Chapter 5), followed by workshops to standardize *each* category of parts and materials.

- Start with the early steps: list existing parts, clean up database nomenclature, eliminate approved but unused parts, eliminate parts not used recently, and eliminate duplicate parts (Section 5.6).

- Prioritize opportunities (Section 5.6) and start from the top of the list creating standard parts lists using the procedures presented in Sections 5.7 and 5.8.

- Similarly, standardize raw materials (Section 5.10), tools (Section 5.13), features (Section 5.14), and processes (Section 5.15).

- For the standardization of expensive parts (Section 5.11), overcome resistance by quantifying the benefits of the standardization in the format of Figure 5-3.

- Issue the standardization lists (Section 5.8, point 14) and incorporate into subsequent DFM training

- Encourage standardization through appropriate material overhead rates, prequalified standard parts, floor stock, personal display boards, spec books, and cost metrics (Section 5.16).

- Perform *product line rationalization* to eliminate or outsource the most unusual *products* that usually have the most unusual *parts* (See Appendix A).

11.10 TOTAL COST MEASUREMENT IMPLEMENTATION

Acknowledge Deficiencies

The first step in quantifying total cost is to get the company to acknowledge deficiencies in current cost measurements, which usually only measure labor and materials and average overhead over all products. Section 7.2A presented many of these deficiencies, such as:

- Distortions in product costing because overhead is averaged

- Cross subsidies, where *good* products subsidize *bad* products, *high-volume* products subsidize *low-volume* products, and *standard* products subsidize *custom* products

- Decisions made "by the numbers" may be way off if "the numbers" are distorted so much that they are irrelevant.

- Cost management is difficult without total cost measurements.

- Downward spirals can occur if good products are overpriced and bad products are underpriced (Figure 7-1).

Estimate the Degree of the Distortion

The above points, and others, could be presented qualitatively, or estimates could be made of the degree of the distortion. If necessary, a suspected distortion could be quantified "the hard way," just to make a point. Polls and surveys could quickly steer the investigation to the worse case offender(s). One way to get the attention of a senior manager or a key decision maker is to estimate the costing/pricing distortion that is happening to that person's favorite product, for instance, that the company's biggest cash cow, which could be unnecessarily priced higher to pay the "loser tax" on weaker products.

Understand the Value of Total Cost Measurements

Summarize several points showing the value of total cost measurements, starting with the generic list in Section 7.2C. The list should be ordered starting with whatever is widely perceived to be of the most value. Any estimates or investigations of current distortions may help. Include the impacts on future programs, like DFM implementation.

Start Total Cost *Thinking*

Until total cost measurements can be implemented, campaign for decisions to be made on the basis of *total cost thinking,* as discussed in Section 7.4. Everyone should be encouraged to do what they think will lower the total cost, even if it can't be justified quantitatively by the current numbers.

Implement Cost Drivers

The "low-hanging fruit" of total cost implementation is the *cost driver* approach, as discussed in Section 7.6. Cost drivers are defined as the *root causes* of a cost – the things that "drive" cost. Identifying cost drivers make the root causes visible, which will (a) allow total costs to be measured and prices set accordingly and (b) encourage behavior that actually lowers total cost.

The cost driver approach identifies key drivers of cost that should be quantified instead of lumped in with all other overhead costs. The cost driver approach is easy to implement and starts with the most important overhead costs that need to be quantified. Cost drivers can provide a more rational basis for performance measures. Examples of cost drivers are presented in Section 7.6.

The cost driver approach can be easier to implement by basing the cost driver data on estimates (that have universal consensus) or *share-of-activity* percentages. For instance, the total cost of material overhead can be calculated by asking the Purchasing Manager what percent of purchasing activities are spent procuring standard parts, as defined by the standard parts lists generated by the procedures presented in Chapter 5. The typical answer would be that the standard parts are the easiest to get and may be resupplied automatically, say, with kanban (Section 4.2). Therefore, standard parts might account for only 10% of Purchasing's activities. So then the overhead charges could be set so that standard parts get one tenth of the material overhead of hard-to-get nonstandard parts. Activities that are homogeneous, like accounts payable, would not need to broken down further.

An approach that first identifies those activities whose costs will make a real difference and then focuses on those activities would be much easier to implement and administer than measuring all activities, which is typical of Activity Based Costing implementations. Therefore, it might be a good idea to avoid even calling the total cost project, "Activity Based Costing," to avoid resistance (Section 7.3), since some ABC program implementations have been so complex that results may have been disappointing or the efforts may have died under their own weight.

Implement the Costing Model

Based on this cost driver approach, create a *costing model* that will accumulate and summarize the total cost data generated by the cost driver approach discussed above. It is intended to break down overhead costs to the product level, so it can assign real costs and relevant pricing. This is to be a costing/pricing model and is not intended to replace the current cost system, which can continue to generate annual reports and filings for regulatory agencies, as it was created to do. The new model may or may not be part of the existing cost system.

The Finance department might seem to be a logical owner of the costing/pricing model, but *costing* (as opposed to *cost accounting*) is not necessarily an accounting function. If Finance does not show in an interest in rapid implementation, or resists for some reason, then the model should be implemented by the most motivated group, which could be Engineering, Manufacturing, Marketing, Product Management, or some staff group. In that case, the model will only need Management's blessing to allow it to assign pricing.

The model can be easily set up on a PC spreadsheet with the help of an excellent how-to book: Douglas Hicks' *Activity-Based Costing, Making it Work for Small and Mid-Sized Businesses.*[17]

Implementation can be fairly quick and cost-effective. One study showed that companies that used "medium involvement" of outside consultants took an average 6.5 months by 2.1 FTEs (full-time equivalent workers) to implement the model. Companies that used "active involvement" of consultants took an average of three months by 1.6 FTEs.[18]

Doug Hicks reports that efforts to implement the basic model have "ranged from 80 hours for a small commercial printer to 500 hours for a large automotive supplier with very poor historical financial and operating records."[19]

ENDNOTES/REFERENCES

1. Sydney Finkelstein, *Why Smart Executives Fail and What You Can Learn from Their Mistakes,* (2003, Portfolio/Penguin), p. 138.

2. Micheline Maynard, *The End of Detroit, How the Big Three Lost their Grip on the American Car Market,* (2003, Currency/Doubleday), page 75 in Chapter 2 on Toyota and Honda.

3. Philip B. Crosby, *Quality is Free; The Art of Making Quality Certain,* (1979, McGraw-Hill).

4. This quote is attributed to both Benjamin Franklin and Albert Einstein.

5. Satoshi Hino, *Inside the Mind of Toyota,* Chapter 1, "Toyota's Genes and DNA," p. 3.

6. Bill George, *Authentic Leadership; Rediscovering the Secrets of Creating Lasting Value;* (2003, Jossey-Bass); Chapter 12, "Innovation

from the Heart," p. 141.

7. Robert W. Hall, AME President, *Medtronic Xomed; Change at "People Speed,"* Target, First Issue 2004, , p. 10.

8. For more information on customized in-house DFM seminars, see page 407 of this book or *www.design4manufacturability.com/seminars.htm.*

9. This data was generated by DataQuest and presented in the landmark article that started the Concurrent Engineering movement: "A Smarter Way to Manufacture; How `Concurrent Engineering' can invigorate American Industry," page 110, *Business Week,* April 30, 1990. In the author's in-house seminars, he presents similar data from Motorola, Ford, General Motors, Westinghouse, Rolls Royce, British Aerospace, the Allison Division of Detroit Diesel, Draper Laboratories, Rensselear Polytechnic Institute, and several other published sources.

10. The colleges that used various editions of this book for courses are listed in the Preface section, "Preface for Instructors."

11. For internally generated DFM training, quantity discounts of this book are readily available from CIM Press, which, unlike resellers, can ship any quantity right away; Phone/fax: (805) 924-0200; e-mail: *andersondm@aol.com.*

12. See the outsourcing article at the author's web-site www.HalfCostProducts.com/outsourcing.htm.

13. See the offshoring article at the author's web-site www.HalfCostProducts.com/offshore_manufacturing.htm.

14. The first section of the outsourcing article shows how "cost reduction"attempts thwart 6 of the 8 cost reduction strategies presented on the home page of www.HalfCostProducts.com/outsourcing.htm.

15. Matthew E. May, *The Elegant Solution*, (2007, Free Press), p. 73.

16. Morgan & Liker, *The Toyota Product Development System,* Chapter 4, "Front-Load the PD Process to Explore Alternatives Thoroughly."

17.Douglas T. Hicks, *Activity-Based Costing, Making it Work for Small and Mid-Sized Businesses,* Second Edition (1998, John Wiley).

18. Cooper, Kaplan, Morrissey, and Oehm, *Implementing Activity-Based Cost Management,* pp. 6, 25, and 256.

19. Hicks, *Activity-Based Costing.*

DFM SUMMARY

This chapter provides a summary of key DFM principles, which can be used as to help plan implementation, get management support, and implement DFM. The copyright policy of this book permits copying such material for internal presentations, meetings, and reports, but does not allow extensive reproductions for training.[1]

12.1 DEFINITIONS

Design for Manufacturability is the process of *proactively* developing products to :

- optimize all the manufacturing functions: fabrication, assembly, test, procurement, shipping, service, and repair;

- assure the best cost, quality, reliability, regulatory compliance, safety, time-to-market, and customer satisfaction; and

- ensure that *lack of* manufacturability doesn't compromise functionality, styling, new product introductions, product delivery, improvement programs, strategic initiatives, and unexpected surges in product demand.

Concurrent Engineering is the proactive practice of:

- Designing products to be built on standard processes, or

- Concurrently developing *new* processes while developing new products

12.2 MYTHS AND REALITIES OF PRODUCT DEVELOPMENT

Myths of Product Development

Myth # 1: To develop products **quicker**, get going soon on the detail design and software coding and then enforce deadlines to keep design release and first-customer-ship on schedule.

Myth # 2: To achieve **quality**, find out what's wrong and fix it.

Myth # 3: To **customize** products, take all orders and use an *ad hoc* approach: marking up existing drawings, or having a separate engineering group perform custom engineering on individual products as needed.

Myth # 4: **Cost** can be easily reduced by cost reduction efforts after the product is designed.

Realities of Product Development

Fact # 1: The only measure of **time-to-market** is the time to stable, trouble free production and that depends on getting the design right the first time.

Fact # 2: The most effective way to achieve **quality** is to design it in and then build it in.

Fact # 3: The most effective way to **customize** products is by the concurrent design of versatile product families and flexible processes, which is known as *mass customization.*

Fact # 4: **Cost** is designed into the product, especially by early concept decisions, and is difficult to remove later.

from, *Design for Manufacturability & Concurrent Engineering,* David M. Anderson (2008, CIM Press)

12.3 WHEN COSTS ARE COMMITTED BY THE DESIGN

Figure 1-1 shows that by the time a product is designed, 80% of the cost has been determined.[2] And by the time a product goes into production, 95% of its cost is determined, so it will be very difficult to remove cost later. The most profound implication for product development is that *60% of a product's cumulative lifetime cost is committed by the concept/architecture phase!*

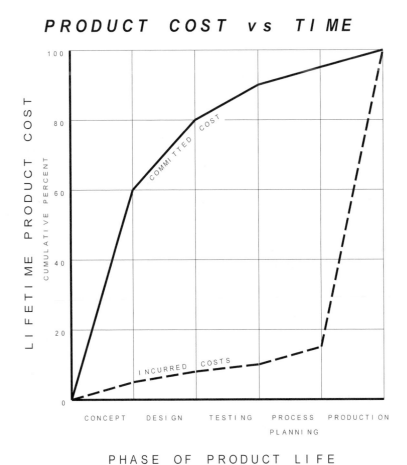

Figure 1-1: When Costs Are Committed

from, *Design for Manufacturability & Concurrent Engineering,* David M. Anderson (2008, CIM Press)

12.4 RESOURCES ALLOCATIONS: BEST AND WORST

The product development benchmarking reported by Womack, Jones, Roos in the first lean production book, *"The Machine That Changed the World, The Story of Lean Production,"*[3] summarized the difference between the best and worst practices they encountered.

In the worst projects,

> *"The number of people involved is very small at the outset but grows to a peak very close to the time of launch, as hundreds or even thousands of extra bodies are brought in to resolve problems that should have been cleared up in the beginning."*

In the best projects,

> *"The numbers of people involved are highest at the very outset. All the relevant specialties are present, and the project leader's job is to force the group to confront all the difficult trade-offs they'll have to make to agree on the project."*

This comparison between the best and the worst coupled with the author's experience with companies practicing both of these extremes inspired the following plot of team participation over time (Figure 2-1), which graphically shows this vivid contrast between what will be designated *traditional* model (which corresponds to the "worst projects" described above) and *advanced* model (which corresponds to the "best projects" described above).

from, *Design for Manufacturability & Concurrent Engineering,* David M. Anderson (2008, CIM Press)

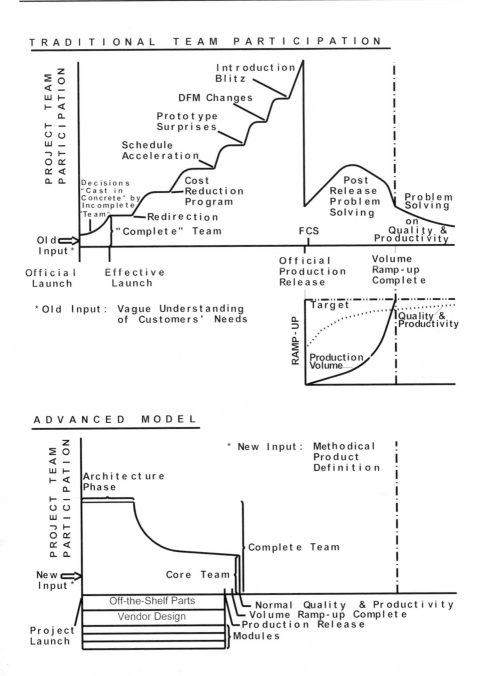

Figure 2-1 Team Participation: Traditional vs Advanced Models

from, *Design for Manufacturability & Concurrent Engineering,* David M. Anderson (2008, CIM Press)

12.5 HOW TO CUT IN HALF, THE *REAL* TIME-TO-MARKET

Time-to-market is heavily affected by early optimization of the early concept/architecture phase as shown by the Lexmark model in Figure 3-1 (repeated below). The projected 40% savings in the *real* time-to-market comes from thorough concept/architecture optimization that minimizes the need for revisions and iterations and makes the manufacturing ramp-up much faster. Note that the architectural phase, labeled "conceptual design," went from 3% in the old model to 33% (of the total development time) in the new model, *an order of magnitude increase!* The more thorough up-front work decreased the post-design activities (the revisions, iterations, and ramp-up) from almost three-fourths to less than a half of the product development cycle. It is more efficient to incorporate a balance of design considerations early than to implement the later with changes, revisions and iterations.

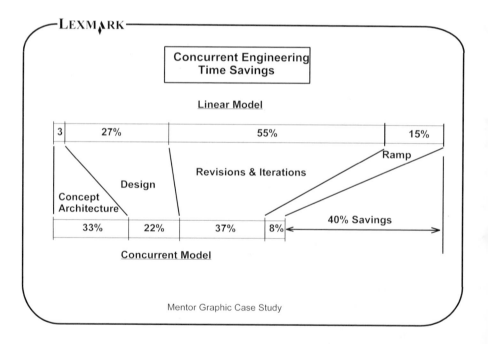

Figure 3-1: The Lexmark Model Showing True Time-to-Market
Differences Between Linear vs. Concurrent Models
(used with permission)

from, *Design for Manufacturability & Concurrent Engineering,* David M. Anderson (2008, CIM Press)

12.6 DFM PRINCIPLES SUMMARY

Ask customers to rank importance factors and plot them against our grade compared to competitors to determine zones of importance.

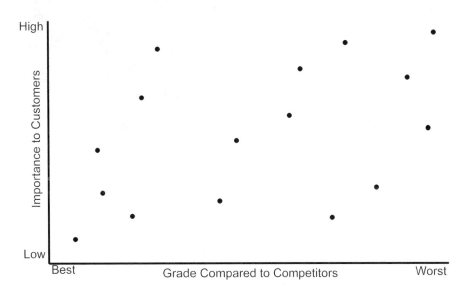

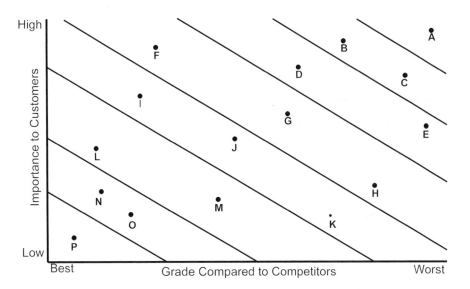

Figure 2-3: Customer Importance vs. Competitive Grade

from, *Design for Manufacturability & Concurrent Engineering,* David M. Anderson (2008, CIM Press)

No Arbitrary Decisions, they make it
difficult to incorporate other
considerations later.

Avoid Late Changes. An engineering
change will cost 10 times more in the
next phase.

Time of Design Change	Cost
During design:	$1,000
During design testing:	10,000
During process planning:	100,000
During test production:	1,000,000
During final production:	10,000,000

Figure 1-3 Cost of Engineering Changes

Specify Good Parts. It costs 10 times more to find and repair a defect
at each subsequent stage of manufacture.

Level of completion	Cost to find & repair defect
the part itself	X
at subassembly	10 X
at final assembly	100 X
at the dealer/distributer	1,000 X
at the customer	10,000 X

from, *Design for Manufacturability & Concurrent Engineering,* David M. Anderson (2008, CIM Press)

Use Standard Parts for New Designs

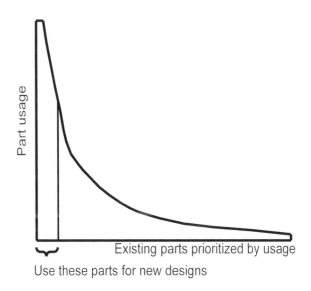

Existing parts prioritized by usage

Use these parts for new designs

Optimize the Utilization of Off-the-Shelf Parts

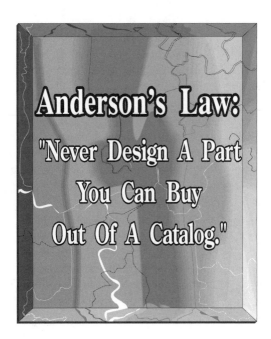

from, *Design for Manufacturability & Concurrent Engineering,* David M. Anderson (2008, CIM Press)

The Usual Cost Breakdown Ignores Overhead and Leads to the Wrong Decisions

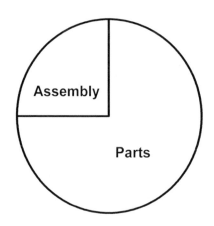

You don't compete on cost; you compete on price.
Customers don't care about *your cost.*
They only care about *their* cost which is *your price.*

The Selling Price Breakdown Shows *All* Costs

from, *Design for Manufacturability & Concurrent Engineering,* David M. Anderson (2008, CIM Press)

Know Tolerance Step Functions to avoid needlessly paying several times too much.

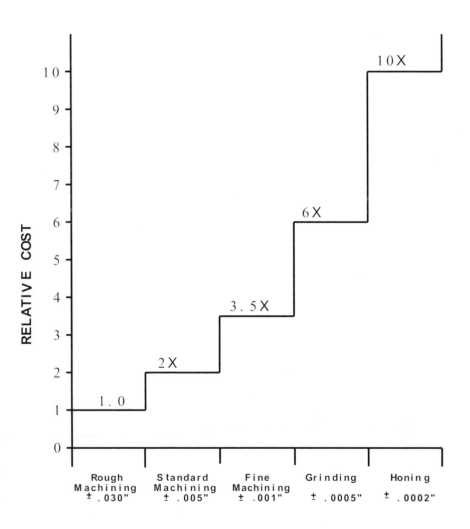

Figure 9-2: Cost as a Function of Process

from, *Design for Manufacturability & Concurrent Engineering,* David M. Anderson (2008, CIM Press)

Product Quality is Determined by
Part Quality *to the exponent of the number of parts.*

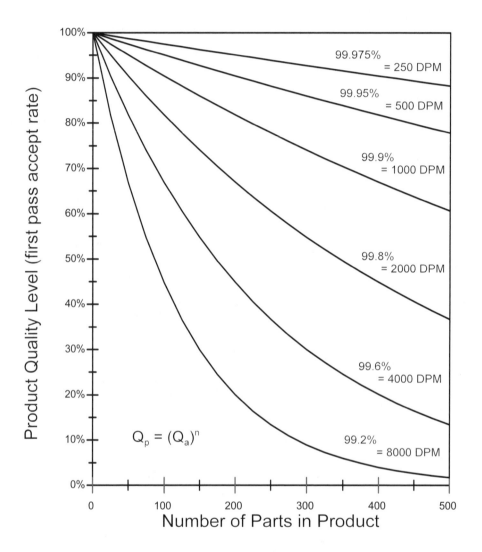

Plotted lines are for average part quality levels
cited as percent good and DPM (Defects/Million)

Figure 10-3: Quality as a Function of Part Count and Part Quality

from, *Design for Manufacturability & Concurrent Engineering,* David M. Anderson (2008, CIM Press)

Other Key DFM Principles

- Do it right the first time; You can't afford to do it over.

- It's *everyone's* responsibility to consider *all* the goals and constraints *early.*

- Define the product well to satisfy the "voice of the customer."

- The most important time-to-market measurement is the time to *stable, trouble-free* production.

- The further into a design, the harder it is to start satisfying additional needs.

- Design to optimize the *system,* not just many parts that are hard to integrate together.

- Break down the walls by working together.

- Make sure all specialties are present to confront all the difficult tradeoffs and resolve the issues *early.*

- Use proven features and modules from previous designs to avoid reinventing the wheel.

- Use methodical approaches to specifying tolerances for an optimal balance of performance, cost, quality and safety.

- Work with other projects to design product *families* to maximize synergies and avoid duplication of effort.

- Proactively manage product variety by designing for lean production, build-to-order, and mass customization.

from, *Design for Manufacturability & Concurrent Engineering,* David M. Anderson (2008, CIM Press)

12.7 DFM METHODOLOGIES SUMMARY

I. Product development management ensures that:

- Selection of product development projects based on rational product portfolio planning
- Diverse teams have the resources so that all relevant specialties are *active early*
- The team leader has leadership abilities, experience, empowerment, and thorough understanding of DFM methodologies
- Vendor/partnerships determined ahead of time to encourage early vendor participation; avoid low-bidding on custom parts
- Timing of phases supports thorough up-front work
- Bottom line metrics/compensation are based on *total cost* and *time to stable production*
- Management has realistic expectations compatible with DFM methodologies

II. Thorough Concept/Architecture Phase with the following deliverables:

- Voice of the customer captured and applied to QFD house-of-quality
- Lessons learned from pervious projects understood with respect to manufacturability, quality, and so forth
- Concept simplification at the product/process level
- Architecture optimization for product families, processes, and supply chains
- All issues raised and resolved *early*
- Optimal utilization of off-the-shelf parts
- Modular strategy optimized
- Manufacturing strategy determined early
- Outsourcing/integration strategy optimizes concurrent engineering, manufacturability, cost, quality, and responsiveness
- Strategy is determined for variety, options, customizations, extensions, and derivatives

from, *Design for Manufacturability & Concurrent Engineering,* David M. Anderson (2008, CIM Press)

III. Products Designed for All Aspects of Manufacturability:

- The product is designed *as a system,* not just a collection of parts

- Vendors are on the team early to help design parts for their processes

- Products are designed for existing processes or concurrently designed new processes

- DFM guidelines are obeyed for all relevant processes

- Quality and reliability targets are achieved *by design*

- Mistake-proofing (*poka-yoke*) by design

- Robust design ensures optimal tolerances and compatibility with process capabilities

- Arbitrary decisions are avoided by early participation of complete teams and early inclusion of all design considerations

- Standard parts lists are determined and used for new designs

- Parts are selected for quality, availability, and supply chain management optimization

- Cost is computed by *total cost* measurements

- Time is measured to *stable, trouble-free* production

- Documentation is complete and unambiguous

- Lean and build-to-order are designed for utilizing: concurrent engineering of product families *and* lean processes; setup/batch elimination by design; aggressive standardization and part consolidation to enable spontaneous (pull system) resupply .

from, *Design for Manufacturability & Concurrent Engineering,* David M. Anderson (2008, CIM Press)

12.8 KEY DFM TASKS, RESULTS, AND TOOLS

TASKS	RESULTS	TOOLS
Get "voice-of-customer;" Perform QFD analysis.	Rational product specs; Best resource prioritization.	Customer input, QFD, & Teamwork.
Raise & resolve issues early.	All issues raised early; All issues resolved early.	Strong team leadership; Team consensus.
Simplify product concepts.	Inherently low product cost; Inherently high quality; Inherently high reliability.	Thorough up-front work; Creative culture; Teamwork.
Optimize product architecture and system design.	Ensure lowest cost; Ensure quick development; Ensure trouble-free launch.	Thorough up-front work; Multi-functional team; Architecture focus.
Optimize product and process design.	Manufacturable designs; Optimized processing; Quality designed in.	Concurrent Engineering; DFM guidelines; Quality guidelines.
Standardize, modularize, re-use engineering.	Minimum material overhead; Quicker product designs; Flexible operations.	Standardization lists; Motivation & discipline; Cross-team cooperation.
Quantify total costs.	Best decisions; Proper costing/pricing.	Activity-Based Costing; Total cost thinking.
Establish vendor/partner partnerships.	Manufacturable part designs; Lowest vendor cost and time; Quality assured at the source	Vendor partnerships; Total cost measurements; Teamwork.
Measure & compensate to encourage teamwork and total goals.	Minimum total cost; Minimum time-to-market; Best decisions.	Metrics & compensation based on total cost and the real time-to-market.
Management supports and understands DFM & Concurrent Engineering.	Product development becomes a potent competitive advantage.	Executive education.

Figure 12-1: Key DFM Tasks, Results, and Tools

from, *Design for Manufacturability & Concurrent Engineering,* David M. Anderson (2008, CIM Press)

12.9 SUMMARY OF DFM BENEFITS

This section repeats the benefits of DFM presented throughout the book in list form without explanations, which are found in the appropriate chapters.

DFM Saves Design Time

1) by using purchased parts,

2) by using standard commonality parts,

3) by reusing previously designed detail,

4) by farming out part design to part vendors,

5) by using modular (building block) design,

6) by more quickly converging on the optimal design,

7) by minimizing test development with higher product quality,

8) with less involvement in factory troubleshooting,

9) with fewer engineering changes to write,

10) by avoiding redesigns.

Benefits of DFM (from Chapter 1)

1) Lower production costs

2) Higher quality products

3) Quicker time to market

4) Lower capital equipment cost through better utilization

5) Greater use of automation

6) Production up to speed sooner

7) Fewer engineering changes

8) Less chance of redesign

9) Fewer parts to purchase from fewer vendors

10) Factory availability will be better due to fewer production problems

from, *Design for Manufacturability & Concurrent Engineering,* David M. Anderson (2008, CIM Press)

Results of "Do it Right the First Time" (from Chapter 1)

The results of doing it right the first time are:

1) No need for costly changes or redesigns

2) Quick & easy product introduction and ramp

3) Trouble-free production

4) Good product cost, quality, and delivery

Benefits of Designing for Lean and Build-to-Order (from Chapter 4)

In Engineering

1) Design time will be reduced with maximum use of standard parts and previous engineering

2) Documentation time will be reduced

3) Prototyping and testing will be reduced

4) Design cost will be lower

5) Cost estimating will be more accurate

In Manufacturing

6) Set-up times will be reduced with similar parts built without setup

7) Lot (batch) sizes will be smaller with less setup

8) Work-in-Process (WIP) inventories will be reduced

9) Thruput will be quicker with less WIP inventory

10) Quality will improve from more rapid feedback

11) Plant layout will be better

12) Less floor space will be needed

from, *Design for Manufacturability & Concurrent Engineering,* David M. Anderson (2008, CIM Press)

13) Product flow will be improved

14) Machine utilization will be higher with less setup

15) Product and part scheduling will be better

16) Responsiveness to customers will improve

17) Product introduction will be quicker

18) Introduction cost will be less

19) Greater purchasing leverage for better price and delivery

20) Product cost will be lower

Benefits of Modular Design (from Chapter 4)

1) Lower engineering cost with greater use of standard modules

2) Quicker time to market for modular products

3) Quicker delivery on standard products assembled from standard modules

4) Lower inventory from modular assembly

5) Easier servicing with module replacement

6) Wider product line with module combinations

7) Easier product upgrading with modular upgrades

from, *Design for Manufacturability & Concurrent Engineering,* David M. Anderson (2008, CIM Press)

Standardization Benefits (from Chapter 5)

Cost Reduction

1) Purchasing costs lower with economies of scale

2) Inventory cost reduction

3) Floor space reduction

4) Overhead cost reduction

Quality

5) Product quality better with fewer parts

6) Continuous Improvement focused better

7) Supplier reduction from fewer part types

Flexibility

8) Eliminating setup easier with fewer parts to change

9) Inventory reduction

10) Internal material logistics simpler

11) Breadtruck deliveries possible

12) Supports Lean Production, BTO, and Mass Customization

Responsiveness

13) Build-to-Order more possible

14) Parts availability better

15) Quicker deliveries from suppliers

16) Stronger suppliers

from, *Design for Manufacturability & Concurrent Engineering,* David M. Anderson (2008, CIM Press)

Cost Savings of Purchased Parts (from Chapter 5)

1) Design costs are reduced since purchased parts do not need to be designed

2) Documentation cost is less with fewer new designs to document

3) Prototyping and testing cost may be eliminated for purchased parts

4) Debugging and correction of part designs may not be necessary

5) Purchasing costs of purchased parts will be less than for the constituents of their manufactured counterparts

6) The part cost will be less because of more efficient and specialized manufacture by the supplier

7) Administrative expense will be less with fewer manufactured parts to administer

8) Quality costs will be less with more refined parts

9) Suppliers may share warrantee costs for their parts

10) Overhead costs will be less because of all of the above.

Time Savings of Purchased Parts (from Chapter 5)

1) Less time spent designing parts that are available

2) Less time spent documenting unnecessary designs

3) Less time spent building and testing prototypes

4) Less time spent debugging and redesigning parts

5) Less time spent by Manufacturing on parts that suppliers are more efficient producing

from, *Design for Manufacturability & Concurrent Engineering,* David M. Anderson (2008, CIM Press)

Conclusions

DFM alone may make the difference between being competitive or not succeeding in the marketplace. Most markets are highly competitive and slight competitive advantages (or disadvantages) can have significant impact.

DFM can have enormous benefits to product cost, quality, and time to market with very little investment. Practiced right, DFM actually takes less effort because products *are designed right the first time.*

ENDNOTES/REFERENCES

1. For internally generated DFM training, quantity discounts of this book are readily available from CIM Press, which, unlike resellers, can ship any quantity right away; Phone/fax: (805) 924-0200; e-mail: *andersondm@aol.com.*

2. This data was generated by DataQuest and presented in the landmark article that started the Concurrent Engineering movement: "A Smarter Way to Manufacture; How `Concurrent Engineering' can invigorate American Industry," page 110, *Business Week,* April 30, 1990. In the author's in-house seminars, he presents similar data from Motorola, Ford, General Motors, Westinghouse, Rolls Royce, British Aerospace, the Allison Division of Detroit Diesel, Draper Laboratories, Rensselear Polytechnic Institute, and several other published sources.

3. James P. Womack, Daniel T. Jones, and Daniel Roos, *The Machine That Changed the World, The Story of Lean Production* (1991, Harper Perennial), Chapter 5, "Designing the Car."

Appendix A

PRODUCT LINE RATIONALIZATION

Product line rationalization is a powerful technique to improve profits, simplify operations and supply chains, and free valuable resources for product development. It does this by *rationalizing* existing product lines to eliminate or outsource products and product variations that are problem prone, have low sales, have excessive overhead demands, have limited future potential, and may really be losing money.

Rationalization can quickly improve profits by stopping the production of money-losing products and eliminating all of the excess overhead costs associated with "fire-drill" products. This, in turn, will allow precious resources to focus on the most profitable products instead of low-leverage products, which will increase sales and further lower costs. After rationalization, the remaining products will cost less because they will no longer have to subsidize the money losers or marginal products.

All these cost savings can be used to lower prices in price-sensitive markets or to increase profits. In fact, rationalization can raise profits enough to be justified as a free standing program. The following scenario will show that, by simply eliminating the lowest leverage products, profits can be tripled!

A-1: PARETO'S LAW FOR PRODUCT LINES

All companies experience some Pareto effect, typically with 80% of profits or sales coming from the best 20% of the products.

This happens because almost all companies keep *adding* products to the portfolio without ever *removing* any. Further, sales incentives and emphases on growth and market share encourage the sales mantra of "take all orders," thus overloading production operations and the supply chain with too many low-volume products that have unusual parts and manufacturing procedures. This results in many setup changes, causes excessive overhead costs, lowers plant capacity, complicates supply chain management, and dilutes engineering and manufacturing resources.

365

Few companies realize these problems because their cost systems allocate (average) overhead costs, which implies that all products have the same overhead costs – a very unlikely situation.

Focus

Product line rationalization encourages companies to focus on their *best* products by eliminating or outsourcing the *marginal* products. The resources that were being wasted on the low-leverage products can then be focused on growing the "cash cows."

Robert Atkins and Adrian Slywotzky, writing in a Wall Street Journal about profiting during a recession contend that *"spreading resources evenly among all customers is bad even in good times; in bad times, it's disastrous."*

A-2 HOW RATIONALIZATION CAN TRIPLE PROFITS!

The following scenario shows the power of this methodology using a simple example illustrated in Figure A-1.

Figure A-1: Pareto's Law for Products

The actual product line rationalization takes many more factors into account, but this example shows the profit increasing potential for rationalization.

If a company kept the 20% of the products that were making 80% of the profits and dropped the other 80% of the product line, it would result in only a 20% drop in revenue.

The cost reduction can greatly exceed the revenue drop because of the way cost is distributed. Direct costs such as materials, parts, and labor would be proportional to revenue – in other words, the more products sold, the more materials, parts, and labor would be consumed. However, overhead has the *opposite* effect. Indirect cost (such as procurement, manufacturing engineering, and other support functions) would be low on the cash-cow products because they are better designed for manufacturability, parts are procured routinely, quality issues have been resolved, and processes have been stabilized due to the focus that is usually applied to higher-volume production. In contrast, overhead cost on the low-volume products is high, probably 80% of the total, because of all the inefficiencies inherent in building many low-volume, seldom-built products. Further, those products may be less well designed for manufacturability and have much higher quality costs.

So the breakdown of direct and indirect costs would be as shown in Figure A-2.

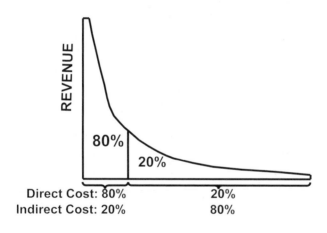

Figure A-2: Cost Breakdown

In order to make this example relevant, Figure A-3 converts these percentages into dollars for a $100,000,000 business, which, according to the common Pareto's law effect experienced by most companies, generates $80 million in revenue from cash-cow products and $20 million from all the others. The cost breakdown shows indirect (overhead) costs as half the total cost, which is not an unreasonable assumption. In fact, in many industries, overhead cost is greater than half of the total cost (as shown in Figure 6-1), thus resulting in an even stronger case.

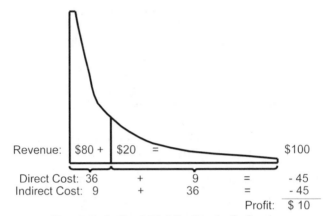

Figure A-3: Cost Distribution in Dollars

Now to show the powerful effect of this procedure, simply eliminating the 80% of the low-volume products and keeping the 20% cast-cows will have the following effect, as shown in Figure A-4.

The bottom line: revenue drops 20% (this will be discussed later) but eliminating the high-overhead products eliminated most of the indirect cost, so that *profits are 3.5 times that of the full product line!*

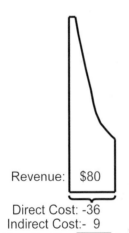

Figure A-4: Results after rationalization

For this motivational scenario, overhead cost savings are assumed to be eliminated to show the effect on profits. This could be realized in a rapidly growing company where the focus shifts from current loser products to upcoming growth products.

However, it would be a shortsighted strategy to lay off the workers to realize a short-term overhead cost savings.[1] Rather, "liberated" workers should be *invested* in growing the remaining aspects of the business. Breakdowns of actual cost savings and reinvestments are discussed next.

A-3 COST SAVINGS FROM RATIONALIZATION

The cost savings from rationalization comes in two forms: cash and human resources, which will be itemized below. Rationalization, like lean production, effectively *liberates* many types of resources and their disposition should be planned ahead of time. *The* lean production guide, *Lean Thinking,* has one section titled, "Deal with Excess People at the Outset." [2]

Product line rationalization results in the following short term cash savings and resource investment opportunities.

Short Term Cash Savings:

• Avoid the purchase of parts and materials for rationalized products, which may have less purchasing leverage, higher procurement costs to find, and higher than normal setup and expediting costs.

• Avoid quality costs of unusual products, which may be higher than normal, for reasons discussed in Section A-10.

• Limit, postpone, or cancel hiring for growth and attrition replacement.

• Avoid overtime.

• Phase out temps (temporary workers) as long as they do not have critical knowledge or skills.

• Bring in-house currently outsourced services, especially when co-location would provide better concurrent engineering.

• Delay facility expansion. Unusual products generally require more space than those that have benefitted from continuous improvements implementing space-saving lean principles.

Investments:

- Focus on improving sales on the remaining products, which now can sell at higher profits (or lower prices) without having to cross-subsidize the "losers" (see the next section on redirecting resources).

- Improve quality and lower the cost of quality.

- Continuously improve operations and productivity.

- Expand into related services.

- Get certificated (ISO 9000, QS 9000, etc.) or win awards (Best Plants, Baldridge, etc.) to improve stature with customers.
- Upgrade CAD tools, information systems, and web presence.

- Upgrade skills with investments in training.

- Implement new capabilities like build-to-order and mass-customization to be able to build a wide variety of mass-customized or standard products on-demand without forecast or inventory.

- Invest in *internal* start-up ventures.

- Use liberated cash and resources to buy and transform related, supportive businesses up and down the supply chain (*not competitors!*). The book *Lean Thinking* cited an example: "Each time Wiremold's vacuum sucks up a batch-and-queue producer, it spits out enough cash to buy the next batch-and queue producer!"[3]

- Improve product development. Without the daily fire-drills in operations and procurement, manufacturing people will be more available to participate in product development teams, which is a key element to successful product development.

A-4 SHIFTING FOCUS TO THE MOST PROFITABLE PRODUCTS

After product line rationalization, resources that were being wasted on the low-leverage products can now be focused on improving the remaining products, as shown in Figure A-5.

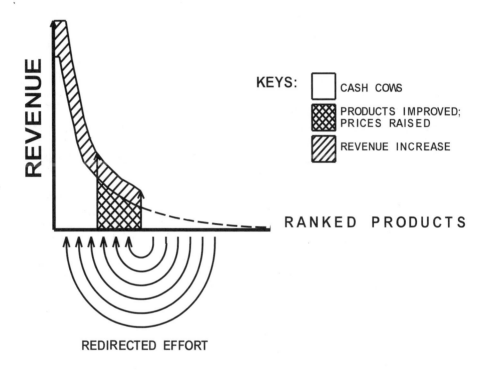

Figure A-5: Redirecting Focus to Cash Cows

One of the author's clients, a telecom equipment company, reported that after dropping their marginal products, they recovered their original revenue within two months! This came from focusing liberated resources (both personnel and money) on the cash cow products with improved efforts in advertising, sales channels, product design, operations, and supply chain management. All of these efforts will be easier and more efficient with fewer products to focus on. Operations and supply chain management will benefit from greatly reduced number of parts and processes to deal with.   Multifunctional product development teams will make faster progress and develop better products with more people available from operations and purchasing. In addition, the money saved not having to subsidize "the losers" can fund improvement activities, be used to lower prices, or simply go to the bottom line to improve profitability.

In addition to improving the known cash cows, it may be possible to "raise worthy dogs," or focus some improvement on selected worthy products, especially if they are related to cash cow products. For instance, consider raising their prices, if the market accepts them; they may survive and simply make more money. Look for products that have *easy* opportunities to lower their total cost, but be wary of any "cost reduction" effort that does not pay off the cost of the effort within the expected life of the product, as discussed in Chapter 6. Make sure good products are not unfairly burdened by inappropriate overhead charges, like paying the "loser tax" to subsidize marginal products. In addition to these techniques, selected products may also benefit from all above mentioned improvements in advertising, sales efforts, product design, operations, and supply chain management.

Professor Kim Cameron of the University of Michigan Business School recommends that during downturns companies should "exit from weak businesses entirely."[4]

Sometimes companies can profit from shifting the focus from products that are only *good* to those that would have the potential to be *great.* Jim Collins, author of *Good to Great,* points out that "few executives have the guts to get rid of profitable businesses where their company can only be good, but never great."[5]

What Is the Goal of a Business?

Many managers still have trouble with the issue of dropping revenue 20% even if it triples profit. And this brings up the issue of what is the goal of a business.

As Eli Goldratt[6] and others have pointed out, the real goal of a for-profit enterprise is to make money, not optimize other common measures like productivity, market share, or "growth at any cost."

The opening chapter in Slywotzky & Morrison's book, *The Profit Zone; How Strategic Business Design Will Lead You to Tomorrow's Profits,*[7] is titled: "Market Share is Dead," in which are found the following quotes.

"The two most valuable ideas in the old economic order,
market share and growth, have become
the two most dangerous ideas in the new order."

"Paradoxically, the devout pursuit of market share
may be the single greatest creator of no-profit zones
in the economy."

Similarly, the book about the largest research project ever devoted to corporate failures, *Why Smart Executives Fail, and What You Can Learn from Their Mistakes,*[8] states that market share is the wrong *scorecard* because *"market share does not translate into profitability, since significant investments are typically needed to build share in the first place."*

One of the themes of Richard Koch's book *The 80/20 Principle,*[9] is:

> *"Successful firms operate in markets where it is possible to generate the highest revenue with the least effort."*

A-5 VOLUME GROWTH STRATEGIES

Another quote from *The 80/20 Principle* is:

"The road to hell is paved with the pursuit of volume." [10]

Of course, "pursuit of volume" here means a volume growth strategy. Many companies, who have been stumbling lately, have volume growth as the cornerstone of their corporate strategy, with quarterly and yearly growth goals. But, the underlying theme of Pareto's law is that:

All opportunities are not equal and do not make an equal contribution to profitability.

But a volume growth strategy encourages the "take all orders" mantra. Thus, when there is pressure to grow the business, the company end up taking any business it can, not just the most profitable. This behavior is built into the system if sales incentives are based on volume growth, instead of profit. This is the sales equivalent of piece-part incentives that have been abandon long ago because they favored one metric (volume) over another (quality).

*The key to **profitable** growth is to focus on the products with the most potential, not to dilute resources on the most products.*

Rationalization Prerequisite - Eliminating Duplicate Products

Before doing the rationalization procedure, there are certain first steps that can simplify the process. Eliminate overlapping or duplicate products. Search out and eliminate or consolidate duplicate products, overlapping products, and superceded products, even if some customers are still using the older product. You may have to encourage or force customers to switch from the older, less-advanced products that they have been ordering because of arbitrary decisions, inertia, or lack of awareness about newer/better replacements.

A-6 THE RATIONALIZATION PROCEDURE

The rationalization procedure divides product line into four zones as shown in Figure A-6.

PRODUCTS, RANKED BY REVENUE

Figure A-6: Rationalization Procedure

The least profitable, lowest-volume products would be mostly dropped (zone 4) subject to certain considerations discussed in the product family section below. Products that need to be in the catalog could be outsourced (zone 3), thus simplifying the in-house supply chain and manufacturing operations. Cash cows would be kept (zone 1). As mentioned in the focus discussion, the remaining products could be improved (zone 2).

Zone 1) "Cash Cow" products should remain since they are probably making 80% of the revenue and profits. Some may be just fine in dedicated mass production lines. No change in production *per se* may be required for some products while others may be made together on flexible lines.

Zone 2) This zone includes products that could be improved and grow with redirected efforts.

Zone 3) This category consists of products that do not fit into either (1) or (2) but still need to be in the catalog for completeness, to satisfy loyal customers, or for service obligations. These products may remain in the catalog, *but they do not have to be designed and built in-house.* They could be outsource and manufactured by a supplier under the company name/label. Or the company catalog could simply carry another source's product to complete product line, assuring customers about appropriate equivalency.

Zone 4) This zone contains the products that should be dropped from product line. Sell off the rights to losing products if possible; someone else may be able to make money if they are a better fit with their products and operations. This certainly would not be a competitive threat, since those products would not be making as much money as new products designed with better focus using the techniques of this book.

A-7 TOTAL COST IMPLICATIONS

Chapter 7 discussed total cost measurements and their impact on business decisions.   The cost accounting system has significant implications for product line rationalization.   Most companies average (allocate) overhead costs so much that the reported "costs" of individual products do not reflect reality.   What happens is that good products usually subsidize bad products.   And since profitability is based on cost, it will be distorted too.   When total cost measurements are implemented, the profitability of products becomes more realistic, as shown in Figure A-7, and it becomes apparent how many of the products are really losing money. These then become the prime candidates for elimination in zone 4 of Figure A-6.

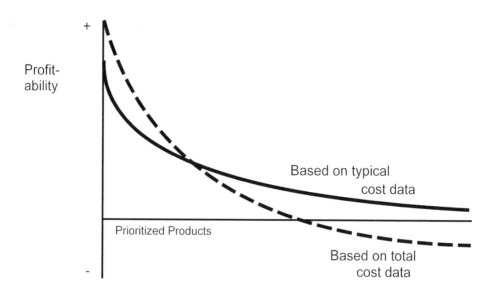

Figure A-7: Prioritized Profitability; Typical vs Total Cost

You cannot have a profitability strategy unless you can have total cost measurements and can break down "corporate profits" into profits for products, market segments, and so forth.

Sometimes implementing total cost measurements can resolve a rationalization impasse. A Harvard case study (9-186-272)[11] analyzed seven products made by Schrader Bellows. In a factory where most products had annual volumes of thousands per year, there was one product that they only build 53 per year. Of course, production management wanted to get rid of it because they understood all the inefficiencies, but the current cost system said, quite illogically, that it had the highest "profit margin" in the plant, so they had to keep building it. However, after the total cost analysis was performed, the product that originally was thought to have the highest profit margin of the group was shown, in reality, to have a negative 59% "margin."[12] This shows the dangers of using profit margins for reasons cited next.

The Margin Trap

Making decisions based on product profit margins can be a dangerous practice when costs are not based on total cost accounting practices and updated often.

Low-profit or money-losing products will keep selling if there is a *perception* that they have high "margins." Reporting profit margins for individual products is a dangerous practice when costs are not based on total cost accounting practices and updated often. Many misleading situations occur when products have margins computed after high-volume builds and these numbers stay in the system, even though the order volumes have since decreased. In this case the obsolete margin data mislead decision makers and may thwart rationalization efforts.

Seldom Built Products

Products "revived from the dead" have very high overhead costs, despite their reported "margins." Another rationalization procedure is to investigate which products have not been built recently, for instance, in the last year, two years, three years, four years, and five years. These products that are "revived from the dead" have very high overhead demands because of the effort to remember how to build them, find all the documentation, procure unusual materials, and find the tooling. In one company, tooling for a seldom built product had been sitting outside in the snow for months and required much rehabilitation. Some companies can simply implement a policy that all products that have not been built in, say three years, will be dropped immediately, or at least discouraged or given special scrutiny.

Obsolescence Costs

When mass producers build too many low-volume products, it increases the risk and cost of obsolescence due to market changes and engineering change orders. An APICS article on "product proliferation" stated:

> *"Low-volume products are particularly prone to [obsolescence] since batch sizes are often increased to produce a six-month or more supply in order to reduce the number of changeovers required in manufacturing. With this amount of inventory on the shelf, the risk of becoming obsolete due to engineering changes or changing levels of demand increases dramatically."[13]*

A-8 OVERCOMING INHIBITIONS, FEARS, AND RESISTANCE

Despite the fact that product line rationalization can easily raise profits, free valuable resources, and simplify operations and supply chain management, many managers have inhibitions, fears and resistance:

Growth Emphasis. When there is too much emphasis on revenue growth, it may be hard to get companies to do what may *appear* to reduce their revenue stream, even temporarily, in order to eliminate the low-leverage products, improve the cash cows, improve profitability, and ultimately grow revenue.

Cost System Deficiencies. When overhead is allocated (averaged), all products will appear to have close to equal profitability. Total cost measurements will then be necessary to flush out the low profit products.

Inertia. Many people resist change in general, especially if the cost system or personal communications do not show them the "big picture," so Rationalization programs need to emphasize benefits stated in Section A-11.

Departmentalism. Often resistance comes from those who have been optimizing their department's performance, for instance Sales, at the cost of the company as a whole. So metrics may need to be changed to direct behavior toward maximizing *company* goals.

Unhealthy Attachments. Every product at one time was the "baby" or someone or several people. But remember that the goal of a business is to produce the most profitable products, not a collection of favorites.

Fears Overstated. Usually fears about negative consequences are overstated, especially the fear of losing customers who, in reality, will most likely switch to better equivalents from the same catalog. When low-leverage products are eliminated:

1) The company can *increase* sales on the remaining products with better a focus in each of the following areas: research, product development, manufacturing, quality, and marketing.

2) Without having to subsidize low-leverage products, the remaining products can generate more profit or be priced lower.

3) Customers can switch to remaining products from older, less-advanced products that they have been ordering because of arbitrary decisions, inertia, or lack of awareness about newer/better replacements.

The following is a list of most common questions that come up in the author's workshops, followed by his answers.

- **What about the "complete product line" argument?**

If the catalog *must* really be complete (zone 3 in Figure A-6), that doesn't mean *you* have to manufacture all the products, options, or variations. Outsource unusual products/options/variations so that the resources that were formerly squandered on them can now be invested in development a *better portfolio* of new products.

- **Won't customer satisfaction drop?**

Overall customer satisfaction will actually be *lower* if you waste your resources making low-leverage products instead of capitalizing on *opportunities* to give customers better innovation, lower cost, and better quality. However, they will probably miss the good deals you were giving them on your money-losing products.

- **Won't we be limiting customer choice?**

Often customers keep ordering older/unusual products because of arbitrary decisions, inertia, and lack of awareness about newer/better replacements. Point out how the remaining products have been improved; drop prices on them.

• **What about loss-leaders?**

If low-leverage products are to be retained as "loss leaders," then management should *know* how much money is really being lost, including the *opportunity* losses of what those resources could have accomplished.   If loss-leaders are still a valid strategy after implementing total cost accounting, then the loss-leader products should be outsourced to avoid distracting the factory from its most efficient tasks.

• **But what about the perception that we have to sell some oddball products to get the big sales.**

First of all, customers may have been spoiled by years of unnecessary concessions made by salespeople who may not know or care about the trauma that low-volume products cause in operations and supply chain management. Customized products would fall into this category if not done efficiently through mass customization.[14]

Second, ask objectively if the customer will really terminate a long and viable relationship over a few low-volume products.

Third, point out that if customers continue to buy older products, they will become increasingly vulnerable to product obsolescence and availability problems.

Finally, if customers still insist on package deals, the manufacture of oddball products could be done by outsourcing so those sales do not distract from new product development.

If all of these arguments are not convincing, then consider the "Competitive Scenario" (next)

Competitive Scenarios

A savvy competitor would not blindly compete against your entire product line. It would offer only the most profitable products. Not burdened by your low-leverage products, it would be able to make the *rationalized* product line quicker, better, and at lower cost.

Another competitive scenario is "cherry picking," when an existing or new competitor skim off the most profitable products.[15]   Thus, competitors could steal your "cash cows" leaving you with the "dogs."

Role Playing. It may be a valuable exercise to role-play competitor scenarios, pretending you, or your brainstorming group, are a well-financed new competitor. Ask the questions:

- Which products would you want to have in your product line?

- How would you group products and structure production lines for the greatest efficiencies?

- How could a concise product line benefit from standardization?

- What is the minimum list of materials needed?

- How would you build them flexibly to be able to reach the broadest possible markets?

- What would you like to do that you cannot do because of existing product line limitations?

Here is what Downes and Mui reported in their book, *Unleashing the Killer App:*[16]

"One organization had teams of executives play the role of well-funded outsiders, both new entrants and existing competitors, and asked them to devise business plans that attacked the organization's prime markets and stole away its most profitable customer segments. Knowing the blinders of the organization, and the exposed flanks of its offerings, these teams easily put together alliances and business propositions that realistically challenged the status quo."

Similarly, General Electric uses "Destroy-Your-Business.com" task forces to identify business threats.[17]

The Dartmouth Business School study that produced the book on corporate failures, cited earlier, recommended as a high-return activity the practice of "convening 'devil's advocate' groups that are assigned the task of spotting vulnerabilities in past and current policies."[18]

Three years after Quaker lost $1.4 *billion* acquiring Snapple, which was a complete mismatch with Quaker's operations, the CEO admitted, "We should have had a couple of people arguing the 'no side' of the evaluation."[19]

A-9 IMPLEMENTATION & CORPORATE STRATEGY

The rationalization approach depends on the business model.

Scenario for Mass Production

For mass production, which builds batches of products for inventory based on forecasts, individual products decisions are made independently. Be sure to quantify the total cost of all setup, inventory and all the other overhead costs to identify which low-volume products are making the least profit. Then eliminate them or, if they must be in the catalog *at any cost*, outsource them to free in-house people for new product development. Note that the "cost" will go up if those products were subsidized before, because outsourcers will charge the true total cost.

Scenario for Mass Customization/Build-to-Order

Flexible cells can build a range of any product in a "family" (or platform) with minimal setup costs and delays. In such an environment some low-volume products can be retained if they can be grouped into a *product family* and quickly and cost-effectively build on either dedicated mini-lines or flexible lines or cells.

Products that do not fit into any family group should be removed from all *flexible* operations, either eliminated or outsourced.

Thus, an inflexible mass production plant will eliminate more low-volume products that a flexible (lean, build-to-order) plant for the same economic benefits.

Implementation Steps

Data gathering. Create Pareto plots by plotting revenue (or sales units) against ranked products in the format of Figure A-6. First, plot all products; this is for motivation and buy-in, so it does not have to be rigorous. Then plot each product family, market segment, or other logical grouping with product identifying numbers displayed.

Polls and surveys. Polls and surveys can quickly identify difficult-to-build products for scrutiny. Just ask the following question to everyone involved in building products, procuring their parts, and performing custom engineering or configurations: "What products or variations cost us more, and delay us more, then we think?" Then plot out the results and start scrutinizing from the top of the list.

Seminar/workshop. Arrange for training on Product Line Rationalization for all people that will be involved. The training should be interactive enough to discuss principles, address concerns, and get buy-in to process. The workshop phase of this event should start the rationalization process based on preliminary data gathered in the previous steps.

Profiles. Profiles can be quickly created to "red flag" certain products for special scrutiny. The profile could be based on any criteria that should raise red flags: low-volume, infrequent manufacture, special materials, hard-to-get parts, unusual processing, difficult customizations, or any other unusual demands. Profiles are valuable because they can be created immediately, before the rationalization process is complete, based on anecdotal criteria in addition to available data. If neither of these are available, conduct polls and ask everyone in operations to vote on which products they think are making less money than assumed and which are distracting them from their jobs and from participation on new product development teams.

At first, red-flagged products would receive special scrutiny and, before the order could be accepted, would require signatures from Manufacturing, Purchasing, Engineering, and so forth. A senior manager may need to be appointed to quickly arbitrate disputes.

As profiles mature, they could automatically block unacceptable orders.

Configurators. Profiles can be built into a *configurator,* which is order-entry software that has the added ability to:

- Contain all the rules, profiles, data, and formulas to certify a valid order and provide customers with instant cost quotes and delivery schedules.

- Quickly provide customers with many "what if" scenarios showing the cost and delivery time for standard or custom orders.

- Transmit the data needed for processing the order, doing engineering work, procuring the materials, setting up production, and launching the product.

Data analysis. Segregate Pareto plots as shown in Figure A-6. Scrutinize the low selling products to see which should be dropped or, if necessary to be in the catalog, which should be outsourced. Look for opportunities to shift resources to improve worthy products as shown in Figure A-5.

Recommendations. Make recommendations on which products to drop, outsource, or improve and how these actions should be executed.

Total cost. Improve the costing system (as discussed in Chapter 7) to the point where all costs are quantified for all product variations, so that:

- All product variations can be plotted by true profitability, which will greatly improve corporate strategy, product portfolio planning, and product line rationalization.

- Pricing can be objectively based on the total cost for all product variations, which will result in an automatic and enduring rationalizing effect. The result of this will be that previously subsidized products, with high overhead costs, will have their prices raised, so the market will rationalize away products that do not provide a good value to customers. On the other hand, efficient products will have their prices lowered (or profit raised) because (a) they will no longer have to subsidize the "losers" and (b) their price will reflect increased efficiencies in manufacturing and supply chain management, which will become even more effective as inefficient products are removed from the system.

Implement recommendations. Get necessary approvals and implement the recommendations. Adjust sales compensation policy as necessary to focus on the most profitable products and products that are compatible with manufacturing and supply chain strategies.

A-10 HOW RATIONALIZATION IMPROVES QUALITY

Quality metrics are a summation of the quality of all products. Rationalization will *raise corporate quality* by eliminating the unusual, low-volume products which usually have the lowest quality because:

- Unusual, lower volume products get less *kaizen* focus (continuous improvement) and have less sophisticated tooling and procedures.

- Infrequently built products may have: missing or vague instructions, procedures, and "know-how;" rusty or damaged tooling; or missing or discarded tooling, build fixtures, test fixtures, or repair tools, resulting in costly and error-prone manual or "plan B" procedures. More difficult setups generate more scrap before first good units can be successfully built.

• Older products may have: worn tooling; less sophisticated diagnostics, tests, and repair tools; less effective design for manufacturability and quality; and old materials that may have deteriorated, which is especially likely after "end-of-life buys" (buying a lifetime supply of parts before they go out of production).

Not only will rationalization raise the quality of *existing* products, it will also make quality improvement programs, like six-sigma, more effective and easier to implement because (a) quality improvement efforts can be better focused on the remaining products, (b) these efforts will not have to deal with products that have inherently lower quality for reasons cited above, and (c) program results will not be pulled down by those products with inherently low-quality and little prospects for improvement.

A-11 THE VALUE OF RATIONALIZATION

Eliminating or outsourcing *low-leverage* products will *immediately:*

• **Increase profits** by avoiding the manufacture of products that have low profit or are really losing money because of their (unreported) high overhead demands and inefficient manufacture/procurement.

• **Improve operational flexibility** and make lean production implementations quicker and more successful, because, typically, low-leverage products are inherently different with unusual parts, materials, set-ups, and processing. Often, these are older products that are built infrequently with less common parts on older equipment using sketchy documentation by a workforce with little experience on those products. Rationalization had the following effect on a drill bit manufacturer:

> *"Efforts to convert to cellular manufacturing using small batch flow became immeasurably easier. By eliminating the very low volume product line, the company was able to set up a simple kanban system between finished goods and the manufacturing cells, which eliminated the need to operate a complicated, computer-based work order system."[20]*

• **Simplify Supply Chain Management.** Eliminating the products with the most unusual parts and materials will greatly simplify supply-chain management. Rationalization enabled the same drill bit manufacturer to reduce bar stock from 24 different types to only six.[21]

- **Free up valuable resources** to improve operations and quality, implement better product development practices, and introduce new capabilities. One of the author's clients summarized the resource gains as follows:

  "Product line rationalization freed up a lot of people!"

  - Jon Milliken, Vice President of Engineering, Fisher Controls Division, Emerson Electric

- **Improve quality** from eliminating older, infrequently-built products, which inherently have more quality problems than current, high-volume products that have benefitted from continuous improvement and current quality programs and techniques.

- **Focus on the most profitable products** in product development, manufacturing, quality improvement, and sales emphases. Focusing on the most profitable products can increase their growth and the growth of similarly profitable products. According to Richard Koch, writing in *The 80/20 Principle*,[22]

  "If you focus on the most profitable segments, you can grow them surprisingly fast -- nearly always at 20 percent a year and sometimes even faster. Remember that the initial position and customer franchise are strong, so it's a lot easier than growing the business overall."

- **Better quality.** Similarly, getting rid of the worst products raises existing quality and enables quality improvements to focus efforts better, as discussed in Section A-10.

- **Protect the most profitable products** from "cherry picking" (launching a competitive attack on the most profitable products), which can be a threat when agile competitors can skim off the most profitable products.[23]

- **Stop cross-subsidizes.** Remaining products will no longer have to subsidize the "dogs" and so they can generate more profit or offer a more competitive selling price.

- **Ensure resource availability** so that multifunctional product development teams have all the specializations available when they need them.

ENDNOTES/REFERENCES

1. David M. Anderson, *Build-to-Order & Mass Customization* (2004, CIM Press); See the section titled, "Downturn Strategies," on why not to lay off workers, in Chapter 13.

2. James P. Womack and Daniel T. Jones, *Lean Thinking, Banish Waste and Create Wealth in your Corporation,* (1996, Simon & Schuster), p. 257.

3. Ibid., p. 147.

4. Jon E. Hilsenrath, "Many Say Layoffs Hurt Companies More Than They Help," *Wall Street Journal,* Feb. 21, 2001.

5. Jim Collins, "Beware of the Self-Promoting CEO," *Wall Street Journal,* November 26, 2001.

6. Eliyahu M. Goldratt, *The Goal,* Second Revised Edition, (1992, North River Press).

7. Adrian J. Slywotzky and David J. Morrison, *The Profit Zone; How Strategic Business Design Will Lead You to Tomorrow's Profits,* (1997, Times Business/Random House), Ch. 1, "Market Share is Dead."

8. Sydney Finkelstein, *Why Smart Executives Fail and What You Can Learn from Their Mistakes,* (2003, Portfolio/Penguin), p. 142.

9. Richard Koch, *The 80/20 Principle; The Secret of Achieving More With Less,* (1998, Currency/Doubleday), p. 53.

10. ibid., p. 93.

11. The Schrader-Bellows case study is described in Harvard Business School Case Series 9-186-272; A summary of the findings appears in "How Cost Accounting Distorts Product Costs," by Robin Cooper and Robert S. Kaplan, *Management Accounting,* (April, 1988).

12. Robin Cooper and Robert Kaplan, "How Cost Accounting Distorts Product Costs," *World-Class Accounting for World-Class Manufacturing,* Edited by Lamont F. Steedle, (Institute of Management Accountants, 1990), p. 122.

13. C. Karry Kouvelas, "Getting a Grip on Product Proliferation," *APICS - The Performance Advantage,* April, 2002, pp. 26 - 31.

14. For more on Mass Customization, see article at www.build-to-order-consulting.com/mc.htm.

15. Downes and Mui, *Unleashing the Killer App*, p. 140.

16. Larry Downes and Chunka Mui, *Unleashing the Killer App, Digital Strategies for Market Dominance,* (1998, Harvard Business School Press), p. 171.

17. Thomas H. Davenport and Laurence Prusak with H. James Wilson, *What's the Big Idea? Creating and Capitalizing on the Best Management Thinking,* (2003, Harvard Business School Press), p. 37.

18. Sydney Finkelstein, *Why Smart Executives Fail and What You Can Learn from Their Mistakes,* (2003, Portfolio/Penguin), p. 185.

19. Ibid., pages 79 and 98.

20. C. Karry Kouvelas, "Product Proliferation," *APICS - The Performance Advantage,* April 2002, pp. 26-30.

21. Ibid.

22. Koch, *The 80/20 Principle*, p. 90.

23. Downes and Mui, *Unleashing the Killer App*, p. 140.

Appendix B
SUMMARY OF GUIDELINES

To help create company specific guidelines, all 140 guidelines presented so far are repeated below in guideline number order without explanation.

Assembly guidelines from Chapter 8

A1) Understand manufacturing problems/issues of current, past, and related products

A2) Design for easy fabrication, processing, and assembly

A3) For critical alignment of parts use round/diamond pins

A4) Provide unobstructed access for parts *and* tools

A5) Make parts independently replaceable

A6) Order assembly so the most reliable part goes in first; the most likely to fail goes in last

A7) Make sure options can be added easily

A8) Ensure the product's life can be extended with future upgrades

A9) Structure the product into modules and subassemblies, as appropriate

A10) Use adhesives as a last resort

A11) Use press fits as a last resort

389

Assembly guidelines (on error prevention) from Chapter 10

A12) Make sure the *wrong part* cannot go into the intended position

A13) Make sure the part cannot go into the *wrong position*

A14) Design so parts cannot be installed in the wrong orientation

A15) Revisions (changes) to the product design are *clearly* conveyed to manufacturing and implemented

A16) Design so that omissions cannot happen

A17) Design so that subsequent part installation will sense previous part omission

A18) Design so that omissions would be visually obvious

A19) Design so that omissions would be easy to see during inspection

A20) Eliminate process steps that depend on operators' memory

A21) Revisions and changes *do* get documented and implemented

A22) Design so assembly or process sequence doesn't matte

A23) Design so assembly steps cannot happen in the wrong order

A24) Design so assembly or process sequence is intuitively obvious

A25) Clearly specify assembly or process order

A26) Design without the need for timed processes

A27) Eliminate operator timed processes

A28) Make all timed operations the same

A29) Make different timings *very* different

Fastening guidelines from Chapter 8

F1) Use the minimum number of total fasteners

F2) Use fewer large fasteners rather than many small fasteners

F3) Maximize fastener standardization with respect to fastener part numbers, fastener tools, and fastener torque settings

F4) Make sure screws are standardized and have the correct geometry so that auto-feed screwdrivers can be used

F5) Design screw assembly for downward motion

F6) Minimize use of separate nuts

F7) Consider captive fasteners when applicable

F8) Avoid separate washers

F9) Avoid separate lockwashers

F10) Use slotted nuts only when necessary

F11) Use self tapping screws when applicable

F12) Eliminate fasteners by combining parts

F13) Consider snap together features

F14) Consider fasteners that push or snap on

F15) Specify proper tolerances for press fits

Assembly Motion guidelines from Chapter 8

M1) Design for easy *and reliable* alignment of parts to be assembled

M2) Products should not need any tweaking or any mechanical or electrical adjustments unless required for customer use

M3) If adjustments are really necessary, make sure they are independent and easy to make

M4) Eliminate the need for calibration in manufacture; if not possible, design for easy calibration

M5) Design for easy independent test/certification

M6) Minimize electrical cables; plug electrical sub-assemblies directly together

M7) Minimize the number of *types* of cables and wire harnesses

Test guidelines from Chapter 8

T1) Product can be tested to ensure desired quality

T2) Subassemblies and modules are structured to allow independent testing

T3) Testing can be performed by standard test instruments

T4) Test instruments have adequate access

T5) Minimize the test effort spent on product testing consistent with quality goals

T6) Tests should give adequate diagnostics to minimize repair time

Standardization Guidelines from Chapter 9

S1) Use standard parts

S2) Standardize design features

S3) Minimize the number of part types

S4) Minimize number of total parts

S5) Standardize on *types* of linear materials & cut and mark as needed

S6) Consider prefinished material

S7) Combine parts

Part Design Guidelines from Chapter 9

P1)   Adhere to specific process design guidelines

P2)   Avoid right/left hand parts and paired parts

P3)   Design parts with symmetry

P4)   If part symmetry is not possible, make parts very asymmetrical. Polarize all connectors.

P5)   Design for fixturing and concurrently design fixtures

P6)   Minimize tooling complexity by concurrently designing tooling

P7)   Make part differences very obvious

P8)   Specify optimal tolerances for a *robust* design.

P9)   Specify quality parts from reliable sources

DFM for Fabricated Parts from Chapter 9

P10) Choose the optimal processing

P11) Design for quick, secure, and consistent work holding

P12) Use stock dimensions whenever possible

P13) Optimize dimensions and raw material stock choices

P14) Design machined parts to be made in one setup

P15) Minimize cutting tools for machined parts

P16) Avoid arbitrary decisions that require special tools and thus slow processing and add cost unnecessarily

P17) Choose materials to minimize total cost with respect to post-processing

P18) Design parts for quick, cost-effective, and quality heat treating

P19) Design and utilize versatile fixtures

P20)Avoid interrupted cuts and complex tapers and contours

P22) Minimize shoulders, undercuts, hard-to-machine materials, specially ground cutters, and part projections that interfere with cutter overruns

P23) Understand tolerance step functions

P24) Specify the widest tolerances

P 25) Be careful about too many operations in one part

P 26) Concurrently engineer the part and processes

P 27) Avoid sharp internal corners that require sharp cutting tools

P28) Proactively deal with burr removal

P29) Specify 45 degree bevels instead of round external corners

P30) Don't overspecify surface finishes

P31) Reference each dimension to the best datum

DFM For Castings from Chapter 8

P32) Obey all the guidelines for design of castings and molds

P33) Standardize cast parts

P34) Design *versatile* raw castings

P35) Capitalize on opportunities to avoid machining with "as cast" shapes

P36) Carefully plan out the sequence of machining castings

DFM for Plastics from Chapter 8

P37) Obey all the guidelines for part design and mold design

P38) Standardize molded parts

P39) Design *versatile* molded parts

P40) Standardize raw materials for all parts

P41) Choose raw materials commonly used

P42) Don't limit thinking to one-for-one replacements when substituting plastics for other materials

P43) Optimize the number of functions in each part.

P44) Methodically *choose* tolerances for molded parts

Quality Guidelines from Chapter 10

Q1) Establish a quality culture

Q2) Understand past quality problems and issues

Q3) Methodically define the product

Q4) Make quality a primary design goal

Q5) Use Multi-functional teamwork

Q6) Simplify the design and processing

Q7) Chose parts for quality

Q8) Optimizing processing

Q9) Minimize Cumulative Effects

Q10) Thoroughly Design the Product Right the First Time

Q11) Mistake-proof the Design with Poka-Yoke

Q12) Optimize tolerances for a *robust* design

Q13) Continuously improve the product

Q14) Document thoroughly

Q15) Implement incentives that reward quality

Reliability Guidelines from Chapter 10

Q16) Simplify the concept

Q17) Make reliability a primary design goal

Q18) Understand past reliability problems

Q19) Simulate early

Q20) Optimize part selection on the basis of substantiated reliability data

Q21) Use proven parts and design features

Q22) Use proven manufacturing processes

Q23) Use pre-certified modules

Q24) Design to minimize errors with Poka-Yoke

Q25) Design to minimize degradation during shipping, installation, or repair

Q26) Minimize mechanical electrical connections

Q27) Eliminate all hand soldering

Q28) Establish repair limits for circuit boards

Q29) Use burn-in wisely

Handling by automation guidelines from Chapter 9

H1)   Design products so that parts are assembled from above or from the minimum number of directions

H2)   Design and select parts that can be oriented by automation

H3)   Design parts to easily maintain orientation

H4)   Use parts that will not tangle when handled in bulk

H5)   Use parts that will not shingle when fed end to end

H6) Use parts that do not adhere to each other or the track

H7) Specify tolerances tight enough for automatic handling

H8) Avoid flexible parts which are hard for automation to handle

H9) Make sure parts can be presented to automation

H10) Make sure parts can be gripped by automation

H11) Make sure parts are within machine gripper span

H12) Make sure parts are within automation load capacity

H13) Make sure parting lines, sprues, gating or any flash do not interfere with gripping

Repair guidelines from Chapter 8

R1) Provide ability for tests to diagnose problems

R2) Make sure the most likely repair tasks are easy to perform

R3) Ensure repair tasks use the *fewest* tools

R4) Use quick disconnect features

R5) Ensure that failure or wear prone parts are easy to replace with disposable replacements

R6) Provide inexpensive spare parts in the product

R7) Ensure availability of spare parts

R8) Use modular design to allow replacement of modules

R9) Ensure modules can be tested, diagnosed and adjusted while in the product

R10) Sensitive adjustments should be protected from accidental change

R11) The product should be protected from repair damage

R12) Provide part removal aids for speed and damage prevention

R13) Protect parts with fuses and overloads

R14) Ensure any module or subassembly can be accessed through one door or panel

R15) Access covers which are not removable should be self supporting in the open position

R16) Connections to modules or subassemblies should be accessible and easy to disconnect

R17) Make sure repair, service or maintenance tasks pose no safety hazards

R18) Make sure subassembly orientation is obvious or clearly marked

R19) Provide means to locate subassemblies before fastening

Maintenance guidelines from Chapter 8

R20) Design products for minimum maintenance

R21) Design self correction capabilities into products

R22) Design products with self-test capability

R23) Design products with test ports

R24) Design in counters and timers to aid preventative maintenance

R25) Specify key measurements for preventative maintenance programs

R26) Include warning devices to indicate failures

Appendix C
FEEDBACK FORMS

The next pages are feedback forms that can be used to solicit feedback from the customers, the factory, vendors, and field service. These can be valuable sources of feedback that can help develop better products. The procedure is as follows:

1. **Circulate to target audiences** with an introduction that asks for their help in making "our products" better, easier to build, and so forth. Emphasize the importance of this input and how it will be acted upon. The Customer Feedback Form should be filled out by customers as discussed in Section 2.11. The Factory Feedback form should be circulated to all manufacturing personnel, from supervisors to assembly-line workers. The Vendor Feedback form should be circulated to all vendors that make parts that your company has designed. The Field Service form should be circulated to field service personnel that are employed by the company, by the customer, or third party service providers.

2. **Analyze feedback throughly.** Follow up and interview sources. Investigate causes, propose solutions, and implement proposals.

3. **Get back to respondents.** At the minimum, thank them for the feedback. State what is being done, even if this is just the beginning of the process. Let them know about any specific solutions that are going to be implemented. Consider some form of recognition and/or reward system for valuable suggestions.

4. **Follow up** with those who indicated a willingness to "give input to new product development teams" (the last question on the forms). Solicit their input at the appropriate times or invite them to participate in design team activities.

CustomerFeedback Form

Date _____

(For Importance and Competitive Grades, see instructions in Section 2.11)

Rating of Importance	Grade	Compared to:
____ Functionality	_____	_____
____ Purchase cost	_____	_____
____ Quality	_____	_____
____ Reliability/Durability	_____	_____
____ Delivery/Availability	_____	_____
____ Appearance/Aestetics		_____
____ Service, repair, maintenance	_____	_____
____ Cost of ownership	_____	_____
____ Technical support	_____	_____
____ Customizability/Options	_____	_____
____ Safety	_____	_____
____ Environmental	_____	_____
____ Other _____	_____	_____

In which areas do our products need to be improved?

☐ more on back
☐ more attached

Which features or functions of our competitors' products do you most appreciated?

☐ more on back
☐ more attached

If we completely re-designed our products, which features would you most value in the new products? Mention features you value, even if they are not available on any product in the market.

☐ more on back
☐ more attached

Name	Title/Position	
Company/Division	e-mail address:	Phone:
Address		

Would you be willing to provide input to New Product Development teams? ☐ yes, contact me

Factory Feedback: *What Would Make Our Products Better and Easier to Build?*

(One problem/issue per form)   Return to: Date:

1. Problem Type (Quality, Assembly, Cost, Throughput, Delivery, etc.) List all that apply.

2. On Which Products, Sub-Assemblies, Parts, Drawings, or Procedures?

3. What is the Problem or Issue?

☐ more on back
☐ more attached

4. Speculate as to the Real Cause:

☐ more on back
☐ more attached

5. Potential Solutions (optional):

☐ more on back
☐ more attached

Name (optional)	Mailstop/Location:	Phone:
Department		

Would you be willing to give input to New Product Development teams? ☐ yes ☐ maybe ☐ no

Vendor Feedback: *What Would Make Our Products Better and Easier to Build?*
(One problem/issue per form)   Return to: Date:

1. Problem Type (Fabrication, Assemblly, Cost, Quality, Tolerances, Time, Documentation, etc.)
2. On Which Products, Sub-Assemblies, Parts, Drawings, Liasons,or Procedures?
3. What is the Problem or Issue?   ☐ more on back ☐ more attached
4. Speculate as to the Real Cause: ☐ more on back ☐ more attached
5. Potential Solutions (optional):   ☐ more on back ☐ more attached

Name (optional)	Mailstop/Location:	Phone:
Company/Division		

Would you be willing to give input to New Product Development teams? ☐ yes ☐ maybe ☐ no

Field Service Feedback: *What Would Make Our Products Better and Easier to Build?*

(One problem/issue per form)   Return to: Date:

1. Problem Type (Service, Repair, Maintenance, Reliability, Customer Satisfaction, etc.)
2. On Which Products, Sub-Assemblies, Parts, Drawings, Liasons,or Procedures?
3. What is the Problem or Issue?   □ more on back □ more attached
4. Speculate as to the Real Cause: □ more on back □ more attached
5. Potential Solutions (optional):   □ more on back □ more attached

Name (optional)	Mailstop/Location:	Phone:
Organization		
Would you be willing to give input to New Product Development teams? □ yes □ maybe □ no		

Appendix D
RESOURCES

BOOKS

The Toyota Product Development System by James Morgan & Jeffrey K. Liker,(2006, Productivity Press) [this is cited 13 times because Toyota's design process closely parallels these DFM & CE principles]

The Machine that Changed the World; The Story of Lean Production, by James Womack, Daniel Jones, and Daniel Roos,(1991, paperback edition, Harper Perennial) [10 citations in this book]

Why Smart Executives Fail, and What you Can Learn from their Mistakes by Sydney Finkelstein,(2003, Portfolio/Penguin Group) [9]

The Connected Corporation; How Leading Companies Win Through Customer-Supplier Alliances by Jordan D. Lewis,(1995, Free Press)[9]

The Elegant Solution by Matthew E. May, (2007, Free Press) [6]

Inside the Mind of Toyota, Management Principles for Enduring Growth by Satoshi Hino,, (2006, Productivity Press) [5]

Lean Thinking; Banish Waste and Create Wealth in Your Corporation by James P. Womack and Daniel T. Jones,(1996, Simon & Schuster)[4]

The Goal, a novel by Eliyahu M. Goldratt,(1992, North River Press)[4]

Authentic Leadership; Rediscovering the Secrets of Creating Lasting Value by Bill George, former CEO, Medtronic; (2003, Jossey-Bass) [3]

ARTICLES

"How Cost Accounting Distorts Product Costs," by Robin Cooper and Robert S. Kaplan, *Management Accounting*, April, 1988. [4]

"How Nokia Thrives by Breaking the Rules," by David Pringle, *The Wall Street Journal,* January 3, 2003. [2]

WEB-SITES by Dr. Anderson

www.HalfCostProducts.com [cited 18 times in this book]

Home page: Eight-step half-cost reduction strategy (with links to related articles) followed by "How Not to Lower Cost" (with links articles on bidding, offshoring, and cost reduction after design)

Statistics: Content equivalent to 250 page book; 700 hyperlinks

Articles:

Build-to-Order	Mass Customization
Build-to-Order Future	Mass Production, end of
Cost of Quality	Mergers & Acquisitions
Cost Reduction; How Not to	Lean Production
Designing for Build-to-Order	Off-Shore Manufacture
Designing for Lean	Outsourcing
Designing for Manufacturability	Rationalization
Designing for Mass Customization	Standardization
Designing for Quality	SCM Cost Reduction
Low-Bidding	Total Cost

www.build-to-order-consulting.com [cited 15 times in this book]

Pages: Home page (with summaries and links), Seminar page (with comments from attendees), Consulting, Implementation, Articles, Books, Credentials, Client List, Site Map

Articles:

Build-to-Order	Standardization
Mass Customization	Kanban resupply
Shortcomings of Mass Production	Hoffman case study
Business Model for BTO& MC	Rationalization
Achieving Growth with BTO & MC	Training for BTO&MC
On-Demand Lean Production	

www.design4manufacturability.com

Pages: Home page (with summaries and links), Seminar page (with comments from attendees), Consulting, Implementation, Books, Credentials, Client List, Site Map

Articles: Design for Manufacturability
Standardization
Product Line Rationalization
Build-to-Order
Mass Customization

SEMINARS

Dr. Anderson has been providing customized in-house training on DFM and Concurrent Engineering for the last 25 year and has honed the two-day seminar into a very effective program. He personally prepares and present all his seminars during which he encourages questions and engages in discussions based on his extensive experience both training companies and designing and building products. The typical baseline agenda includes:

Product Development Strategy. Managers and Executives join the class for this session on how to raise product development effectiveness to the highest level. Topics include ensuring the availability of resources to form complete multifunctional teams early, thorough up-front work, how to cut time-to-market in half, and how to greatly lower total cost.

Multifunctional Teams. This *concurrent engineering* session shows how to optimize product development by creatively simplifying concepts, methodically optimizing product architecture, raising and resolving issues early to avoid later changes, concurrently planning manufacturing strategies, optimizing the utilization of existing engineering, modules, and off-the-shelf parts, and doing it right the first time.

Designing for Low Cost. This seminar will show how to minimize cost *by design* with thorough architecture optimization, designing for easy fabrication and assembly, designing to minimize the cost of quality, designing right the first time without costly changes, and focusing on designing to minimize all the elements of *total* cost.

Designing in Quality & Reliability. The seminar will show how quality and reliability can be assured *by design* through integrated product/process design, concept simplicity, optimizing tolerances, quality part selection, minimize cumulative effects, and mistake-proofing the design with *poka-yoke*.

Designing for Lean. Dr. Anderson is in a unique position to show how to develop products for lean production, BTO, and Mass Customization, having written two books on Mass Customization and Build-to-Order.

Design Guidelines. The seminar will present dozens of design guidelines for assembly, part fabrication, quality, and reliability.

Standardization. This session presents a practical and effective procedure he developed to generate standard parts lists that are only a few percent of proliferated parts lists that are common in most companies.

What Happens Next. The seminar concludes with discussions on "What happens next," in which attendees suggest what should change and then vote on their choices, which provides a prioritized list which can be used as a good starting point for facilitated implementation meetings.

Tel: **805-924-0100**   e-mail: *anderson@build-to-order-consulting.com*

Dr. Anderson's

WORKSHOPS

After providing DFM training (described on the previous page), Dr. Anderson can facilitate a *product-specific workshop* to immediate apply DFM principles to a specific product development project that is just starting. The workshop includes brainstorming sessions on concept idea generation and optimizing product architecture, which usually are not done well enough despite the fact that this work determines 60% of the cost. He also facilitates DFM implementation meetings and workshops to implement standardization and product line rationalization.

CONSULTING TO TEAMS

After providing DFM training and possibly workshops, companies will benefit from on-going consulting advice to product development teams to help teams apply DFM principles, optimize designs, and make the best decisions throughout their projects.

COMMERCIALIZATION

Both new ventures and existing companies will benefit from this consulting to *commercialize* research and prototypes into viable products that can be designed quickly and be manufacturable enough for rapid ramps that can quickly reach even best-case-scenario demand volumes. This work can be either hourly consulting working with product development teams or as independent design studies (next).

DESIGN STUDIES

He applies all the principles he teaches and writes about, coupled with his Doctorate in Mechanical Engineering, thesis research on mechanisms, four patents, and 35 years of design and manufacturing experience, to offer leading-edge development work ranging from concept studies to innovative product architecture development studies. The deliverables from this work will allow client company to easily complete the inherently manufacturable design work.

His bio-sketch appears opposite page one in this book and at his three web-sites, which are described on page 406.

Tel: **805-924-0100**   e-mail: *anderson@build-to-order-consulting.com*

INDEX